Get **more** out of libraries

Please return or renew this item by the last date shown.

You can renew online at www.hants.gov.uk/library

Or by phoning 0300 555 1387

Hampshire
County Council

Philippe Sands is Professor of Law at University College London and a practising barrister at Matrix Chambers. He has been involved in many important cases of recent years, including Pinochet, Congo, Yugoslavia, Rwanda, Iraq, Guantanamo and the Yazidis. His previous books include *Lawless World* and *Torture Team*. He is a frequent contributor to the *Financial Times, Guardian, New York Review of Books* and *Vanity Fair*, makes regular appearances on radio and television, and serves on the boards of English PEN and the Hay Festival.

@philippesands

By Philippe Sands

Books
City of Lions (with Józef Wittlin)
Torture Team
Lawless World
Principles of International Environmental Law
Justice for Crimes Against Humanity (ed.)
From Nuremberg to the Hague (ed.)
Bowett's Law of International Institutions

Film
My Nazi Legacy

Performance
East West Street: A Song of Good and Evil

'Deeply compelling . . . As Philippe Sands' fascinating and moving book makes clear, those who laboured to submit the worst atrocities to the rule of law knew the human cost of mass crimes all too intimately'   Lawrence R. Douglas, *TLS*

'Gripping, profound and deeply personal . . . *East West Street* is especially interesting and readable as much of it is a detective story of Sands' investigation into his family history . . . The unravelling of these secrets, and the remarkable way that Sands' family history interweaves with those of Lemkin and Lauterpacht, make for gripping reading'   Holocaust Memorial Day Trust

'Intellectual thriller, family story, legal history, political tour de force, *East West Street*, winner of the Baillie Gifford prize for non-fiction, is all of these things . . . It makes a compelling case for international law and the rights of the individual as it sweeps you along with its astonishing narrative'   *The Times* Books of the Year

'An extraordinary work of research and evocative empathy, in which consciousness of present effects is never allowed to trump the complexities of the past'   *Guardian* Books of the Year

genocide

'Genocide' in the handwriting of Rafael Lemkin, c. 1945, and
'crimes against humanity', Hersch Lauterpacht, July 1946

crimes against humanity

EAST WEST STREET

On the Origins of
GENOCIDE *and*
**CRIMES AGAINST
HUMANITY**

PHILIPPE SANDS

WEIDENFELD & NICOLSON

First published in Great Britain in 2016
This paperback edition first published in 2017
by Weidenfeld & Nicolson
an imprint of The Orion Publishing Group Ltd
Carmelite House, 50 Victoria Embankment
London EC4Y 0DZ

An Hachette UK Company

1 3 5 7 9 10 8 6 4 2

A CIP catalogue record for this book is
available from the British Library.

ISBN 978 1 474 60191 7

Typeset by Input Data Services Ltd, Somserset

Printed and bound by CPI Group (UK) Ltd, Croydon CR0 4YY

MIX
Paper from
responsible sources
FSC® C104740
www.fsc.org

www.orionbooks.co.uk

The little town lies in the middle of a great plain . . . It begins with little huts and ends with them. After a while the huts are replaced by houses. Streets begin. One runs from north to south, the other from east to west.

Joseph Roth, *The Wandering Jews*, 1927

What haunts are not the dead, but the gaps left within us by the secrets of others.

Nicolas Abraham, 'Notes on the Phantom', 1975

CONTENTS

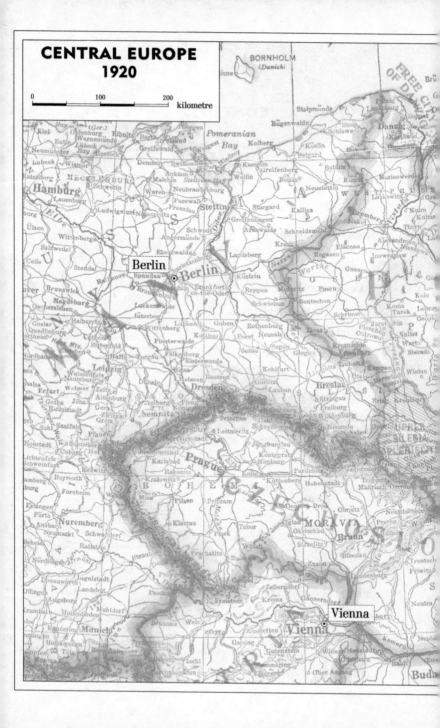

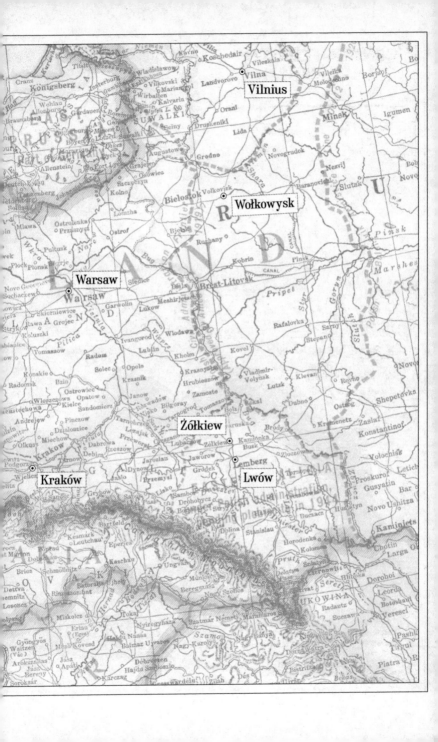

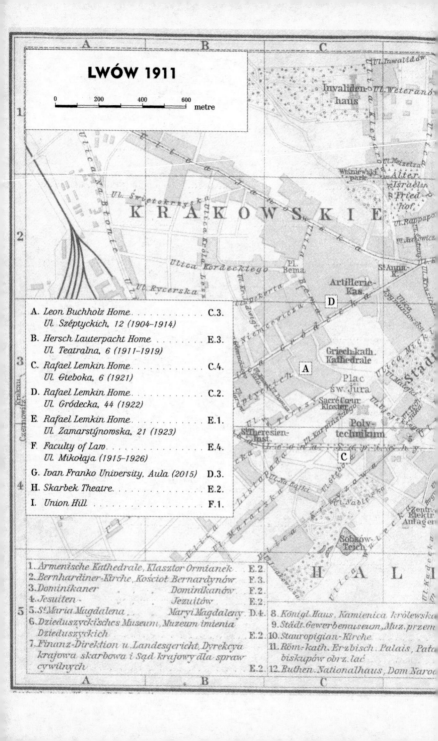

LWÓW 1911

0   200   400   600   metre

A. *Leon Buchholz Home* . . . . C.3.
   Ul. Széptyckich, 12 (1904–1914)

B. *Hersch Lauterpacht Home* . . . . E.3.
   Ul. Teatralna, 6 (1911–1919)

C. *Rafael Lemkin Home* . . . . C.4.
   Ul. Głeboka, 6 (1921)

D. *Rafael Lemkin Home* . . . . C.2.
   Ul. Gródecka, 44 (1922)

E. *Rafael Lemkin Home* . . . . E.1.
   Ul. Zamarstýnowska, 21 (1923)

F. *Faculty of Law* . . . . E.4.
   Ul. Mikołaja (1915–1926)

G. *Ivan Franko University, Aula (2015)* . D.3.

H. *Skarbek Theatre* . . . . E.2.

I. *Union Hill* . . . . F.1.

1. *Armenische Kathedrale, Klasztor Ormianek* . . E.2.
2. *Bernhardiner-Kirche, Kościoł Bernardynów* . . F.3.
3. *Dominikaner . . . . Dominikanów* . . F.2.
4. *Jesuiten - . . . . Jezuitów* . . . . E.2.
5. *St Maria Magdalena . . . . . Maryi Magdaleny* . D.4.
6. *Dzieduszyckisches Museum, Muzeum imienia
   Dzieduszyckich* . . . . E.2.
7. *Finanz-Direktion u. Landesgericht, Dyrekcya
   krajowa skarbowa i Sąd krajowy dla spraw
   cywilnych* . . . . E.2.
8. *Königl. Haus, Kamienica królewska*
9. *Städt. Gewerbemuseum, Muz. przem.*
10. *Stauropigian-Kirche*
11. *Röm.-kath. Erzbisch. Palais, Pała
   biskupów obrz. łac*
12. *Ruthen. Nationalhaus, Dom Naro*

Note to the Reader

The city of Lviv occupies an important place in this story. Through the nineteenth century, it was generally known as Lemberg, located on the eastern outskirts of the Austro-Hungarian Empire. Soon after the First World War, it became part of newly independent Poland, called Lwów, until the outbreak of the Second World War, when it was occupied by the Soviets, who knew it as Lvov. In July 1941, the Germans unexpectedly conquered the city and made it the capital of Distrikt Galizien in the General Government, known once more as Lemberg. After the Red Army vanquished the Nazis in the summer of 1944, it became part of Ukraine and was called Lviv, the name that is generally used today.

Lemberg, Lviv, Lvov and Lwów are the same place. The name has changed, as has the composition and nationality of its inhabitants, but the location and the buildings have remained. This is even as the city changed hands, no fewer than eight times in the years between 1914 and 1945. What to call the city in the pages of this book posed a number of difficulties, so I have used the name by which it was referred to by those who controlled it at the time of which I am writing. (I generally adopt the same approach for other places: nearby Żółkiew is now Zhovkva, after an interregnum from 1951 to 1991, when it was called Nesterov in honour of a Russian First World War hero, the first pilot to fly a loop.)

I thought of calling it Lemberg throughout, because the word evokes a gentle sense of history, as well as being the city of my grandfather's childhood. Yet such a choice could be taken as sending a signal which might cause offence to others, all the more unfortunate at a time when the territory of Ukraine is being fought over with Russia. The same went for the name Lwów, which it was called for two decades, and also for Lviv, which had been the name of the city for just a few tumultuous days in November 1918. Italy never controlled the city, but if it had, it would be called Leopolis, the City of Lions.

Principal Characters

Hersch Lauterpacht, professor of international law, was born in August 1897 in the small town of Żółkiew, a few miles from Lemberg, to which the family moved in 1911. The son of Aron and Deborah (née Turkenkopf), he was the second of three children, between his brother, David, and his sister, Sabina. In 1923, he married Rachel Steinberg in Vienna, and they had one son, Elihu, who was born in Cricklewood, London.

Hans Frank, a lawyer and government minister, was born in Karlsruhe in May 1900. He had an older brother and a younger sister. In 1925, he married Brigitte (née Herbst), and they had two daughters and three sons, the last of whom was named Niklas. In August 1942, he spent two days in Lemberg, where he delivered several speeches.

Rafael Lemkin, a prosecutor and lawyer, was born in Ozerisko near Bialystok, in June 1900. The son of Josef and Bella, he had two brothers (the older, Elias, and the younger, Samuel). In 1921, he moved to Lwów. He never married and had no children.

Leon Buchholz, my grandfather, was born in Lemberg in May 1904. The son of Pinkas, a distiller of spirits and later an innkeeper by trade, and Malke (née Flaschner), he was the youngest of four children, after his older brother, Emil, and two sisters, Gusta and Laura. He married Regina 'Rita' Landes in Vienna in 1937, and a year later their daughter, Ruth, who is my mother, was born there.

PROLOGUE

An Invitation

Tuesday, 1 October 1946, Nuremberg's Palace of Justice

A little after three o'clock in the afternoon, the wooden door behind the defendants' dock slid open and Hans Frank entered courtroom 600. He wore a grey suit, a shade that was offset by the white helmets worn by the two sombre-faced military guards, his escorts. The hearings had taken a toll on the man who had been Adolf Hitler's personal lawyer and then personal representative in German-occupied Poland, with his pink cheeks, sharp little nose and slicked-back hair. Frank was no longer the slender and swank minister celebrated by his friend Richard Strauss. Indeed, he was in a considerable state of perturbation, so much so that as he entered the room, he turned and faced the wrong direction, showing his back to the judges.

Sitting in the packed courtroom that day was the professor of international law at Cambridge University. Balding and bespectacled, Hersch Lauterpacht perched at the end of a long wooden table, round as an owl, flanked by distinguished colleagues on the British prosecution team. Seated no more than a few feet from Frank, in a black suit, Lauterpacht was the one who came up with the idea of putting the term 'crimes against humanity' into the Nuremberg statute, three words to describe the murder of four million Jews and Poles on the territory of Poland. Lauterpacht would come to be recognized as the finest international legal mind of the twentieth century and a father of the modern human rights movement, yet his interest in Frank was not just professional. For five years, Frank had been governor of a territory that came to include the city of Lemberg, where Lauterpacht had a large family, including his parents, a brother and sister, and their children. When the trial had opened a year earlier, their fate in the kingdom of Hans Frank was unknown.

Another man with an interest in the trial was not there that day.

Rafael Lemkin listened to the judgement on a wireless, from a bed in an American military hospital in Paris. A public prosecutor and then a lawyer in Warsaw, he fled Poland in 1939, when the war broke out, and eventually reached America. There he worked with the trial's American prosecution team, alongside the British. On that long journey he carried a number of valises, each crammed with documents, among them many decrees signed by Frank. In studying these materials, Lemkin found a pattern of behaviour to which he gave a label, to describe the crime with which Frank could be charged. He called it 'genocide'. Unlike Lauterpacht, with his focus on crimes against humanity, which aimed at the protection of individuals, he was more concerned with the protection of groups. He had worked tirelessly to get the crime of genocide into Frank's trial, but on this last day of the trial he was too unwell to attend. He too had a personal interest in Frank: he had spent years in Lwów, and his parents and brother were caught up in the crimes said to have been committed on Frank's territory.

'Defendant Hans Frank,' the president of the tribunal announced. Frank was about to learn whether he would still be alive at Christmas, in a position to honour the promise he had recently made to his seven-year-old son, that all was fine and he would be home for the holiday.

Thursday, 16 October 2014, Nuremberg's Palace of Justice

Sixty-eight years later I visited courtroom 600 in the company of Hans Frank's son Niklas, who was a small boy when that promise was made.

Niklas and I began our visit in the desolate, empty wing of the disused prison at the rear of the Palace of Justice, the only one of the four wings that still stood. We sat together in a small cell, like the one in which his father spent the best part of a year. The last time Niklas had been in this part of the building was in September 1946. 'It's the only room in the world where I am a little bit nearer to my father,' he told me, 'sitting here and thinking of being him, for about a year being in here, with an open toilet and a small table and a small bed and nothing else.' The cell was unforgiving, and so was Niklas on the subject of his father's actions. 'My father was a lawyer; he knew what he did.'

Courtroom 600, still a working courtroom, was not greatly changed since the time of the trial. Back in 1946, the route from the cells required each of the twenty-one defendants to travel up a small lift that led directly to the courtroom, a contraption that Niklas and I were keen to see. It remained, behind the dock at which the defendants sat, entered through the same wooden door, which slid open as noiselessly as ever. 'Open, shut, open, shut,' wrote R. W. Cooper of *The Times* of London, the former lawn tennis correspondent who reported each day on the trial. Niklas slid the door open and entered the small space, then closed the door behind him.

When he came back out, he made his way to the place where his father sat during the trial, charged with crimes against humanity and genocide. Niklas sat down and leaned forward on the wooden rail. He looked at me, then around the room, and then he sighed. I had often wondered about the last time his father passed through the lift's sliding door and made his way to the defendants' dock. It was something to be imagined and not seen, because cameras were not allowed to film the last afternoon of the trial, on Tuesday, 1 October 1946. This was done to protect the dignity of the defendants.

Niklas interrupted my thoughts. He spoke gently and firmly. 'This is a happy room, for me, and for the world.'

Niklas and I were together in courtroom 600 because of an invitation I had unexpectedly received several years earlier. It came from the law faculty of the university in the city now known as Lviv, an invitation to deliver a public lecture on my work on crimes against humanity and genocide. They asked me to talk about the cases in which I'd been involved, about my academic work on the Nuremberg trial, and about the trial's consequences for our modern world.

I had long been fascinated by the trial and the myths of Nuremberg, the moment in which it was said our modern system of international justice came into being. I was mesmerized by odd points of detail to be found in the lengthy transcripts, by the grim evidence, drawn to the many books and memoirs and diaries that described in forensic detail the testimony that was laid before the judges. I was intrigued by the images, the photographs and black-and-white newsreels and movies like *Judgment at Nuremberg,* the 1961 Oscar winner made memorable by its subject and Spencer Tracy's momentary flirtation with Marlene Dietrich. There was a practical reason for my interest, because the trial's influence on my work had been profound: the Nuremberg judgement blew a powerful wind into the sails of a germinal human rights movement. Yes, there was a strong whiff of 'victor's justice', but there was no doubting that the case was catalytic, opening the possibility that the leaders of a country could be put on trial before an international court, something that had never happened before.

Most likely it was my work as a barrister, rather than my writings, that prompted the invitation from Lviv. In the summer of 1998, I had been peripherally involved in the negotiations that led to the creation of the International Criminal Court (ICC), at a meeting in Rome, and a few months later I worked on the Pinochet case in London. The former president of Chile had claimed immunity from the English courts for charges of genocide and crimes against humanity laid against him by a Spanish prosecutor, and he had lost. In the years that followed, other cases allowed the gates of international justice to creak open, after a period of quiescence in the Cold War decades that followed the Nuremberg trial.

Cases from the former Yugoslavia and Rwanda soon landed on my desk in London. Others followed, relating to allegations in the Congo, Libya, Afghanistan, Chechnya, Iran, Syria and Lebanon, Sierra Leone, Guantánamo and Iraq. The long and sad list reflected the failure of good intentions aired in Nuremberg's courtroom 600.

I became involved in several cases of mass killing. Some were argued as crimes against humanity, the killings of individuals on a large scale, and others gave rise to allegations of genocide, the destruction of groups. These two distinct crimes, with their different emphases on the individual and the group, grew side by side, yet over time genocide emerged in the eyes of many as the crime of crimes, a hierarchy that left a suggestion that the killing of large numbers of people as individuals was somehow less terrible. Occasionally, I would pick up hints about the origins and purposes of the two terms and the connection to arguments first made in courtroom 600. Yet I never enquired too deeply as to what had happened at Nuremberg. I knew how these new crimes had come into being, and how they subsequently developed, but little about the personal stories involved, or how they came to be argued in the case against Hans Frank. Nor did I know the personal circumstances in which

Hersch Lauterpacht and Rafael Lemkin developed their distinct ideas.

The invitation from Lviv offered a chance to explore that history.

I seized it for another reason: my grandfather Leon Buchholz was born there. I knew my mother's father for many years – he died in 1997 in Paris, a city he loved and called home – but I knew little about the years before 1945, because he did not wish to talk of them. His life spanned the entire twentieth century, and by the time I knew him, his family had diminished in size. That I understood, but not the extent or the circumstances. A journey to Lviv was a chance to learn more about those painful years.

A few scraps of information were available, but for the most part Leon locked the first half of his life into a crypt. They must have been significant for my mother in the years after the war, but they were also important for me, events that left lingering traces and many un-answered questions. Why had I chosen the path of the law? And why law of the kind that seemed to be connected to an unspoken family history? 'What haunts are not the dead, but the gaps left within us by the secrets of others,' the psychoanalyst Nicolas Abraham wrote of the relationship between a grandchild and a grandparent. The invitation from Lviv was a chance to explore those haunting gaps. I accepted it, then spent a summer writing the lecture.

A map showed Lviv to be right in the centre of Europe; not easily accessible from London, it stood at the midpoint of imaginary lines connecting Riga to Athens, Prague to Kiev, Moscow to Venice. It was the crossing of the fault lines that divided east from west, north from south.

Over the course of a summer, I immersed myself in the literature about Lviv. Books, maps, photographs, newsreels, poems, songs, in fact anything I could find about the city of 'blurred borders', as the writer Joseph Roth called it. I was particularly interested in the first years of the twentieth century, when Leon lived in this city of bright colours, the 'red-white, blue-yellow and a touch of black-gold' of Polish, Ukrainian and Austrian influences. I encountered a city of mythologies, a place of deep intellectual traditions where cultures and religions and languages clashed among the groups that lived to-gether in the great mansion that was the Austro-Hungarian Empire.

The First World War collapsed the mansion, destroying an empire and unleashing forces that caused scores to be settled and much blood to be spilled. The Treaty of Versailles, the Nazi occupation and Soviet control combined in quick succession to work their mischiefs. The 'red-white' and 'black-gold' faded, leaving modern Lviv with a Ukrainian population, a city now dominated by 'blue-yellow'.

Between September 1914 and July 1944, control of the city changed hands eight times. After a long spell as the capital of the Austro-Hungarian Empire's 'Kingdom of Galicia and Lodomeria and the Grand Duchy of Kraków with the Duchies of Auschwitz and Zator' – yes, it is *that* Auschwitz – the city passed from the hands of Austria to Russia, then back to Austria, then briefly to the Western Ukraine, then to Poland, then to the Soviet Union, then to Germany, then back to the Soviet Union, and finally to Ukraine, where control resides today. The kingdom of Galicia on whose streets Leon walked as a small boy was one shared by Poles, Ukrainians, Jews and many others, yet by the time Hans Frank entered courtroom 600 on the last day of the Nuremberg trial, which was less than three decades later, the entire Jewish community had been extinguished, and the Poles were being removed.

The streets of Lviv are a microcosm of Europe's turbulent twentieth century, the focus of bloody conflicts that tore cultures apart. I have come to love the maps of those years, with streets whose names often changed, although the course they followed did not. One park bench, a fine art nouveau relic from the Austro-Hungarian period, became a place that I came to know well. From here I could watch the world go by, a fine vantage point on the city's changing history.

In 1914, the bench was in the Stadtpark, the city park. It stood across from the grand Landtagsgebäude, the parliament of Galicia in the easternmost province of the Austro-Hungarian Empire.

A decade later, the bench hadn't moved, but it was in a different country, in Poland, in Park Kościuszki. The parliament had disappeared, but not the building, now the home of the Jan Kazimierz University. In the summer of 1941, as Hans Frank's General Government took control of the city, the bench was Germanized, now in the Jesuitengarten across from a former university building stripped of its Polish identity.

Those interwar years were the subject of a significant literature,

Lwów, Gmach sejmowy. — Lemberg, Landtags-Gebäude

Parliament of Galicia, Austro-Hungarian Empire

but no work described more evocatively what had been lost than *Mój Lwów* (My Lwów). 'Where are you now, park benches of Lwów, blackened with age and rain, coarse and cracked like the bark of mediaeval olive trees?' the Polish poet Józef Wittlin enquired in 1946.

Six decades later, when I arrived at the bench on which my grandfather could have sat a century earlier, I was in the Ivan Franko Park, named in honour of a Ukrainian poet who wrote detective novels and whose name now graced the university building.

Wittlin's idyllic reminiscence, in its Spanish and German translations, became my companion, a guide across the old city and the buildings and streets scarred by the fighting that erupted in November 1918. That vicious conflict, between Polish and Ukrainian communities with Jews caught or targeted in the middle, was grave enough to be reported in the *New York Times*. It caused the US president, Woodrow Wilson, to set up a commission of inquiry. 'I do not wish to disturb the wounds on the living body of these memories, and so I won't talk about 1918,' Wittlin wrote, and then proceeded to do exactly that. He evoked 'fratricidal fighting between Poles and Ukrainians' that cut the city into parts, leaving many caught between the warring factions. Yet common courtesies remained, as a

Ukrainian school friend briefly halted the fighting near the bench on which I sat to allow young Wittlin to pass and make his way home.

'Harmony reigned among my friends, although many of them belonged to different ethnicities that were at loggerheads, and professed different faiths and views,' wrote Wittlin. Here was the mythical world of Galicia, where National Democrats loved Jews, socialists tangoed with conservatives, Old Ruthenians and Russophiles wept alongside Ukrainian nationalists. 'Let's play at idylls,' Wittlin wrote, evoking 'the essence of being a Lvovian'. He depicted a city that was sublime and loutish, wise and imbecilic, poetic and mediocre. 'The flavour of Lwów and its culture is tart,' he concluded wistfully, like the taste of an unusual fruit, the *czeremcha,* a wild cherry that ripened only in Lwów's Klepary suburb. Wittlin called the fruit a *cerenda,* bitter and sweet. 'Nostalgia even likes to falsify flavours too, telling us to taste nothing but the sweetness of Lwów today. But I know people for whom Lwów was a cup of gall.'

The bitterness festered after the First World War, suspended but not settled at Versailles. Periodically it flared up with a vengeance, as when the Soviets rolled into town on white horses in September 1939 and again two years later with the arrival of the Germans in their tanks. 'In early August 1942 Governor General Dr Frank arrived in Lvov,' a Jewish resident recorded in a rare surviving diary. 'We knew that his visit did not bode well.' That month, Hans Frank, Hitler's lawyer of choice and now Governor-General of occupied Poland, ascended the marble steps of the university building to deliver a lecture in the great hall in which he announced the extermination of the city's Jews.

I arrived in Lviv in the autumn of 2010 to deliver my lecture. By then, I had unearthed a curious and apparently unremarked fact: the two men who put crimes against humanity and genocide into the Nuremberg trial, Hersch Lauterpacht and Rafael Lemkin, had been residents of the city in the period of which Wittlin wrote. Both men studied at the university, experiencing the bitterness of those years.

This would not be the last of many coincidences that passed across my desk, but it would always be the one that cut deepest. How remarkable that in preparing a journey to Lviv to talk about the origins of international law, I learned that the city itself was intimately connected to those origins. It seemed more than just a coincidence that two men who did more than any others to create the modern system of international justice should have origins in the same city. Equally striking was the sense that in the course of that first visit, not a single person I met at the university, or indeed anywhere in the city, was aware of its role in the founding of the modern system of international justice.

The lecture was followed by questions, generally directed to the lives of the two men. On what streets did they live? What courses did they take at the university, and who were their teachers? Did they meet or know each other? What happened in the years after they left the city? Why did no one talk about them at the law faculty today? Why did one of them believe in the protection of individuals and the other in the protection of groups? How had they become involved in the Nuremberg trial? What became of their families?

I didn't have answers to these questions about Lauterpacht and Lemkin.

Someone then asked a question I could answer.

'What's the difference between crimes against humanity and genocide?'

'Imagine the killing of 100,000 people who happened to come from the same group,' I explained, 'Jews or Poles in the city of Lviv. For Lauterpacht, the killing of individuals, if part of a systematic plan, would be a crime against humanity. For Lemkin, the focus was genocide, the killing of the many with the intention of destroying the group of which they were a part. For a prosecutor today, the difference between the two was largely the question of establishing intent: to prove genocide, you needed to show that the act of killing was motivated by an intent to destroy the group, whereas for crimes against humanity no such intent had to be shown.' I explained that proving intent to destroy a group in whole or in part was notoriously difficult, since those involved in such killings tended not to leave a trail of helpful paperwork.

Does the difference matter? someone else asked. Does it matter whether the law seeks to protect you because you are an individual or because of the group of which you happen to be a member? That question floated around the room, and it has remained with me ever since.

Later in the evening, a student approached me. 'Can we speak privately, away from the crowd?' she whispered. 'It's personal.' We moved towards a corner. No one in the city knew or cared about Lauterpacht and Lemkin, she said, because they were Jews. They were tainted by their identities.

Maybe, I responded, not knowing where she was headed.

She said, 'I want to let you know that your lecture was important to me, *personally* important for me.'

I understood what she was telling me, sending a signal about her own roots. Whether a Pole or a Jew, this was not a matter to be spoken of openly. Issues of individual identity and group membership were delicate in Lviv.

'I understand your interest in Lauterpacht and Lemkin,' she continued, 'but isn't your grandfather the one you should be chasing? Isn't he the one closest to your heart?'

I

LEON

My earliest memory of Leon dates back to the 1960s, when he was living in Paris with his wife, Rita, my grandmother. They lived in a two-bedroom apartment with a tiny kitchen on the third floor of a worn nineteenth-century building. Halfway up the rue de Maubeuge, the home was dominated by a musty smell and the sound of trains from the Gare du Nord.

Here were some of the things I could recall.

There was the bathroom with pink-and-black tiles. Leon spent a great deal of time here, sitting on his own, occupying a small space behind a plastic curtain. This was a no-go area for me and my more curious younger brother. Occasionally, when Leon and Rita were out shopping, we'd sneak into the forbidden space. Over time we became more ambitious, examining items on the wooden table that served as his desk in a corner of the bathroom, on which scattered indecipherable papers lay, in French or more foreign languages (Leon's handwriting was different from anything we'd seen, spidery words stretched across the page). The desk was also littered with watches, old and broken, which fed our belief that our grandfather was a smuggler of timepieces.

Occasional visitors would arrive, elderly ladies with odd names and faces. Madame Scheinmann stood out, dressed in black with a strip of brown fur that hung off the shoulder, a petite face powdered white and a smear of red lipstick. She spoke in a strangely accented whisper, mostly of the past. I didn't recognize the language (it was Polish, I later learned).

The absence of photographs was another memory. I recalled only one, a black-and-white photograph that stood proud in a bevelled glass frame above the unused fireplace, Leon and Rita on their wedding day in 1937. Rita wasn't smiling in the photograph, or later when I knew her, something I noticed early and never forgot. There seemed to be no scrapbooks or albums, no pictures of parents or siblings (long gone, I was told), and no family memories on public display. There was a black-and-white television, odd copies of *Paris Match,* which Rita liked to read, but no music.

The past hung over Leon and Rita, a time before Paris, not to be talked about in my presence or in a language I understood. Today, more than forty years later, I realize with a sense of shame that I never asked Leon or Rita about their childhoods. If curiosity existed, it was not permitted to express itself.

There was a silence about the apartment. Leon was easier than Rita, who gave the impression of being detached. She spent time in the kitchen, often preparing my favourite Wiener schnitzel and mashed potato. Leon liked to wipe his plate with a piece of bread, so clean it didn't need to be washed.

A sense of order and dignity abounded, and pride. A family friend who had known Leon since the 1950s remembered my grandfather as a man of restraint. 'Always in a suit, beautifully turned out, discreet, never wanting to impose himself.'

Leon encouraged me in the direction of the law. In 1983, when I graduated from university, he offered me a gift of an English-French legal dictionary. 'For your entry into a professional life', he scrawled on the flyleaf. A year later, he sent me a letter with a cutting from *Le Figaro,* an advertisement looking for an English-speaking international lawyer in Paris. 'Mon fils,' he would say, what about this? 'My son'. That was what he called me.

Only now, many years later, have I come to understand the darkness of the events through which Leon lived before this time, to emerge with a dignity intact, with warmth and a smile. He was a generous, passionate man with a fiery temper that sometimes burst forth unexpectedly and brutally, a lifelong socialist who admired the French prime minister Léon Blum and loved soccer, an observant Jew for whom religion was a private matter not to be imposed on others. He was uninterested in the material world and didn't want to be a burden on anybody. Three things mattered to him: family, food and home.

I had plenty of happy memories, yet Leon and Rita's home never seemed to me to be a place of joy. Even as a young boy I could sense the heaviness, a tension that hung around the rooms, of foreboding and silence. I would visit once a year, and I still recall the absence of laughter. French was spoken, but if the subject was private my grandparents reverted to German, the language of concealment and history. Leon didn't seem to have a job, or not the kind that required an early-morning departure. Rita didn't work. She kept things tidy, so the edge of the rug in the living room was always straight. How they paid the bills was a mystery. 'We thought he smuggled watches in the war,' my mother's cousin told me.

What else did I know?

That Leon was born in a distant place called Lemberg and moved to Vienna when he was a young boy. It was a period he would not talk about, not with me. 'C'est compliqué, c'est le passé, pas important.' That was all he said: it's complicated, it's the past, not important. Best not to pry, I understood, a protective instinct. Of his parents and a brother and two sisters, there reigned a complete and impenetrable silence.

What else? He married Rita in 1937 in Vienna. Their daughter, Ruth, my mother, was born a year later, a few weeks after the Germans arrived in Vienna, to annex Austria and impose the *Anschluss*. In 1939, he moved to Paris. After the war, he and Rita had a second child, a son they called Jean-Pierre, a French name.

Rita died in 1986, when I was twenty-five.

Jean-Pierre died four years later, in a car accident, with both his children, my only cousins.

Leon came to my wedding in New York in 1993 and died four years later, in his ninety-fourth year. He took Lemberg to the grave, along with a scarf given to him by his mother in January 1939. It was a parting gift from Vienna, my mother told me as we bade him adieu.

This was about what I knew when I received the invitation from Lviv.

2

A few weeks before the journey to Lviv, I sat with my mother in her bright living room in north London, two old briefcases before us. They were crammed with Leon's photographs and papers, newspaper clippings, telegrams, passports, identity cards, letters, notes. Much dated to Vienna, but some documents went back further, to Lemberg days. I examined each item with care, as a grandson but also as a barrister who loves the muck of evidence. Leon must have kept certain items for a reason. These mementoes seemed to hold hidden information, coded in language and context.

I put a small group of items of special interest to one side. There was Leon's birth certificate, which confirmed his birth in Lemberg on 10 May 1904. The document also offered an address. There was family information, that his father (my great-grandfather) was an innkeeper called Pinkas, which could be translated as Philip or Philippe. Leon's mother, my great-grandmother, was called Amalie, known as Malke. She was born in 1870 in Żółkiew, about fifteen miles north of Lemberg. Her father, Isaac Flaschner, was a corn merchant.

Other documents made their way into the pile.

A worn Polish passport, old and faded, light brown, with an imperial eagle on the cover. Issued to Leon in June 1923 in Lwów, it described him as a resident of the city. I was surprised, having believed him to be Austrian.

Another passport, this one a dark grey, a shock to behold. Issued by the *Deutsches Reich* in Vienna in December 1938, this document had another eagle on the cover, this one perched on a golden swastika. This was a *Fremdenpass,* a travel pass, issued to Leon because he'd been stripped of his Polish identity and made stateless *(staatenlos),* deprived of nationality and the rights it offered. There were three such passes among Leon's papers: a second issued to my mother, in December 1938, when she was six months old, and a third that went to my grandmother Rita three years later, in Vienna, in the autumn of 1941.

I added more items to the pile.

A small scrap of thin yellow paper, folded in half. One side was blank; the other contained a name and address written firmly in pencil, in a writing that was angular. 'Miss E. M. Tilney, Norwich, Angleterre.'

Three small photographs, each of the same man, taken in a formal pose, with black hair, strong eyebrows and a faintly mischievous air. He wears a pin-striped suit and is partial to bow ties and handkerchiefs. On the back of each, a different date seems to have been written in the same hand: 1949, 1951, 1954. There is no name.

My mother told me she didn't know who Miss Tilney was or the identity of the man in the bow tie.

I added a fourth photograph to the pile, a larger one but also in black-and-white. It showed a group of men, some of whom are in uniforms, walking in a procession among trees and large white flowers. Some look towards the camera; others have a more furtive air, and one I recognized immediately, the tall man right at the centre of the picture, a leader in a military uniform that I imagine to be green, and tightly around his waist is a black belt. I know this man, and the one who is standing behind him, the indistinct face of my grandfather Leon. On the back of the photograph, Leon wrote 'de Gaulle, 1944'.

I took these documents home. Miss Tilney and her address hung on the wall above my desk, alongside the photograph of 1949, the man in a bow tie. I gave de Gaulle the distinction of a frame.

3

I left London for Lviv in late October, during a gap in my work schedule, after a hearing in The Hague, a case brought by Georgia against Russia claiming racial discrimination against a group. Georgia, my client, alleged that ethnic Georgians in Abkhazia and South Ossetia were being mistreated in violation of an international convention. I spent much of the first flight, from London to Vienna, reviewing the pleadings in another case, brought by Croatia against Serbia, on the meaning of 'genocide'. The allegation related to killings that occurred in Vukovar in 1991, which led to the filling of one of the largest mass graves in Europe since 1945.

I travelled with my mother (sceptical, anxious), my widowed aunt Annie, who had been married to my mother's brother (calm), and my fifteen-year-old son (curious). In Vienna we boarded a smaller plane for the 650-kilometre trip east, across the invisible line that once marked the Iron Curtain. To the north of Budapest, the plane descended over the Ukrainian spa town of Truskavets, through a cloudless sky, so we could see the Carpathian Mountains and, in the distance, Romania. The landscape around Lviv – the 'bloodlands' described by one historian in his book on the terrors visited upon the area by Stalin and Hitler – was flat, wooded and agricultural, a scattering of fields pockmarked with villages and smallholdings, human habitations in red, brown and white. We might have passed directly over the small town of Zhovkva as Lviv came into sight, a distant sprawl of an ex-Soviet metropolis, and then the centre of the city, the spires and domes that jumped 'out of the undulating greenery, one after another', the towers of places I would come to know, 'of St George's, St Elizabeth's, the Town Hall, the Cathedral, the Korniakt and the Bernardine' that were so dear to Wittlin's heart. I saw without knowing them the cupolas of the Dominican church, the City Theatre, the Union of Lublin Mound and the bald, sandy Piaskowa Hill, which 'soaked up the blood of thousands of martyrs' during the German occupation. I would grow familiar with all these places.

The plane taxied to a stop before a low building. It would not have been out of place in a *Tintin* book, as though we were back in 1923, when the airport enjoyed the evocative name of Sknyliv. There was a familial symmetry: the city's imperial railway station opened in 1904, the year of Leon's birth; the Sknyliv air terminal opened in 1923, the year of his departure; the new air terminal emerged in 2010, the year in which his descendants returned.

The old terminal hadn't changed much in the intervening century, with its marbled hall and large wooden doors and the officious, fresh-faced guards dressed in green, à la *The Wizard of Oz,* barking orders without authority. We passengers stood about in a long line that snaked slowly towards a patch of wooden cubicles occupied by grim immigration officers, each under a giant ill-fitting green cap.

'Why here?' the officer asked.

'Lecture,' I replied.

He stared blankly. Then he repeated the word, not once, but three times.

'Lecture? Lecture? Lecture?'

'University, university, university,' I responded. This prompted a grin, a stamp and a right of entry. We wandered through customs, past dark-haired men in shiny black leather coats who smoked.

In a taxi, we headed to the old centre, passing dilapidated nineteenth-century buildings in the style of Vienna and the great Ukrainian Catholic Cathedral of St George, past the old Galician parliament, into the main thoroughfare, bookended by the opera house and an impressive monument to the poet Adam Mickiewicz. Our hotel was close to the medieval centre, on Teatralna Street, called Rutowskiego by the Poles and Lange Gasse by the Germans.

To follow the names and maintain a sense of historical bearing, I took to wandering around with three maps: modern Ukrainian (2010), old Polish (1930), ancient Austrian (1911).

On our first evening, we searched for Leon's house. I had an address from his birth certificate, an English translation prepared in 1938 by one Bolesław Czuruk of Lwów. Professor Czuruk, like many in that city, had a complicated life: before the Second World War he taught Slavic literature at the university, then served as a translator for the Polish Republic, helping hundreds of Lwów Jews to obtain false papers during the German occupation. For these efforts, he was repaid with a period of incarceration by the Soviets after the war. With his translation, Professor Czuruk told me that Leon was born at 12 Szeptyckich Street and that he was delivered into the world by the midwife Mathilde Agid.

Today Szeptyckich Street is known as Sheptyts'kykh Street, close to St George's Cathedral. To walk there, we circled Rynok Square, admired fifteenth-century merchants' houses, passed city hall and the Jesuit church (which was shuttered during the Soviet era, used as an archive and book depository), then into a nondescript square in front of St George's, from which the Nazi governor of Galicia, Dr Otto von Wächter, recruited members of the 'Waffen-SS Galician Division'.

From this square it was but a short walk to Sheptyts'kykh Street, named in honour of Andrey Sheptytsky, the renowned metropolitan archbishop of the Ukrainian Greek Catholic Church who, in November 1942, published a pastoral letter titled 'Thou Shalt Not Murder'. No. 12 was a two-storey late-nineteenth-century building, with five large windows on the first floor, next to a building with a large Star of David spray-painted onto a wall.

From the city archives, I would obtain a copy of the construction plans and early permits. I learned that the building was constructed in 1878, that it was divided into six flats, that there were four shared toilets, and that there was an inn on the ground floor (perhaps the one run by Leon's father, Pinkas Buchholz, although a 1913 city directory listed him as the proprietor of a restaurant a few buildings up, at No. 18).

We entered the building. On the first floor, an elderly man answered our knock, Yevgen Tymchyshn, born there in 1943 he told us, during German rule. The Jews had gone, he added, the apartment

12 Sheptyts'kykh Street, Lviv, April 2015

was empty. Inviting us in, his friendly yet shy wife proudly showed us around the extended single room that was the couple's home. We drank black tea, admired pictures on the wall, talked of the challenges of modern Ukraine. Behind the tiny kitchen at the back of the house was a small balcony, where Yevgen and I stood. He wore an old military cap. Yevgen and I smiled, the sun shone, St George's Cathedral loomed as it had in May 1904.

4

Leon was born in this house, and his family roots led to nearby Zhovkva, known as Zółkiew when his mother, Malke, was born there in 1870. Our guide, Alex Dunai, drove us through a misty, tranquil rural landscape of low brown hills and scattered woods, towns and villages long ago famed for their cheeses, sausages, or bread. Leon would have taken the same road a century earlier, on visits to the family, travelling by horse and cart, or maybe by train from the new railway station. I tracked down an old Cook's railway timetable that included the line from Lemberg to Zółkiew, which led to a place called Bełzec, later to be the site of the first permanent extermination camp to use gas as an instrument of mass killing.

I found only a single family photograph from that period of Leon's childhood, a studio portrait with a painted background. Leon must have been about nine years old, seated in front of his brother and two sisters, between his parents.

Buchholz family, Lemberg, c. 1913 (from left: Pinkas, Gusta, Emil, Laura and Malke, with Leon at the front)

Everyone looked serious, especially Pinkas the innkeeper, with his black beard and the garb of a devout Jew, staring quizzically into the camera. Malke looked tense and formal, a buxom and well-coiffed lady in a lace-edged dress and heavy necklace. An open book sat in her lap, a nod to the world of ideas. Emil was the oldest child, born in 1893, in a military collar and uniform, about to go off to war and death, although he didn't yet know it. Next to him stood Gusta, younger by four years, elegant and an inch taller than her brother. In front of him was Laura, the younger sister, born in 1899, holding on to the arm of the chair. My grandfather Leon was at the front, a small boy in a sailor's uniform, eyes wide open, ears protruding. Only he smiled as the lens clicked, as though he didn't know what the others did.

In a Warsaw archive, I came across birth certificates for the four children. All were born in the same Lemberg house, each introduced into the world by the midwife Mathilde Agid. Emil's birth certificate was signed by Pinkas, which stated that the father was born in 1862 in Cieszanów, a small town to the north-west of Lemberg. The Warsaw archive threw up a marriage certificate for Pinkas and Malke, a civil ceremony conducted in Lemberg in 1900. Only Leon was born in civil wedlock.

Archival material pointed to Żółkiew as the family hub. Malke and her parents were born there, she the first of five children and the only girl. In this way, I learned of Leon's four uncles – Josel (born in 1872), Leibus (1875), Nathan (1877) and Ahron (1879) – all married with children, which meant Leon had a large family in Żółkiew. Malke's uncle Meijer also had many children, providing Leon with a multitude of second and third cousins. On a conservative count, Leon's Żółkiew family, the Flaschners, numbered in excess of seventy individuals – 1 per cent of the town's population. Leon never mentioned any of these people to me, in all the years I knew him. He always seemed to be a man who stood alone.

Żółkiew flourished under the Habsburgs, a centre of commerce, culture and learning, important still in Malke's day. Established five centuries earlier by Stanisław Żółkiewski, a renowned Polish military leader, it was dominated by a sixteenth-century castle with a fine Italian garden, which were both still standing in decrepitude. The town's numerous places of worship reflected its varied population: Dominican and Roman Catholic temples, a Ukrainian Greek church and, right at the centre, a seventeenth-century synagogue, the last reminder of Żółkiew's prominence in Poland as once being the only place where Jewish books were printed. In 1674, the great castle became the royal residence of Jan III Sobieski, the Polish king who defeated the Turks at the Battle of Vienna in 1683, ending three centuries of conflict between the Ottomans and the Habsburg Holy Roman Empire.

Żółkiew had a population of around six thousand when Leon visited his mother's family, made up of a mix of Poles, Jews and Ukrainians. Alex Dunai gave me a copy of an exquisite town map, hand-drawn in 1854. The palette of greens and creams and reds, names and numbers etched in black, evoked a painting by Egon Schiele, *The Artist's Wife*. The detail was striking: each garden and

Zółkiew, Lembergerstrasse, 1890

tree marked, every building numbered, from the royal castle at the
centre (No. 1) to the lesser places on the outskirts (No. 810).

Joseph Roth described the layout of such a town. Typical for the
area, standing 'in the middle of a great plain, not bounded by any
hill or forest or river', it began with just a few 'little huts', then a
few houses, generally ordered around two main streets, one that ran
'from north to south, the other from east to west'. A marketplace
stood at the intersection of the two roads, and invariably a railway
station was located 'at the far end of the north-south street'. This
perfectly described Zółkiew. From a cadastral record drawn up in
1879, I learned that Malke's family inhabited house No. 40 on parcel
762 of Zółkiew, a wooden construction in which, most likely, she
was born. It lay at the western limit of the town on east-west street.

In Leon's day, the street was called Lembergerstrasse. We entered
from the east, passing a large wooden church, shown as the Heilige
Dreyfaltigkeit on the map prepared with much care in 1854. After
the Dominican convent, on our right, we entered the Ringplatz,
the main square. The castle came into view, close to St Laurence's
Cathedral, the burial place of Stanisław Żółkiewski and a few lesser
Sobieskis. A little beyond stood the Basilian convent, crowning what
must once have been a glorious space. On a cold autumn morning

the square and the town felt faded and sad: a micro-civilization had become a place of potholes and roaming chickens.

5

In January 1913, Leon's older sister Gusta left Lemberg for Vienna to marry Max Gruber, a *Branntweinverschleisser* (seller of spirits). Pinkas attended the ceremony, signing the marriage certificate against a backdrop of unrest in the Balkans. Serbia had allied with Bulgaria and Montenegro and, supported by Russia, gone to war against the Ottoman Empire. A peace treaty was signed in London in May 1913, offering new boundaries. Yet just a month later, Bulgaria turned on Serbia and Greece, its former allies, catalysing the Second Balkan War, which lasted until August 1913. This was a precursor to the greater upheavals about to be unleashed on the region, as Bulgaria was defeated by Serbia, which acquired new territories in Macedonia, a matter seen as a threat to the all-powerful Austro-Hungarian Empire.

Vienna concocted the idea of a preventive war against Serbia, to rein in Russia and the Slavs. On 28 June 1914, Gavrilo Princip assassinated Archduke Franz Ferdinand in Sarajevo. Within a month, Vienna had attacked Serbia, prompting Germany to attack Belgium, France and Luxembourg. Russia entered the war alongside Serbia, taking on Vienna and the Austro-Hungarian army and, by the end of July, invading Galicia. In September 1914, the *New York Times* reported that Lemberg and Zółkiew were occupied by Russian forces, following a 'most colossal battle' that involved over a million and a half men. The newspaper described a 'thousandfold, cosmic destruction and wrecking of human life, the most appalling holocaust history had ever known'. One of the casualties was Leon's brother Emil, killed in action before he reached his twentieth birthday. 'What was a single murder,' Stefan Zweig asked, within 'the cosmic, thousandfold guilt, the most terrible mass destruction and mass annihilation yet known to history?'

Pinkas Buchholz fell into despair and died of a broken heart just a few weeks later, overwhelmed by guilt for having prevented his son Emil from emigrating to America a year earlier. Despite my efforts, I found no more information about the deaths of Pinkas and

Emil, and no graves, beyond confirmation in a Viennese archive that Pinkas died in Lemberg on 16 December 1914. I was unable to find where Emil fell. The Kriegsarchiv (War Archive) in Vienna offered a crisp explanation that 'no personal files are available'. This was a quirk of history: when the Austro-Hungarian Empire collapsed, the 1919 Treaty of Saint-Germain determined that all Galician files were to remain in the various successor states. Most have been lost.

In the space of three months, Leon had lost his father and brother. At ten years old, he was the last man in the family. He left for Vienna with his mother and sister Laura as the First World War pushed the family westward.

6

In Vienna, they moved in with Gusta and her husband, Max Gruber. In September 1914, Leon enrolled at the local *Volksschule* (elementary school) on Gerhardusgasse, in Vienna's 20th District. His school reports recorded his *mosaisch* (Jewish) origins and modest academic abilities. That month, a first child was born to Gusta and Max, Leon's niece Therese, known as Daisy. Leon lived with the Grubers at 69 Klosterneuburger Strasse, close to school, in an apartment on the first floor of a large building that was later purchased by Max and Gusta, with the help of a mortgage.

Leon's family was one among the tens of thousands to emigrate from Galicia to Vienna, a migration of *Ostjuden,* eastern Jews. The war caused large numbers of Jewish refugees to come to Vienna in search of a new home. Joseph Roth wrote of the Nordbahnhof train station, 'where they all arrived', its lofty halls infused with the 'scents of home'. The new inhabitants of Vienna made their way to the Jewish districts of Leopoldstadt and Brigittenau.

In 1916, at the age of twelve, Leon graduated to the nearby Franz Joseph Realschule. Throughout his life, he held on to the *Schulerausweiskarte,* the school identity card issued on 19 December. A line in faded ink struck out the words 'Franz Joseph', to indicate the death of the emperor a few weeks earlier. The photograph shows a thin boy in a dark, buttoned tunic. With his prominent ears, he carries a defiant look, with arms crossed.

The Realschule, which specialized in maths and physics, was

located at 14 Karajangasse, close to the family house. Today it's the Brigittenauer Gymnasium, and when I visited with my daughter, she noticed the small plaque on the wall near the entrance. It marked the use of the basement as a Gestapo prison in 1938, a place of incarceration for Bruno Kreisky, who became chancellor of Austria after the next war. The school's current director, Margaret Witek, found the class registers for 1917 and 1919. These showed that Leon did rather better in the sciences than in the arts, that he spoke German to a 'satisfactory' level and that his French was 'good'.

Malke returned to Lwów after the First World War, to an apartment at 18 Szeptyckich Street, the building where Pinkas had once run a restaurant. She left Leon in Vienna under the guardianship of Gusta, who soon produced two more nieces, Herta born in 1920, then Edith in 1923. Leon lived with them for several years, a youthful uncle for the small girls, but he never spoke of them, to me at least. In the meantime his other sister, Laura, married Bernard Rosenblum, a swing operator. In due course, Malke returned to Vienna from Lwów.

Max Gruber outside his liquor store,
69 Klosterneuburger Strasse, Vienna, c. 1937

The gaps in my knowledge about Leon's family, in Lemberg, Żółkiew and Vienna, were gradually being filled in. With family papers and public archives I had names, ages, places and even occupations. As the details began to emerge, I learned that the family was larger than I had known.

7

In 1923, Leon was studying electrical and technical subjects and helping his brother-in-law Max at the liquor store, hoping to follow in his father's educational footsteps. I found photographs in his album, including one of a man who seemed to be a teacher. He had a distinguished air, a man with whiskers, standing in a garden, a small wooden table before him laden with the stuff of distillation, the burners, bottles and tubes. The teacher might begin with a liquid of fermented grains, which contained ethanol. This liquid was purified to produce a spirit, the liquor that emerged from the process of separation.

The act of purification was the opposite of life in Vienna. In hard economic times, with inflation rampant and tensions high, new refugees arrived from the east in great numbers. Political groupings struggled to form working governments as conditions conspired to promote nationalist and anti-immigrant feelings, along with a rising tide of anti-Semitism. A local National Socialist German Workers' Party, which was formed in Austria in 1918, merged with its German counterpart. The leader was a charismatic Austrian named Adolf Hitler.

In the summer of 1923, two weeks after attending the wedding of his sister Laura to Bernard Rosenblum, Leon returned to Lwów to obtain a passport. Even after a decade in Vienna, he discovered that he didn't have Austrian nationality. An obscure treaty signed in June 1919 on the same day as the Treaty of Versailles, the Polish Minorities Treaty, made Leon a Polish citizen.

That treaty had been forced on Poland, imposing obligations to protect minorities. An early precursor to modern human rights conventions, Article 4 provided, in effect, that anyone born in Lwów before the treaty was signed in 1919 would be deemed a Polish citizen. There were no forms to be completed, no applications to be made. '*Ipso facto* and without requirement of any formality', the treaty declared, Leon and hundreds of thousands of other citizens of Lwów and Zółkiew and other lands became Polish citizens. A surprise and a nuisance, this legal quirk would later save his life and that of my mother. My own existence owed something to Article 4 of this Minorities Treaty.

Leon had left Austrian Lemberg on the eve of the First World War, before it was plunged into a murderous conflict between Poles, Ukrainians and Jews. By the time he returned to collect a passport, the city was a thriving Polish metropolis, filled with the rasping sound of trams and the 'aromas of patisseries, fruit sellers, colonial stores and Edward Riedl and Julius Meinl's tea and coffee shops'. The city entered a period of relative stability after the end of the wars against the Soviets and the Lithuanians. On 23 June 1923, the Police Directorate of Lwów issued Leon's new Polish passport. It described a young man with blond hair and blue eyes, although the photograph showed him in glasses and with dark hair. A natty dresser, he wore a dark jacket, a white shirt and a strikingly modern tie, with thick horizontal stripes. Although he was nineteen years old, his profession was listed as *écolier,* schoolboy.

He spent the rest of the summer in Lwów, with friends and family, including his mother, who still lived on Szeptyckich Street. In Zółkiew, he would have visited Uncle Leibus and the large, extended family on Piłsudski Street, in a wooden house a little north of the great synagogue (decades later the street was a muddy path, the house long gone). Leon could take to the hills around the town, passing through fine local woods of oaks and birches on its eastern edge, known as the *borek*. This was where the children of Zółkiew often played, on the wide plain between low-lying hills, along the main road to Lwów.

In August, Leon visited the Austrian consulate on the first floor of 14 Brajerowska Street, near the university. In these rented rooms, a last bastion of Austrian authority, he was issued the stamp that allowed a single return trip to Austria. The Czechoslovak consulate, located close to the law faculty, offered a transit visa. Amid the hubbub, Leon might have passed two other young men on the city streets, early on career paths that would lead to significant roles in the Nuremberg trial: Hersch Lauterpacht had left the city in 1919 to study in Vienna, and might have been back to visit his family and take forward his candidacy for the chair in international law at

Leon's Polish passport photograph, 1923

Lwów University; Rafael Lemkin, a student at the university's law faculty, was living near Malke, in the shadow of St George's Cathedral. This was the formative period, touched by events in the city and Galicia, in which the ideas on the role of the law in combating mass atrocity were being formed.

Leon left Lwów at the end of August. He travelled by train to Kraków, a ten-hour journey, then on to Prague and Czechoslovakia's southern border, at Břeclav. On the morning of 25 August 1923, the train pulled in at the Nordwestbahnhof. From there, Leon walked the short distance to Gusta's home on Klosterneuburger Strasse. He never returned to Lwów or Żółkiew and, as far as I know, never saw any member of that family again.

8

Five years on, Leon had become a distiller of spirits, with his own shop at 15 Rauscherstrasse, in Vienna's 20th District. He kept one photograph from that period, taken in March 1928, a time of renewed economic depression and hyperinflation. It showed him and his brother-in-law Max Gruber at the annual meeting of the Association of Viennese Liquor Sellers. In the company of elderly men, he was on the up, seated in a wood-panelled hall under a brass candelabra with twenty-seven glass bulbs, the youngest man present in a room without women, a regular guy, twenty-four years old. A shadow of a smile passes his lips. If times were anxious, they didn't show on his face. Leon retained the receipt issued to him by the association on the day he became a member, 27 April 1926. For eight schillings, he joined the alcohol establishment.

Eight decades later, I visited 15 Rauscherstrasse with my daughter. We peered into the window of rooms being refurbished, transforming the place into a club. A new oak entrance door was being installed, with lyrics from a Led Zeppelin song, 'Stairway to Heaven', carved into it. There's a feeling I get when I look to the west, the song went, as my spirit cries for leaving.

Leon remained at 15 Rauscherstrasse for several years, as political and economic unrest grew in Austria and its environs. In his photo album, I found images suggesting a carefree period of happiness and assimilation. There were photographs of aunts and uncles and nieces, family members without names, images of walking holidays with friends. Several showed Leon with his closest friend, Max Kupferman. Two dapper young men, laughing, often in suit and tie, summers spent in the hills and lakes of Austria.

The two took excursions to nearby Leopoldsberg, north of Vienna, and the Leopoldskirche, the church at the summit with fine views over the city. I followed them up that hill to see for myself, a big hike. Sometimes they ventured farther north, to the small town of Klosterneuburg on the Danube, a place with an Augustine monastery, or west towards the village of Pressbaum. The photographs were familiar and modern, young men and women in bathing costumes, arms entwined, intimate, carefree.

I came across images of family holidays, farther afield, to Bodensdorf on Lake Ossiach, north of Trieste. There were a few sporting moments, Max and Leon playing football, his friend the more accomplished player, appearing for the Whiskey Boys Football Club, an amateur team whose matches were reported in the *Österreichische Spirituosenzeitung*.

They were images of a regular life, of Leon having escaped his origins. There is 'no harder lot than that of the Eastern Jew newly arrived in Vienna', Joseph Roth wrote of the interwar years, yet Leon created a life among those Jews who had 'their feet safely pushed under desks in the First District', the ones that had 'gone "native"'. Seemingly on the up, he occupied a position between the desk sitters and the *Ostenjuden*, politically active, a reader of the socialist *Neue Freie Presse* (New Free Press), and a supporter of the progressive Social Democrats, a party distinct from the Christian Socialists and the German Nationalists who placed identity, anti-Semitism and purification at the centre of their political programmes.

9

At the end of January 1933, President Paul von Hindenburg appointed Adolf Hitler chancellor of Germany. Leon now occupied a larger shop at 72 Taborstrasse, in the heart of the Leopoldstadt district. As the liquor trade flourished, he must have viewed events in neighbouring Germany with trepidation. The Reichstag was burned down, the Nazis won the largest share of the vote in German federal

Leon and Max Kupferman, Vienna, 1929

elections, Austrian Nazis gained ever more support. Demonstrations in the Leopoldstadt were frequent and violent.

Four months later, on Saturday, 13 May 1933, representatives of the new German government made a first visit to Austria. A tri-motored German government plane landed at the Aspern Airfield, not far from Leon's shop. It carried seven Nazi ministers, led by Dr Hans Frank, the newly appointed Bavarian minister of justice, Hitler's former lawyer and confidant.

Frank's arrival prompted demonstrations, with large crowds of supporters, many of whom wore the white knee-length socks that indicated support for the Nazis. The Austrian chancellor, Engelbert Dollfuss, soon banned the Austrian Nazi Party, and other measures followed. Dollfuss was dead a little more than a year after Frank's visit, murdered in July 1934 by a group of Austrian Nazis led by Otto von Wächter, a local lawyer who would, a decade later, as Nazi governor in Lemberg, create the Waffen-SS Galician Division.

I found little information on Leon's life during these turbulent days. He was a single man, and although the odd document offered a snippet about his family in his papers I found no letters or other

Hans Frank (standing in car) arrives in Vienna, May 1933

accounts, no details of political or other activities. There were several photographs, later inserted into an album in random fashion. Leon wrote a few words on the back of some, a date or a place. I rearranged the images chronologically as best I could. The earliest photograph, of his friend Max Kupferman, dated to 1924. Most were taken in the 1930s, but after 1938 the images tailed off.

Several photographs were work-related. A black-tie gathering, men with their ladies, taken in December 1930, with names and signatures on the back: Lea Sochi, Max Kupferman, Bertl Fink, Hilda Eichner, Grete Zentner, a Metzl and a Roth. Another picture showed Leon outside his brother-in-law Max Gruber's liquor store on Klosterneuburger Strasse. Others were of family members. His nieces Herta and Edith Gruber outside their father's shop, on their way to school. His sister Gusta, elegant in a black coat on a Viennese street. A note from his niece Daisy, on holiday in Bodensdorf: 'To my dear uncle . . .' Three photographs of Malke, dressed in black, a widow with a furrowed brow. Malke on a street, Malke in an apartment, Malke walking with her son on Leopoldsberg. I found only one image of Leon with his mother, taken in 1938, silhouetted with small trees.

Several pictures showed Leon with friends, many in Klosterneuburg in the 1930s. In bathing suits, men and women laughed, touched, posed. Leon with an unnamed woman, but no clue as to their relationship.

Max. Through the years, from 1924 to 1938, at least one photograph a year of his best friend, a straight run. He was a constant. Leon and Max on the banks of the Danube at Kritzendorf, north of Vienna. Leon, Max and a young woman with a leather soccer ball at their feet. Leon and Max hiking in the Wachau valley. Leon and Max standing in front of a shining black automobile. Leon and Max joking around with a football. Max standing. Max in portrait. Max laughing, smiling.

I noticed how elegant and well dressed Leon always was, neat and dignified. On a Viennese street in a boater. In a suit at a railway station, or maybe it was a marketplace. He looked happy, usually with a smile, more so than the way I remembered him in later years. At my wedding in New York, in his ninetieth year, I recall seeing him sitting alone in a reflective mood, as though looking back across a century.

The last photograph of that period, of Leon's bachelor days, was of two attractive young women, on the streets. They wore fur, and behind them, approaching in the background, a storm cloud looms.

Leon and Malke, Vienna, 1938

10

The darkness grew more ominous in 1937. Hitler denounced various agreements on the protection of minorities, freeing Germany from the constraints of international law and allowing it to treat minority groups as it wished. Yet in Vienna, daily life and love went on. At this moment, as Europe stumbled towards war, Leon chose to marry.

His bride was Regina Landes, the marriage celebrated on 23 May 1937 at the Leopoldstempel, a fine Moorish-style synagogue on Leopoldsgasse, the largest Jewish temple in Vienna. My grandmother Rita emerged from nowhere. The first image of her was in a white wedding dress.

I knew this photograph well, she in a flowing wedding dress, holding white flowers, he in black tie. Neither of them smiled on this happy day. This was the single photograph on display in their apartment in Paris, the one I often stared at as a child.

The bride was twenty-seven, Viennese and Austrian, the daughter of Rosa Landes, a widow with whom she lived on Habichergasse in the 16th District. The marriage was witnessed by Leon's brother-in-law Max and by Rita's older brother Wilhelm, a dentist. Malke attended with Gusta and Laura, accompanied by their husbands and Leon's four nieces. Rita was given away by her mother and three brothers: Wilhelm, his wife Antonia, and their young son, Emil; Bernhard and his wife Pearl (known as Fini) and Susanne; and Julius. This was Leon's new Viennese family.

The Lembergers and Żółkiewers weren't able to make the trip to Vienna, but they sent telegrams. I found two. 'Wishing you much luck,' Uncle Leibus wrote from Żółkiew. Another came from Uncle Rubin, in Lwów.

Leon kept these congratulatory telegrams, a record of the secure, middle-class community of which the new couple was a part. A world of doctors and lawyers, shopkeepers and furriers, engineers and accountants, a world of yesterday, about to disappear.

11

On the morning of 12 March 1938, the German Wehrmacht entered Austria and marched into Vienna, met by huge and enthusiastic

Leon and Rita, wedding day, May 1937

crowds. Rita was five months pregnant on the day Austria became a part of the Greater German Third Reich. The *Anschluss* (linkup) followed a coup d'état by the Austrian Nazi Party, to prevent a referendum on the country's independence from Germany. The 'first great breach of the peace', the German writer Friedrich Reck noted in his diary on 20 March 1938, in a state of despair. It was a day on which 'the criminal has been let go unpunished and is thus made to appear more powerful than he is'.

Three days later, Hitler arrived in Vienna to address a vast crowd on the Heldenplatz. He stood alongside Arthur Seyss-Inquart, the newly appointed governor, with Otto von Wächter behind them, just returned from German exile. Within days a plebiscite ratified the takeover, and German law was applied across Austria. A first transport of 151 Austrian opponents of the Nazis was taken from Vienna to the Dachau concentration camp near Munich. Jews were harassed, forced to scrub the streets, then hit by new laws that banned them from the universities and participation in the professions. Within weeks, Jews were required to register their assets, property and businesses, a death knell for the liquor stores run by Leon and brother-in-law Max.

As businesses were confiscated without compensation, Arthur Seyss-Inquart's new government entrusted to Adolf Eichmann the task of running the Zentralstelle für judische Auswanderung, the body responsible for implementing the 'solution of the Jewish problem'. Persecution was embraced as policy, along with 'voluntary' emigration and deportation. A Vermögensverkehrsstelle (asset transfer office) transferred Jewish property to non-Jews. Another commission oversaw the removal of Jews from public positions in Austria, headed by Otto von Wächter.

Many Jews emigrated, or tried to do so, among them Leon and his brothers-in-law on Rita's side. Bernhard Landes left in April 1939, preceded by his wife and daughter. Wilhelm's family followed in September 1938. They obtained tourist visas for Australia but only got as far as London, where they remained. Wilhelm's son, Emil, was six. 'I remember being in your grandparents' apartment on Taborstrasse, at nighttime,' he recalled. 'I remember marching feet outside the building and a general sort of atmosphere of fear and emotion around me.' He remembered too the September night that his family left Vienna from the Westbahnhof. 'I looked down from the train compartment, which was high up, and saw the worry and the crying faces, probably my father's mother [Rosa] was standing there, probably your grandmother [Rita] was standing there. There were lots of crying adults. They just stood there, crying.'

The brothers did what they could to obtain a visa for their mother, Rosa, but no visa ever reached Vienna. Leon's three nieces, the daughters of Gusta and Max, did manage to get out. Daisy, who was twenty-five, went to London to study (she later emigrated to Palestine). Herta (who was eighteen) and Edith (fifteen) together made their way to Italy and then Palestine. Their parents, Gusta and Max, remained in Vienna.

I located the form Leon filed with the Israelitische Kultusgemeinde Wien (the Vienna Jewish Community), a prerequisite of emigration. He declared himself to be a 'liquor and spirits' manufacturer who had studied electrical and radio repairs and spoke Polish and German. He was willing to go to Australia, Palestine, or America (the only overseas relative identified was a 'cousin' of Rita's, one P. Weichselbaum of Brooklyn, New York, a name I didn't recognize). He also applied for permission to emigrate on behalf of his two dependants, Rita (who was pregnant) and Malke. In the space left to declare his financial and other resources, he offered a single word: 'None.' The shop on Taborstrasse was gone, along with the stock. Leon was destitute.

On 19 July 1938, Rita gave birth to a daughter, Ruth, my mother. Four months later, a lowly official at the German embassy in Paris was murdered, unleashing *Kristallnacht* and the destruction of Jewish property and businesses. That night, 9 November, the Leopoldstempel where Rita and Leon were married was burned down, and thousands were rounded up. Among the hundreds who were killed or 'disappeared' were two of Leon's brothers-in-law. Max Gruber was arrested on 12 November, spending eight days in prison before being released. He was forced to sell off his shop and the building he owned with Gusta, and to do so cheaply. Rita's youngest brother, Julius Landes, was less fortunate: he disappeared a few days after *Kristallnacht,* never to be heard from again. The only trace that remained was a single document, which revealed that a year later, on 26 October 1939, he was transported eastward to a camp near the town of Nisko, between Kraków and Lemberg. Seven decades later, he remains a disappeared person.

Leon and Rita were ensnared. Within a week of *Kristallnacht,* Rita was forced to change her name, and birth and marriage certificates, with 'Sara' being added to indicate Jewish origins. For reasons that are unclear, neither Leon nor their daughter was subjected to this humiliation. On 25 November, Leon was summoned to appear before the authorities. The president of the Vienna Police, Otto Steinhaus, issued an order of expulsion:

> The Jew Buchholz Maurice Leon is required to leave the territory of the German Reich by 25 December 1938.

Leon kept a copy of the order, but I only saw it when my mother gave me his papers in preparation for the trip to Lviv. The paper was folded in half, kept with a certificate of good character that was issued by the head of the local Jewish community. On a careful reading, I noticed that the expulsion order was judicially confirmed by the registry of the Leopoldstadt district court.

Order expelling Leon from the Reich, 25 November 1938

12

The exact circumstance of Leon's departure from Vienna had always been a mystery, but I assumed he left for Paris with his wife and daughter.

Passport No. 3814 was issued to his daughter, Ruth, on 23 December 1938, suggesting she would leave with her father. Below her photograph, overstamped with a swastika, the space left for a signature was filled in by an official: 'The passport holder is unable to write.' Ruth was six months old, identified as 'small' and 'stateless'.

Passport No. 3816 was issued on the same day to Leon, on the authority of the president of the Vienna Police, the same man who ordered his expulsion. Leon signed with a large, proud, firm *B*. The document, like his daughter's, allowed travel within the country and abroad and described Leon as 'stateless'. He'd lost his Polish nationality – as suddenly as it was obtained in 1919 – a consequence of the Polish foreign minister Józef Beck's September 1934 speech to the Assembly of the League of Nations, renouncing the 1919 Polish Minorities Treaty. The loss of status would have one unintended benefit: as a stateless individual, Leon could only be issued a foreigner's passport (a *Fremdenpass*), which was not required to be stamped with a big red *J*, the mark of a Jew. Leon's passport, as well as that of his daughter, was not stamped with a red *J*.

The third passport would have been No. 3815, in Rita's name, but it was missing. The passport that was among Leon's papers that bore Rita's name was issued much later, in August 1941, three years after the others. It carried a different number. Rita stayed behind, to care for her mother, Rosa, at least that is what I was told. I had assumed the period of separation was short, but now I learned that it extended over three years. How did Rita leave Vienna in late 1941? Ruth's cousin Emil, who left Vienna in September 1938, was surprised. 'It was a mystery, and it has always been a mystery,' he said quietly. Had he known that Leon and Rita did not leave Vienna together. 'No, did they?' he asked. Did he know that Rita remained in Vienna until the end of 1941? 'No.'

I tried to find out what happened to passport No. 3815, but without success. Most likely it was issued to Rita, not used, then discarded. A kind lawyer in Germany's Federal Foreign Office looked into the matter but found nothing in the Federal Archives. 'It would appear close to improbable that this file is preserved in German public archival funds,' he wrote.

Passports 3814 and 3816 offered a further surprise: they revealed that Leon left without his daughter. The only stamp in Leon's passport from the currency office in Vienna was dated 2 January 1939. Beyond that it was empty, without anything to indicate when he left or the route he took. His daughter's passport, on the other hand, bore a stamp to show that she left Austria much later, on 22 July 1939, entering France the following day. Because she did not travel with her father, the obvious question was, who accompanied the infant on the trip?

'I have absolutely no idea how your grandfather contrived to get out of Vienna,' Ruth's cousin Emil told me. 'Nor do I know how your grandfather got his daughter out of Vienna, or how your grandmother escaped Vienna.'

13

Leon was thirty-four years old at the end of January 1939, when he arrived alone in Paris, a place of safety even as Prime Minister Édouard Daladier's government faced up to political realities, negotiating with Hitler and preparing to recognize Franco's government in Spain. Leon arrived with a passport, a copy of the order expelling him from the *Reich* and two certificates, one of which confirmed his good character, and the other attesting to the fact that he ran a liquor store in Vienna from 1926 to 1938. He had no money.

I had often imagined Leon's escape from Vienna to Paris, without knowing the details. After I attended a conference in Vienna on the accident at the Chernobyl nuclear plant in Ukraine, a spur-of-the-moment decision took me to Vienna's rebuilt Westbahnhof station, where I bought a one-way, overnight train ticket to Paris. I shared the compartment with a young German woman. We talked about the war years, their effect on our families, the sense of connection with that past. It was an intimate journey, a moment of acknowledgement and remembrance, and we never exchanged names.

In Paris I went to the building where Leon stayed when he arrived, 11 rue du Malte, a four-storey building behind the Cirque d'Hiver,

Ruth, Paris, 1939

not far from place de la République. From here, he made repeated applications to remain in France, retaining the many rejection slips handed to him by the Préfecture de Police, small pieces of paper covered in blue ink. Given five days to leave, he challenged each decision every month for a year. Eventually he received permission to remain.

In July 1939, his infant daughter arrived in Paris. Where they lived, and how he survived, I did not know. In August he rented a room at 29 rue de la Lune, a tall and thin building on a narrow street, where he was living when Germany invaded Poland on 1 September. A few days later, France and Britain declared war on Germany, making communications with Rita difficult, because Vienna was in enemy territory. No letters remained, just a photograph of their daughter, sent to Rita in October. 'Ruthi running to a better future', Leon wrote on the back. He added a few affectionate words for other family members, unaware they'd left for England.

Leon entrusted his daughter to the care of others, then enlisted in the French army to join the struggle against Germany. The French military issued him an identity card that described him as an 'electrician'. In March 1940, he joined the Troisième Régiment de Marche de Volontaires Étrangers (RMVE: the Third Marching Regiment of Foreign Volunteers), an offshoot of the Foreign Legion. A few days later he was transferred to a camp on the south-west coast, near the Pyrenees and the border with Spain, based at Camp Barcarès, a long strip of sand that divided the Mediterranean from a voluminous freshwater pond. The Seventh Company, of which he was a member, comprised several thousand men drawn from across Europe. They included Spanish Republicans and Communists and Jews from Hungary, Czechoslovakia and Poland. He kept a few photographs, looking dandy in a large-brimmed hat, breeches and greatcoat.

Within a month he was decommissioned, deemed too old for combat at thirty-five. A few weeks later, Germany marched into France, Belgium and Holland, as Leon's former regiment was renamed the Twenty-Third RMVE and sent north to active engagement against the Germans at Soissons and Pont-sur-Yonne. Hostilities ended on 22 June with an armistice. The regiment was dissolved.

Leon was back in Paris when the Germans entered on 14 June

Leon, Barcarès, 1940

1940, causing many Parisians to flee. Within weeks the roads outside Paris were deserted, and an 'air of venality' hovered over the capital as German soldiers took over the restaurants on the Champs-Élysées and teenagers of the Gardes Françaises (a French equivalent to the Hitler Youth) sold copies of *Au Pilori,* a furiously anti-Semitic and anti-Freemason weekly that called for the lynching of Léon Blum and Édouard Daladier.

Leon worked at a language school, the École Saint-Lazare at 102 rue Saint-Lazare, making use of his German-language skills. In his papers I found a note from the school's director, Monsieur Edmond Melfi, certifying his role as a teacher. Ruth was sent into hiding outside Paris, to nearby Meudon. She was two years old, able to walk but not speak, hidden at a *pouponnière,* a private nursery called L'Aube de la Vie, the 'Dawn of Life'. It was the first of several places of hiding, all traces of which evaporated from her memory. For the next four years, my mother was a hidden child, separated from her father, given the false name of Jocelyne Tévé.

14

Leon kept only one document that offered information on the *pouponnière,* a postcard of a young woman with a big smile. She wore a pin-striped jacket and a white shirt, with a large black bow tie. Her hair was dark, pulled back behind her head. She was pretty, and on the back of the card she wrote a few words: 'To Ruth's father, with all my friendship, S. Mangin, Director of the Pouponnière "L'Aube de la Vie", Meudon (Saône et Oise).'

The town hall in Meudon directed me to the municipal archivist, who located the nursery's file. Between 1939 and 1944, Mademoiselle Mangin looked after several small children at her premises at 3 rue Lavoisier, a small, detached house with a small front garden in the centre of town. 'We have found no trace of Ruth Buchholz in the register of children maintained by this "nourrice",' Madame Greuillet informed me. 'Maybe she was declared to the municipality under a different name,' something that happened frequently. She sent me the names of all the children who registered at the nursery between September 1938 (the first was Jean-Pierre Sommaire) and August 1942 (the last was Alain Rouzet). Of the twenty-five, eight were girls. If Ruth was registered, it was under a secret name. More likely, she was kept off the books.

15

In Zhovkva, a thousand miles to the east of Paris, a woman who lived on the street where Malke was born gave me another account of the events of 1939. Sixteen years old when the Germans arrived in September 1939, ninety-year-old Olga offered a clear first-hand account of the occupation of Poland. She did so as she stood at a large urn of boiling cabbages, protected from the autumn chill by a layer of bright scarves, tightly wound.

'I'll tell you the truth,' Olga said. 'There were maybe ten thousand people in Zółkiew, half Jewish, the rest Ukrainians and Poles. The Jews were our neighbours; we were friends with them. There was a doctor, he was respected, we went to him. There was a watchmaker. They were honest, all of them.'

Olga's father got on with Jews. When Poland became independent in 1919, he was arrested because his first wife – not Olga's mother – was an active supporter of the short-lived West Ukrainian People's Republic, which existed for less than a month, in November 1918 (we spoke shortly before Russia occupied the Crimea in 2014, an act that would cause others I met in Ukraine to suggest that a western republic might yet re-emerge). 'When my father was in prison, the Jew Gelberg, his neighbour, took money and food to the prison for him, because he was alone. So my father was fine with the Jews.'

As our conversation meandered, Olga drank tea, tended to the cabbages, and reminisced about the war.

'First the Germans came,' which scared the Jews. 'The Germans stayed in Zółkiew for a week, didn't do much, then left, back west. Then the Russians arrived in town.'

Olga was at school when the Soviets entered the town.

'It was a woman who came first, a beautiful woman soldier on a great white horse who led the Soviets into town. Then came the soldiers, then the big guns.'

She was curious about the artillery, but the woman on the horse left a greater impression.

'She was beautiful, and she carried a big gun.'

For eighteen months, Zółkiew was under Soviet control, a Communist-run municipality in which private enterprise was eliminated. Other parts of Poland were occupied by Nazi Germany, the General Government under the rule of Governor-General Hans Frank. The division was agreed to by Stalin and Hitler in the secret Molotov-Ribbentrop Pact, a non-aggression agreement that divided Poland with a line drawn to the west of Lemberg and Zółkiew, leaving Leon's family safe on the Soviet side. In June 1941, Germany broke the pact, launching Operation Barbarossa. Its forces moved eastward at speed, so by the end of June, Zółkiew and Lemberg were under German control.

The return of the Germans brought fear to the Jews. Olga remembered restrictions, the creation of the ghetto, and the burning of the synagogue after they arrived. She didn't personally know the Flaschners, Malke's family, but the name rang a bell. 'One was an innkeeper,' she said suddenly, recalling that there were many with that name. 'They went into the town ghetto, all the Jews did,' she said of Leon's uncle Leibus, of the aunts and cousins, of all the relatives, of the thirty-five hundred other Jews from the town. In faraway Paris, Leon knew nothing of these events.

16

Vienna in the summer of 1941 was no less difficult for Rita. Separated from Leon and her daughter for nearly three years, she lived with her mother, Rosa, and mother-in-law, Malke. Nothing in Leon's papers shed any light on those years, of which Rita never spoke, not to her daughter, not to me. By other means, I traced some of what came next.

In September, an ordinance was passed requiring all Jews in Vienna to wear yellow stars. The use of public transportation was curtailed as they were prohibited from leaving the area where they lived without authorization. The city archive in Vienna offered more details. After Leon left, Rita was forced out of the Taborstrasse apartment. She moved in with Malke; they lived first on Franz Hochedlinger Gasse, then on Obere Donaustrasse, both in the Leopoldstadt district, where many of the Jews lived. Malke was evicted from the apartment she'd lived in for a quarter of a century on Romanogasse and forced into a 'collective' apartment on Denis-gasse. Deportations to the east had been halted in October 1939, but in the summer of 1941, under the rule of Baldur von Schirach, the new gauleiter of Vienna, rumours about a fresh wave of deport-ations began to circulate.

On 14 August, Rita was issued a *Fremdenpass,* a travel pass valid for one year, allowing travel in and out of the *Reich.* It bore no red *J* stamp, despite her being registered as a Jew. Two months later, on 10 October, the Vienna police authorized her to make a one-way trip out of the country, travelling via Hargarten-Falck in the Saarland on the German border with France. The journey was to be completed by 9 November. The passport photograph was strikingly sad, Rita with pursed lips and eyes full of foreboding.

I found another copy of that photograph in Leon's papers, one she sent from Vienna to Paris. On the back she had written an inscrip-tion, 'For my dearest child, for my golden child.'

I was surprised that Rita, a registered Jew, could be issued so late a document that allowed her to travel. An archivist at the US Holocaust Memorial Museum in Washington described the journey as 'improbable', setting out the multitude of steps she would have had to go through to obtain the *Fremdenpass,* obstacles imposed by Adolf Eichmann. The archivist directed me to a large chart titled *Die jüdische Wanderung aus der Ostmark, 1938–1939* (The Jewish migration from Austria, 1938–1939), as prepared by Eichmann. A stateless person like Rita, who lost her Austrian nationality after the *Anschluss* by reason of her marriage to a now-stateless Jew, was required to take even more steps than others.

To leave Vienna, Rita must have had help from someone with con-nections. In October 1941, Eichmann and his deputy Alois Brunner, who would soon move to Paris, issued a raft of orders for large-scale Jewish deportations. That month, some fifty thousand Jews were deported from Vienna. Among them were Leon's sister Laura and her daughter, his thirteen-year-old niece, Herta Rosenblum. The two were sent to Litzmannstadt (Lodz) on 23 October.

Rita avoided deportation. She left Vienna on 9 November. The very next day 'the borders of the German Reich were closed for refu-gees', all emigration ended, all departure routes were blocked. Rita got out at the last minute. Her escape was either very fortunate or based on assistance from someone with inside information. I don't

Unterschrift des Inhabers
Signature du porteur

Regine Buchholz

Nr. 09438 6/40

Rita's passport, 1941

know when Rita arrived in Paris or how she made it there. The *Fremdenpass* bore no stamps or other clues. Other documents confirmed that by early 1942 she was in Paris, reunited with her husband.

Malke was now the last member of Leon's family in Vienna. Her children and grandchildren having left the city, her companion was Rosa Landes, Rita's mother. The gaps created by the silence of the family as to the events of that time could be filled by documents available in numerous archives, offering grim details, in black and white, of what followed. But first, I wanted to see where these events unfolded.

17

I travelled to Vienna with my fifteen-year-old daughter to visit the addresses thrown up by the archives. Triggered by school history lessons, she wanted to visit a 'museum of the *Anschluss*', but no such institution existed. We made do with the wall of a single room at the small, private, and rather wonderful Third Man Museum, a homage to the Orson Welles film that was one of Rita's favourites, and mine. The room traced the unhappy events from 1938 to 1945 by means of photographs, newspapers and letters. A copy of the voting form for the plebiscite that followed the *Anschluss,* organized to ratify the union with Germany, declared the support of the Catholic Church, firm and unambiguous.

Later we walked through Viennese streets, to 69 Klosterneuburger Strasse, the building where Leon lived when he arrived from Lemberg in 1914. Once the home of his sister Gusta and brother-in-law Max, the liquor store was now a convenience store. Close by was Leon's school, the *Realschule* on Karajangasse, and his first shop, on Rauscherstrasse. We went to Taborstrasse, where Leon and Rita first lived together, the building where my mother was born. The street was elegant, but No. 72 was among the buildings destroyed by war. Later we stood outside 34 Rembrandtstrasse, Malke's last Viennese home, a *Wohngemeinschaft* (shared apartment) she occupied with other elderly residents. It wasn't too difficult to imagine the last day, which began early in the morning of 14 July 1942, the street closed by the SS to prevent escapes. 'They are going to take the whole street, whoever is a Jew,' a panicked resident of a nearby street recalled as an SS man marched around with a pizzle shouting, 'Alles raus, alles raus.'

Malke was seventy-two years old, allowed to travel east with a single suitcase. Escorted to the Aspangbahnhof, behind the Belvedere Schloss, she and other deportees were spat at, jeered, and abused by spectators, who applauded the departures. One comfort was that she was not entirely alone, travelling with Rita's mother, Rosa. It was a haunting image, two elderly ladies on a platform at the Aspangbahnhof, each hanging on to a small suitcase, two among 994 elderly Viennese Jews heading east.

They travelled on Transport No. IV/4, a regular train with a seat in a normal compartment with lunch boxes and refreshments, a deceptively comfortable 'evacuation'. The journey lasted twenty-four hours and led to Theresienstadt, sixty kilometres north of Prague. On arrival, they were searched. The first hours were uncertain and traumatic, waiting around, eventually directed to their quarters, a single room, empty save for a few old mattresses on the floor.

Rosa survived for a few weeks. According to a death certificate she died on 16 September of pericolitis. It was signed by Dr Siegfried Streim, a dentist from Hamburg who spent two more years at Theresienstadt before being deported to Auschwitz, where he died in the autumn of 1944.

A week after Rosa died, Malke was deported from Theresienstadt on Transport Bq 402. By train, she headed east, beyond Warsaw, entering the territory of Hans Frank. The train journey extended over a thousand kilometres, twenty-four hours locked into a cattle wagon with eighty other frail, elderly *Untermenschen*. Among the 1,985 other people who travelled on that transport were three of Sigmund Freud's sisters: seventy-eight-year-old Pauline (Pauli), eighty-one-year-old Maria (Mitzi) and eighty-two-year-old Regina (Rosa).

The train stopped at a camp, two and a half kilometres from the railway station of the small town of Treblinka. The routine that followed was well rehearsed, under the personal direction of Commandant Franz Stangl. If she was still alive, Malke would have joined the Freud sisters in getting off the train within five minutes of its arrival. They were ordered to line up on the platform, divided into separate groups of men and women, forced to strip naked under the threat of lashes. Jewish workers collected their discarded clothes and carried them off to barracks. Those able to do so walked naked into the camp, along 'Himmelfahrtstrasse', the 'street to heaven'. The women's hair was shaved by barbers, to be packed into bundles for the manufacture of mattresses.

Reading an account of this process, I recalled a scene in Claude Lanzmann's film *Shoah*. Among the very few to survive Treblinka, the barber Abraham Bomba was interviewed as he cut a man's hair, being pressed for details of the task he carried out, matters that he plainly did not wish to talk of. Bomba refused to answer, yet Lanzmann persisted. Eventually the barber cracked, weeping as he described his own actions, the shaving of the hair of women.

'I was obsessed by the last moments of those who were to die,' Lanzmann wrote of his visit to Treblinka, 'by their first moments in the death camps.' Those moments were taboo. The cutting of hair, the naked walk, the gas.

Malke's life was over within fifteen minutes of stepping off the train.

18

Malke was murdered in the forest of Treblinka on 23 September 1942, a point of detail about which Leon did not learn until many years later. Within six months of her death, her brother Leibus and the entire Flaschner family in Żółkiew were also dead. While the exact circumstances were not knowable, I learned about the fate of Żółkiew's Jews from one of the few Jewish residents to survive, Clara Kramer, now a resident of Elizabeth, New Jersey.

I came across Clara by chance, a consequence of a photograph bravely posted in Zhovkva's tiny museum, a couple of gloomy rooms on the ground floor of a wing of Stanisław Żółkiewski's crumbling castle. On the museum wall hung a few dismal black-and-white photographs, small and indistinct, three or four grainy, unfocused images taken in the early days of the German occupation, the summer of 1941. They showed armoured vehicles, grinning soldiers, the seventeenth-century synagogue on fire. There was also a picture of one of the entrances to the town through which I walked, the Brama Glińska (Glinske Gate), taken shortly after the Germans arrived.

Glinske Gate, Żółkiew, July 1941

At the top of the imposing stone gate three banners were hung, offering a local message of welcome to the new arrivals, in Ukrainian. *HEIL HITLER! Glory to Hitler! Glory to Bandera! Long live the Independent United Ukrainian State! Long live the Leader Stepan Bandera!*

It required courage for a museum curator to display such photographs, evidence of local Ukrainian support for the Germans. Eventually I located her, Lyudmyla Baybula, a municipal employee who worked in another wing of the castle. Luda, as she asked me to call her, was in her forties, a strong, attractive woman with jet-black hair, a proud, open face and truly amazing blue eyes. She had devoted her life to learning about her town's lost wartime years, having grown up in a place without Jews, a subject of silence. One of the few Jews to remain was a friend of her grandmother's, an elderly lady whose stories of childhood ignited Luda's interest in what had been lost.

Luda began to collect information and then decided to display some of what she found on a wall of the museum. During one of our conversations, over a lunch of pickles and borscht, she enquired if I'd read *Clara's War,* a book about a young girl from Żółkiew who survived the German occupation. She told me that Clara Kramer was one of eighteen Jews who spent two years hidden under the floorboards of a house occupied by a Polish couple, Mr and Mrs Valentin Beck, and their daughter. In July 1944, when the Russians arrived from the east, she was liberated.

I bought Clara's book and read it in a single sitting. Curiously, one of the eighteen was a young man called Gedalo Lauterpacht, who turned out to be a distant relative of Hersch's. I visited Clara in New Jersey, wanting to learn more, and found an engaging, sprightly and talkative ninety-two-year-old. She was fit and beaming, with a good memory, but sad because her husband had died a few weeks earlier.

'Żółkiew was nice in the 1930s,' she recalled, with its fine city hall with a tall tower and the balcony on the top, around all four sides. 'Every day at noon a policeman played Chopin on a trumpet,' she said with a smile. 'He walked round all four sides of the balcony and just played his trumpet, always Chopin.' She hummed the piece but couldn't recollect the name.

As a child, Clara walked to school, past the Lemberg Gate and the municipal theatre. She took day trips to Lwów. 'There was a train about three times a day, but nobody used it,' she explained, 'the bus was every hour on the hour, so we always used that.' There was no real tension among the different communities. 'We were Jewish, the Poles were Polish, and the Ukrainians knew they were Ukrainian. Everybody was observant, religious.' She had Polish and Ukrainian friends, and at Christmas her family visited Polish homes to admire the decorated trees. The summer brought trips to other parts of Poland, places with beautiful forests that were different from Galicia. There, she remembered, the Jews were less free to trade or travel. That was the first time she was called names.

She spoke fondly of the old wooden church on east-west street, 'It was next to where we lived.' One of her neighbours was an old Lauterpacht, Hersch's uncle David, it turned out, who greeted them each morning on the street. She recalled the name Flaschner and Leon's uncle Leibus, but not his face. Did he run an inn? she enquired. She knew the street where the Flaschners lived with their children, then called Piłsudski Street, located between her house and the main square.

The Germans arrived but left abruptly, just as Olga described. 'It was a relief to get the Soviets; we were so scared of the Germans.' They'd heard about the *Anschluss* on the radio and from a few Viennese refugees who arrived in 1938. A Viennese couple was assigned to them, the Rosenbergs, a doctor and his wife. They came for supper every Wednesday evening. Initially, Clara and her parents didn't believe their tales of life in Vienna.

When the Germans returned in June 1941, life became more difficult. School friends ignored her on the street, turning their heads as she approached. 'I wore the white armband,' she explained. A year later, they went into hiding under the Becks' floorboards, opposite the old wooden church – eighteen of them, including Gedalo Lauterpacht and Mr and Mrs Melman, also relatives of Hersch Lauterpacht's.

She vividly remembered a day in March 1943, awoken by footsteps outside the house, the sound of crying and wailing. 'We knew our day would come in Żółkiew. It was maybe three o'clock in the morning. I was woken by the noise and then some shots. They were being taken to the forest; it was the only place to dig a grave.' She knew that forest, the *borek*, where children played. 'It was a beautiful wood. We had fun there. Now there was not a thing we could do. We could join them from our hiding place. At least three or four times, we were sure this was the end. I knew this was it.'

That was 25 March. The Jews of Zółkiew, thirty-five hundred of them, were marched into the wood, to a clearing and the sandpits. They were lined up, two kilometres from the centre of their little town, then shot.

19

Leon knew nothing of the events in Zółkiew, Lemberg and Vienna. Rita had been with him in Paris for a year, but their situation was precarious as they took steps to avoid regular roundups of Jews, the *rafles*. A year earlier, in July 1942, thirteen thousand Parisian Jews were interned at the Vélodrome d'Hiver, then deported to Auschwitz.

That summer, Leon and Rita obtained official documents. Two tiny identity cards were issued on 6 July 1943, in Courrières, a small town in north-west France, the site of Europe's worst mining disaster, forty years earlier. The cards were in Leon's papers, each with a diminutive photograph and two sets of fingerprints, one for each hand. Leon's card was No. 433, citing his birthplace as Lemberg, in the Départment of 'Autriche'; Rita had card No. 434, her maiden name misstated as Kamper (not Landes as it should have been), with an obviously false signature. Both cards stated their nationality to be French (untrue) and misspelled their surnames as Bucholz (omitting an *h*).

The cards folded to close, thin blue card, and cheap. When I contacted the *mairie* in Courrières, I was told that the SS destroyed the town hall on the rue Jean Jaurès in May 1940 and executed dozens of local residents who resisted German advances. Monsieur Louis Bétrémieux, a local historian, told me the cards could not be genuine; they were almost certainly forgeries: because the town was a centre of French Resistance, many forged cards were being issued. Thus I connected Leon to an underground life.

Leon and Rita's identity cards, 1943

20

I discovered little about Leon's life in the difficult period before the liberation of Paris by American troops in August 1944. Leon's teaching career was over, and he worked in some capacity for a Jewish organization. There was nothing about this in the papers my mother kept, but when I asked my aunt Annie (the widow of Leon and Rita's son Jean-Pierre, born after the war) whether Leon ever mentioned this period, she produced a bundle of documents that Leon gave her before he died. They were in a plastic shopping bag.

The documents were unexpected. The bulk of the papers comprised copies of a roughly printed newsletter, the *Bulletin* of the Union Générale des Israélites de France (UGIF), the Union of French Jews. The organization was established during the Nazi occupation to provide assistance to Jewish communities, and the *Bulletin* was published each Friday. Leon had a near-complete collection, from issue 1 (published in January 1942) to issue 119 (May 1944). Never more than four pages long, the *Bulletin* was printed on cheap paper, with articles on Jewish themes, advertisements (restaurants in the

4th arrondissement, a funeral parlour) and death notices. As the number of deportations rose, the *Bulletin* provided details of letters that couldn't be delivered, the addressees having been sent to distant 'work camps' in the east.

The *Bulletin* offered a platform for Nazi regulations, with warnings about the dangers of noncompliance, a snapshot of life in occupied Paris. One early ordinance prohibited Jews from leaving their homes between 8 p.m. and 6 a.m. (February 1942). A month later, a new rule banned the employment of Jews. From May 1942, every Jew was required to wear a Star of David on the left side of the chest (to be obtained from the main UGIF office at 19 rue de Téhéran, the elegant nineteenth-century building where Leon worked). In July, Jews were banned from attending theatres or other places of public performance. From October, they were limited to making purchases for an hour each day, prohibited from having a telephone, then required to travel in the last carriage of each train on the métro. The following year, in August 1943, special identity cards were issued.

As the number of deportations increased, the UGIF was subjected to increased restrictions, particularly after its leadership refused to give effect to an order to fire its foreign Jewish employees. In February 1943, the local Gestapo commander Klaus Barbie led a raid on the main office, arresting more than eighty employees and beneficiaries. A month later, on 17 and 18 March, former employees of UGIF were arrested (I noticed that issue 61 of the *Bulletin,* published that week, was missing from Leon's collection). Later that summer, Alois Brunner ordered the arrest of several UGIF leaders, sent to Drancy, then Auschwitz.

As a Polish Jew, Leon was under particular threat, yet somehow he evaded arrest. My aunt recalled him telling her how, on one occasion in the summer of 1943, Brunner personally descended on the offices at 19 rue de Téhéran to oversee arrests. Leon avoided him by hiding behind a door.

The plastic bag offered other evidence of activity. It held sheets of unused notepaper from the American Jewish Joint Distribution Committee, the Mouvement National des Prisonniers de Guerre et Déportés, and the Comité d'Unité et de Défense des Juifs de France. Each of these organizations, with which he must have worked, had offices at 19 rue de Téhéran.

Among the papers were two personal statements, each offering a detailed description of the treatment of deportees sent east. One was prepared in Paris in April 1944, recording testimony that at Auschwitz 'they hang for no reason, to the sound of music'. The other was prepared shortly after the war ended. 'At Birkenau, we worked in filth, at Auschwitz we died in cleanliness and order.' It ended with a statement of evidence: 'In short, this young man confirms all that is said on the radio and in the newspapers on the subject of concentration camps.'

Leon kept receipts of the postal packages he sent to camps and ghettos in the General Government in Nazi-occupied Poland. In the summer of 1942, he made twenty-four trips to the post office on the boulevard Malesherbes to send packages to Lina Marx, a woman in the Piaski ghetto near Lublin (the ghetto was liquidated the following summer, and Lina Marx was not among the few to survive).

Two postcards caught my eye, sent from the small town of Sandomierz, in Nazi-occupied Poland, by a Dr Ernst Walter Ulmann, deported from Vienna in February 1941. In the first, sent in March 1942, Dr Ulmann explained that he was an elderly, retired Viennese lawyer. 'Please help me.' The second card came four months later, in July, personally addressed to Leon at 19 rue de Téhéran. Dr Ulmann thanked him for a care package of sausage, canned tomatoes and small quantities of sugar. By the time Leon received the card, courteous Dr Ulmann was dead: the ghetto from which the card was sent had been emptied that month, its occupants dispatched to the concentration camp at Bełzec, farther along the railway line that connected Lemberg to Żółkiew.

At the bottom of the bag I found a bundle of yellow cloth, small sections cut into squares, with fraying edges. Each had a black Star of David printed onto it, with the word 'Juif' at its centre. There were forty-three of these stars, each in pristine condition, unused, ready to be distributed and worn.

21

Leon and Rita were separated from their daughter during their first years in Paris, although it seems they occasionally spent a little time with her. A few photographs remained – tiny square images, black-and-white, no more than two dozen. Undated, they showed a little girl with her parents, a toddler, two or three years old. She wore a white bow in her hair as Rita hovered near her with an anxious face. One image showed my mother standing with an older boy. In another, she was with her smartly attired parents, sitting at a café in a park, along with an older couple, the woman crowned with a box-like hat. A third set showed Ruth with her mother in Paris, five or six years old, perhaps towards the end of the occupation.

In none of the photographs did Rita smile.

Leon and Rita now lived on the rue Brongniart, the shortest street in Paris, close to their friends Monsieur and Madame Boussard, who were not Jewish and kept an eye on them. In later years, Leon told his daughter that Monsieur Boussard would warn him of roundups, telling him to stay off the streets and away from the apartment. Yet there was nothing about the Boussards in Leon's papers or any mention of them elsewhere. Leon and Rita remained close to the Boussards after the war, but my mother lost contact after they declined to attend her wedding to an Englishman, my father. The English were an even more detestable lot than the Germans, they explained. That was in 1956. I laughed out loud when my mother told me the story, but she said it was no laughing matter, that it put a strain on the friendship between the older couples, and that she never saw Monsieur Boussard again. Many years later, when she took tea with Madame Boussard at La Coupole, the famous café on the boulevard du Montparnasse, Madame Boussard told her that Rita had always loved her son, Jean-Pierre, more than her daughter. My mother never saw her again.

On 25 August 1944, Leon and Rita celebrated the liberation of Paris with the Boussards. They joined the throngs on the Champs-Élysées, greeted American troops, and wondered how they might collect their daughter from Meudon. Leon stopped a US army truck filled with young GIs, one of whom spoke Polish.

'Hop in,' the GI said, 'we'll take you to Meudon.' An hour later, the soldiers dropped the couple in the town centre. One more 'Good luck' in Polish, then they were off.

That night the family slept together in their home at 2 rue Brongniart, a tiny two-room apartment on the fourth floor. It was the first time in five years that they had slept under the same roof.

22

I returned to a photograph in Leon's papers, one I had seen in my mother's living room before I first travelled to Lviv.

I sent the image to an archivist at the Fondation Charles de Gaulle in Paris. She told me it was taken on 1 November, in the cemetery of Ivry-sur-Seine, just outside Paris. De Gaulle had visited the Carré des Fusillés, a memorial to foreign resistance fighters executed by the Germans during the occupation.

'The person with the moustache is Adrien Tixier, appointed by General de Gaulle as minister of the interior in the provisional government of the French Republic in September 1944,' the archivist explained. 'Behind him is the head of the police in Paris, [Charles] Luizet' (on the left of the picture, in peaked cap), and the prefect of the Seine, Marcel Flouret (on the right, white scarf). 'Behind Flouret with the moustache is Gaston Palewski,' a name that rang a bell: Palewski was director of de Gaulle's cabinet, Nancy Mitford's lover,

Charles de Gaulle, Cimetière d'Ivry, 1944

later immortalized as Fabrice, the fictional duc de Sauveterre in her novel *Love in a Cold Climate*.

What was Leon doing in such company?

One clue came with the identity of those interred at the Carré des Fusillés. Among those executed were twenty-three French résistants, members of the Franc-Tireurs et Partisans de la Main d'Oeuvre Immigrée, foreign fighters living in Paris. The group included eight Poles, five Italians, three Hungarians, a Spaniard, three French and two Armenians, one of whom was Missak Manouchian, the leader of the group. The only woman was Romanian. Half the group was Jewish.

The twenty-three members of the Resistance were apprehended in November 1943. Three months later, bright red posters appeared around the city and other parts of France, with names and faces under a bold headline, 'L'armée du crime' (The army of crime). This was *L'affiche rouge*, the famous red poster that called on Parisians to hunt out these foreigners before they destroyed France, its women and children. 'It is always foreigners who take command of such actions, always the unemployed and professional criminals who execute them, and always the Jews who inspire them', the back of the poster declared.

A few weeks later, in February, all but one of the group were executed by firing squad at Fort Mont-Valérien. They were buried at the Ivry cemetery, and de Gaulle visited their graves, accompanied by Leon. The solitary exception was Olga Bancic, the only woman in the group, briefly spared. She was beheaded in Stuttgart a few weeks later, on her thirty-second birthday.

The executions were memorialized by Louis Aragon's poem 'L'affiche rouge'. Written in 1955, the poem drew on Manouchian's last letter to his wife, Mélinée, lines that later inspired the singer Léo Ferré, who wrote a song that was familiar from childhood, perhaps because Leon knew it:

> *Happiness to all, Happiness to those who will survive,*
> *I die without hatred for the German people,*
> *Adieu to pain and unhappiness.*

When de Gaulle visited the graves, Leon was among the entourage. Did he know the twenty-three? One person on the poster was familiar, Maurice Fingercwajg, a Polish Jew, who was twenty when executed. I recognized the name: Lucette, a childhood friend of my mother's, walked her to school each morning after the occupation was over, and later married Lucien Fingercweig, a cousin of the executed young man. Lucette's husband later told me that Leon had been in touch with the group, but he was unable to offer more detail. 'That was why he was near the front of the procession at the Ivry cemetery,' Lucien added.

23

When the occupation of Paris ended, Leon had no information as to the fate of Malke, Gusta, or Laura, or any of the family in Lemberg and Żółkiew. Newspaper articles reported mass killings at concentration camps, and names of towns like Treblinka and Auschwitz began to appear in the press. Leon must have feared the worst but hoped for something better.

New organizations sprang up. In March 1945, the American Jewish Joint Distribution Committee set up the Comité Juif d'Action Sociale et de Reconstruction (the Jewish Committee for Social Assistance and Reconstruction). Leon was working with the Comité Juif in the centre of Paris at the Hôtel de Lutèce, which had been a Gestapo headquarters, when he heard the news of Hitler's suicide, on 30 April. A week later, General Alfred Jodl signed an unconditional surrender. In July, Leon was appointed *chef de service,* although which department he headed was not clear from the one document he retained in his papers, a fading grey identity card. He never spoke to me of this organization, said to have grown out of the French Resistance, which worked to reintegrate refugees and concentration camp survivors into postwar life. My mother's recollection of those days was limited to the memory of an occasional visitor to their home on the rue Brongniart, a destitute man or woman invited to share a meal and conversation. More than one committed suicide.

Leon did receive one piece of encouraging news. Separated from his friend Max for six years, in April he found an address in New York, to which he wrote. In July a response arrived, joyful about the renewal of contact, tinged with fear about the fate of lost family members. 'As long as I don't have any bad news,' Max wrote to

Leon, 'I will not lose hope.' What news of your family? Max enquired. He listed those for whom he sought information, including his missing brothers. The letter ended with affectionate sentiments, encouragement that Leon and Rita should move to America, and an offer of help with visas. In January 1946, Leon and Rita registered at the American consulate in Paris to apply for emigration, Rita as an Austrian, Leon as a Pole.

24

Around this time, *Le Monde* and other newspapers reported that the Allies were thinking of creating an international tribunal to prosecute the leading Nazis. Speculation hardened into fact: the tribunal would have eight judges, two of whom were French. Leon might have known one, by name at least, Robert Falco, a former judge at the court of appeal in Paris.

In October 1945, the indictment of the twenty-two defendants was put before the tribunal. *Le Monde* described the crimes with which they would be charged, noting a new one called 'genocide'. What did the crime signify, the newspaper enquired, and what were its origins? The answer came in an interview with the man who was said to have invented the word, Rafael Lemkin, identified as an American professor. Asked about the practical consequences, Lemkin referred the journalist to events occurring in places with which Leon was so closely connected, Vienna and Poland. 'If in the future a State acts in a manner that is intended to destroy a national or racial minority within the population,' Lemkin told French readers, 'any perpetrator can be arrested if he leaves the country.'

The reference to events in Vienna and Poland would have offered Leon another reminder of a family about which he had no news. His father, Pinkas, and his brother, Emil, were both dead by the end of 1914, but what of those who remained in Vienna, Lemberg and Zółkiew?

In 1945, Leon had no information, but I now did. He never told me that every single person from his childhood, each and every member of the extended Galician family of Buchholzes and Flaschners was murdered. Of the seventy or more family members living in Lemberg and Zółkiew when the war began, the only survivor was Leon, the smiling boy with big ears.

Leon never spoke to me of that period, nor did he mention any of these family members. Only now, as a consequence of accepting the invitation to deliver a lecture in Lviv, could I begin to comprehend the scale of the devastation that he lived with for the remainder of a life that ran to the end of the twentieth century. The man I came to know in the second half of his life was the last person standing from the years in Galicia. This was the cause of the silence I had heard as a child, a silence that dominated the small apartment he shared with Rita.

From the few documents and photographs, I was able to reconstruct the outlines of a disappeared world. The gaps were many, and not just of individuals. I noticed the absence of affectionate exchanges between Leon and Rita in his papers. To her 'golden child' Rita sent heartfelt love, but if a similar sentiment was communicated to Leon, no written trace remained. The same went the other way.

I had a sense that something else had intervened in their lives before they separated in January 1939. Why did Leon leave Vienna on his own? How did his infant daughter get to Paris? Why did Rita stay behind? I returned to the documents, seeking clues in the scrap of paper with Miss Tilney's address and the three photographs of the man in a bow tie.

They led nowhere, so I turned to another place connected with this early life, the small town of Zółkiew. This was the birthplace of Leon's mother, Malke, and also of Hersch Lauterpacht, the man who put the words 'crimes against humanity' into the Nuremberg trial.

II

LAUTERPACHT

The individual human being . . . is the ultimate unit of all law

Hersch Lauterpacht, 1943

25

On a warm summer's day in 1945, a few weeks after the war in Europe had ended, a middle-aged law professor who was born in Żółkiew but now lived in Cambridge, England, awaited the arrival of lunch guests. I imagined him in his study on the upper floor of a solid, semi-detached house on Cranmer Road, sitting at his large mahogany desk, gazing out of the window, Bach's *St Matthew Passion* playing on the gramophone. Forty-eight years old and anxious, Hersch Lauterpacht awaited the arrival of the US Supreme Court justice Robert Jackson, recently appointed by President Truman as chief prosecutor of German war criminals at the International Military Tribunal in Nuremberg.

Jackson was on his way to Cambridge with a specific problem, one for which he sought Lauterpacht's 'good judgment and learning'. Specifically, he needed to persuade the Soviets and the French of the charges to be brought against the Nuremberg defendants for international crimes perpetrated by the German Nazi leadership. The relationship between Jackson and Lauterpacht was one of trust, going back several years. They would discuss the list of crimes, the roles of the prosecutors and the judges, the treatment of evidence, points of language.

The one matter they would not talk about was Lauterpacht's family: like Leon and millions of others, he awaited news about his parents and siblings, uncles and aunts, cousins and nephews, a large family lost in silence, in Lemberg and Żółkiew.

Of this he did not wish to speak to Robert Jackson.

26

Lauterpacht was born in Żółkiew on 16 August 1897. A birth certificate, unearthed in an archive in Warsaw, declared that his parents were Aron Lauterpacht, a businessman, and Deborah Turkenkopf.

The birth was witnessed by Barich Orlander, an innkeeper who happened to be a distant relation of Leon's mother.

Aron worked in the oil business and managed a sawmill. Deborah attended to the family, Lauterpacht's older brother, David (Dunek), and a younger sister, Sabina (Sabka), born three years after Hersch. A fourth child had been stillborn. Lauterpacht's family was large, middle-class, literate and devoutly Jewish (Deborah maintained a kosher home and modest appearance, following the tradition of wearing a wig). A photograph of the family showed Lauterpacht aged five, his feet pointing in different directions, holding on to the arm of a father with a solid appearance.

Lauterpacht family, Żółkiew, 1902: Hersch is far left

Lauterpacht's sister, the little girl perched on the stool, would eventually produce a daughter of her own called Inka. When I met her, she described Aron and Deborah as 'wonderful' grandparents, 'kind and loving' people who were hardworking, generous and 'very ambitious' for their children. Inka recalled a lively home, filled with music and books, talk of ideas and politics, and an optimistic future. The family spoke Yiddish, but the parents switched to Polish if they didn't want the children to understand.

The cadastral records of Żółkiew disclosed that the Lauterpacht family lived at house No. 158 on parcel 488. This turned out to be the eastern end of the same east-west street on which my great-grand-mother Malke Buchholz (Flaschner) had lived, the other end of town.

Lyudmyla, Żółkiew's fine and friendly historian, identified the precise spot, now covered in tarmac on the eastern edge of the town, on the road by which I'd arrived from Lviv.

'A fine place to put a statue,' Lyudmyla observed wryly, and we agreed it would happen one day. The spot was close to the Alter Friedhof (the old cemetery) and the old wooden church of the Holy Trinity, to which Lyudmyla took me. With its worn brown-shingle exterior, the church interior was infused with cosy smells of wood and spice. There was a striking altar of painted icons; it was a warm place of gold embellishments, with deep reds and blues, a place of safety, unchanged in a hundred years. Lauterpacht's uncle David lived right opposite, Lyudmyla added, a house long gone. Nearby she pointed out another house, which we should visit. She knocked vigorously on the front door, eventually opened by the owner, a round and jolly man with a big smile. Come in, he said, before leading us to the front bedroom, overlooking the wooden church, then to a small area between bed and wall. On his knees, he prised up a section of the parquet, revealing an irregular hole in the floor, just large enough for an adult to pass. In this space, in the darkness, Clara Kramer and seventeen other Jews hid for nearly two years. Among them were various members of the Lauterpacht family, not more than a stone's throw from where Lauterpacht was born.

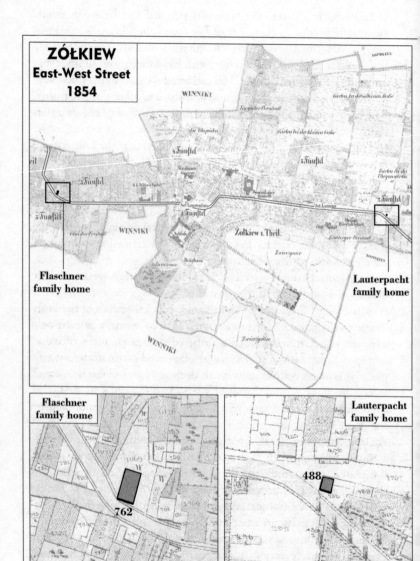

ZÓŁKIEW
East-West Street
1854

WINNIKI

SOROSZYN

Garten In der silbernen Ruhe

Turynher-Vorstadt

Au Blapoka

Garten bei der kleinen Ruhe

3 Fünftel

Garten bei der
Chrynomicka
at

Rosshauer
Vorstadt

Spitaldiste

5 Fünftel

3 Fünftel

K.K. Militär Spital

Rosswolauer
Garten

Sct. Laurentius

Sct. Lazarus

2 Fünftel

5 Fünftel

1 Fünftel

Ost. Spital

Heisse Vorstadtchen

Lemberger Vorstadt

Glinher-Vorstadt

WINNIKI

Schloss

Zólkiew I. Theil.

Zwierzyniec

MOROSZYN

Brauhaus

Zwierzyniec

Flaschner
family home

Lauterpacht
family home

WINNIKI

Zwierzyniec

Flaschner
family home

762

Lauterpacht
family home

488

27

Lauterpacht left Żółkiew in 1910, with his parents and siblings. He was thirteen, off to Lemberg for a better education, in the sixty-second year of the Emperor Franz Joseph's liberal reign. That year, the Epsom Derby was won by a horse called Lemberg, owned by an English bachelor called Alfie Cox with no obvious connection to the city.

As Aron managed a sawmill on the outskirts of the city, his son enrolled at the Humanist Gymnasium, already a distinct and articulate boy. He was a voracious reader, confident, politically engaged and disinclined to follow a religious path. His peers recognized him as a leader, a boy who was cultured, strong-willed, intolerant, with 'a very big intellect' and a conscience. Social inequalities coursed through Lemberg's streets, built on foundations of xenophobia, racism, group identity and conflict. These elements touched him from an early age.

In Żółkiew, Lauterpacht had learned about friction between groups, divisions carved into everyday life by matters of religious faith and political belief. Lemberg offered a more bloody account, a city built on the fault line of nationalist and imperialist ambitions, as Leon too had learned. Yet even as an Orthodox Jewish family tucked between Roman Catholic and Eastern Orthodox civilizations, the Lauterpachts believed themselves to be living in a metropolis that was the epicentre of liberal civilization, a firmament of inventive mathematicians and fearless lawyers, of cafés filled with scientists, of poets and musicians, a city with a fine new railway station and a magnificent opera house, a place that Buffalo Bill Cody might visit (as he did in 1905, with his Wild West show).

It was also a city of sounds and smells. 'I can hear the bells of Lwów ringing, each one rings differently,' wrote Józef Wittlin. 'I can hear the splash of the fountains on the Market Square, and the soughing of the fragrant trees, which the spring rain has washed clean of dust.' Young Lauterpacht could have frequented the same cafés as Wittlin, all now long gone: the Europejska at the corner of Jagiellońska and May the Third Streets (where 'the appearance of a member of the fairer sex was a disturbing rarity'), the Sztuka on an upper floor of Andriolli Passage ('where the atmospheric lighting was dimmed whenever the long-haired violinist Wasserman played Schumann's *Träumerei*'), and the Renaissance on May the Third and Kościuszko Streets (where waiters from other cafés would appear in challengingly bright jackets and colourful ties and order their colleagues to wait on them).

War came to Lemberg three years after the family's arrival. Lauterpacht was in the city when the Russians occupied it in September 1914, Emperor Nicholas receiving the news that the Austrians had been totally routed and were 'retreating in complete disorder'. This was a reference to the great battle in which Leon's older brother, Emil, was probably killed. The *New York Times* reported that the Russian 'invaders' showed 'kindness', respected churches and 'little wayside praying centres', allowing Lemberg to remain as peaceful and busy as London amid the bloody mayhem of war.

In June 1915, the Austro-Hungarian army retook the city, with help from German troops, producing 'an outburst of wild joy throughout Austria and Germany'. A month later, Lauterpacht was conscripted into the Austrian army, although he seems to have spent most of his time billeted at his father's sawmill. A friend observed him there in the engine room, 'oblivious' to the sounds of machinery and war, immersed in books, teaching himself French and English. Lauterpacht kept a detailed notebook, now in the possession of his son, in which he recorded the books he read, across a wide range of areas, including war and economics, religion and psychology, Adam Smith's *Wealth of Nations* and a treatise on Marxism. Music offered an escape, in particular the Bach and Beethoven that would come to offer passion and solace over a lifetime. He was said to have a 'phenomenally good ear and musical memory', but his playing didn't extend beyond a two-fingered *Kreutzer Sonata*.

As the time came for him to decide on a life at the university, his parents persuaded him to follow in his brother's footsteps. In the autumn of 1915, he enrolled at the law faculty of Lemberg University.

28

The writings on Lauterpacht's life had little to say about his university days, what he studied or where he lived, so I decided to explore the city archives of Lviv. Without Polish or Ukrainian language skills, I came to rely on Ihor and Ivan, admirable students at the same law faculty where Lauterpacht had studied a century earlier (Ivan's Ph.D., on the Soviet naval base at Sebastopol in the Crimea, proved to be timely, coinciding with the renewal of Russia's territorial forays, this time into the unlawful occupation of the Crimea). Ivan eventually took me on a trail that led to the meandering edifice that was the State Archive of Lviv Oblast.

Muzeina Square, just north of the town hall, was familiar to me, the home to a flea market, an open-air library of postcards, newspapers and books that offered a full account of the city's anguished twentieth century. My son bought a Soviet cuckoo clock (blue and red, metal) as I foraged for scraps from the Austro-Hungarian period, Polish postcards, a few Jewish and Yiddish objects. The premium objects – if price was the measure – were from the three years of Nazi control: I spotted the distinctive shape of a dark green *Stahlhelm* with a swastika on one side and an SS symbol on the other, but the seller shooed me away when I got too close.

The State Archive occupied a dilapidated eighteenth-century building abutting a former Dominican monastery, part of the Baroque Church of the Blessed Eucharist. In the Soviet era, the church served as a museum of religion and atheism; now it was a Ukrainian Greek Catholic church. A scarfed babushka guarded the entrance. 'Your business?' she shouted. Ivan mouthed the password – 'Archiv' – with sufficient authority that we were allowed to enter. The secret was to carry on walking, not to stop.

The reading room was reached through an overgrown rose garden and up a metal staircase over which a rain-sodden carpet had been laid. Ivan and I entered on the first floor, a place with no signs, the corridor unlit, a hallway lined with the detritus of Lembergiana. Documents lined the walls: the final retreat of the Austro-Hungarian army, November 1918; the proclamation of the independent but short-lived West Ukrainian People's Republic, same date; the German encirclement of Soviet Lviv, June 1941; Governor Hans Frank's order incorporating Galicia into the territory of his General Government, August 1941; another order, closing all Lemberg's schools and universities, September 1941.

At the end of the corridor, a neon light flickered above the entrance to the reading room. Here the archivist took our book orders, in the presence of five readers, including one nun and two sleepers.

Lemberg, 1917. Law faculty on left, second from top; railway station on right, second from top; George Hotel, bottom right.

All was quiet until the electricity died, a short, daily occurrence that prompted gentle commotion, although on one occasion I noticed that the nun managed to sleep through the entire disturbance. Return tomorrow at ten, the archivist instructed, to collect the books. The next day a pile of volumes awaited, neatly laid out on wooden desks, three towers of dust, leather and crumbling paper. These were the student records of the law faculty from 1915 to 1919.

We began in the autumn of 1915, working our way through hundreds of forms filled in by hand, the pages arranged alphabetically by the name of each student, identified as a Pole or Mosaic (Jewish), with only a few Ukrainians. It was painstaking work. Names were written out, with lists of the courses taken, class hours, the names of the professors. The back of each form was signed and dated.

Ivan spotted a first Lauterpacht document, based on the work of his friend Ihor, which dated to the autumn of 1915, shortly after the Russians had been removed. We gathered a near-complete set, seven semesters of study from 1915 to 1919, Lauterpacht's formative years. There was a home address, 6 Rutowskiego Street, now Teatralna Street, just a few doors from my hotel. I'd walked past it, even noticed the fine metal doors with their two large Ls at the centre, mounted in circular metal frames. Lauterpacht? Lemberg? Lwów?

I learned that Lauterpacht's studies began with Roman law and German public law, followed by one course on soul and body, and another on optimism and pessimism. Of the early teachers, only one had a familiar name, Professor Oswald Balzer, teacher of the legal histories of Poland and Austria, distinct subjects. Balzer was a practising advocate who argued esoteric cases for the governments of Austria and Galicia. The most notable, which I'd come across in my own work on boundary disputes, was a nineteenth-century conflict over the ownership of two lakes in the Tatra Mountains. Balzer was a practical man, an influence on Lauterpacht.

The second year of studies, from September 1916, was dominated by war and the death of the Emperor Franz Joseph, after a record-inducing reign over sixty-eight years. Change was in the air as battles continued to rage around the city, yet classes continued. I was struck by the seam of religious themes (Catholic Christian law, then the History and Culture of Israel) and by the daily lecture on pragmatism and instinctivism, the two poles between which Lauterpacht's intellectual development oscillated like a sharp current of electricity.

In April 1917, he passed a state exam in historical and legal science, obtaining the highest mark ('good').

His third year began in September 1917 as Austria's hold on the city became more tenuous. Lauterpacht took a first class on criminal law, taught by Professor Dr Juliusz Makarewicz, a well-known authority on Austrian criminal law. A second followed, with the same teacher, on the science of the prison. A third course, on Austrian adversary proceedings, was taught by Professor Dr Maurycy Allerhand. I mention these names because they will return.

The fourth and final year of studies opened on the cusp of dramatic changes, for Lemberg, Europe and the world. In November 1918, as the First World War ended – along with the Austro-Hungarian Empire – control of Lemberg changed as each week passed.

29

Lauterpacht's life was transformed by a secret decision taken by Archduke Wilhelm of Austria, the twenty-three-year-old 'Red Prince', one that would catalyse a bloody conflict between Poles and Ukrainians in Lemberg. This was in November 1918, four years after Leon had left for Vienna, when Wilhelm ordered Polish units of the Austro-Hungarian army to withdraw from Lemberg, replacing them with two Ukrainian regiments of Sich Riflemen. On 1 November, the Ukrainians took control of Lviv and declared it the capital of the West Ukrainian People's Republic, a new country.

Heavy fighting followed between Polish and Ukrainian factions, with Jews caught between the two, fearful of choosing the wrong side, the one that lost, opting for neutrality. The conflict continued beyond the armistice signed by Germany and the Allies on 11 November, the day Poland declared independence. Bloodshed came to Teatralna Street, where the Lauterpachts lived, causing much damage to property. Lauterpacht's school friend Joseph Roth (a namesake of the novelist born in nearby Brody) described the period that followed, days of 'friction and conflict' as the Austro-Hungarian Empire disintegrated. 'To protect the Jewish population,' Roth explained, 'a voluntary Jewish militia was organized.' It included Lauterpacht, who patrolled the Jewish quarters 'day and night'.

Within a week, the Ukrainians had lost control to the Poles, and an agreement was reached to end the fighting. As Lviv became Lwów, looting and killing came to the streets.

I found a picture of a barricade, on the street where the Lauterpacht family would later live, dusted with a light fall of early snow. With this photograph, it was easier to imagine the events over those three days, described by the *New York Times* under the headline: '1,100 Jews Murdered in Lemberg Pogroms'. The words heaped pressure on President Woodrow Wilson to stop the bloodshed.

Barricade on Sykstuska Street, Lemberg, November 1918

Lauterpacht ploughed on with his studies as these bloody events underscored the dangers for minority groups. Confronted by the harsh realities for tens of thousands of individuals caught up in a struggle between groups, and now a leader of the Organization of Zionist Academics in Galicia, he established a Jewish high school (Gymnasium) and organized a boycott of Polish schools. Jewish youths could not 'sit on the same benches with those who participated in the pogroms against Jews', a friend of his explained.

The collapse of established authority unleashed a violent

nationalism as the possibility of a new Polish or Ukrainian state came into view. Among the Jewish population, there were differing reactions. As the anti-nationalist community of Orthodox Jews hoped for a quiet life alongside the Poles and the Ukrainians, some argued for the creation of an independent Jewish state somewhere in the former Austro-Hungarian Empire. Others wanted greater autonomy for Jews in newly independent Poland, whereas for the Zionists nothing less than a separate Jewish state in Palestine would suffice.

Such issues of group identity and autonomy, along with the rise of nationalism and the emergence of new states after the end of the First World War, combined to move the law to the centre of the political stage. This was a new development in scale and scope. How might the law protect minorities? it was asked. What languages could they speak? Would they be able to educate their children in special schools? Such questions continue to resonate today around the world, but back then no international rules offered guidance on how to address them. Each country, old or new, was free to treat those who lived within its borders as it wished. International law offered few constraints on the majority's treatment of minorities and no rights for individuals.

Lauterpacht's intellectual development coincided with this crucial moment. Engaged in Zionist activity, he nevertheless feared nationalism. The philosopher Martin Buber, who lectured and lived in Lemberg, became an intellectual influence, opposing Zionism as a form of abhorrent nationalism and holding to the view that a Jewish state in Palestine would inevitably oppress the Arab inhabitants. Lauterpacht attended Buber's lectures and found himself attracted to such ideas, identifying himself as a disciple of Buber's. This was an early fluttering of scepticism about the power of the state.

In the meantime, classes at law school continued. Lauterpacht immersed himself in Professor Roman Longchamps de Berier's course on Austrian private law, even as Austria withered. Professor Makarewicz offered a daily lecture on Austrian criminal law, even as that law ceased to be applicable in Polish Lwów, giving the class a surreal air. Lauterpacht also took a first course on international law, taught in the autumn of 1918 by Dr Józef Buzek, politically active in Vienna and about to become a member of the new Polish parliament. The classes must have underscored the marginality of the subject, at a university where discrimination was rife and individual professors were free to decide that Ukrainians and Jews were not permitted to attend their courses.

Lauterpacht imagined a move elsewhere, perhaps inspired by one of the books he listed as having read in his notebook. *Ghetto Comedies,* written by Israel Zangwill, whose face would soon appear on the cover of *Time* magazine, offered a collection of stories that touched on the glories of 'Anglicization'. In 'The Model of Sorrows', Zangwill wrote the story of an innkeeper who left Russia for England because of the 'intolerable' situation at home. Another story ('Holy Wedlock') posed a question: 'Would you not like to go and see Vienna?'

30

In 1919, Vienna was the capital of a rump state, the last territory of a monarchy that had lasted nearly a thousand years. It was a place of dilapidated buildings, filled with demobilized soldiers and prisoners of war streaming home, with galloping inflation and an Austrian Crown 'dissolving like jelly in your fingers'. Stefan Zweig described a 'distressing' foray into an Austrian city overwhelmed by famine and the 'yellow, dangerous eyes of the starving', of bread that was but a few 'black crumbs tasting of pitch and glue', frozen potatoes, men going around in old uniforms and trousers made of old sacks, and a 'general breakdown of morale'. Yet it still offered hope to Leon and his family, who had been there for five years. To someone like Lauterpacht, the lure of a liberal culture, literature, music and cafés, and of universities open to all, would have been strong.

In the summer of 1919, after his course ended, Lauterpacht left Lwów. Europe's boundaries were being redrawn and the issue of Lwów's control became unclear: in January 1918, the US president, Woodrow Wilson, had addressed Congress, setting out his Fourteen Points, ideas on the 'autonomous development' of 'the peoples of Austria-Hungary' that also took account of the aspiration for a new state 'inhabited by indisputably Polish populations'. Wilson's proposals had an unintended consequence: the modern law of human rights was born on the anvil of Lwów and its environs.

In April 1919, as the Versailles negotiations moved to a close, an intergovernmental Commission on Polish Affairs drew a line as Poland's eastern boundary. It was known as the Curzon Line, in honour of the British foreign secretary, and Lauterpacht played a minor role in its preparation (although he never wrote of this), working as an interpreter. He knew the territory and had the language skills. 'Hersch, then aged 21, was chosen as interpreter and fulfilled his task satisfactorily,' a friend reported. By then he spoke French, Italian, Polish and Ukrainian, with knowledge of Hebrew, Yiddish, German and Italian. He even had a little English. The Curzon Line was drawn to the east of Lwów, bringing the city and surrounding areas, including Zółkiew, into Poland. Russian control was avoided.

These developments coincided with attacks on Jews across Poland, raising concerns in the United States and elsewhere as to the ability of a newly independent Poland to safeguard its German and Jewish minorities. In the shadow of Versailles, a quid pro quo emerged: Poland would get independence if it protected the rights of minorities. At the behest of President Wilson, the Harvard historian Archibald Coolidge reported on conditions in Lwów and Galicia, calling for minorities to be assured basic protections, of 'life, liberty, and the pursuit of happiness'.

President Wilson proposed a special treaty to link Poland's membership in the League of Nations with a commitment to bestow equal treatment on racial and national minorities. Wilson was supported by France, but Britain objected, fearful that similar rights would then be accorded to other groups, including 'American negroes, Southern Irish, Flemings and Catalans'. The new League of Nations must not protect minorities in all countries, a British official complained, or it would have 'the right to protect the Chinese in Liverpool, the Roman Catholics in France, the French in Canada, quite apart from more serious problems, such as the Irish'. Britain objected to any depletion of sovereignty – the right to treat others as it wished – or international oversight. It took this position even if the price was more 'injustice and oppression'.

This was the background against which pro-Zionist and national Jewish delegations arrived in Paris in March 1919, calling for greater autonomy, language and cultural rights and principles of self-government and representation. As these matters were being debated, a report circulated that 350 kilometres to the north of

Lwów, in the town of Pinsk, a group of Polish soldiers had massacred thirty-five Jewish civilians. This caused the pendulum to swing as the Versailles negotiations produced a draft treaty for the protection of minorities in Poland. On 21 May, the Polish delegation at Versailles was handed a copy of the draft treaty, reflecting President Wilson's call for 'rigid protection' for minorities. This was seen by the new Polish government as an unwarranted interference in its internal affairs. Ignacy Paderewski, the classical pianist and head of the Polish delegation, wrote directly to the British prime minister, David Lloyd George, to object to every clause of the draft treaty. Don't create a 'Jewish problem', he warned, in Poland or elsewhere. Fearful that Warsaw might not sign the treaty, Lloyd George agreed to concessions.

A month later, the Versailles Treaty was signed. Article 93 required Poland to sign a second treaty, to protect 'inhabitants' who differed from the majority of the population in race, language, or religion. The Allies would be entitled to 'protect' these minorities, a further humiliation in the eyes of Poland because lopsided obligations were imposed: rights were given to some groups, but not all, and the victorious powers would escape equivalent obligations for their own minorities.

Poland was basically forced to sign the document, known as the Little Treaty of Versailles. Article 4 imposed Polish nationality on all people born in and around Lwów, including Lauterpacht and Leon. Poland was required to take steps to protect all its inhabitants, 'without distinction of birth, nationality, language, race or religion'. Minorities could run their own schools and religious and social institutions and would have language rights and religious freedom. Yet the Polish Minorities Treaty went further: it made the rights of such minorities into 'obligations of international concern', to be protected at the League of Nations. Any disputes could go to the Permanent Court of International Justice, newly created in The Hague.

Such revolutionary obligations allowed some minorities in Poland to have a right of access to international protection but not the Polish majority. This produced a backlash, a little treaty, a little time bomb, the unintended consequence of well-intentioned international legislation. A few days after signing the Minorities Treaty, President Wilson established a commission to investigate the situation of the

Jews in Poland, supposedly at the request of President Paderewski, to be headed by Henry Morgenthau, the former US ambassador to the Ottoman Empire. Marshal Józef Piłsudski, head of the new Polish government, complained bitterly about the Minorities Treaty. 'Why not trust to Poland's honour?' he asked Morgenthau. 'Every faction within Poland was agreed on doing justice to the Jew, and yet the Peace Conference, at the insistence of America, insults us by *telling* us that we must do justice.'

The commission visited Lwów on 30 August 1919. The members appreciated the 'exceedingly pretty and modern looking' city, largely undamaged by the events of the previous November except for the Jewish quarter, which was 'burnt down'. The commission concluded that although 'excesses' had occurred, only sixty-four people were killed, far fewer than the thousand reported in the *New York Times*. It also found that those responsible were soldiers, not civilians, so it would be 'unfair to condemn the Polish nation as a whole' for the violence of a few troops or local mobs.

Shortly before leaving, the commission's young legal adviser, Arthur Goodhart, walked up Vysoky Zamok, the large hill to the north that overlooked the city, in the company of Dr Fiedler, the president of Lwów Polytechnic. Trouble was brewing, Dr Fiedler told Goodhart, because of the separate schools the Jews had asked for. Assimilate, or face difficulties.

31

Nearly a century later, I walked up the same path taken by Fiedler and Goodhart to the top of the hill, to look across a city that was, back in 1919, on the cusp of great changes. 'I was unable to take my final examinations,' Lauterpacht complained, 'because the University closed its doors to the Jews of Eastern Galicia.' He followed the suggestion of the writer Israel Zangwill and headed to Vienna.

I visited the home he left behind in Lwów, a grey four-storey neo-classical building on Teatralna Street, largely unscathed today, now home to a 'Cossack hostel'. A photograph from that period showed the building framed between two churches, the town hall's impressive tower to the rear. A plaque in the lobby recorded the name of the architect (the engineer A. Piller, 1911), introducing a mighty stairwell capped by a glass skylight. The first-floor apartment had a balcony, allowing a fine view across the city.

I imagined Lauterpacht leaving behind this view. He would have made his way to the station, through the vibrant scene described by the writer Karl Emil Franzos, passing hussar officers alongside elegant gentlemen; Moldovan boyars with 'dark, cunning faces' and 'heavy gold rings'; dark-eyed women in 'heavy silk clothing and dirty slips'; long-bearded Ruthenian priests; faded coquettes on their way to Bucharest or Iaşi to seek their luck. He might also have encountered a few 'civilized travellers', emancipated Polish Jews like Lauterpacht who were heading west.

Lauterpacht arrived at the Nordwestbahnhof of Vienna, the city dominated by Freud, Klimt and Mahler. It was passing through troubled economic times, the trauma of empire's end. Lauterpacht was in *Rote Wien* – Red Vienna – a city with a Social Democratic mayor, bustling with refugees from Galicia, inflation and poverty rampant. The Russian Revolution provoked agitation for some, hope for others. Austria was on its knees, an empire dissolved. The country now depended on the Czechs and the Poles for coal, on the Banat for cereal. It had no access to the sea, having lost most of its former territory, including the German-speaking Sudetenland and south Tyrol, Hungary, Czechoslovakia and Poland, as well as the State of Slovenes, Croats and Serbs. Bukovina and Bosnia and Herzegovina were also gone. Prohibited from entering a union with Germany, the country wasn't even allowed to call itself *Deutschösterreich* (German Austria).

Feelings of subjugation and humiliation further inflamed nationalist sentiment. The influx of *Ostjuden* from Galicia – young men like Lauterpacht and Leon – made for easy targets. Around the time of Lauterpacht's arrival, five thousand gathered at the city hall to call for all Jews to be expelled from the city. Two years later, in March 1921, the numbers had grown as forty thousand attended a rally of the *Antisemitenbund* to applaud the call by the director of the Burgtheater, Hofrat Milenkovich, for strict limits on jobs for Jews.

The journalist Hugo Bettauer published a best-selling novel, *Die Stadt ohne Juden,* which imagined the city without Jews. 'If I was able to get out of the burning Lemberg ghetto and reach Vienna,' one of Bettauer's characters declared, 'I guess I'll find some place to go from Vienna.' In the novel, the city falls apart without its Jews, and in due course they are invited to return, their expulsion recognized as a mistake. Bettauer paid a price for such ideas: he was murdered in 1925 by Otto Rothstock, a young National Socialist, who was tried but acquitted on grounds of insanity (he later became a dentist). The nationalist newspaper *Wiener Morgenzeitung* warned that Bettauer's murder sent a message to 'every intellectual who wrote for a cause'.

Such events coloured Lauterpacht's life in Vienna. He was now enrolled at the law faculty of the university, and his teacher was the renowned legal philosopher Hans Kelsen, a friend and university colleague of Sigmund Freud's. Kelsen combined academic life with practical work, having been legal adviser to the Austrian war minister during the war. He helped draft Austria's revolutionary new constitution, a model that was followed by other European countries, the first with an independent constitutional court with the power to interpret and apply the constitution and to do so at the request of individual citizens.

In 1921, Kelsen became a judge on the Constitutional Court, bringing Lauterpacht into direct contact with a new idea, in Europe if not America: individuals had inalienable constitutional rights, and they could go to a court to enforce those rights. This was a different model from that which protected minority rights, as in Poland. The two key distinctions – between groups and individuals, between national and international enforcement – influenced Lauterpacht's thinking. In Austria, the individual was placed at the heart of the legal order.

By contrast, in the rarefied, conservative world of international law – dominated by the idea that the law served the sovereign – the notion that an individual had rights enforceable against the state was inconceivable. The state must be free to act as it wished, unless it voluntarily accepted rules of constraint (or if such rules were imposed, as they were for Poland under the Minority Rights Treaty). In short, the state could do whatever it wanted to its nationals. It could discriminate, torture, or kill. Article 93 of the Versailles Treaty, as well as the Polish Minorities Treaty that would later cause my grandfather Leon to be stripped of his Polish nationality in 1938, might have offered protection for some minorities in some countries, but it offered no protection for individuals generally.

Lauterpacht caught the eye of his professor. Kelsen noted his 'extraordinary intellectual capacity', a young man from Lemberg with a 'truly scientific mind'. He also noticed the German spoken with the 'unmistakable accent of his origin', for the pupil was an *Ostjude,* a 'serious handicap' in 1920s Vienna. It's the likely reason why the degree he was awarded in June 1921 was graded only as a pass, not a distinction.

Lauterpacht immersed himself in the study of international law and a doctoral thesis on the new League of Nations. He worked under two supervisors: Professor Leo Strisower, who was Jewish, and Professor Alexander Hold-Ferneck, who was not. In July 1922, he was awarded a doctorate in political science, graded 'excellent'. The mark surprised Kelsen, who knew Hold-Ferneck to be a vigorous anti-Semite (fifteen years later, after the *Anschluss,* Hold-Ferneck would publicly – and erroneously – accuse his university colleague Eric Voegelin of being a Jew, causing the distinguished philosopher to flee to America).

In an environment that required Gustav Mahler to be baptized into Roman Catholicism to be able to direct the Wiener Staatsoper, Lauterpacht was confronted once more by the reality of ethnic and religious discrimination. This propelled him towards a new idea, on the 'vital necessity' of rights for individuals. Not lacking in self-confidence, he saw himself as an intellectual leader. Contemporaries recognized a fine advocate, a young scholar with a 'biting' sense of humour, fuelled by a desire for justice. Dark-haired and bespectacled, with a strong face and powerful eyes, he was a private man who inhabited 'a world of his own' yet was also politically engaged and actively involved in Jewish student life. He became president of the Hochschulausschuss, the coordination committee for Jewish student organizations, and in 1922 was elected chairman of the World Union of Jewish Students, with Albert Einstein as honorary president.

On the side, he participated in more mundane activity, helping to run a dormitory for Jewish students, which meant hiring a housekeeper. They appointed a young woman called Paula Hitler, unaware that her brother was the leader of the fast-growing National Socialist Party. Adolf Hitler turned up unexpectedly in Vienna in 1921, a visitor 'fallen from heaven', as his sister put it, not yet notorious.

32

Sought after as a speaker, at a university event Lauterpacht was introduced to Rachel Steinberg, an intelligent, strong-willed, attractive music student from Palestine. She was much taken by the young law student, 'so quiet, so gentle – not a movement of hand – so unlike the other students from Eastern Europe'. She liked the absence of emotion in his character, and both were soon smitten. On their first date she played an early Beethoven piano sonata, as set by her teacher, unnamed but described in a letter only as 'very lovely but not too easy to execute' (maybe it was Sonata no. 8, the *Pathétique*?). Lauterpacht invited Rachel to a concert at the Vienna Symphony Hall, with a programme that included Beethoven's Seventh Symphony, perhaps conducted by Wilhelm Furtwängler. She was entranced by the music and her companion, who was polite and correct, with a quiet and acute sense of humour. He dressed well, too.

When Lauterpacht invited her to accompany him to Berlin, she accepted. They lodged separately (she at the Excelsior Hotel, he at a boarding house in the Charlottenburg district), remaining in Berlin for three weeks. On the evening of 17 December 1922 – a day after the assassination of the Polish president, Gabriel Narutowicz, by a nationalistic art critic – Lauterpacht dared to take her hand, kiss her on the lips, and declare his love. Knowing of her desire to study at the Royal College of Music, he offered a quick engagement, marriage and a move to London. She said she'd think about it, wondering if he was serious.

He was. The next morning he returned to the Excelsior with a telegram from his parents in Lwów, expressing happiness at news of the engagement. Lauterpacht was surprised, and probably irritated, that she'd not yet written to her parents. She agreed to the engagement.

A month later, Rachel's parents in Palestine too agreed to the marriage. Lauterpacht wrote from Berlin to thank them, 'from my heart'. In February 1923, the couple returned to Vienna, where they married on Tuesday, 20 March. Two weeks later, they journeyed by train through Germany and then by boat to England.

Engagement photo, Berlin, 18 December 1922

33

The newlyweds arrived in the north-eastern English fishing port of Grimsby on 5 April 1923. Lauterpacht travelled on a Polish passport, Rachel on a document issued by the British mandate government in Palestine. He enrolled at the London School of Economics and Political Science (LSE), she at the Royal College of Music. During the first months in London they lived at various addresses around the city, including one flat off Regent Square and another close to the Caledonian Road. The LSE was then under the influence of Sidney and Beatrice Webb, progressive socialists, a happening campus on Houghton Street, opposite what would become the BBC's Bush House.

Lauterpacht's courses began in October, after he had failed in his effort to be appointed to the chair in international law at Lwów. At the LSE he studied with Arnold McNair, a lecturer in international law who came from a distinguished family of Scottish intellectuals. An intensely practical man with no great interest in theory or the philosophy of law, McNair introduced Lauterpacht to the Anglo-Saxon method, with its emphasis on cases and pragmatism. McNair recognized his pupil as an exceptional intellect, although something of an introvert among strangers. Those who met Lauterpacht casually might not appreciate 'his real quality', McNair noted, but he and his wife, Marjorie, became 'great and loyal' friends, as Rachel would recall, and 'a great admirer of mine'. The McNair children and grandchildren called her 'Auntie Rachel'.

McNair's pragmatic approach was reflected in his writings, important reference works still today, on treaties and on war. He was a man of balance, moderation and independence, traits that Lauterpacht appreciated as British, rather different from the passions of Lwów and Vienna.

When Lauterpacht arrived in London, his English was so poor that he couldn't easily be understood, even in asking for directions. He might have read English before coming to London, but he'd obviously not heard it spoken. 'At our first meeting we could hardly communicate,' McNair reported, his pupil's spoken English 'barely intelligible'. Yet within two weeks, McNair was 'staggered' by Lauterpacht's fluency, the beautifully constructed English sentences that became a feature of his writing. This was achieved by attending a multitude of lectures, up to eight a day, to develop his vocabulary and an ear for the sounds. Evenings were spent 'unendingly in the cinema', although quite how this helped was unclear: the great films of the year, Harold Lloyd's *Safety Last!* and James Cruze's landmark western *The Covered Wagon,* were silent movies.

Several people who knew him told me that Lauterpacht had a soft and guttural voice and never lost his distinct accent. He only became aware of how he sounded many years later, after recording a talk for the Third Programme of the BBC, now Radio 3. He was 'astonished' when he listened to the broadcast, dismayed by the 'strong continental accent'. He was said to have switched off the wireless, poured himself a generous whisky, and vowed never to be recorded again. The upshot was that no recording of his voice is known to exist.

34

Within a few years Lauterpacht felt at home in London, away from the continuing tumult of central Europe. He and Rachel lived in a small house in Cricklewood, at 103 Walm Lane, a leafy suburb of north-west London, not far from my home. On visiting, I noticed that the entrance tiles were gone, but the wooden embellishments around the front entrance remained, now painted green. If occasionally impecunious, McNair helped with a small loan.

The summer of 1928 was busy, with travel to Warsaw for a conference of the International Law Association, now as a member of the British group. From there he travelled to Lwów to visit the family. His brother, David, was married to Ninsia, a law student, with a young daughter, Erica. His sister, Sabina, was also married, to Marcele Gelbard (their only child, a girl called Inka, was born two years later, in 1930). On the trip he met old friends and surprised new acquaintances with his fluency in Polish, his first childhood language in Żółkiew and Lemberg. A senior member of the Polish judiciary enquired how it was that he spoke 'such good Polish', to which he responded tartly, 'Thanks to your *numerus clausus*' (a reference to the rules that precluded further studies in Lwów).

Lauterpacht had by then acquired a third doctoral degree, under McNair's supervision. His thesis was called 'Private Law Sources and Analogies of International Law', perhaps not a winning title but a work of real significance. It traced the influence of national rules on the development of international law, looking for bridges between the two systems, hoping in this way to fill the gaps in the international rules. He continued to be influenced by Kelsen's belief in the power of constitutional review and perhaps also by Sigmund Freud's ideas, casting light on the importance of the individual and the relationship with the group. Lauterpacht would run with this theme, focusing on the one amid the many.

One catalyst for his work was the creation of the first global court of law, a product of the Versailles Treaty. Based in The Hague, the Permanent Court of International Justice opened its doors in 1922, aspiring to resolve disputes between states. Among the sources of international law it applied – the main ones were treaties and customary law – were 'general principles of law recognized by civilised nations'. These were to be found in national legal systems, so that the content of international law could draw on the better-established rules of national law. Lauterpacht recognized that this connection between national and international law offered a 'revolutionary' possibility of developing the rules so as to place more limits on the supposedly 'eternal and inalienable' powers of the state.

Pragmatic and instinctive, a creature of his life and law courses in Lemberg, Lauterpacht believed in the possibility of reining in the power of the state. This would be achieved not by aspiration, whether of writers or pacifists, but through ideas that were rigorous and rooted, to do justice and contribute to 'international progress'. To this end, he wanted an international law that was less isolated and elite, more open to 'outside influence'. His thesis – to use general principles of national law to strengthen international obligations – was published in May 1927, to great scholarly acclaim. Today, nearly a century on, it continues to be recognized as a work of fundamental importance.

The book brought wider recognition and, in September 1928, a job as an assistant lecturer in law at the LSE. McNair thought him to be fortunate in his choice of country. 'I do not think that outside the sporting set and the Stock Exchange set there is very much feeling against individual foreigners,' he explained, perhaps optimistically, even if there was a 'good deal of anti-foreign feeling' in Parliament and in the press. 'Happily for us', McNair thought, Lauterpacht chose a life in Britain. Still, McNair teased him about his continental pretensions. Why use the word 'norms', he asked, far too 'highbrow' for the philistine British. Practical McNair encouraged Lauterpacht to become a barrister and assimilate into London's legal life, to embrace the establishment. This was achieved, but only up to a point (in 1954, as a candidate to be the British judge at the International Court of Justice, Lauterpacht was opposed, unsuccessfully as it turned out, by Attorney General Sir Lionel Heald, M.P., on the grounds that Britain's 'representative' on the Hague court should 'be and be seen to be thoroughly British, whereas Lauterpacht cannot help the fact that he does not qualify in this way either by birth, by name or by education').

McNair identified his protégé as a man without 'a trace of the political agitator in his temperament', yet with a 'passion for justice' and the 'relief of suffering'. McNair believed the events he lived through in Lemberg and Vienna from 1914 to 1922 prompted a belief in protecting human rights as a matter of 'vital necessity'. Individuals should 'possess international rights', an innovative and revolutionary idea then and, in many quarters, still now.

If Lauterpacht missed Lwów, it was for the family, not the place. His anxieties were hardly helped by letters from his mother, who wrote that things were 'not too well at home for the moment', a reference to economic troubles. In 1928, she made a first visit to London to see her new grandson, Elihu, born that year. Her son welcomed her but railed against his mother's expressions of individuality, objecting strongly to her 'painted nails', forcing her to remove the nail polish.

He was equally resistant to his mother's efforts to influence Rachel, who adopted a fashionable Louise Brooks bob and fringe. 'Incandescent' when he saw the new style, Lauterpacht insisted that she return to the bun, prompting a major row between the couple and a threat from Rachel to leave him. 'I can and must have my private harmless life without you bullying me.' In the end, however, Rachel conceded: the bun was still in place when I met her, more than fifty years later.

Individual rights for some, but not for the mother or the wife.

35

Five years later, in January 1933, Hitler came to power, a matter of great concern to Lauterpacht. An avid reader of *The Times,* he might have read the paper's lengthy extracts from *Mein Kampf,* describing Hitler's years in Vienna and the observation that Jewish culture was a 'spiritual pestilence, worse than Black Death'. One extract, setting out Hitler's views on Jews and Marxism, explicitly denied 'the value of the individual among men', emphasizing the importance of 'nationality and race' and the role of religious destiny. 'By fighting against the Jews I am doing the Lord's work,' Hitler wrote.

The National Socialists were on the rise, with serious implications for Lwów and Żółkiew. Poland signed a non-aggression pact with Germany and cast aside the 1919 Minorities Treaty. In September 1935, the Nuremberg decrees were passed in Germany, to protect the purity of the Aryan race. Marriage and sexual relations between Jew and German were prohibited; Jews were stripped of citizenship and most rights and banned from employment as lawyer, doctor, or journalist. It was a far cry from Cricklewood in north London, where he lived.

In 1935, Lauterpacht's parents, Aron and Deborah, visited London, reporting that life in Lwów was more difficult than ever, with a collapsing economy and rising discrimination. The family had moved from Teatralna Street to May the Third Street as a period of relative stability ended with the death in May of Marshal Piłsudski. By contrast, life in Walm Lane was comfortable. Lauterpacht was on the up, promoted to reader in law at the LSE, with a blossoming reputation. In 1933, he'd published a second book – *The Function of Law in the International Community* – to further acclaim, a work that Lauterpacht considered his most important, touching on the theme of the individual in international law. He'd launched a pioneering collection of reports of international law cases from national and international courts – the *Annual Digest and Reports of Public International Law Cases,* today called the *International Law Reports.* He also completed a new edition of volume 2 of Oppenheim's *International Law,* the treatise used by foreign ministries around the world, a volume on war law, in which the protection of civilians had a central place. 'The well-being of an individual is the

Rachel, Lauterpacht and Eli, Walm Lane, 1933

ultimate object of all law,' Lauterpacht wrote in the preface. The words were prescient, a radical vision for an increasingly establishment figure.

Lauterpacht didn't shirk the big issues of the day. He wrote a paper titled 'The Persecution of the Jews in Germany', proposing action by the League of Nations to prevent discrimination on grounds of race or religion. When one reads the paper today it feels tentative, for Lauterpacht was a pragmatist who knew that international law as it then was allowed Germany to persecute anyone not deemed to be an Aryan. Yet he believed that such persecution disturbed international relations and should be prohibited by 'the public law of the world'. He hoped Spain, Ireland, or Norway might act on an issue of political morality. They didn't, and the paper had no discernible impact.

Lauterpacht had his critics. As Jews flooded out of Germany, the League of Nations official with responsibility for refugees, James G. McDonald, decided to resign in protest at governmental inactions. To prepare a strong letter, he sought the help of Oscar Janowsky, a historian from the City College of New York, who travelled to London to enlist the support of Lauterpacht. The encounter went badly. Lauterpacht might be a 'brilliant youngish man on the rise', Janowsky wrote, but he was an 'overbearing' man of self-importance who 'pontificated like a judge' when he should be advocating a cause. Lauterpacht declined to work with one of Janowsky's graduate students, prompting a tirade about Lauterpacht's pomposity and arrogance, the absence of moral stature or generosity of spirit. A 'libellous stereotype of the Galitzianer', Janowsky wrote of him.

Lauterpacht wanted to 'steam-roller' his own views and dismiss those of others. 'Fidgety and impatient' during meetings, he 'showed that he was no gentleman' and became patronizing and angry if he didn't get his own way. Sensing he'd misbehaved, Lauterpacht sent Janowsky a grudging letter of apology. 'I love to see my own work torn to pieces when I submit it to criticism,' he wrote. 'I may be committing the mistake of thinking that others approached it in the same way.'

Despite the pressure, Lauterpacht resisted calls to support Germany's treatment of the Jews being referred to the international court in The Hague. The idea was 'inadequate, impracticable and highly dangerous'. He was not the easiest of colleagues, as he recognized the limits of international law, with gaps allowing states to discriminate and adopt measures such as the Nuremberg decrees.

In 1933, he qualified as a barrister. An early brief came from Haile Selassie, who wanted an opinion on Italy's annexation of Ethiopia. In November 1936 another brief arrived, a request from a distinguished Swiss academic for a legal opinion on the protection of Jews in Upper Silesia. If they couldn't get diplomatic protection, could they at least leave Germany with their possessions? Lauterpacht declined to give a legal opinion aimed at influencing the British government: the aims sought by the Swiss academic were simply not attainable.

Amid the gloom of world politics, Lauterpacht tried to persuade his parents to move permanently to England. Poland had by now shredded the 1919 Minorities Treaty, so the Jews and other minorities of Lwów were stripped of international legal protection. But Aron and Deborah decided to stay put in Lwów, which was home.

36

On a bright autumn day, I sat with Lauterpacht's son, Eli, in a book-lined study at his home in Cambridge, looking across the apple trees in the garden. Eli reminisced about Walm Lane, the trams and daily journeys to kindergarten with his father, 'on his way to the LSE'.

He recalled a father 'totally wrapped up' in his work, spending most of the time in a study at the back of the house, the 'quiet room'. He worked 'too intensely' to put his son to bed, but there was a closeness, a relationship that was 'loving' if not 'intellectual', with lighter moments. Eli recalled his parents dancing around the living room to the sound of Bizet's *Carmen* and walks in the local park, a time for Latin declensions and conjugations. 'He would make me recite them, very insistent.'

What about the family in Poland? Eli was vaguely aware of the situation. 'My grandparents came to visit us twice,' but he only remembered 1935, when his father 'begged them to stay'. They decided against it, to remain with their two other children. Young Eli had no sense of what lay over the horizon. 'My father must have been aware of the incipient danger, but that sort of thing never came through to me.'

Did they talk about Lwów?

'Never.'

Its influence?

'Not really, no.'

Did the fear of war weigh on his father's mind? The question produced a quizzical look, then silence. That's interesting, he said, but no. 'He kept that to himself. Maybe he shared it with my mother, but what was happening in Poland was completely shut off. We never talked about the situation in Lemberg. He found other things to talk about.'

I persisted.

'Well, it was a horrendous period,' Eli eventually conceded. 'He knew that something terrible could happen, not necessarily that it would happen or that it would happen the way it did.'

His father was detached, for protective reasons. Eli explained, 'He went about his life and his business, tried to persuade his parents to come. There was occasional correspondence, of which, alas, we have no copies. He didn't return to Poland to see his parents. I don't know that he was detached, but the relationship with his parents was one of detachment, although I knew he loved them very much. I doubt if he and my mother ever sat down to discuss "should we tell the boy about this?"'

Did he talk about his Polish past?

'No. What was part of the household was the fact that he had been brought up in an Orthodox Jewish household in Poland. He would take us through the Passover Seder, singing it in the traditional way, which I loved, the melody still persists in my head. But I have no recollection of any substantive conversation about his Polish life.'

Never?

'No, not ever.'

Eli was silent for a little, then said, 'He was busy, getting on with his work.' This was followed by a weary, soft sigh.

37

'Getting on with his work' brought further success. In late 1937, the boy from Żółkiew was elected to the prestigious chair of international law at Cambridge University. In January 1938, Lauterpacht travelled by train from King's Cross Station to take up his new post, which came with a fellowship at Trinity College. Letters of congratulation arrived from Kelsen and colleagues at the LSE. Philip Noel-Baker, the director, offered warm congratulations, as did Sir William Beveridge, a colleague who helped accommodate German refugees when he wasn't thinking about creating a modern system of welfare.

'My feeling towards you has always been one of profound gratitude', Lauterpacht told Beveridge in reply, for the help with academic refugees, and 'great affection'.

The Cambridge news brought a proud and happy response from Lwów. 'My dearest and beloved son!' Deborah wrote, 'for this piece of good news I thank you a thousand times.' The letter hinted at financial difficulties, with Aron at work in distant Gdańsk. 'We cannot be happy together,' she wrote.

In September, the family moved to a larger, semi-detached house at 6 Cranmer Road in Cambridge, bought from the McNairs for eighteen hundred pounds, on a tree-lined street of generously proportioned homes, many with their own driveways. There were sitting rooms, a dining room, a butler's pantry and a scullery for the cooking. Meals were served punctually – one o'clock for lunch, seven o'clock for supper – announced by a brass gong. Tea was served at half past four, often with a slice of Victoria sponge cake from Fitzbillies, the local bakery that still operates today.

The first floor had a bedroom each for Lauterpacht, Rachel and Eli, and a study for Lauterpacht. This was where he worked, often with classical music in the background, seated in an elbow chair made of walnut, behind a large, leather-topped mahogany desk, looking out over the garden. It was stocked with apple, plum and greengage trees, which Lauterpacht liked to prune, and daffodils, roses and lilies of the valley, his favourite flowers. He attached importance to a weed-free lawn, mowed by a gardener, retaining throughout his life a fear of catching cold if his feet touched wet grass. For this reason, in such conditions he always walked on his heels, toes tipped upward to minimize contact with the ground. 'Picturesque,' Eli recalled.

The Lauterpachts were comfortable but not wealthy. The decoration was modest, and for the first decade there was no central heating. A rare concession to extravagance was the purchase of a motor car for ninety pounds, a second-hand blue Standard 9 Saloon manufactured in Coventry. Hersch was not a relaxed driver and would become highly agitated if the speed ever exceeded fifty miles an hour.

The street's other residents reflected Lauterpacht's varied new world. Their immediate neighbour, at No. 8, was Dr Brooke, a retired cleric. David Winton Thomas, Regius Professor of Hebrew and once a rugby player for Wales, lived across the street at No. 4. Farther along, at No. 13, lived Sir Percy Winfield, the Rouse Ball Professor of English Law, the country's leading authority on the law of tort (*Winfield on Tort*, still in use today, was credited by the historian Simon Schama as the book that finally extinguished any interest he might have in the law).

Sir Ernest Barker, Professor of Political Science, lived at No. 17, hard at work on *Britain and the British People*. Professor Arthur B. Cook, Professor Emeritus of Classical Archaeology, lived at No. 19. No. 23 was occupied by Professor Frank Debenham, Professor of Geography and the first director of the university's Scott Polar Research Institute (as a young man he accompanied Robert Falcon Scott on his last expedition to the Antarctic, missing out on the ill-fated final leg to the South Pole because of an injury suffered while playing football in deep snow).

Lauterpacht liked to walk to Trinity and the nearby law faculty. Punctilious and always attentive to appearance – he lectured in a dark suit and gown – he was often seen in a much-loved homburg hat. On one occasion, during a train journey from The Hague to Switzerland, the beloved hat 'flew out of the window and lay beautifully on the line', an event worth writing about to Rachel, as was the time spent at the Bureau des Objets Trouvés in Lausanne. The hat was never found.

Rachel was still living in London when her husband delivered his first lecture in Cambridge. Not overly burdened by modesty, he thought it to have been a 'quite eloquent' affair. The student newspaper *Varsity* reported him to be a 'first-class lecturer, with a well-practised and polished technique', one who made great use of his hands, 'to good purpose'. If there was a discernible fault, it was that he 'window gazes'. *Varsity* noticed another trait: 'What private joke causes that little smile to hover eternally on his lips?'

Astonishment perhaps that he had made the journey from Żółkiew to Cambridge.

In this idyllic environment, the background noises were increasingly ominous. Germany occupied the Sudetenland, then attacked Czechoslovakia. Lwów and Żółkiew were much on Lauterpacht's mind.

38

Germany invaded Poland on 1 September 1939. Two days later, on a Sunday morning, Prime Minister Neville Chamberlain announced that Britain had declared war on Germany. The family gathered in the study at Cranmer Road to listen to the broadcast, Lauterpacht in a high-backed chair, his wife and son in deep, square green armchairs, facing the Pye wireless. Eli was eleven years old. He recalled the excitement, although not understanding 'what it would mean in terms of human suffering'. His father received the news calmly. The house was put on a war footing, food supplies brought in, blackout curtains hung. Life went on, lodgers arrived, Lauterpacht taught and wrote. Forty-two years old, he was too old to fight, but he did join the Home Guard, where he was known affectionately as 'Lumpersplash'.

The Germans entered Lwów and Żółkiew in September but quickly retreated, as ancient Olga of Żółkiew had told me. The Soviets took charge as Poland's independence was extinguished, a country divided by Hitler and Stalin. Letters from Lvov, as it now was, described life under the Soviets as difficult but without grave dangers.

In June 1940, Germany overran France, the moment when Leon was separated from my mother, his infant child. The occupation of Paris prompted a decision to evacuate Eli and Rachel to America. Lauterpacht accepted a lecture tour with the Carnegie Foundation, so in September that year the family sailed to America on the RMS *Scythia* of the Cunard White Star Line. Three days later, another ship from Liverpool, the *City of Benares*, was torpedoed by a German U-boat, killing 248 people, including many children. The Lauterpachts arrived in New York in early October, moving into an apartment in Riverdale in the Bronx, near the Hudson River. Eli enrolled at Horace Mann, missing the former pupil Jack Kerouac by a year. Lauterpacht went off to lecture.

In Washington, the British political scientist Harold Laski introduced him to the upper echelons of the American legal community. Not at war with Germany, the United States was intent on helping London, but within the bounds permitted by the rules on neutrality. Lauterpacht spent time with British embassy officials and visited Justice Felix Frankfurter at the Supreme Court. Frankfurter, whose wife had a Lemberg connection, thanked Laski for the introduction, prompting the LSE academic to express the hope that Lauterpacht's sanity and tolerance might make the Americans understand the values for which Britain was fighting.

Lauterpacht lectured across America for two months, covering six thousand miles and fifteen law schools and universities. The central theme of his lectures offered a riposte to critics of international law, stressing its importance at a time of crisis, not least for the protection of individuals. Yet letters home reflected doubts and anxiety at the war's direction. 'Will there be a Cambridge to go back to?' he asked Rachel. To Eli, he offered simple advice: 'Do your best; be modest; try to win friends and keep their friendships.'

In December 1940, Laski introduced Lauterpacht to Robert Jackson, President Roosevelt's attorney general. 'I'm going to be in Washington in the first week of January, can I pay you a courtesy call?' Lauterpacht wrote to Jackson, who responded positively. A few weeks later he travelled to Washington, where he called on the State Department legal adviser and met again with Justice Frankfurter.

Looking for ways to help the United States support the British without getting dragged into the war, Jackson had his own reasons for meeting Lauterpacht. 'What is wanted', he told Lauterpacht, was 'a philosophy' to give effect to America's policy of 'all aid to the Allies short of war'. Jackson mistrusted American international lawyers, many of whom resisted engagement.

Lauterpacht wanted to help but knew the situation to be delicate. He got a green light from the British embassy in Washington to prepare a legal memorandum on options for the United States to help Britain without violating the rules on neutrality. Jackson introduced some of these ideas into the Lend-Lease Bill that President Roosevelt got through Congress a few weeks later, controversial legislation that allowed the administration to support Britain and China. The first effort at cooperation between Lauterpacht and Jackson bore fruit.

Lauterpacht passed along other ideas, some of which made their way into a speech Jackson delivered in March 1941. The attorney general pleaded with lawyers present – a conservative group – to adopt a modern approach, drawing on Lauterpacht's ideas. Those who broke the law must pay a price, Jackson explained, so America must be allowed to aid the victims. The *New York Times* reported Jackson's speech as 'extraordinarily significant', applauding the rejection of outdated, nineteenth-century conceptions of law and neutrality. No doubt delighted by the endorsement of his ideas, Lauterpacht refused the honorarium offered by Jackson. When the speech was delivered he was on his way back to Britain, although Rachel and Eli remained in New York.

39

Lauterpacht returned to Cambridge at the end of January 1941, three flights on an Atlantic clipper, via Bermuda, the Azores and Lisbon. His travel companions included Wendell Willkie, the Republican candidate defeated by Roosevelt in the presidential elections just a few weeks earlier. They spent much of the flight in animated conversation about the state of the world. Willkie never did make good on his acceptance of an invitation to visit Trinity.

Lauterpacht's return coincided with the arrival of an increasingly rare communication from Lvov. 'My Dear!' his brother wrote, with news that the family was 'relatively well' and that 'our dear old ones have aged in this period by twenty years'. Under the gaze of the Soviet censors, the letter offered coded messages. 'We would like to see you so that we could be together again,' David hinted, 'in what way it is up to you.' If they were to be reunited, it would be for Lauterpacht to make the arrangements. The family preferred 'to be together in such times', could Lauterpacht come to Lvov to get them? 'You know our wishes,' David concluded, somewhat cryptically due to the censorship, 'stay healthy, we send you our kisses'.

The letter caused concern, but any steps he took to get the family to Britain went unrecorded. He put effort into lectures, the 'troublesome' but distracting work on the *Annual Digest* and a new edition of Oppenheim's *International Law*. Food was comforting; because stocks in Cambridge were limited, he made regular trips to his favoured delicatessen in Cricklewood, run by Mr Ziedman. He is a 'blessing', Lauterpacht told Rachel, somehow able to get 'all the frying oil I wanted' and other unobtainable items.

Writing also gave him comfort. One letter went to Leonard Woolf, whom he had known during his days at the LSE, expressing condolence at the death of Virginia. Another was sent to Rachel in New York, worrying about the war's direction as Yugoslavia entered on the side of the Germans, more positive as to the recapture of Addis Ababa, a rare success for his one-time client Haile Selassie. A letter to Eli berated him for complaining about life in New York while people in Britain lived 'in a state of more immediate anxiety and worries of all kinds'.

In April 1941, he received an invitation to lecture at Wellesley College in Massachusetts. In May, he gave a talk at the Royal Institute of International Affairs in London on 'The Reality of the Law of Nations', in which he once more focused on the plight of individuals. He railed against despondency and cynicism, putting the positive case for international law and hope. This was something of a challenge, given widespread reports that circulated as to the 'grievous violations' occurring across Europe. Such acts by lawless states had to be confronted by governments, he told the audience, by international lawyers and 'the will and exertion of the citizen'.

Lauterpacht found a voice that drew strength in adversity, speaking to the 'rights and duties of man'. The passion was fuelled by the arrival of a short letter from his father, written on 4 January 1941. 'Dearest!' he wrote lovingly to his son, your letters 'rejoiced us extraordinarily'. He was 'totally becalmed' by the news that the family was safe in America. In Lvov everyone was 'perfectly sound', but no more than that. They hoped for the best. Greetings were sent from Uncle David in Żółkiew. 'We heartily greet and kiss you all.' His mother added a line of kisses.

Then came silence. 'Write often to my family,' he urged Rachel, offering an address in Lvov now in 'Soviet Russia': ulica Obrony Lwów, a street named in honour of the '"Defenders of Lvov"'. The family still lived on May the Third Street.

40

In June, Hitler cast aside the Molotov-Ribbentrop Pact and ordered German troops eastward into Soviet-occupied Poland. Within a week, Żółkiew and Lvov were in German hands and academics rounded up, including Lauterpacht's teacher of Austrian private law, Professor Roman Longchamps de Berier. Arrested for the crime of being a Polish intellectual, he was executed a day later in the 'Massacre of the Lwów Professors', along with his three sons.

Lauterpacht's niece Inka gave me a first-hand account of those days, a parallel to Clara Kramer's account of the arrival of the Germans in Żółkiew. I met Inka – the only child of Lauterpacht's sister – in the summer of 2010 in Paris, in her tidy, small apartment near the Eiffel Tower. She was intense and sparrow-like, flitting around the room with great energy. Eventually we settled at her dining-room table, draped in a fresh white cloth, illuminated by a single ray of bright, clean sun. She offered black tea in a delicate porcelain cup. Under an open window, she spoke softly, without emotion.

On the table we'd spread out a 1938 map of Lwów. She was eight years old then, she told me, as she pointed out my grandfather Leon's home, a street on which she walked. She asked to see the meagre documents I'd brought. I showed her a certificate issued to Leon's father, Pinkas Buchholz, in 1890. 'It says he was born in 1862,' she exclaimed, with an accent that reminded me of my grandfather. He passed the exam for the manufacture of eau-de-vie, but only with an '*assez bon,* good enough'. She smiled. 'Not the same as "good"!'

Her father, Marcele Gelbard, was a lawyer, in the family tradition, like his father. Both men were blond; Gelbard meant 'yellow beard' in German, a name bestowed during the Austro-Hungarian period. Inka's memory of Lauterpacht in those days was vague, because he left for Britain before she was born. As we talked of Żółkiew, she said, 'Oh dear, you have said it wrong. You don't pronounce the Z, it is pronounced "Julkiev", the Z is like a J. A soft J.' Then she added, with a sigh, 'I know it well, the town of my mother, uncles and grandparents, where I went after the war.'

We worked our way around the 1938 map of Lwów. Although she never returned after 1945, she could show me the street where Lauterpacht's parents, her grandparents Aron and Deborah, lived,

64 May the Third Street, where they moved after Teatralna Street. It was close to Szeptyckich Street, a few minutes' walk from the house where Leon was born, a 'less prestigious area'. 'We used to eat at the Bristol or the George,' she recalled, the fancy hotels.

'I could wander around Lwów until I was nine years old, then it changed, when the Russians came, the end of the life we knew.'

She took a small sip of tea, then another.

'Let me show you some photographs.' We passed to her bedroom and a wardrobe, from which she removed a small wooden box containing photographs of her parents. There was a letter from Lauterpacht, sent in the 1950s, and a photograph at the Palace of Westminster in London with her aunt and uncle, in the wig of a newly appointed king's counsel, a senior barrister.

We returned to the living room. Life before the Soviets occupied Lwów in September 1939 was good. Inka attended a small private school, unaware of discrimination. 'My parents hid it from me, and at school no one talked about those things.' Her father was respected, a fine lawyer, had good friends, most of whom were Jewish. There were a few non-Jews around, Poles who 'came for cocktails', followed by the Jews who came later in the evening for dinner. There were no Ukrainians in her life.

Things changed 'immediately' with the arrival of the Soviets. 'They let us stay in the same apartment, except we couldn't occupy the whole of it. First we got two rooms, then we were allowed one room and the kitchen and the right to use the toilet and bathroom.' She remembered the address, 258 May the Third Street, or maybe it was No. 87, close to the Lauterpachts, also on that street. It ran parallel to Sykstuska Street, on which the photograph of the barricade was taken during the battles of November 1918.

Her mother, 'madly charming', received a great many invitations from the Russians. 'The colonel who lived in our apartment fell in love with her,' Inka exclaims, those years were not too bad. Then the Germans arrived, in July 1941, and the situation got much worse.

'Life carried on, because my father spoke German, but not for most Jews. They had to leave their neighbourhoods unless they lived in the Jewish quarter. For some reason, we were allowed to stay in a room in our apartment; it was never fully requisitioned.'

Every so often, over a period of several days, *Aktionen* were initiated, to round up Jews on the streets, those not wearing Star of

Inka (right), with Rachel and Lauterpacht, London, 1949

David armbands. Her father was well-known and had to be careful, but fewer people knew her mother, so she sometimes went out
without wearing 'le truc'. 'The thing', that was what Inka called the
armband.

'It was unpleasant and dangerous. We were not liked. Before the
war, they didn't know who on the streets was Jewish. Now they
knew.'

We looked at a few black-and-white photographs I'd brought.
One was a postcard of the famous seventeenth-century Zółkiew
synagogue in a state of dilapidation. Did she remember the building?
'No.'

As Inka examined the postcard, close to her face, something

strange occurred. The doorbell rang. It was the concierge, holding a single letter. Inka looked at it and said, 'It's for you.' Curious, it was the first time I'd met Inka. She handed me the letter, which was addressed to her, from the Association of the Martyrs of Żółkiew. I opened it, removed a pamphlet, placed it on the table.

On the front was a picture of the old synagogue in Żółkiew. It was the same one I'd just shown her, the one she couldn't remember. A simple coincidence, and now she had two copies.

41

In August 1941, Lemberg and Galicia were incorporated into Germany's General Government. As Hans Frank became the ruler, Lauterpacht planned a return to America, to lecture at Wellesley College and take up a small space to work at the Harvard Law Library.

The days before departure dragged, as the implications of the German occupation sank in. 'You know all about Lwów,' he wrote to Rachel. 'I do not like to express my sentiments, but the thing is constantly with me like a nightmare.' It was not possible to hide the fears, yet life went on, as though he had 'split his personality'. He was 'perfectly normal' in daily intercourse with people, going through the motions, helping colleagues at Trinity, entertaining generals. There was more political engagement: before leaving for America, he added his name to a list of Cambridge academics offering support to the Soviet Academy of Sciences for that country's 'heroic fights against the common foe'.

Lauterpacht arrived back in New York in August 1941 and spent the autumn term at Wellesley. He visited Harvard, spending weekends in New York with Rachel and Eli. In October he travelled to Washington to meet Francis Biddle, Jackson's successor as attorney general, who wanted legal arguments that would allow America to attack German submarines. Lauterpacht had stayed in touch with Jackson, sending congratulations to him on his appointment as an associate justice of the US Supreme Court. Jackson responded with a friendly note and an offprint of the Havana speech. Lauterpacht offered help with another speech, on ending 'international lawlessness', but by the time he passed on his ideas the war had taken a decisive turn: on 7 December, Japan attacked US naval forces at Pearl Harbor, causing the United States to declare war on Japan. Within days, Germany had declared war on America. The military and political situation was transformed when the two men met in Washington early in 1942.

Around that time, nine European governments in exile – including those of Poland and France – came together at St James's Palace in London to coordinate their response to reports of Germany's 'regime of terror'. Terrible stories were circulating, accounts of mass imprisonments and expulsions, of executions and massacres. These caused the governments in exile to issue a declaration, in January 1942, expressing a common desire to use the criminal law to punish those 'guilty' of and 'responsible' for atrocities. Perpetrators would be 'sought for, handed over to justice and judged', an idea that became an official aim of the war.

The nine governments established a commission on war crimes to collect information on atrocities and perpetrators, a body that would become the United Nations War Crimes Commission. Churchill authorized British government lawyers to investigate German war crimes under the direction of Solicitor General David Maxwell Fyfe. Within months, the *New York Times* reported that the Polish government in exile had identified ten leading criminals. The first name on the list was that of Hans Frank, just above Governor Otto von Wächter, Lauterpacht's classmate from Vienna.

Against this background, Jackson delivered a speech titled 'International Lawlessness' at the Waldorf Hotel in late January. Written with the assistance of Lauterpacht, who attended as a guest, the speech described war and atrocity and the need for law and courts, 'the best instrumentalities . . . yet devised to subdue violence'. Lauterpacht now had a supporter for his ideas at the highest level of American government. What he and Jackson didn't know was that the atrocities were about to go up the scale of horror: three days earlier, at a villa on the Wannsee, near Berlin, a conference of senior Nazis had secretly agreed on the 'Final Solution'.

Lauterpacht spent several weeks in New York, working with staff at the British embassy, attending conferences, meeting the governor of New York, Herbert Lehman. There was even time to relax with Rachel, to see films. Not much taken by Bette Davis in *The Man*

Who Came to Dinner, the couple did enjoy *'Pimpernel' Smith* at the Rivoli Theater on Broadway.

I understood why, watching it seven decades later. The hero, a Cambridge academic played by the heartthrob actor Leslie Howard (who was killed a year later when his plane was shot down over the Atlantic by the Luftwaffe), takes on the 'gutturals and brown shirts' and smuggles victims out of the Nazi terror, including his own daughter. 'Singapore may fall,' the *New York Times* reviewer chirped, 'but the British can still make melodramas to chill the veins.'

42

In March 1942, Lauterpacht returned to England, soon after Japan occupied Singapore and as Germany sought to extend its control over the eastern parts of Europe. Without any news from Lemberg, Lauterpacht wrote frequently to Rachel and Eli, who was enrolled at Phillips Academy in Andover. 'I am slightly depressed . . . because of the war news,' he told them; they were 'passing through a very bad period.'

The food situation, limited by tight rations, did not improve his mood. 'I have altogether abandoned house-keeping,' and shops no longer delivered. 'You have to get everything yourself.' The garden offered a ray of light, with daffodils providing 'a glorious show', a modest compensation for the loss of his luggage at sea, somewhere between America and Britain.

He focused on another edition of Oppenheim's *International Law* and a ninth volume of *International Law Reports,* to include cases from the opening years of the war. These touched on the civil war in Spain, Italy's conquest of Abyssinia and the 'legislation and practices of the Nazi regime in Germany', with their 'ominously general characteristics'. Lauterpacht selected the cases with care. He chose one judgement of the German Supreme Court, an appeal by a German Jew convicted of having sex with an Aryan woman in violation of the 1935 Nuremberg decrees. The case raised a somewhat novel legal issue: What if the act of sex occurred outside Germany? The Supreme Court ruled that the Nuremberg decrees applied to a sexual act that occurred in Prague, the reasoning a marvel of teleological simplicity: the purpose of the Nuremberg decrees would be undermined if they didn't apply to acts committed abroad. Thus, a German Jew who cohabited with a German national of German blood outside the *Reich* 'must be punished . . . if he has persuaded the German woman to join him abroad for this purpose.' A decision such as this, Lauterpacht commented, confirmed the need for an international court of review.

Lauterpacht was active beyond scholarship. He continued to offer advice to Jackson, whom he saw as a bastion against American isolationism as the United States entered the war, a man with 'the ear of the Administration'. He wrote to Eli and Rachel in America, telling them of his involvement in a new project, to examine 'the question of so-called War Crimes' and how to punish Germans guilty of international crimes in occupied territories. The project started in June 1942, when Arnold McNair was appointed to chair the 'Committee on War Crimes' to implement the Declaration of St James's Palace. McNair invited Lauterpacht to join his team, and in early July he attended a first meeting of the committee. McNair asked him to prepare a memorandum on legal issues.

'I got quite a swollen head,' he told Rachel, as the committee decided to 'model' its work on his approach. The meeting offered other opportunities, because it involved lawyers from the governments in exile based in London. In this way, he wrote to his wife, he hoped to do 'much good . . . for the minorities of eastern Poland', because the Poles would be 'the principal factor' in the postwar settlement of the minorities. This work caused him to focus in a practical way on justice and the responsibility of individuals, not just the states they served.

That summer another new project landed on his desk: the American Jewish Committee invited him to write a book on the international law of human rights and offered a generous fee (twenty-five hundred dollars, plus expenses). This was an enticing new subject, so he accepted. He said he would write a book 'on the International Bill of Rights of the Individual (or something like that)'. He started work on 1 July, optimistically hoping to complete it by the end of the year.

In December he tested out some new ideas on international law at a lecture in London, delivered in an atmosphere of 'solemnity'. It

went rather well, he told Rachel; there was 'some embarrassing worship of your husband'. His central theme was a call for governments
to embrace the 'revolutionary immensity' of a new international law
that would protect the fundamental rights of man.

43

Lauterpacht didn't know that his work on the new book in the
summer of 1942 coincided with a visit to Lemberg by Governor-
General Hans Frank to celebrate the first anniversary of Galicia's
incorporation into the General Government. At the very moment
that Lauterpacht turned to an international bill of rights, Frank
set in train the implementation of the Final Solution in Galicia, as
agreed to at the Wannsee Conference. The impact on Lauterpacht's
family was immediate and devastating.

Inka Katz told me what happened. She remembered Frank's
visit, the fear it engendered, the consequences that followed. Her
grandfather Aron was the first to be taken, on 16 August, from the
apartment he shared with Lauterpacht's brother, David, an old man
removed from a wardrobe in the bathroom, where he was hidden.

'Two days later, on 18 August, Hersch's sister, my mother, Sabina,
was taken by the Germans.' Inka spoke with absolute calm. 'It was
on the street; my mother was rushed by Ukrainians and German
soldiers.' She was alone at home, saw the events from the house,
looking out of a window. Her father was at work a few houses away,
in their old apartment. 'Someone went and told him that my mother
had been taken,' Inka said; a concierge told him. 'I understood what
had happened. I saw everything looking out of the window.'

How old was she?

'I was twelve, not a child any more. I stopped being a child in
1939. I understood what was happening, I knew the dangers and all
the rest. I saw my father running after my mother, behind her, on
the street.'

She paused and looked out of the elegant window, across Paris,
sipping black tea. 'I understood it was over.'

She observed from the upper window, remembering points of
detail for which a child has a special memory.

'I was watching discreetly; I wasn't brave. If I had been, I would have run after her. But I knew what was happening. I can still visualize the scene, my mother's dress, her high heels . . .'

Did she know that maybe she might not see her mother again?

'There was no "maybe". I knew.'

Lauterpacht's sister was taken by the Germans as her daughter watched.

'My father didn't think about me. You know what? I rather liked that. For him, it was simply that they had taken his wife, the woman he loved so much. It was just about bringing her back.'

She admired the fact that her father, in his dark grey suit, went looking for his wife.

Then her father was taken. He never returned; Inka was on her own.

'I heard nothing more from them. They had taken thousands of people. Who knows what became of them? But I knew what was going to happen to them. A few days later, I left the apartment, as I knew the Germans would come and take it. My grandmother went to the ghetto; I refused, could not imagine myself there. I went to my governess, the ex-governess; she remained close to my parents because my father was good to her. She wasn't Jewish, although she could have been. I told her what had happened, and she said, "Come and stay with me." She wasn't just a governess, it was more than that. She was . . . what do you call it, a nursemaid? My mother didn't breast-feed me; she did. She gave me her breast.'

As we talked, Inka poured cups of dark Russian tea.

'I went there, not for very long, because of the searches. "She's my little niece," the governess told anyone who asked. I didn't really look Jewish at all, but I certainly didn't look like her niece. They didn't really believe her, so she sent me off to the countryside to be with her family.' Inka couldn't stay there long.

'I left for other reasons. There was a man who liked young children. I knew about that; I'd read about these things, knew the jokes about such men. So I left. I went to stay with someone else my father had helped. It was the end of 1942, still around Lwów, but not in the Jewish ghetto. I didn't stay long. The woman pretended I was a cousin, or a niece, or her cousin's daughter. It didn't work. Her family got anxious. I would listen through the door; I could hear them say, "She doesn't look like family." It was true.'

So Inka left. 'It was very difficult. I didn't know where to go any more. I would wander in the streets all day long and sleep where I could. In Poland, in those days, the front entrances of apartment buildings were locked at night, at ten or eleven, so I could go in before then, very quietly up to the attic, in a building where they didn't know me. I could sleep there, on the stairs next to the *grenier*. It was frightening when someone came in the night. I was scared, alone, worried I'd be handed over to the police.'

She continued, calmly, 'That lasted for a month or two. It was the end of the autumn. My mother had told me where her jewellery was, where the money was. I lived off that. Then I was robbed. One morning I woke up and everything had been taken. There was nothing left.'

Alone and desperate, the twelve-year-old girl found a client and friend of her father's, an elderly lady, willing to take her in for two months.

'People started talking, so then I had to leave her. She was a Catholic; she talked about putting me into a convent. We went together. The nuns said yes, we will take her.'

The convent was on the outskirts of the town.

'I don't remember the name,' Inka says. 'It was very small, not well-known. There were twelve nuns, connected to the Jesuits.'

Inka speaks slowly, in a whisper, as though approaching an awkward denouement.

'The nuns said there was one condition to my staying. My family never knew this.' Inka was momentarily uncomfortable, on the verge of breaking a lifelong silence.

'They said I must be baptized. I had no choice. Maybe it was fortunate that I wasn't any more observant then than today. I was lucky to grow up in a household that wasn't too religious.'

Seventy years on, she retained a sense of discomfort. One woman, coming to terms with a feeling that somehow she had abandoned her group to save herself.

44

Lauterpacht, who knew nothing about what was happening to the niece he had never met, decided to give up alcohol and start a slimming cure. This was not on doctor's orders, merely a sensible precaution. That was what he told himself, as he continued with Home Guard duties and thought about what a bill of rights might contain. He didn't know that his father had been taken on 16 August. That same day he sent a memorandum to the War Crimes Committee in London, setting out the paucity of international practice on the prosecution of war crimes.

From the east, bits of news and rumour trickled through. In September, an article appeared in *The Times* on Nazi atrocities in Poland. This ignited a feeling of kinship with Jewish colleagues in Cambridge, reflected in a letter to Rachel. 'Last night I went to the Synagogue of the German refugees as a sign of my feeling of solidarity with their sufferings.' He sent food parcels into the Lemberg void, addressed to David, unaware of the situation in the city.

Eighteen months had now passed with no news from the family. Solace was hard to find. He listened to music, which generated a feeling of sentimentality, remembrance of a life past.

'It is 6 p.m. on a Sunday and I have been fasting all day,' he wrote to Rachel in December, a day of fast and intercession for the murdered Jews in Poland. 'I felt I would like to join in.'

Lwów was perpetually on his mind. 'My very dear ones are there, and I do not know whether they are alive. The situation there is so terrible that it is quite conceivable that they may prefer death to life. I have been thinking the whole day about them.'

45

Over the next year, the direction of the war turned. Rachel returned to Cambridge in the summer of 1943, although Eli remained in America. Lauterpacht spent many hours alone in his study, listening to Bach, writing and looking over the garden, watching the leaves change, worrying in silence about the family stuck somewhere in Lwów. The greengage tree lost its fruit, the grass was mowed less frequently, yet as the dark days of winter enveloped Lauterpacht he focused on positive developments. In September, Italy capitulated. A 'day of elation', Lauterpacht exclaimed. It felt 'good to be alive', he wrote, for the first time in ages, beginning to 'witness the downfall of evil'. It offered a tangible sign of 'the triumph of the forces of progress'.

He delivered a series of lectures to test out the emerging ideas on the rights of man. The project was taking longer than expected, the main challenge being to find practical ways of putting the individual at the heart of a new legal order. A lecture in London, then another in Cambridge, during which he 'solemnly' read out a draft of his International Bill of Rights of Man, described by a member of the audience as 'a historic occasion'. His thinking had evolved. 'The Bill of Rights, if it is to be effective, must be enforced not only by the authorities of the State, but also by international actors.' This evoked the possibility of an international court. To Eli, he offered a simple description of his working conditions: 'Imagine the study, with windows open, and with the moving strains of Bach's *St Matthew Passion* filling the room, and you will have an idea of the atmosphere.'

The Germans were now in retreat across Europe. The work of the War Crimes Committee became more pressing as Lauterpacht's ideas filtered into the work of the United Nations War Crimes Commission, created a year earlier by the Allied governments. The international dimension allowed a renewal of contacts with American members of the commission and with Philip Noel-Baker, his former LSE colleague, now a member of the British government, offering access to power and influence.

In March 1944, he completed a 'biggish article' on war crimes, hoping to influence a possible decision on a trial. He offered help to the World Jewish Congress for its investigations of the atrocities, telling Rachel, who was back in New York, that the congress wanted a special committee to investigate 'the terrible war crimes which Germany has perpetrated against the Jews'. Yet his focus was on the protection of individuals, not groups or minorities, recognizing that the Polish Minorities Treaty had not achieved its aims. Still, the situation of groups could not be ignored, and he reasoned that because the Jews were 'the greatest victim of the German crimes', it was 'proper' that 'anti-Jewish atrocities should be made the subject of a special investigation and report.'

Lauterpacht was not alone in thinking about these matters. In November, another book was published in America, by a former Polish prosecutor named Rafael Lemkin. Titled *Axis Rule in Occupied Europe,* the work adopted a different approach from Lauterpacht, with the aim of protecting groups, for which he invented a word for a new crime, 'genocide', the destruction of groups. Lauterpacht wrote a review of Lemkin's book for *The Cambridge Law Journal*, hinting that he wasn't a great supporter of Lemkin's ideas.

Lemkin's book was 'imposing' and offered an 'informative' survey of German laws and decrees, with 'interesting and sound observations'. It was an 'invaluable' product of 'prodigious industry and ingenuity'. Yet Lauterpacht's tone was detached and lukewarm, especially about the new word, 'what he calls "genocide" – a new term for the physical destruction of nations and ethnic groups'. It may be 'a scholarly historical record', Lauterpacht concluded, but it 'cannot be accurately said that the volume is a contribution to the law'. He commended the Carnegie Endowment for International Peace for publishing the book but made no mention of the author by name. The review was sceptical about the new term and its practical utility. The implication was clear: Lauterpacht was concerned that the protection of groups would undermine the protection of individuals. It should not be the primary focus of the law.

I mentioned this to Eli. He thought his father's failure to mention Lemkin by name reflected nothing more than 'a detached academic assessment'. 'My father never met Lemkin, and I never heard of him coming to the house,' he added. I sensed in Eli a certain reluctance, so I pushed him a little harder.

'I have a very vague recollection that my father didn't think much of Lemkin,' Eli said. 'He thought him to be a compiler, not a thinker.' Lauterpacht the father was not keen on the concept of genocide. 'He may have resented the intrusion into the field of international law of a personal notion like genocide, not supported by practice. He probably felt it was impracticable, an unrealistic approach. He was pragmatic, always careful not to push things too far.'

A 'personal notion' because it was one that touched the situation of his own family? I enquired.

'He may have thought that genocide was going a bit far.'

Going a bit far because it was impracticable?

'Exactly. My father was a very practical man, and he worried whether judges could deal with certain issues, knowing that judges can't resolve all problems.'

Did his father fear that elevating the role of groups would undermine the individual?

'Yes, that would have been a factor,' Eli replied. He referred me to the seventh edition of Oppenheim's *International Law,* written after the war, which was very dismissive of genocide. The concept was replete with 'gaps, artificialities and possible dangers', Lauterpacht wrote it would constitute a 'recession' from the protection of individual human rights.

At the end of 1944, Lauterpacht had submitted the corrected page proofs of his book on individual rights. By then, as Leon was reunited with his wife and daughter in newly liberated Paris, Eli was back in Cambridge, the strands of another family being reunited.

46

In February 1945, Churchill, Roosevelt and Stalin met at Yalta in the Crimea, where they took a number of important decisions. Europe would be divided. Lvov, liberated by the Red Army a few months earlier, would be in Ukraine and under Soviet domination, not in Poland as the Americans had wanted. German leaders would be treated as criminals and prosecuted.

Three months later, the fighting in Europe was over. On 2 May Harry Truman, who became president following the death of Roosevelt, appointed Robert Jackson to head the prosecution team in the trial of major German war criminals. A few weeks later, on 26 June, the United Nations Charter was signed in San Francisco, by which governments agreed to introduce a new commitment to 'fundamental human rights', to respect the 'dignity and worth of the human person'.

In June, Columbia University Press published Lauterpacht's book on an international bill of the rights of man. Reflecting his hope for a new international legal order, he invoked Churchill's commitment to the 'enthronement of the rights of man', to place the protection of the individual at the centre of the international legal order. Lauterpacht's preface set out as his aim an end to the 'omnipotence of the State'. Reactions were largely positive. 'Persuasive', 'penetrative', 'breath-taking', 'full of ideas', a 'pragmatic and realistic' combination of legal theory and political knowledge. Yet there were also critics of his hope that 'Jim Crowism and extermination camps' would no longer be matters governed exclusively by national laws. His ideas, it was claimed, were dangerous, and no more than a harking back to a long-disappeared constellation of seventeenth-century ideas. Lauterpacht was 'an echo of the past rather than a portent of the future', it was said.

The draft articles set out in the book were presented as a 'radical innovation in international law'. With little to go on by way of precedent, beyond a modest effort of the Institut de Droit International and the ideas of H. G. Wells and various wartime international committees, Lauterpacht's draft bill included nine articles on civil rights (liberty, religion, expression, assembly, privacy, equality and so on). Some matters were left out, with no mention of any prohibition on torture or discrimination against women. Equally striking, with the benefit of hindsight, was his approach to the situation of non-whites in South Africa and 'the thorny problem of actual disenfranchisement of large sections of the Negro population in some States of the United States', recognition of the realpolitik necessary to allow those two countries to engage with an international bill. Five more draft articles covered other political rights (elections, self-government, minority rights and so forth) and, to a limited extent, economic and social rights relating to work, education and public assistance in case of 'undeserved want'. Lauterpacht was silent about property rights, a nod perhaps to the political wind from the east and to political considerations in the UK.

Against the background of the UN Charter and the ideas set out in his book, Lauterpacht welcomed the idea of a war crimes trial and the appointment of Jackson as prosecutor. The American judge turned to him for help. The two men met in London on 1 July as work began on the drafting of an agreement to create the first international criminal tribunal to try the German leaders. Yet even then, a year after Lemberg had been liberated from German rule, he had no word as to the fate of the family.

At the end of July, on a warm Sunday morning, Jackson left Claridge's hotel in Mayfair to be driven to Cambridge for a meeting with Lauterpacht. Jackson sought the benefit of the academic's assistance in resolving difficulties faced by the Four Powers, particularly the charges to be brought against the defendants. No such case had ever been brought, and there were 'stubborn and deep' differences with the Soviets and the French.

The Four Powers agreed on some points. The tribunal would exercise jurisdiction over individuals, not states, and the defendants would not be allowed to hide behind the authority of the state. There would be eight judges, two from each of the Allies, a principal and an alternate. The Americans, British, French and Soviets would each nominate a prosecutor.

Differences remained, however, as to the procedures to be followed. Would the German defendants be examined by the judges, as in the French system, or by the prosecutors, as in the Anglo-American system? Of all the difficulties, the most serious concerned the list of crimes with which to charge the defendants. The differences centred on the wording of draft Article 6 of the Charter of the International Military Tribunal, the governing instrument of the new international court.

The Soviets wanted three crimes: aggression; atrocities against civilians in pursuance of the aggression; and violations of the laws of war. The Americans wanted these three crimes, as well as two more: waging an illegal war, and the criminality of membership in the SS or the Gestapo. Jackson sought Lauterpacht's help to bridge the gap, worried that the French would support the Soviets. Jackson had recently returned from Germany, where he visited Hitler's private offices, to the news that Churchill and the Conservatives had lost the general election to Labour, who might be more sympathetic to the French and the Soviets. He feared the new British government would support the Soviets. On his return to London, on Saturday, 28 July, he received new British proposals on the trial, which had, worryingly for Jackson, been accepted by the French.

These were the matters that occupied Jackson as he drove to Cambridge the next day, accompanied by his son, Bill, two secretaries and a staff lawyer. He took Lauterpacht to lunch at 'a lovely old country inn', which might have been in Grantchester, then they headed back to Cranmer Road. On a warm summer's day, they sat in the garden, on a freshly cut lawn 'as smooth as a tennis court and closely cropped'. A sweet smell permeated the garden, Lauterpacht delighted that the visitors noticed. As they talked, a young child wandered in from a neighbouring garden, and Rachel served tea and coffee. Accounts did not record whether a Victoria sponge cake from Fitzbillies was served.

Jackson set out the difficulties. There was general support from the French and the British for the Soviet approach, so the issue was how best to package a solution. Lauterpacht suggested that titles be inserted into the text, a way of introducing compromises. This might help to develop the law in a progressive way.

He suggested that the word 'Aggression' be replaced with 'The Crime of War' and that it would be preferable to refer to violations of the laws of warfare as 'War Crimes'. Titles would make it easier for the public to understand the actions being prosecuted, useful to garner support, adding to the legitimacy of the proceedings. Jackson responded positively to his idea of titles.

Lauterpacht offered a further thought. What about introducing a new term into international law to address atrocities against civilians, a matter on which the Russians and the Americans were divided and on which he had an unspoken personal interest? He pitched it. Why not refer to the atrocities against individual civilians as 'Crimes Against Humanity'?

A version of the formulation had been used in 1915, when the British and the Americans decried Turkish actions against Armenians, but that declaration was not legally binding. The term was also used in the work of the United Nations War Crimes Commission, but again not in a form that was legally binding. Jackson liked this idea too, a practical and attractive way forward. He said he'd think about it.

Later, the entourage visited Trinity College, walked through the great Christopher Wren library, toured the private college gardens. Jackson admired the trees. Katherine Fite, one of Jackson's lawyers, loved the 'backs' and the little bridges over the River Cam, 'the most beautiful thing I remember in England,' she wrote to her mother.

47

Back in London, on 31 July Jackson circulated a revised draft of the statute. He used Lauterpacht's idea of titles and included the new definitions of the crimes. There, in black and white, for the first time, was a reference to 'Crimes Against Humanity'. 'We should insert words to make clear that we are addressing persecution, etc. of Jews and others in Germany, as well as outside of it,' Jackson explained to the Allies, 'before as well as after commencement of the war.'

Such language would extend the protections of international law.

It would bring into the trial Germany's actions against its own nationals – Jews and others – before the war began. It would cover Leon's expulsion from the *Reich* in November 1938 and the measures taken against millions of others that occurred before September 1939. No longer would a state be free to treat its people entirely as it wished.

On 2 August, the Four Powers met in a final effort to reach agreement. Sir Hartley Shawcross, the strong-willed new British attorney general, who liked to ruffle feathers and was described as 'the best looking man in English public life', attended with David Maxwell Fyfe, his predecessor, retained for continuity. The discussion of draft Article 6 – with Lauterpacht's titles – was highly contentious, so left to the end. The Soviet general Iona Nikitchenko was strongly against titles; they should be removed because they 'complicate things'. His deputy, Professor A. N. Trainin, welcomed the titles from a 'theoretical point of view' but objected to their vagueness. They should be removed. Jackson disagreed, firmly. The classification was useful. The titles, suggested to him by an eminent scholar of international law whom he did not name, were 'convenient'. They would help the public to understand differences between the crimes; public support was important.

The Soviets relented, allowing crimes against humanity to become a part of international law, aimed at the protection of individuals. A week later, on 8 August, the final text was adopted, signed, made public – a historic day. By Article 6(c) of the charter, the tribunal's judges were given power to punish individuals who had committed crimes against humanity, defined to cover

> murder, extermination, enslavement, deportation, and other
> inhumane acts committed against any civilian population, before
> or during the war; or persecutions on political, racial or religious
> grounds in execution of or in connection with any crime within
> the jurisdiction of the Tribunal, whether or not in violation of the
> domestic law of the country where perpetrated.

The paragraph is worth reading very carefully. In particular, look out for the lonely semi-colon in the third line, which will cause a problem. Lauterpacht thought the text to be overly broad but wasn't worried that the use of the semi-colon might give the tribunal jurisdiction over acts that occurred before the war began. 'Paragraph 6(c) of the Agreement – Crimes against Humanity – is clearly an innovation,' he told the British Foreign Office, but it was an enlightened innovation, one that offered 'a fundamental piece of international legislation'. It affirmed that international law was not only law 'between States' but 'also the law of mankind'. Those who transgressed it would have no immunity, even if they were leaders, a reflection of the 'outraged conscience of the world'.

Shawcross gave Lauterpacht a seat on the new British War Crimes Executive, which replaced McNair's committee. Would he assist with the preparation of the trial, Shawcross asked, and help write the British arguments? Lauterpacht accepted the invitation. A few days later he received a note from Jackson, offering thanks for the hospitality in Cambridge and the 'painstaking memorandum' on crimes. Not all of your suggestions were heeded, Jackson noted, but 'all helped to clarify our thinking on the subject'. Jackson hinted at future cooperation. 'I shall be in London from time to time and will be seeing you again.'

Article 6 of the statute offered a professional and intellectual leap but little by way of personal comfort. Four years had now passed without word from Lemberg or Żółkiew. 'Daddy does not say much,' Rachel told Eli, 'he never displays much emotion.'

48

A few days after the charter was adopted, someone noticed a minor discrepancy in the texts of Article 6(c) on crimes against humanity, the problem of the semi-colon. This caused a discrepancy between the Russian version, on the one hand, and the English and French texts, on the other. An amendment was quickly agreed on, to bring the English and French versions into line with the Russian text. This was achieved on 6 October, when the semi-colon was removed and replaced with a comma.

The consequence could be significant. The semi-colon seemed to allow a crime against humanity that occurred before 1939, when the war began, to come within the jurisdiction of the tribunal; the replacement comma, however, seemed to have the effect of taking events that occurred before the war began outside the jurisdiction of the tribunal. There would be no punishment for those actions if crimes against humanity had to be connected to war. Whether this was intended, or would have this effect, would be for the judges to decide.

A few days after the disappearance of the semicolon, Shawcross complained to Lauterpacht about another development, the terms of the specific charges against the individual defendants. The Four Powers were having 'very great difficulty' with the indictment, a document Shawcross didn't like 'at all'. 'Some of the allegations in it will, I think, hardly pass the test of history or, indeed, of any serious legal examination.' Shawcross could have been referring to the unexpected introduction of a new word in the indictment, 'genocide'. It had been added at a late stage at the insistence of the Americans over strong British objections. Lauterpacht would not have let it in. 'We shall just have to make the best of this rather unsatisfactory document,' Shawcross told Lauterpacht.

It was decided that the trial would be held in Nuremberg's Palace of Justice, to open in November 1945. The Allies identified twenty-four lead defendants, to include Hermann Göring (Hitler's vice-chancellor), Albert Speer (minister of armaments and war production), and Martin Bormann (personal secretary to the Führer). The seventh name would interest Lauterpacht: Hans Frank, governor-general of occupied Poland, whose territory included Lemberg and Zólkiew.

'If you could find it possible to be there for a few days at the commencement,' Shawcross suggested, 'it will be of great assistance to us.' There would be no fee, but expenses would be covered.

Once again, Lauterpacht accepted the invitation.

III

MISS TILNEY OF NORWICH

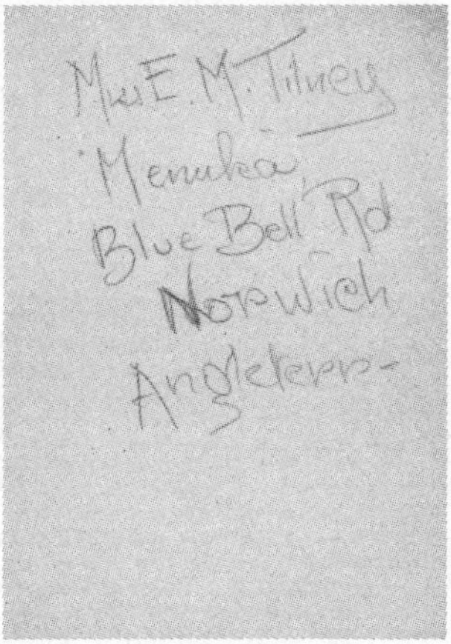

Mrs E. M. Tilney
'Menuka'
Blue Bell Rd
Norwich
Angleterre—

49

'Who was Miss Tilney?' I asked my mother.

'No idea,' she replied, without much enthusiasm.

Then she said, 'I think she was the woman who brought me from Vienna to Paris in the summer of 1939,' insisting there was no more information. This was what Leon had told her, many years after the event. 'Pas important.' Not important.

Apparently, Miss Tilney collected Ruth, just a year old, from her mother, Rita. The handover occurred at the Westbahnhof station. Farewells exchanged, Miss Tilney and the infant boarded the train to Paris, an impossibly difficult moment for a mother. On arrival at the Gare de l'Est, the infant was delivered to Leon. Miss Tilney wrote her name and address on a scrap of paper, in pencil. Au revoir. They never saw each other again.

'She saved your life?'

My mother nodded.

'You didn't want to know who she was, to see her, to find out more, thank her?'

'No.'

'You didn't want to know why she did what she did?'

'No.'

50

The manner of my mother's departure from German-occupied Vienna, three days after her first birthday and without the company of a parent, was obscure. I understood the reluctance to unlock the memory.

No one left alive knew the details, and the documents I could find offered few clues. There was the passport issued in my mother's name in December 1938, with three fading stamps and a few swastikas. One stamp was dated 4 May 1939, a permit that allowed the infant a single trip out of Austria, with a right of return. There was an exit stamp issued two and a half months later on 22 July, in the Austrian town of Feldkirch, on the Swiss border, east of Zurich. An entry stamp, marked 'Entrée', was issued the next day, 23 July, in France. The passport had a swastika on the cover, but no bright red *J*. The infant was not identified as *Jude*.

Rita remained in Vienna. That fact had always troubled my mother, raising questions as to the circumstances in which Rita had chosen – if she had a choice – not to accompany her only child to Paris. Necessity or choice? Necessity had its attractions.

Beyond the passport, the only other clue was the yellowing scrap of paper that waited patiently in Leon's documents. No more than two inches square, it was folded in half with a few words written firmly in pencil on one side. 'Miss E. M. Tilney, "Menuka", Blue Bell Rd, Norwich, Angleterre'. No message, only a name and an address.

For two years, the yellow scrap hung above my desk. Occasionally I looked at it, wondering where it was written, who wrote it, and what might have caused Miss Tilney to undertake so perilous a journey, if indeed she did. The information must have been important, because Leon kept the scrap for the rest of his life, six decades.

The Norwich address was a hundred miles to the north-east of London, beyond Cambridge, off the Norfolk Broads. I could find no house named Menuka, with its middle-class, English connotation.

I started with census records and phone directories for Norwich for the early twentieth century, surprised to find no fewer than five women with the name E. M. Tilney. Two could be discounted on grounds of age: Edna M. Tilney would have been too young to travel to Vienna (born in 1924), and Edith M. Tilney too old (born in 1866). That left three names:

1. E. M. Tilney, born in 1915, from the nearby village of Blofield.
2. Elsie M. Tilney, born in 1893, aged seven in the 1901 national census, living at 95 Gloucester Street, Norwich, with her parents.
3. Edith M. V. Tilney, no date of birth, who married Mr Hill in 1940.

The telephone directory listed an E. M. Tilney in Blofield. If it was

Unterschrift des Inhabers
Signature du porteur

Paß-Inhaberin kann nicht
schreiben

3

the same person, she would now be ninety-five years old. I called the number over several days and eventually spoke to Desmond Tilney, who had a fine Norfolk accent. 'My sister Elsie May died three years ago,' he said sadly. Did she make a trip to Vienna in 1939?

'Oh, I don't know, never heard anything about that.' He would ask around. Two days later he called, disappointed to report that his sister didn't travel abroad before the war.

I moved on to Elsie M. Tilney, born in 1893. The 1901 national census recorded that she lived in a detached house with her parents, Albert (a stationer's clerk) and Hannah, and four brothers and sisters. The name and birth date turned up two further hits on the Web. On 1 January 1960, a woman of the same name and age disembarked from the MV *Stirling Castle* (of the Union Castle line) at Southampton docks, having travelled from Durban, South Africa. The ship's manifest identified Miss Tilney – middle name Maud – as a 'Missionary' returning from Basutoland. Fourteen years later, in October 1974, a woman of the same name and age died in Dade County, Florida.

The information on this woman's demise offers a zip code. For a fee of six dollars, I obtained five numbers and a city: 33134, Miami. A search for the name Tilney and that zip code turned up several Tilneys in the area, two of whom died in 1974. One was Frederick, the name of Elsie Maud Tilney's younger brother, according to the 1901 national census. In the Miami white pages I found several Tilneys in the same zip code area. The first I reached, a few days later, was Germaine Tilney.

51

'Yes, I knew Elsie Tilney,' Germaine Tilney told me, crisply. Elsie was her late husband's aunt, the older sister of her father-in-law, Dr Frederick Tilney. Forty years had passed since she died, so Germaine didn't remember too much about Aunt Elsie, a 'gracious lady' who came into their lives in the mid-1960s. She devoted herself to missionary work, as an evangelical Christian, then retired in Florida to be with her brother Fred. 'She was quiet, kept herself to herself, and proper.' Occasionally she visited for family meals, usually on a Sunday.

Germaine had no photograph and recalled little about Miss Til-ney's earlier life, apart from a brother in Norwich, a preacher called Albert, and missions to obscure places. 'Maybe she spent time in North Africa,' Germaine wondered, digging deep, but had no infor-mation about the wartime years or any trip to Vienna. The subject of the war was somewhat delicate, because Germaine had German origins. 'Very early on,' Germaine explained, 'my husband, Robert, gathered the family together to say that we would never talk about the war.' During the war her father-in-law, Frederick, and his wife, Nora, hosted visiting British soldiers stationed in Miami.

Germaine asked how much I knew about Miss Tilney's brother Frederick.

'Nothing,' I responded. He had an interesting life, she explained. He came to America in the 1920s, 'became a famous bodybuilder, and discovered Charles Atlas, who was his friend.' Germaine referred me to Fred's autobiography, *Young at 73 – and Beyond!* I found a copy (later offered to my mother for her seventy-third birthday) and a picture of Fred. In the book he described a tough, rough, poor childhood in Norwich, an overbearing father (also a preacher), and his long partnership and friendship with Charles Atlas.

Germaine introduced me to her nephew John. Our only telephone conversation was cut short – whether by intention or accident was unclear. Nevertheless, it threw up a single, excellent clue.

'Elsie Tilney hated the Germans,' John said suddenly and without explanation. 'She just hated them.' Did something happen during the war? He remembered no details.

The vague outlines of a life emerged. Miss Tilney came from a family of preachers, went on mission in southern Africa, disliked Germans, lived her last years in Coconut Grove, Miami. I trawled through African mission archives (more plentiful and enticing than might be imagined), which offered a lead to an archive at the Univer-sity of the Witwatersrand library. There I found documents about Miss Tilney's mission to South Africa after the war. Among the papers were several handwritten letters.

I compared the handwriting in the letters with the scrap of paper. They were identical. The missionary and Miss E. M. Tilney of Bluebell Road were the same person. The letters suggested a strong-willed character and provided information about time spent in Portugal and before that in France. So I turned to French archives,

from which a single letter emerged, dated February 1942, written by
a French military officer to one Otto Landhäuser, the commandant
of Frontstalag 121. This, I discovered, was a German internment
camp in the spa town of Vittel. The letter identified twenty-eight
female prisoners held at the camp whom the Germans wished to
exchange for prisoners held by the British. Among the names was
'Elsie M. Tilney, née en 1893', holder of a British passport, interned
by the Germans at Vittel.

Germaine had mentioned a brother, the preacher Albert Tilney,
and this opened another line of inquiry. Albert turned out to have
been associated with the Surrey Chapel in Norwich, founded by
Robert Govett, a fellow of Worcester College, Oxford. Govett established the chapel because of his desire to be more faithful to the
Scriptures, motivated by logic ('fearless in pursuing a point to its rational conclusion'), independence (refusing 'the ordinary doctrines
of post-Reformation Protestantism') and simplicity (employing
'language direct and plain such as all could understand'). I came
across a copy of the chapel's centenary pamphlet, published in 1954,
which included information about a missionary band established
in 1903. It listed all the chapel's missionaries. Among them was
one who left Norwich for Algeria in 1920, and there was a grainy
black-and-white photograph. It showed a purposeful young woman
with a strong face, hair swept across her forehead, in a simple,
elegant dress. I was looking at Miss Elsie Tilney, after two years
of searching.

52

The Surrey Chapel turned out to be a thriving community in the
heart of Norwich, under the direction of its pastor, Tom Chapman,
to whom I sent an e-mail. He replied within the hour, excited about
a 'fascinating inquiry', hoping that it was 'the same Elsie Tilney!'
He forwarded my e-mail to Dr Rosamunde Codling, the chapel's
archivist. The next morning I received an e-mail from Miss Codling,
who was 'almost certain' that their Miss Tilney and mine were the
same.

Dr Codling connected Miss Tilney to her preacher brother,
Albert (she directed me to one of his tracts, *Believers and Their*

Elsie Tilney, 1920

Judgment, available years ago from 'Mr A. J. Tilney, 66 Hall Road, Norwich, for 6d per doz. 3/6 per 100, 'post free'). Other references to Miss Tilney followed, found in the chapel's newsletter. She was a 'doughty' opponent of modernism, Dr Codling explained. Her 'sphere of work' was simply stated: 'Jews'.

A few weeks later, I made the first of several trips to Norwich. Dr Codling was keen to help, because this was the first she (or anyone at the Surrey Chapel) had heard of the story I was now sharing, delighted that the child of a 'saved Jew' had made contact. I was welcomed with great warmth by the pastor and Dr Codling, who brought Eric to our meeting, an older member of the congregation. Eric remembered Miss Tilney as 'a pretty young lady, with a sweet mellow voice'. He said this a little mischievously. 'You don't associate missionaries with being pretty, do you?' he added, wondering aloud whether she ever married (there was no record that she did). Eric recalled Miss Tilney at Sunday School, talking about Africa, an exotic subject of which the children knew little. 'We had a map of the British Empire but knew nothing about African culture, the people, or Islam,' Eric explained. 'Everything we knew we got from her, the pictures she brought and the pictures she painted.' She was 'special', passionate about Algeria. This was the mid-1930s.

Dr Codling accompanied me to the Surrey Chapel archives at the Norwich Records Office, where we spent an afternoon plough-ing through a great number of documents, looking for any sign of Miss Tilney's activities. These weren't hard to find: she was an avid letter writer who also wrote short articles for various evangelical magazines, an articulate and astute observer. As Europe embraced fascism and anti-Semitism, she chose another path. The archive ma-terial made clear that she was living in Paris in the spring of 1939, when Leon arrived in the city.

She joined the Surrey Chapel in February 1903 as a ten-year-old, then left on mission to Algeria and Tunisia in 1920, where she worked for more than a decade. In November 1927, she was based in the small town of Nabeul, on Tunisia's Mediterranean coast, working with a Madame Gamati. She wrote of visits to Jewish homes, of the 'great' welcome she received as she sought to save Jews by bringing them to Jesus (there is no mention of any success). Occasionally she returned home, spending the summer of 1929 in Bournemouth, at the summer convention of the North Africa Mission. Someone took a group photograph, in which she holds an infant in her arms, one of the few images I found.

In the 1930s, she devoted her activities to the well-being of Jews, having joined the well-established Mildmay Mission. A farewell note prepared by the Surrey Chapel began with a reference to the governing credo: 'To the Jew first'. She stayed in close contact with David Panton, the chapel's pastor, influenced by his writings in *The Dawn*, which he edited. She must have seen the piece Panton wrote after *The Times* published the article on 25 July 1933 (the one likely read by Lauterpacht in Cricklewood), on a speech by Hitler, under the headline 'By Fighting Against the Jews I Am Doing the Lord's Work'. Panton attacked the Führer's 'anti-semitic fury' as irrational and insane, a hatred that was 'purely racial and fanatical', with no religious basis. Hitler's views were 'entirely independent of the individual Jew's character or conduct,' Panton wrote. The article would have spurred Miss Tilney, who was living in Djerba, Tunisia. A year later, in the spring of 1934, she moved to France to take up a new activity, to devote herself to 'work amongst Jewish people in Paris'.

By October 1935, Miss Tilney had settled in Paris. The chapel's 'Missionary Notes' reported an article in *Trusting and Toiling*, another journal, which described a narrow escape from a serious accident. Walking along a busy thoroughfare in Paris, Miss Tilney was about to step off the pavement into the road when 'a gentleman pulled her back only just in time to prevent her being knocked down by a motor-car'. Of particular interest, indeed a matter for rejoicing, was the fact that the rescuer was 'a JEW!!'

In 1936, she moved into the North Africa Mission house in Paris. Speaking excellent French and Arabic, she reported on a visit to the Paris mosque, a building that held no charms for her because of its 'Gospel-denying doctrine'. It did, however, offer an excellent couscous in an Arab setting and opportunities for silent prayer and witness (she took pleasure in offering the Gospel of Luke to a 'genuinely delighted' waiter from Tunis). She wrote of the mosque's interior, its 'exotic loveliness of flowers, foliage and fountains in the sun-flooded courtyard', but left feeling 'sad, sad' because everything 'seemed to bespeak an insidious denial of our Lord'.

The years 1936 and 1937 were divided between Paris and Gabès in southern Tunisia, where her work was dominated by an outbreak of typhoid. She spent time with Arabs in quarantine, tended to 'a dear frightened old Jewess', yet was still able to look on the bright side because a typhoid outbreak opened 'many Jewish and Moslem doors', allowing her to observe 'a young Jewish lad . . . intently reading the Gospel of St Matthew'. In Paris she worked at the Baptist church on the avenue du Maine in the 14th arrondissement. 'I was privileged to help and witness to the suffering German Jewish refugees,' she wrote to her friends in Norwich.

In September 1937 she was back in Paris, interviewing German and Austrian Jewish refugees at the Baptist church, working along-side Deacon André Frankl, the American Board of Missions to the Jews' representative in Paris (born in 1895, the grandson of a Hungarian rabbi, Frankl converted from Judaism and fought in the Austro-Hungarian army in 1914 on the eastern front, like Leon's brother, Emil). Miss Tilney reported that the pastor at the Baptist church, Monsieur Vincent, was 'throwing open his Church – and heart – to Jewish people'. She spoke at meetings for Jews, worked with refugees, and assisted at interviews to decide on what help could be offered. In January 1939, when Leon arrived in Paris, she was still working at the Baptist church, and it must have been here that she met him as he sought assistance in exile. Miss Tilney's activities were occasionally reported in *Trusting and Toiling,* alongside items about the dire situation in Lemberg, where 'Jewish students at Lwów University, in Poland, were attacked by anti-Semitic rioters.'

The Baptist church on the avenue du Maine was a hub for refugees from Austria and Germany, including intellectuals, academics and doctors, aided by the Service d'Aide aux Réfugiés (Assistance for Refugees). The church offered a daily 'soup kitchen' for hundreds of refugees like Leon. Friday-evening meetings were 'especially moving, as the largest part of the hall included Jewish refugees from Germany, Austria and Czechoslovakia'. Seven decades later, I spent an afternoon at the Baptist church with Richard Gelin, its current pastor. He shared archival material, including information on the numerous baptisms undertaken by Jews, hoping by this act to save themselves from the coming danger. The archives included much about the church's assistance to Jewish refugees and their children and several books describing the brave work of Henri Vincent. I found no reference to Leon or Miss Tilney, but several photographs showed Jewish refugees from Austria and Germany, offering a powerful impression. One showed a group sitting in the church hallway, 'people in difficulty waiting to be received'. I could imagine Leon in this room, impecunious and quiet, alone in Paris.

On 15 July 1939, *Trusting and Toiling* reported that Miss Tilney was working in Paris. A week later, at some risk, she travelled to Vienna's Westbahnhof train station to collect a young child. She met Rita, who entrusted to her care an infant who'd just passed her first birthday. I learned from my mother that it was said that Rita went to the station with Leon's sister Laura, who brought her only child, eleven-year-old Herta, who also expected to travel to Paris with Miss Tilney. At the last minute Laura decided that Herta wouldn't travel, the prospect of separation being too painful. The decision was understandable but catastrophic: two years later, in October 1941, young Herta was deported to the ghetto in Litzmannstadt (Lodz) with her mother. Within a few months, Herta and Laura had been killed.

Miss Tilney travelled by train to Paris with only one of the children. At the Gare de l'Est she was met by Leon. I don't know how he expressed his thanks or if he ever saw her again. She wrote out her name and address on the scrap of paper, which she then gave to him, and they headed off to different parts of Paris.

53

I might have ended the research on Miss Tilney at this point but was curious to know what came next, why she had acted as she did, what motivated her compassionate actions. She was in Paris when the war began a month later, working with the North Africa Mission and hoping to obtain a French *carte d'identité* that would allow her to remain in France. The range of her work was 'big', looking after 'her Jewish protégés' to whom she was close. She travelled often to Le Havre and other French ports, to bid her 'protégés' a safe farewell as they left for America. In June 1940, the German army occupied Paris.

She was stuck in the city for several months, with no outside contact. The silence worried her friends, and readers of *Trusting and Toiling* were invited to pray for her and those 'whose lot is now more bitter than ever'. The chapel voted to send relief money – the grand sum of ten pounds – but it took over a year to arrive, leaving her dependent on support from the American embassy. In September 1940 she finally wrote that she'd been unwell but was now better, enjoying the sunshine, racking up debts and 'thinking constantly of family, and friends, especially Surrey Road'.

The chapel members were so worried that they reached out to Lord Halifax, Churchill's foreign secretary, but without success. The record noted drily that the secretary of state for foreign affairs 'presented his compliments to all and sundry, but that is about all'. This was followed by more silence. Enemy aliens in France were being interned, and in early 1941 Miss Tilney was sent to a military barracks in Besançon, with several hundred other British women. In May, she was transferred to Frontstalag 121 in the eastern French spa town of Vittel, interned at the Grand Hotel (it is now a part of Club Med), where she would spend four years.

In February 1942, the British and the Germans tried to agree to a prisoner exchange, but nothing came of the plan. The Surrey Chapel sent her two pounds for dental treatment, and in early 1943 worrying reports arrived that she was suffering from malnutrition.

Her letters were short; she was 'longing for the day of peace'. The third anniversary of internment brought ominous developments. Twenty-five hundred enemy aliens were being held in the camp's ten hotels, separated from the spa town by a three-metre fence topped with barbed wire. Most of the women were from Britain, Canada and the United States, but in April 1943 a group of four hundred Jewish men, women and children arrived, mostly Poles from the Warsaw ghetto, allowed out because they held South American passports. They brought unbelievable stories of murder and mass killing. Miss Tilney, who worked in the main office, the *Kommandantur*, with the records and archives, learned that the man in charge of the camp, Commandant Landhäuser, had been ordered by Alois Brunner and Adolf Eichmann to round up all the Warsaw Jews held in Vittel, to be transported to the east. It was said that they held forged passports.

In January 1944, Commandant Landhäuser transferred the Warsaw Jews from the Hotel Providence to the Hotel Beau-Site, separated from the general site. This caused much commotion in the camp. In March, a first group of 169 Warsaw Jews were loaded onto the trains of Transport No. 72, destined for Auschwitz. Among them was the poet Isaac Katznelson, who hid his last poems in a bottle on the site of the camp, later recovered. One of those poems came to be widely celebrated, 'The Song of the Slaughtered Jewish People'.

There was some resistance. Several of the Warsaw Jews committed suicide, jumping from the upper floors of a hotel or taking poison. Others tried to escape, among them a young Pole called Sasha Krawec, who sought help from his teacher of English, Miss Tilney. This I learned in *Sofka: The Autobiography of a Princess*, a book by Sofka Skipwith, another internee (who was, by happy coincidence, the great-aunt of my neighbour in London). The book offered an account of the disappearance of Sasha Krawec shortly before the Auschwitz transport. 'We felt that Miss Tilney, a middle-aged worker in the Kommandantur who had been extremely friendly with Sasha, must have some part in this.'

Sofka Skipwith was right. Miss Tilney hid Sasha Krawec for more than six months, until 18 September 1944, when US troops arrived. 'It was only after the camp was liberated that it was discovered that he had spent those months in her bathroom,' Sofka wrote. One internee would tell Miss Tilney's brother Albert that his sister had 'always put herself last', that she saved everyone's passports and 'at great personal risk ... hid for a period of sixteen weeks a young Jew condemned to be sent to an annihilation camp in Poland. She was given away to the Germans by an unknown internee, but fortunately she was accused of hiding a girl, and could therefore deny the charge.' Another internee told Albert that saving Sasha Krawec was one of the 'outstandingly brave deeds of this war', that he never met anyone 'so courageous and hard-working, so unsparing of herself in the good work she has been doing'. Miss Tilney was 'one of the bravest persons I have ever met'.

After liberation, she was among the last to leave the camp at Vittel, working for the US Sixth Army and then as a 'secretary and hostess' at the Ermitage Hotel, a unit of the US Seventh Army's Rest Hotel Group (where she was considered conscientious, capable, imaginative, and loyal). She then headed back to Paris and the Baptist church on the avenue du Maine, bringing with her some possessions of others who had been interned. Later, Miss Tilney left France for mission in southern Africa, where she spent much of the 1950s. After retiring, she moved to Florida to be near her brother Fred in Coconut Grove (a colourful character, in 1955 Fred was convicted of mail fraud by a Miami judge and ordered to stop selling his fake 'body-building liquids', called Vi-Be-Ion, a mixture of brewer's yeast and vegetable flavouring). 'They would hang out together here in Coconut Grove,' Germaine Tilney explained, 'Dr Tilney, Mr Atlas and Elsie.'

Miss Tilney died in 1974, her papers destroyed. Unable to find where she was buried, I contacted the obituarist at the *Miami Herald*. After a few enquiries she established that Miss Tilney was cremated and her ashes scattered over Biscayne Bay, on the Atlantic coast of southern Florida.

There was no record that she ever told anyone about Vienna or Vittel. Not at the Surrey Chapel, not in Florida.

54

Few other internees mentioned in *Sofka* were still alive, but I located Shula Troman, an artist in her ninetieth year. Interned in Vittel for three years until 1944, she lived in the small village of Ploumilliau in Brittany, a short walk from the Atlantic. We met in Paris, in the Marais district, at Chez Marianne, her favourite restaurant, on the rue des Rosiers. She arrived in a bright red outfit, with a great smile and much energy. A sense of adoration was the feeling that best described my first impression of Shula, and it lasted.

Shula's internment at Vittel was the result of a clerical error. Living in a small French village, she applied for a *carte d'identité*, and the town clerk saw on her birth certificate that she was born in British Palestine (to which her father moved in 1923 from Warsaw). Shula didn't disabuse him when he listed her nationality as British. Later, because she was a Jew obliged to wear a yellow star, the accidental reference to British nationality saved her life after she was apprehended in Paris by the Germans.

Eventually, in the spring of 1941, she was sent to Vittel and the sixth floor of the Grand Hotel. 'A lovely big room with a view on a courtyard, a kind of suite, with a bathroom,' she explained, quite gaily. Life in the camp wasn't too grim, although there were difficult periods, especially when the Warsaw ghetto Jews arrived in 1943 with 'unbelievable' stories. She took art lessons from a dashing young Englishman, Morley Troman, with whom she fell in love. Later they married. She was part of a literary and political group, one that included Sofka Skipwith and her closest friend, Penelope 'Lopey' Brierley.

She showed me a photograph of her with her friend Lopey, who wrote out a poem by Charles Vildrac on the back of the image. 'Une vie sans rien de commun avec la mort' – 'A life that has nothing in common with death' – she wrote.

Occasionally they put on innocuous, mischievous shows, which Miss Tilney attended, including an evening of 'Oriental songs'. 'It was marvellous,' Shula recalled, her eyes bright, 'in the front row sat all the dignitaries, Commandant Landhäuser in the middle, the Gestapo people next to him as guests of honour. We hadn't provided the lyrics, so they had no idea what we were singing. They really liked one song, with the lyrics "Long life to the people of Israel! Israel will live for ever!" We sang in Hebrew so they didn't understand. The whole front row stood and applauded and cheered and asked us to do it again. It was marvellous.'

She laughed. 'We sang so strong; they applauded so loudly. The

Shula (right) with Lopey Brierley, Vittel, 1943

real joy was that later they found out. We were prohibited from doing more shows!'

Shula recalled with some affection Landhäuser, the hotel keeper who became a camp commandant and had been a POW interned in England in the First World War. 'He liked the English detainees, Christian or Jewish,' Shula explained. 'After the liberation, he gave me his card and invited us to visit.'

Early on, however, she had become aware of a very odd English spinster – she pronounced the name as 'Mees Teel-nay' – about whom she was cautious. 'Miss Tilney was working in the *Kommand-antur,* on the internees' documents and files; I was frightened of her, suspicious.' The woman was ageless, grey-haired, a 'very thin' and 'withdrawn' lady who kept herself to herself and was deeply religious. She was *rétrécie,* tense, coiled up. Shula was concerned that the Englishwoman might be an informer, and she had another worry: she hoped to keep her Jewish background a secret.

The relationship with Miss Tilney changed in the summer of 1941, unexpectedly. 'I was walking along a corridor when I noticed Miss Tilney coming towards me. I was nervous, because I knew she worked in the *Kommandantur,* and wanted to keep my distance. As she got closer to me, I became more anxious. Then a very strange thing happened. Just as she reached me, she fell to her knees, reached out, took my hand and kissed it. This left me feeling *estomaquée* – flabbergasted – and I didn't know what to do or say. Then Miss Tilney said, "I know you are part of the people who will save the world; you are one of the chosen people."'

Shula looked at me across the restaurant table. 'Do you realize how frightening that was?' she asked. 'Here I was,' she continued, 'hoping that no one would know my secret, that I was Jewish, and not really British. Can you imagine how terrifying that was, what it could mean?' She worried she would be reclassified as stateless, with all that implied for possible deportation. 'Then Miss Tilney said, "Don't worry, I will look after you, I will do everything to protect you." It was very strange. For everyone else, being a Jew was danger, but for Miss Tilney it was special.'

Shula paused, then said, 'She was the very opposite for those times.'

Miss Tilney kept a protective eye out for the young woman. Later, after the liberation, Shula learned how she saved Sasha Krawec. 'We were in the yard of the camp, free, amazed, in a sort of no-man's-land under English control. My friend Rabbit [Madeleine Steinberg] was distraught when the Jews were moved to another hotel, then came the transports to Auschwitz. We thought Sasha was taken. And then, all of a sudden, six months later, there he was in the yard, white-skinned, exhausted, half-crazy, at his wits' end. He was like a drugged crazy person, but he was alive, saved by Miss Tilney. And then we learned how she saved him, told him if there was another transport he should give her a sign, which he did, and she summoned him to her, which he did, dressed as a woman.'

Shula was silent again and then said quietly, 'That is what Miss Tilney did.' She wept. 'Une femme remarquable.' The words were barely audible.

55

Rosamunde Codling of the Surrey Chapel arranged a meeting with another member of the congregation, someone else who remembered Elsie. Grace Wetherley was in her late eighties, initially resistant to meeting me because she distrusted lawyers. She relented, and we met after a Sunday-morning service. Her face stood out in the crowd, strong and lined, eyes alert and bright, her hair a beautiful, deep white. Yes, she remembered Miss Tilney, from the early 1930s, at Sunday School, back from trips to North Africa.

'I remember her brother better, although I didn't go much on Bert,' Grace said pointedly. 'He didn't have the character his sister had, a bit erratic.' The memories returned with the questions. 'In 1935, I was made to sit by her,' Grace said precisely, with excitement. 'She was absolutely fearless and devoted to children, that's what drove her.' She paused. 'That's what drives *us*.' A smile illuminated her face. 'As I was growing up as a teenager, I wouldn't say I idolized her, that's the wrong word, but I was full of admiration for the woman. She was fearless.'

Grace knew of the talk around the congregation about Miss Tilney's activities, of the rumours. 'They said she was saving Jewish babies.' She had no details; none of the babies ever turned up at chapel. 'It was during the war, because she was abroad, and the idea was to get rid of the Jews. She was fearless, and she saw these poor children, and she saved them. She did a tremendous work, putting her own life on the line.'

We sat, contemplative. 'Now you've come to see us,' Grace said with a smile. 'I don't think it was just because they were Jewish children who were dying,' she added. 'It was a question of Hitler getting it all wrong, as usual. She was driven by human compassion. After all, Christians are supposed to go for whoever is in trouble.' She thought back to that time and her own endeavours. 'What challenges have I faced?' she asked aloud. 'Nothing much. I wasn't going to be marched off by the Gestapo. She had everything to lose; she could have lost her life at any minute.'

Grace knew that Miss Tilney was interned. 'I don't know why,' she continued, 'but she was a thorough nuisance on the Continent, trying to save the lives of those whom Hitler wanted dead.' She was proud to have known Miss Tilney, a woman who was 'fortunate to escape with her life'. She brought our conversation to a close. 'She was compassionate, brilliant, gracious.' Pause. 'And a thorough nuisance.'

Grace was happy I had made my way to her congregation.

'How nice that you have found us, how very nice that you have seen the light.'

56

'You weren't interested in what motivated Miss Tilney?' I asked my mother. 'What difference would it make?' she replied. Yet I still wanted to understand why Miss Tilney acted as she did, taking a journey to Vienna to save a Jewish baby and hiding Sasha Krawec, at great personal risk.

There were clues, from Grace Wetherley and others, so it was to Rosamunde Codling at the Surrey Chapel that I turned once again. She foraged and came back with some information, a little hesitant.

'It's a bit delicate,' she said, but she had an answer, quite specific, in a textual sense. 'It was about Miss Tilney's great love in Christ for the Jewish people.' Go on, I said. 'It seems she was driven by a literal interpretation of Paul's Letter to the Romans.'

Rosamunde directed me to the relevant lines of the famous epistle, lines for which it became apparent my mother – and by extension I – were indebted. Together we read Romans 1:16: 'For I am not ashamed of the Good News of Christ, for it is the power of God for salvation for everyone who believes; for the Jew first, and also for the Greek.'

She directed me to another line, Romans 10:1: 'Brothers, my heart's desire and prayer to God is for Israel, that they may be saved.'

Rosamunde believed these were the lines that caused Miss Tilney to see her mission as working with Jewish people 'to win them for Christ'. I understood the hesitation in raising this, that I might be offended by the thought that Miss Tilney was motivated by religious ideology. She had no reason to be concerned.

Tom Chapman endorsed the detective work. He believed Miss Tilney was motivated by human compassion, coupled with a strong belief – shared by others at the Surrey Chapel – in the epithet 'For

the Jew first'. His predecessor David Panton adopted a literal interpretation of Romans that pointed to a deep sympathy for Jews and
their crucial role in fulfilling God's purposes. Tom thought it to be
the very opposite of the Nazi credo.

'What Paul is saying,' Tom explained, 'is that you show your faith
to God as a Christian by expressing sympathy and kindness to the
Jewish people.'

Had Miss Tilney travelled to Vienna in the hope that the infant
would become a Christian? The question was awkward. 'She had
an exultation of the Jewish people, a general desire to do good to
those who were struggling,' Tom continued, 'and this was coupled
with a theological position that heightened sensitivities.' A mix of
compassion and theology, then?

Yes, but the basic motivation was compassion, tweaked by a
theological element. 'She was aware of the persecution of Jews in
Germany and Austria, and her position was the very antithesis of
the anti-Semitism dominant in Germany.'

I knew Paul's Letter to the Romans to be controversial, not least
because it dealt with matters such as homosexuality and the rights
of women in church. I knew it also to be significant, in the sense of
prophesying that Christ would not come again until the Jews had
been converted, that the Second Coming wouldn't happen until all
Jews accepted the same God. This posed a challenge for Miss Tilney,
whose Christian doctrine directed that salvation was a one-to-one
business, that each Jew had to decide on his own, as an individual
act. The one, not the many. So Miss Tilney had much work on her
hands, a consequence of the split between Martin Luther and the
Catholic Church during the Reformation. This focused on an interpretation of the Scriptures that pointed to individual conscience, the
negation of the group.

'This was the beginning of our idea of the individual in the
modern world,' a theologically inclined acquaintance explained, the
origins of modern human rights, the focus on the individual.

Like Tom Chapman, I understood Miss Tilney to have been motivated by something beyond ideology. Her writings, the decision
to move to Paris, the fact she spoke Arabic and French, all pointed
to something more. In writing about her visit to the mosque, she
noticed its beauty and the loveliness of particular individuals. She

was ideological and certain about the things she believed, but those matters didn't blind her to the nuances and variety of life, to the individuals who didn't think the way she did, and she wanted to spend time with them.

Miss Tilney was a compassionate woman, not an ideologue out to do the missionary thing. It wasn't only that she hid people but that she went out of her way to hide people. 'People are only capable of great heroism when they believe something passionately,' a friend suggested, when I told her the story. 'An abstract principle is not enough to be heroic; it has to be something which is emotional and deeply motivated.'

IV

LEMKIN

[A]ttacks upon national, religious and ethnic groups should be made international crimes

Rafael Lemkin, 1944

57

On a warm spring day in New York City, Nancy Lavinia Ackerly, a student from Louisville, Kentucky, sat on the grass of Riverside Park close to the campus of Columbia University. It was 1959, and Nancy was with an Indian friend, enjoying a modest picnic. As an elderly man ambled over to them, dressed elegantly in a suit and tie, Nancy noticed his warm eyes. In a heavy central European accent he said, 'I know the words for "I love you" in twenty languages, may I share them with you?'

Please do, Nancy said, please do. He joined them, and over the course of a meandering conversation Nancy learned that he was the author of the Genocide Convention. His name was Rafael Lemkin, and he came originally from Poland.

Nancy and Lemkin became acquaintances. She would visit him on West 112th Street, a space filled with books and papers, a single room with a daybed but no telephone or water closet. He was destitute and ill, but Nancy didn't know this. A few months into their friendship, he enquired whether she might assist on his memoir: Would she be willing to help 'smooth out the language'? Over the summer they worked together on the manuscript, to which Lemkin gave the title *Totally Unofficial*.

Unable to find a publisher, the book ended up several dozen blocks south of Columbia University, in the bowels of the New York Public Library. Many, many years later, a generous American academic mentioned the manuscript and sent me a photocopy. It reached me in London, where I read it with care and much interest. The gaps were immediately apparent, and I enjoyed a typewritten text heavily marked up by Lemkin's hand. One passage was particularly enticing, no more than a few lines about Lemkin's studies in Lwów, which captured a conversation with an unnamed professor (some versions of the text referred to more than one professor), no doubt written with the benefit of a lengthy hindsight. Still, the passage captured my attention and eventually led me to learn that

Lemkin and Lauterpacht had had the same teachers at the same
law school.

58

'I was born . . . [and] lived my first ten years on a farm called Ozerisko,
fourteen miles from the city of Wołkowysk,' Lemkin wrote in the
memoir. Life began in the clearing of a forest in June 1900, not far
from Białystok. This was several hundred miles north of Lemberg,
on land that Russia had annexed from Poland a century earlier, in
1795. The territory was known as White Rus, or Litva. East Prussia
lay to the north, modern Ukraine to the south, Russia to the east and
modern Poland to the west. Ozerisko, which is now Azyaryska in
Belarus, was so small that it was more or less unmarked.

This was the birthplace of Lemkin, the second of Bella and Josef's
three sons, tucked between Elias and Samuel. His father worked as
a tenant farmer in lands over which Poles and Russians had long
fought, with the Jews caught in the middle. Life was a constant
struggle, as his father put it, like three in a bed sharing a single blanket. 'When the man to the right pulls the blanket to himself,' only
the one in the middle could be sure of being covered.

The Lemkins lived with two other families the children formed
a 'happy gang'. Lemkin recalled an idyllic childhood, of roosters
and other animals, a large dog called Riabczyk, a great white horse,
the 'metallic whisper' of swinging scythes cutting through fields of
clover and rye. Food was plentiful, black bread, raw onions, potato
pudding. He helped out on the farm, near a large lake sheltered by
white birches on which he and his brothers built small barges and
played pirates and Vikings. Occasionally, the idyll was interrupted
by a tsarist official, who came to enforce the rules that precluded
Jews from owning a farm. Josef Lemkin circumvented the law with
bribes, paid to a mustachioed police officer in uniform and shiny
black boots who sat astride a large horse. He was the first official to
be feared by Lemkin.

Bible study began at the age of six, introducing Lemkin to proph-
ets who preached justice among men and peace among nations. He
graduated to lessons in a neighbouring village, where his grandparents ran a boarding house, and from his mother, Bella, who was

a voracious reader, he first heard the fables of Ivan Krylov, tales of justice and disappointment. To the end of his life, he would recite the story of the fox who invited the stork to lunch, offering food on a flat plate. The stork reciprocated, with an invitation to eat from a bottle with a narrow neck. Injustice didn't pay, such was the lesson of a childhood fable.

Bella often sang to him, simple melodies that might be built around the poems of Semyon Nadson, a nineteenth-century Russian romantic writer, whose poem-song 'The Triumph of Love' repudiated violence. 'Look how evil oppresses mankind,' Nadson wrote of the world, so 'sick of torture and blood'. Nadson's writings later inspired Sergei Rachmaninoff who, in the year of Lemkin's birth, drew on another poem ('Melodiya') to craft opus 21, no. 9, a romantic piece for piano and tenor that expressed hope for the possibility of a better humankind.

At my instigation, a colleague from Belarus travelled to Azyaryska, three hours by car from Minsk, to take a look. There he found a group of wooden houses, each occupied by an elderly widow. One of them, in her eighty-fifth year, told him with a smile that she was too young to remember Lemkin. She directed him to an abandoned Jewish cemetery. That might be helpful, she said.

Close to the hamlet, my friend came across the village of Miżeryčy, home to a noble Belarus family, the Skirmunts, famous in an earlier age for their collection of French and Polish books. 'Maybe that is why Lemkin's mother spoke so many languages,' my friend suggested.

The years were not pure idyll. Lemkin heard of pogroms and mob violence against Jews. In Białystok in 1906, when Lemkin was six years old, a hundred Jews were killed in one incident. He imagined stomachs split apart and stuffed with pillow feathers, although it seems more likely that the impressions were drawn from a poem by Bialik, *In the City of Slaughter,* which offered a graphic account of a different atrocity a thousand miles south, with a line about 'cloven belly, feather-filled'. Lemkin knew the works of Bialik, and his first published book (in 1926) would be a translation from Hebrew into Polish of a novella by the poet, a book called *Noach i Marynka*. I tracked down a copy in the university library in Jerusalem, a tale of young love, a Jewish boy and a Ukrainian girl (the English title is *Behind the Fence*), a story of conflict between groups.

Azyaryska, Belarus, 2012

In 1910, the Lemkins left Ozerisko for another farm in nearby Wołkowysk. The move was prompted by a desire to improve the children's education, to enable Lemkin to enrol in a city school. There he became an admirer of Tolstoy (to 'believe an idea means to live it,' he liked to say) and of *Quo Vadis,* a historical novel by Henryk Sienkiewicz, about love and ancient Rome. He told Nancy Ackerly that he was eleven when he read the novel, which caused him to ask his mother why the police hadn't intervened when the Romans threw the Christians to the lions. Lemkin touched on analogous matters in his memoir – for example, an account of a Jewish 'ritual killing' that was claimed to have taken place in Kiev in 1911 – events that caused him and other Jewish pupils at the school to be taunted because of their religious affiliation.

59

In 1915, the First World War reached Wołkowysk. In his memoir, which was both incomplete and, I came to believe, not entirely free from a touch of creative embellishment, Lemkin wrote that the

Germans damaged the family farm on arrival, then again in 1918 when they left, although Bella's books were left intact. A good student with a phenomenal facility for languages, he attended a Gymnasium in Białystok. With the end of the war, Wołkowysk became part of Poland, and Lemkin, like Lauterpacht and Leon, acquired Polish nationality.

Lemkin, Białystok, 1917

The end of the First World War brought a different tragedy to the Lemkin family. In July 1918, the global influenza pandemic reached Wołkowysk, and among the many victims was Lemkin's younger brother, Samuel.

It was around this time, when he was eighteen years old, that Lemkin said he began to think about the destruction of groups. One point of focus was the mass murder of Armenians in the summer of 1915, which was in the news. 'More than 1.2 million Armenians' killed, as he put it, 'for no other reason than they were Christians'. Henry Morgenthau, the American ambassador to the Ottoman Empire who would prepare a report on the Lwów killings of 1918, described the Armenian massacres as 'the greatest crime of all ages'. For the Russians, they were 'crimes against Christianity and civilization', a formulation that the French used but changed to a 'crime against humanity and civilization', concerned about Muslim sensitivities. 'A nation was killed and the guilty persons set free,' Lemkin wrote, identifying the 'most frightful' perpetrator as Talaat Pasha, an Ottoman minister.

60

Lemkin's account skipped lightly over the period that followed the end of the First World War. There was a passing mention of studies in Lwów and various biographical sketches written by others suggested he studied philology, but they offered no detail. I returned to the archives in Lviv with the help of Ivan and Ihor, my two Ukrainian assistants, to see what might be found, but we left empty-handed. Could the accounts of Lemkin's life have been wrong? Was he a fantasist? Over a full summer, we drew a blank, until I chanced across a reference in a university yearbook that mentioned a doctoral degree in law being bestowed on him in the summer of 1926. It offered the name of a supervisor, Professor Dr Juliusz Makarewicz, the man who taught criminal law to Lauterpacht. This was curious, remarkable even: the two men who brought genocide and crimes against humanity into the Nuremberg trial and international law happened to share a common teacher.

We returned to the city archive to search again. Ivan systematically examined every single volume that related to students at the law faculty from 1918 to 1928, a painstaking task. On an autumn day, Ivan led me to a table loaded with piles of books, thirty-two bound volumes, each containing hundreds of pages of student records.

In search of Lemkin, we worked our way through thousands of pages. Many volumes hadn't been opened for years; others bore the mark of a recent researcher, a tiny shred of paper inserted as a place marker. After several hours we reached volume 207, the decanal catalogue for the academic year 1923–24, H to M. Ivan turned a page and yelped – he had a signature, 'R. Lemkin'.

The confident black scribble confirmed the studies in Lwów. Ivan and I hugged; an elderly lady in a pink blouse smiled. He signed in 1923, writing out the date and place of birth (24 June 1900, Bezwodne), the names of his parents (Josef and Bella), their hometown (Wołkowysk), an address in Lwów and a complete list of courses taken that academic year.

We soon gathered a complete academic record, from enrolment in October 1921 to graduation in 1926. A 1924 document – the *Absolutorjum* – listed all the courses he took, and a 1926 *Protokol egzaminu* (certificate of examination) confirmed the award of a doctoral degree in law on 20 May. The documents included other new information: a high school diploma obtained from the Białystok Gymnasium on 30 June 1919; enrolment three months later at the law faculty of the Jagiellonian University in Kraków; arrival at the law faculty in Lwów on 12 October 1921.

Yet a whole year was missing from his life, from the summer of 1920 onward. Lemkin made no mention of Kraków in his memoir or, apparently, anywhere else. There he studied legal history and various Polish subjects but not criminal law or international law. One Polish scholar claimed that he fought as a soldier in the Polish-Soviet war, and Lemkin himself once suggested he was wounded in 1920, as Marshal Piłsudski pushed Bolshevik forces out of eastern Poland. Yet of such matters his memoir was silent. Professor Marek Kornat, a Polish historian, told me that Lemkin was expelled from the Kraków university when it emerged that his account of service in the Polish military in 1919 was inaccurate (he only served as a volunteer assistant to a military judge). Confronted by this fact, the Kraków university authorities expelled him (a 'very conservative place' compared with liberal Lwów, Professor Kornat suggested).

61

'In Lwów,' Lemkin wrote in his memoir, 'I enrolled for the study of law.' He offered few details, but, armed with the newly discovered university records, I was able to learn about the courses he took and the addresses where he lived.

He spent five years at Lwów University, from 1921 to 1926, arriving two years after Lauterpacht left. Over eight semesters he took forty-five courses, starting in September 1921, with courses on such diverse matters as church law, the Polish judiciary and Roman law, the classes being taught by many of the men who taught Lauterpacht. That first year he lived on the western side of the city, at 6 Stebona Street (now Hlyboka Street), as Poland was emerging from a long war with Russia, eventually settled by the drawing of a new boundary. Located some 150 miles to the east of the original Curzon Line, on which Lauterpacht had worked in 1919, this new boundary brought four million Ukrainians under Polish control.

The four-storey building in which Lemkin lived had ornate

features, with a stone-carved young woman above its entrance and flowers sweetly carved above each window, a mirror to the busy flower market that occupied the derelict space opposite when I visited. It was near the Lemberg Polytechnic, whose president, Dr Fiedler, had in 1919 shared a walk to the top of Vysoky Zamok (also known as the Castle Hill) with Arthur Goodhart, a young lawyer working for President Woodrow Wilson, to warn of troubles ahead.

The following year, Lemkin studied Polish criminal law with Professor Dr Juliusz Makarewicz, who had reinvented himself after teaching Austrian criminal law to Lauterpacht. Other courses covered international commercial law (with Professor Allerhand) and property law (with Professor Longchamps de Berier), two teachers whose lives would be cut short after the arrival of the Germans in 1941. That year he lived at 44 Grodecka Street (now Horodotska Street), an imposing Palladian building on a major road leading to the opera house, under the long shadow cast by St George's Cathedral. This was but a short distance from the house where my grandfather Leon was born, on Szeptyckich Street.

Lemkin's third year, from the autumn of 1923, was devoted to criminal law, with two more courses taught by Professor Makarewicz. He also took a first course in international law, taught by Ludwik Ehrlich, the man who held the chair that Lauterpacht had unsuccessfully applied for. Lemkin had by now moved again, to a poorer working-class neighbourhood on the wrong side of the rail tracks, reached by passing under the arch of a bridge that would serve, two decades later, as the gateway to the Jewish ghetto in German-occupied Lemberg. Today 21 Zamarstynowska Street (now Zamarstynivs'ka Street) has a dark and gloomy feel to it, a tenement in need of care and attention.

Each new home seemed less grand than the previous one, as though Lemkin were on a downward trajectory.

62

In his memoir, Lemkin made no mention of any of these places or of his life in Lwów. What he did mention was a 'picturesque and most sensational' trial held in Berlin in June 1921, three months before he started his studies. The defendant was a young Armenian,

21 *Zamarstynivs'ka, Lviv, 2013*

Soghomon Tehlirian, who had assassinated a former Ottoman government minister called Talaat Pasha in the German capital. The trial was conducted in a packed courtroom (a young German law student called Robert Kempner sat in the public gallery, a man who would help Lemkin a quarter of a century later in Nuremberg). It was presided over by the aptly named judge Dr Erich Lehmberg. Tehlirian, an 'undersized, swarthily pale faced' student who was partial to dance lessons and the mandolin, argued that he had killed Talaat Pasha to avenge the murder of his family and the Armenians of Erzurum, his hometown.

Tehlirian's defence lawyer played a group identity card, arguing that the defendant was merely an avenger of the 'large and patient' family of Armenians. His star witness was Johannes Lepsius, a sixty-two-year-old German Protestant missionary who implicated the Turk in the massacre of Armenians in 1915. Judge Lehmberg directed the members of the jury to free Tehlirian if they thought he'd acted without free will, because of an 'inner turmoil'. The jury took less than an hour to reach a 'not guilty' verdict, a finding that provoked much commotion.

The trial was very widely reported in the press and became a subject of classroom debate.

'I discussed this matter with my professors,' Lemkin wrote in his memoir. He offered no clue as to the professors' identities but expressed concern about the fairness of rules that allowed Turkey to mistreat so many of its Armenian citizens with impunity. Lemkin doubted that Tehlirian should have acted as a 'self-appointed legal officer for the conscience of mankind', seeking to uphold global moral order. What bothered him more, however, was the idea that the murder of innocent Armenians should go unpunished.

In later years, he frequently evoked the conversations with the professors. Tehlirian did the right thing, Lemkin told the teachers. What about sovereignty, one of the unnamed professors asked, the state's right to treat its citizens as it wished? Strictly speaking, the professor was correct: international law allowed a state to do what it wished back then. Amazingly, there was no treaty to prevent Turkey from acting as it had, from killing its own citizens. Sovereignty meant sovereignty, total and absolute.

Sovereignty was intended for other things, Lemkin retorted, like foreign policy, or building schools and roads, or providing for the welfare of people. It wasn't meant to allow a state the 'right to kill millions of innocent people'. If it did, the world needed a law against such behaviour. On Lemkin's account of an exchange with one professor, which could not be verified, the argument escalated into a grand epiphanic moment.

'Did the Armenians ever try to have the Turk arrested for the massacre?'

'There wasn't any law under which he could be arrested,' the professor replied.

'Not even though he had a part in killing so many people?' Lemkin countered.

'Let us take the case of a man who owns some chickens,' the professor retorted. 'He kills them. Why not? It is not your business. If you interfere, it is trespass.'

'The Armenians were not chickens,' Lemkin said sharply.

The professor allowed the youthful comment to pass, then changed tack. 'When you interfere with the internal affairs of a country, you infringe upon that country's sovereignty.'

'So it's a crime for Tehlirian to strike down one man, but not a crime for that man to have struck down one million men?' Lemkin asked.

The professor shrugged. Lemkin was 'young and excited'. 'If you knew something about international law . . .'

Was the account accurate? Lemkin returned to the exchange throughout his life, explaining that the Tehlirian trial changed his life. Bob Silvers, editor of the *New York Review of Books*, remembers hearing the same tale in a class taught by Lemkin at Yale Law School in 1949 (Silvers's memory of his teacher was of a 'lonely, driven, complicated, emotional, isolated, effusive' man, someone who was not exactly charming but '*tried* to charm people'). Lemkin mentioned the story to a playwright, to diplomats, to journalists. I was curious about the identity of the unnamed professor with whom he had this specific conversation. There was one obvious clue: in so formal a setting as a classroom, he must have known the professor well enough to feel able to challenge him.

63

I turned to Professor Roman Shust, dean of the history faculty at Lviv University, a man who was said to know 'everything' about the institution's past. We met on the same day that the European Court of Human Rights revisited the issue that so exercised Lemkin, ruling that Turkey could not criminalize references to the Armenian killings as a 'genocide', a word that had not been invented when the killings occurred in 1915.

Dean Shust occupied a small office in the old Austro-Hungarian parliament building, now part of the university. A large man with ample grey hair and a friendly, inviting smile, he sprawled across a chair, apparently amused that a distant London academic might be interested in old stories about his city. He'd heard of Lemkin but not Lauterpacht and expressed much interest in the archival material Ivan and I had uncovered.

'Did you know that when the Nazis were here in 1941 they went through the student files to find the Jews?' Dean Shust mused. He pointed to the line in a form where Lemkin wrote 'Mosaic' to identify his nationality. Students came to the archives to get rid of their papers, so did the teachers, like Professor Allerhand, who taught both men.

'Do you know what happened to Professor Allerhand?' the dean asked. I nodded.

'Murdered in the Janowska camp,' he continued, right here, at the centre of this town. 'A German police officer was killing a Jewish man,' he continued. 'Professor Allerhand wanted to get his attention, so he went up to him and asked a simple question: "Have you no soul?" The officer turned to Allerhand, took out his gun and shot him dead. The account was given in the memoir of another prisoner.'

He sighed.

'We will try to help you find the professor who spoke with Lemkin.' He went on to explain that professors held a range of political views in the 1920s, as they did today. 'Some never accepted Jewish or Ukrainian students in their classes; others made the Jewish people sit at the back of the teaching rooms.' Dean Shust peered at Lemkin's forms. 'Poor grades,' he exclaimed, probably due to his 'nationality', which would have engendered a 'negative attitude' from some professors, likely supporters of the National Democratic Party. He explained that the party's leader, Roman Dmowski, was an arch-nationalist with 'ambivalent' feelings towards minorities. I recalled Henry Morgenthau's conversation with Dmowski in Lwów in August 1919. Poland is for the Poles alone, the American diplomat recorded Dmowski as saying, along with an explanation that his 'anti-Semitism isn't religious: it is political'. Dmowski claimed to feel no prejudice, political or otherwise, towards any Jew who wasn't Polish.

The dean brought the conversation back to the events of November 1918, the Jewish 'eliminations', as he referred to them. Students were exposed to the 'negative views' of some professors, mainly the younger ones, less tolerant than professors from the Austrian era. 'When Lemkin was here, Lwów was a multilingual and multicultural society, a third of the population of the city were Jews.' Remember this, the dean said, always.

Together we admired a photograph of the Lemberg professors, taken in 1912.

The dean homed in on Juliusz Makarewicz, in the middle of the group, the longest beard. It was likely he was the unnamed professor

quoted at length by Lemkin, the dean said, because he taught criminal law to Lauterpacht and Lemkin. He made a quick telephone call,
and a few minutes later a colleague entered the room. Zoya Baran,
an associate professor, was the resident expert on Makarewicz. Elegant, authoritative, interested, she summarized a long article she
had recently written on Makarewicz in Ukrainian.

She couldn't say 'for certain' that Makarewicz was the unnamed
professor, Professor Baran explained, but it was 'likely'. 'Makarewicz was born Jewish, then baptized a Catholic. He published works
on national minorities, and these became the ideological platform
for the political party he supported, the Polish Christian Democratic
Party, known as Chadecja.'

What were his views on minorities, the Jews and the Ukrainians?

'National minorities who never intended to rule the country were
tolerated,' she said bluntly. 'The Slavonic minority? Hated. The
Jews? Emigration.' She waved a hand in the air dismissively.

Makarewicz believed national minorities to be 'dangerous', she
continued, especially when they were the 'biggest part' of the population in a specific region, and all the more so 'when they lived

*Faculty of Law, Lemberg, 1912: Juliusz Makarewicz, bearded, is in the
centre, one up from the bottom row*

on the borders of the state'. Lwów was treated as a border city, so Makarewicz would have considered Jews and Ukrainians in Lwów to pose a particular 'danger' to newly independent Poland. She offered another thought: Makarewicz 'had right-wing politics'; he detested the 1919 Polish Minorities Treaty because it discriminated *against* Poles. Minorities could complain to the League of Nations if their rights were violated, but Poles couldn't.

Makarewicz was a nationalist and a survivor. In 1945, the KGB arrested him and banished him to Siberia. Freed following the intervention of a group of Polish professors, he returned to Soviet-controlled Lvov to continue teaching at the law faculty. He died in 1955.

'Would you like to see the classrooms where Lauterpacht and Lemkin studied?' the dean enquired. Yes, I replied, very much.

64

The next morning, I met Zoya on Prospekt Shevchenka, in the shadow of the monument to Mykhailo Hrushevsky, Ukraine's most distinguished twentieth-century historian. We stood close to the building that once housed the Scottish Café, where scholars met in the 1930s to solve obscure and complicated mathematical problems. She was accompanied by a doctoral student called Roman, who had found a list of all the courses taught by Professor Makarewicz between 1915 and 1923, in room N13 of the old law faculty building, at 4 Hrushevskoho Street (formerly Sw Mykolaja Street). A short walk away, it was an imposing three-storey, nineteenth-century Austro-Hungarian building with a two-tone exterior – creamy ground floor, ochre upper floors. On the outside wall, a few plaques record the luminaries who passed through its doors, without mention of Lauterpacht or Lemkin, or any lawyers.

The dark interior was lit by glass globes that hung from the ceiling, with enough light to illuminate the dilapidated classrooms and paint that cracked and peeled along the walls. It wasn't hard to imagine law students taking refuge from the cold and the conflict on the streets in this temple of order and rules. Now it housed the faculty of biology, whose dean welcomed us and accompanied us to the zoological museum housed on an upper floor. This remarkable

Former law faculty building, 4 Hrushevskoho Street, 2012

collection dated back to the Austro-Hungarian period, five rooms packed with deathly artefacts. Butterflies and moths, then fish, including the fearsome *Lophius piscatorius,* the vicious-toothed frog-fish otherwise known as the angler. A troop of lizards and reptiles, followed by mammal skeletons, mighty and small. A stuffed pelican gazed out of the window over the city, improbable monkeys clambered the walls, birds of every possible hue and colour, shape and size hung from ceilings and perched in glass coffins. Thousands of eggs, meticulously arranged according to genus, size and geography. An eagle swooped, observed by pure white owls. We admired *Schlegelia wilsonii,* a bird of paradise caught in Papua New Guinea, a nineteenth-century creature of exquisite beauty and colour.

'The Austrians were inspired by these birds in the design of their hats,' the director explained. A small black-and-yellow-feathered bird bore two spiral feathers on its head. One twirled left, the other right. In such an incongruous place, it offered a stark reminder that Lviv had no museum dedicated to its former residents, the groups that had long gone, the Poles and Jews and Armenians. What it did have was a superb zoological collection, a reminder of the hats worn by the disappeared.

Schlegelia wilsonii, *department of biology, Lviv, 2011*

Our next stop was the classroom in which the famed Ukrainian writer Ivan Franko studied, preserved as it was at the beginning of the twentieth century. Franko was a Ukrainian writer and political activist who died in Lemberg in 1916 in abject poverty. There was now a large statue of him, across the street from Dean Shust's office and this dedicated classroom. We knocked and entered. Students looked up, a class interrupted, seated as Lauterpacht and Lemkin might have been, on wooden rows in a room overlooking an internal courtyard. Bright sunlight shot across the room, cutting through the light of eight brass lanterns that hung from the ceiling. The room was elegant and simple, bright and airy, a place of learning, of calm and order, of structure and hierarchy.

In a room like this, if not this very one, Lauterpacht and Lemkin learned about the law. In the autumn of 1918, in this building, Makarewicz gave his last lecture on the criminal law of the Austro-Hungarian Empire. In November, as violence engulfed the city, Lauterpacht left the barricades to sit in such a classroom, and that month power shifted on a weekly basis, from the Austro-Hungarians to the Poles, then to the Ukrainians, then back to the Poles. As the city changed hands, Professor Makarewicz carried on teaching the criminal law of an empire that had ceased to exist.

By the time Lemkin sat on the same wooden bench four years later, Makarewicz was teaching Polish criminal law. The hour might have changed – Lauterpacht's class with Makarewicz was at ten in the morning, Lemkin's at five in the afternoon – but room N13 was a constant. A bit like Count Morstin, the old Galician governor in Joseph Roth's novella *The Bust of the Emperor,* who performs a daily ritual before a stone bust of the Emperor Franz Joseph years after his death. 'My old home, the Monarchy, alone, was a great mansion,' Morstin mused, but now the mansion was 'divided, split up, splintered'.

As control of the city passed from one group to another, Makarewicz ploughed on. The country changed, the government changed, the students changed, the laws changed, yet room N13 remained. In later years too, in the time of Soviet laws, then the German decrees of Hans Frank, then more Soviet laws, Makarewicz adjusted his courses to take account of new realities. After each class the great survivor left the law faculty, walked up Drahomanova Street, past the university library, trundling up the hill to the house he built for himself, at No. 58. There he could enter his home and shut out the world.

65

Lemkin graduated from the university in 1926. Around then, he completed the translation of Bialik's novella and a book on Russian and Soviet criminal law, for which Juliusz Makarewicz contributed the preface. The times were harsh, economically and politically, as Marshal Piłsudski led a coup that toppled an elected government. Lemkin believed the alternative – Dmowski's anti-Semitic National Democrats – would have been even worse.

Two weeks after the coup, another political murder caught Lemkin's attention. This time it was closer to home, because the victim was the anti-Bolshevist president of the short-lived 1918 West Ukrainian People's Republic, General Symon Petliura, shot dead on the rue Racine in Paris. Worse still, the assassin was Samuel Schwartzbard, a Jewish watchmaker who wanted to avenge the murder of Jews in Russia, allegedly on Petliura's orders. Schwartzbard's trial offered another media sensation, six years after the Tehlirian affair, to be closely observed by Lemkin. The witnesses included famed writers, Israel Zangwill for the prosecution and Maxim Gorky for the defence, but the star turn was a nurse with the Ukrainian Red Cross. Haia Greenberg claimed to have witnessed a pogrom in February 1919 and testified that Petliura's soldiers killed as a military band played.

The jury deliberated for less than an hour, then declared Schwartzbard 'not guilty', because his actions weren't premeditated. The *New York Times* reported that four hundred spectators squeezed into the Paris courtroom – 'white-bearded Jews from Central and Eastern Europe', 'flappers with bobbed hair' and 'Slavic featured Ukrainians' – and received the verdict with 'cheers for France'. Lemkin was satisfied. 'They could neither acquit Schwarzbard [*sic*] nor condemn him,' he wrote, unable to punish an avenger of the deaths of 'hundreds of thousands of his innocent brethren, including his parents'. Equally, the court would not sanction 'the taking of the law in one's hands in order to uphold the moral standards of mankind'. In Lemkin's view, the ingenious conclusion was to declare Schwartzbard insane, then set him free.

Lemkin observed the trial from Warsaw, where he worked as a secretary at the court of appeals, after stints as a court clerk and public prosecutor in Brzezany, sixty miles south-east of Lwów. Under the patronage of Professor Makarewicz, the two trials catalysed his thinking. 'Gradually, but surely,' he explained, a decision was 'maturing' in him to do something to develop new international rules to protect groups. His 'judicial career' at the Warsaw courts offered a platform, along with the numerous books written to develop a 'following and influence'. Scholarship was a platform for advocacy.

By the time Hitler took power, Lemkin had six years under his belt as a public prosecutor. The farm boy from Wołkowysk was established and connected to Poland's top lawyers, politicians and judges. He published books on the Soviet criminal code, Italy's fascist penal code and Poland's revolutionary law on amnesties, usually more descriptive than analytical. He found a new mentor, Emil Stanisław Rappaport, judge on the Supreme Court of Poland and founder of the Free Polish University in Warsaw, where Lemkin taught.

On the side, he participated in efforts at the League of Nations to develop the criminal law, attending conferences, building up a

network of contacts around Europe. In the spring of 1933, antici-
pating a meeting to be held in Madrid in October, he wrote a
pamphlet proposing new international rules to prohibit 'barbarity'
and 'vandalism'. These were more necessary than ever, he believed,
as attacks on Jews and other minorities multiplied in the shadow of
Hitler. He feared *Mein Kampf* as a 'blue-print for destruction', implemented by the new Enabling Law adopted by a supine Reichstag
to give Hitler dictatorial powers.

Lemkin, a practical idealist, believed that proper criminal laws
could actually prevent atrocity. In his view, the minorities treaties
were inadequate, so he imagined new rules to protect 'the life of
the peoples': to prevent 'barbarity', the destruction of groups, and
to prevent 'vandalism', attacks on culture and heritage. The ideas
weren't entirely original, drawing on the views of Vespasian V. Pella,
a Romanian scholar who promoted the idea of 'universal jurisdiction', a principle that national courts around the world should be
able to try perpetrators of the most serious crimes (six decades later,
'universal jurisdiction' for the crime of torture ensnared Senator
Pinochet in the English courts). Lemkin didn't cite Pella's earlier
work on 'acts of barbarism or vandalism capable of bringing about
a common danger', although he gave the Romanian credit for the
list of crimes to which 'universal jurisdiction' would apply (such as
piracy, slavery, trading in women and children, and drug trafficking).
Lemkin's pamphlet was published by Pedone, a publishing house on
the rue Soufflot in Paris, official publisher to the League of Nations.

Lemkin expected to be a member of the Polish delegation at the
Madrid conference, but as he prepared to travel, Emil Rappaport
called to alert him to a problem. The minister of justice opposes you
going, the judge told him, a consequence of efforts by the *Gazeta
Warszawska,* the daily paper associated with Dmowski's National
Democratic Party. Lemkin didn't travel to Madrid but hoped his
pamphlet would be discussed, that it might create 'a movement of
ideas'. The formal record of the meeting documented that the paper
was circulated but offered no evidence that it was discussed.

A few days after the conference ended, as Germany announced
its departure from the League of Nations, the *Gazeta Warszawska*
attacked 'Prosecutor Lemkin' personally. 'It is not difficult to guess
at the motives that induced Mr Lemkin to present this project,' the
paper complained on 25 October, 'considering that he belongs to

the "racial group" most endangered by the "barbarism" and "vandalism" practised by some nations.' The paper reported it to be a 'doubtful honour' for Poland that one of its representatives, Mr Lemkin, was the 'author of this kind of project'.

Within a year, Poland signed a non-aggression pact with Germany and denounced the 1919 Minorities Treaty. The foreign minister, Beck, told the League of Nations that Poland hadn't turned against minorities but wanted equality with other countries: if they weren't required to protect their minorities, Poland shouldn't be required to do so either. As the *New York Times* reported a 'drift towards the Reich', Lemkin left his job as a public prosecutor.

66

Moving into private practice as a commercial lawyer, Lemkin took an office on Jerozolimskie (Jerusalem) Avenue in Warsaw. He was successful enough to buy a small house in the country, build up an art collection and move to an apartment in a modernist block at 6 Kredytowa Street, closer to the city centre. From here, he ran his law office (in 2008, when a plaque was placed there to celebrate the 'outstanding Polish jurist and scholar of international repute', the building housed an office of the National Rebirth of Poland party – Narodowe Odrodzenie Polski – a minor neo-fascist political party).

Lemkin tried to publish a book a year, honing his interest in law reform and terrorism, a topical concern in the face of numerous high-profile political killings (the 1934 murder of King Alexander I of Yugoslavia, whose son Crown Prince Peter would be tutored at Cambridge by Lauterpacht, was the first to be captured on film). Lemkin's connections widened and included visitors from distant lands who arrived with inducements. Professor Malcolm McDermott, of Duke University in North Carolina, came to Warsaw to translate one of Lemkin's books into English, bringing an offer of a teaching position at Duke. Lemkin declined, because his mother wanted her son in Poland.

Bella was a frequent visitor to Warsaw, nursing her son when he fell ill with double pneumonia in the summer of 1938. On returning to Wołkowysk, she shared stories with her grandson Saul about Uncle Rafael's apartment and its fabulous modern lift, Lemkin's reputation with the Warsaw intelligentsia, his impressive circle of friends. Lemkin bent the ears of important men, she told the young boy, with his campaign against 'barbarity' and 'vandalism'. According to Saul, some listened, but his uncle faced stiff opposition: his ideas belonged 'to the past', he was told, and Hitler was only using hatred for political purposes and didn't really intend to destroy the Jews. He should rein in his 'fantastic predictions'.

In March 1938, Germany annexed Austria. Six months later, as the British prime minister, Neville Chamberlain, accepted Hitler's demand that the Sudetenland be ceded to Germany from Czechoslovakia, Lemkin travelled to London for work. On Friday, 23 September, he dined at the Reform Club on Pall Mall with Herbert du Parcq, a court of appeals judge, and they were joined by John Simon, the chancellor of the Exchequer. Simon told them about Chamberlain's meeting with Hitler, explaining that the British negotiated because they weren't ready for war.

A week later, Chamberlain stood outside the famous black door of 10 Downing Street after another rendezvous with Hitler. 'Peace for our time,' he declared; the people of Britain could sleep quietly in their beds. Within a year, Germany was at war with Poland. A million and a half German Wehrmacht troops entered the country alongside the SS and the Gestapo, as the Luftwaffe brought fear and bombs to Warsaw, Kraków and other Polish cities in the east, including Lwów and Zółkiew. Lemkin remained in Warsaw for five days, then left on 6 September as the Germans approached the city.

He made his way towards Wołkowysk, north of Lwów, through the swampy district of Polesie, when the skies fell silent. Lemkin was caught between the Germans in the west and the Soviets, who were now approaching from the east. Poland's independence was extinguished as the country was carved in two by the pact between Stalin's and Hitler's foreign ministers, Molotov and Ribbentrop. As Britain and France entered the war, Lemkin continued northward; in city clothes and glasses with expensive rims, he feared the Soviets would identify him as a Polish intellectual and a 'big city dweller'. He was detained by a Russian soldier but managed to talk himself out of harm.

In the province of Wolynia, he rested near the small town of Dubno, taking refuge with the family of a Jewish baker. Why would the Jews want to escape from the Nazis? the baker asked. Lemkin told him about *Mein Kampf* and the intention to destroy the Jews 'like flies'. The baker scoffed; he knew nothing of such a book, couldn't believe the words to be true.

'How can Hitler destroy the Jews, if he must trade with them? People are needed to carry on a war.'

This wasn't like other wars, Lemkin told him. It was a war 'to destroy whole peoples' and replace them with Germans. The baker wasn't persuaded. He had lived under the Germans for three years during the First World War, not good, but 'somehow we survived'. The baker's son, a boy in his twenties with a bright face, enthusiastic and anxious, disagreed. 'I do not understand this attitude of my father and of all the people like him in the town.'

Lemkin spent two weeks with the baker's family. On 26 October, Hans Frank was appointed governor-general of German-occupied Poland, to the west of a new boundary line that left Zółkiew, Lwów and Wołkowysk under Soviet control. Stranded on the Soviet side, Lemkin took a train to Wołkowysk packed with fearful travellers. The train arrived during curfew, so Lemkin spent the night in the station toilets to avoid arrest. Early in the morning, he walked to his brother Elias's house, at 15 Kościuszko Street, avoiding the main streets. He knocked quietly on the window, put his lips to the glass and whispered, 'Rafael, Rafael'.

Bella expressed a joy that Lemkin wouldn't forget. He was put to bed, drifting off to sleep in a familiar old blanket, worrying about the disaster that had befallen Poland. He awoke to the smell of pancakes, devoured with soured cream. Bella and Josef felt safe in Wołkowysk; they didn't want to leave with him. I'm retired, Josef explained, not a capitalist. Elias was a mere employee, he gave up ownership of the store, the Soviets would leave them alone. Only Lemkin would leave, to head for America, where Josef's brother Isidor lived.

Bella agreed he should go but had another concern. Why wasn't he married? This was a touchy subject. Years later, Lemkin would tell Nancy Ackerly that he was so fully absorbed in his work that he had 'no time for married life, or the funds to support it'. It was a striking feature of all the material I found on Lemkin that none contained any hint of an intimate relationship, although a number of women seem to have expressed interest. Bella persisted, telling her son that marriage was a means of protection, that a 'lonely and loveless' man would need a woman after his mother's support was 'cut off'. Lemkin offered no encouragement. A line from Goethe's epic poem *Hermann and Dorothea* entered his mind, as it always did when Bella raised the subject: 'Take a wife so that the night might become the more beautiful part of your life.' I read the poem, unable to discern any immediate clue that might explain his solitary state or the poem's relevance. He responded to Bella's effort with affection, placed his hands on the back of her head, stroked her hair, kissed each eye, yet offered no promise. 'You are right.' That was all he could muster, with the hope that the coming life of a nomad might bring more fortune.

He left Wołkowysk in the evening. The moment of parting lingered, a casual kiss, a meeting of eyes, silence, finality denied.

67

Present that autumn day in Wołkowysk was Lemkin's nephew Saul. With some effort, I located him in Montreal, living in a small apartment on the ground floor of a building that had seen better days, in a district filled with immigrants. His appearance was striking, the deep, sad eyes hewn into an intelligent face, a straggling grey beard redolent of a nineteenth-century Tolstoy character. Time had not been generous to this gentle, literate man.

Well into his eighties, he sat on a cluttered sofa, surrounded by books. He mourned the recent passing of his lady friend, the subject he really wanted to talk about, along with his ocular problems and the meaning of life with a single kidney (the other was 'lost in 1953', the details not offered). Yes, he remembered Uncle Rafael's visit in the autumn of 1939, when he was twelve, living on a street 'named after a famous Polish hero'. When Rafael left, they knew they might not see each other again.

Until 1938, Saul and his parents lived in a house in Wołkowysk with Bella and Josef. Then Lemkin bought the parents a house of their own, for about five thousand zlotys (approximately one thousand dollars). A lot of money back then, Saul said, he must have been doing well as a lawyer. His grandparents were 'wonderful', farmers from around Wołkowysk. Bella was the more literary of the couple, constantly reading, whereas Josef found interest in politics, Yiddish newspapers and the life of the synagogue. 'Rafael wasn't a believer,' Saul said, without prompting.

His uncle visited twice a year, around the time of the festivals. At Passover, Bella sent Saul to the busy store to 'stock up for uncle's visit'. The arrival of the 'professor and lawyer', as he was reverentially referred to, was always a big occasion, one that brought politics and 'a little friction' into the family home. On a previous visit, in April 1939, Lemkin turned up with a French newspaper, an unusual item. Views were divided about an article on Marshal Pétain being appointed ambassador to Madrid, as a right-winger, to appease Franco. 'My uncle didn't like Pétain or Franco.'

Saul thought Lemkin was 'very well known' in Poland. Uncle lived in a grand building on a famous street – with a fabulous lift! – although Saul never visited Warsaw or got to meet the 'friends in high society'. I enquired about his uncle's romantic life, mentioning the account in Lemkin's memoir of a visit to Vilnius as a teenager and the walk on a hillside with a girl in a brown school uniform. Lemkin wanted to kiss her, but then the instinct was 'stifled in me by something that I could not understand,' he wrote. The words were ambiguous.

'I don't know why my uncle never married,' Saul said, disinterestedly. 'I suppose he had a chance, since he was connected,' but there never was any talk of lady friends. Saul vaguely remembered an event in Vienna, when Edward VIII and Madame Simpson were present, but lady friends? Saul knew nothing. 'There was probably a woman friend,' he added but couldn't remember any information. 'Exactly why he didn't get married? I don't know.'

The Soviets expropriated the family home but allowed the family to remain. An officer moved in; Saul attended a Russian-speaking school. 'When my uncle came in October 1939, having escaped from Warsaw, we talked. The Russians and the Germans joining together meant that it was going to be very bad. This is what I heard, what I remember him saying.'

There was a mournful air about Saul.

Did he have a photograph of Bella and Josef? 'No.'

Of his uncle? 'No.'

Any other member of the family from that period? 'No,' he said sadly. 'There's nothing left.'

68

Lemkin travelled by train from Wołkowysk to Vilnius, the city of the near-kiss, which was occupied by the Soviets. It brimmed with Polish refugees and black-market goods, visas, passports, and the 'noodles' (dollars) that Lemkin recognized as a symbol of freedom, America on his mind. He met acquaintances from League of Nations days, among them Bronisław Wróblewski, a distinguished criminologist. I failed in my efforts on 'barbarity' and 'vandalism', he told Wróblewski, but 'I *will* try again.'

Bella and Josef wrote of the happiness they felt to have spent time with their son. The letter carried a familiar tone, subdued optimism, anxieties barely concealed. There was news too that Lemkin's friend Benjamin Tomkiewicz was on his way to Vilnius with a gift, a small cake with the smell of Bella's oven. Tomkiewicz's deep pessimism offered a counterpoint to Lemkin's brighter disposition: the difficult situation offered some opportunities and real challenges, Lemkin thought, an end to the cushy life of Warsaw, with its generous lawyer's fees, fine furniture and country house. He had become too accustomed to a life of authority and connections, with its 'false prestige'. Such days were gone but not mourned.

Lemkin wrote his way out of Vilnius. On 25 October, he applied for a temporary visa for Norway or Sweden. 'I managed to save my life by a miracle,' he explained in French, and it was vital that he find a way out. 'I will be grateful for my whole life,' he added, emphasizing that all he needed was a visa, 'my financial situation is not bad' (his return address was listed as the Latvian consulate, Vilnius). A letter also went to Karl Schlyter, the former Swedish justice minister, seeking a Swedish visa; another to Count Carton de Wiart, a Belgian diplomat, enquiring about travel to Belgium; a third to Professor McDermott in North Carolina, asking for a teaching position at Duke. He also wrote to the mother-and-daughter team who ran the Pedone publishing house to let them know he was alive and well. Had they received the manuscript sent before the Germans reached Warsaw, the new book on international contracts? Life went on.

From Vilnius he headed west to the Baltic coast, towards Sweden. In Kaunas he told an acquaintance that refugee life bothered him, like being a ghost in search of certainty and hope. The three things in life he'd wanted to avoid had all come to pass: 'to wear eyeglasses, to lose my hair, and to become a refugee'. Another acquaintance, Dr Zalkauskas, a retired judge, asked him how Poland could 'disappear in three weeks'. Such things happen, Lemkin replied stoically. (Lemkin next saw the judge years later in Chicago, a lift man at the Morrison Hotel.)

A letter from the Pedones returned the page proofs of his new book, along with several offprints of his 1933 pamphlet on barbarity and vandalism. The proofs were corrected and returned to Paris, the book published a few months later. Lemkin left Kaunas with a visa for Sweden. Stopping in Riga, the capital of Latvia, he took tea with the historian Simon Dubnow, the author of *History of the Jews in Russia and Poland*. 'The lull before the storm,' Dubnow warned Lemkin, Hitler would soon be in Latvia.

69

Lemkin arrived in Sweden in the early spring of 1940. Stockholm was neutral and free, allowing him to enjoy the customs and food, awaiting a hoped-for invitation from North Carolina, enjoying time with his hosts, the Ebersteins. The possibility of getting to America by boat from Belgium was extinguished: the Germans occupied Belgium and Holland in May 1940; France fell the following month, then Denmark and Norway, and later Lithuania, Latvia and Estonia. All the friends he had visited were – or would soon be – under Nazi rule. Simon Dubnow's pessimism proved well founded: he was murdered two years after Lemkin left Riga, close to his home.

Weeks of waiting in Stockholm turned into months. Karl Schlyter suggested he might lecture at the university, so he took an intensive course in Swedish. By September 1940, he was proficient enough to lecture in Swedish on foreign exchange controls and to write a book on the subject, also in the newly learned language. Letters arrived from Bella and Josef, offering rare moments of happiness, tinged with anxiety about their well-being under the Soviets.

Restless and driven, incapable of indolence, Lemkin sought a bigger project. A map of Europe offered an idea as 'the blood red cloth with the black spider on a white field' extended its reach across the Continent. Lemkin's innate curiosity confronted the nature of the German occupation. How exactly was German Nazi rule imposed? Believing the answer might be found in the minutiae of legal enactments, he started to gather Nazi decrees and ordinances, as others might collect stamps. As a lawyer, he understood that official documents often reflected underlying objectives without stating them explicitly, that a single document might be less revealing than a collection. The group was more valuable than the sum of its individual parts.

He spent time at the central library in Stockholm, gathering, translating, and analysing, looking for patterns of German behaviour. The Germans were orderly, putting many decisions in writing, producing documents and a paper trail, clues to a bigger conception. This might lead to 'irrefutable evidence' of crime.

He sought the assistance of others. One source was an unnamed Swedish company with a Warsaw office that had previously retained his services as a lawyer. Visiting the headquarters in Stockholm to ask a favour, he enquired whether the company's offices across Europe might collect copies of the official gazette published by the Germans in occupied countries, then send them to Stockholm? His acquaintance said yes.

Decrees and ordinances and other documents from across Europe arrived in Stockholm. Lemkin read each one, took notes, annotated the text, translated. The piles multiplied, supplemented by materials obtained from Stockholm's central library, which held texts originating in Berlin.

As Lemkin worked his way through the decrees, he found common themes, the elements of 'a concentrated plot'. Conducted in parallel with Lauterpacht's efforts on the protection of individuals, of which he was not then aware, Lemkin's work identified the wholesale destruction of the nations over which the Germans took control as an overall aim. Some documents were signed by Hitler, implementing ideas aired in *Mein Kampf* on *Lebensraum,* the creation of a new living space to be inhabited by Germans.

A first Polish decree was signed by Hitler on 8 October, a month after Lemkin left Warsaw. German-occupied Poland got a new name, Incorporated Eastern Territories (Eingegliederte Ostgebiete), then absorbed into the *Reich.* It was a territory where the soil and people could be 'Germanized', Poles rendered 'headless or brainless', the intelligentsia liquidated, populations reorganized as slave labour. Another decree was signed on 26 October by the newly appointed governor-general, Hans Frank, who declared with glee that his territory would soon be free from 'political agitators, shady dealers and Jewish exploiters'. 'Decisive steps' would be taken, Frank announced. A copy of a third decree, dated 1 August 1941, and incorporating Galicia and Lemberg into the General Government, remained among Lemkin's papers in the Columbia archives.

Lemkin followed the trail, the 'decisive steps' that formed a pattern. The first step was usually the act of denationalization, making individuals stateless by severing the link of nationality between Jews and the state, so as to limit the protection of the law. This was followed by 'dehumanization', removing legal rights from members of the targeted group. The two-step pattern was applied across Europe. The third step was to kill the nation 'in a spiritual and cultural sense': Lemkin identified decrees from early 1941 pointing to the 'complete destruction' of the Jews in 'gradual steps'. Individually, each decree looked innocuous, but when they were taken together and examined across borders, a broader purpose emerged. Individual Jews were forced to register, wear a distinctive Star of David badge, a mark of easy identification, then move into designated areas, ghettos. Lemkin found the decrees creating the Warsaw ghetto (October 1940), then the Kraków ghetto (March 1941), noting the death penalty for those who left the ghettos without permission. 'Why the death penalty?' Lemkin enquired. A way of 'hastening' what was 'already in store'?

Seizure of property rendered the group 'destitute' and 'dependent on rationing'. Decrees limited rations of carbohydrates and proteins, reducing the members of the group to 'living corpses'. Spirits broken, individuals became 'apathetic to their own lives', subjected to forced labour that caused many deaths. For those who remained alive, there were further measures of 'dehumanization and disintegration' as they were left to await the 'hour of execution'.

Immersed in these materials, Lemkin received a letter from Professor McDermott in North Carolina, offering him a teaching position and a visa.

70

This time, Bella and Josef agreed he should go, although Lemkin felt torn at the prospect of not being able to 'watch over them' from distant America. Yet a journey to America posed challenges, with the Atlantic route barred by war and Stockholm awash with rumours that passage through the Soviet Union would soon be curtailed. Lemkin decided to leave immediately by the long route: to Moscow, across the Soviet Union, to Japan, over the Pacific to Seattle, then by train across America.

He would make the journey with few personal belongings and many decrees, packed into several large, leather valises together with pages of his notes. Visas were obtained and the Ebersteins offered a farewell dinner in his honour. The dining table festooned with little Polish flags – red and white – left an enduring memory.

After a brief stop in Latvia, allowing a last glance in the 'general direction' of Wołkowysk, he arrived in Moscow. Lodging in an old-fashioned hotel with a cold lobby and a huge bedroom, he walked the streets, admired Red Square and the Kremlin and the pointed domes of St Basil's Church, which reminded him of childhood books, of the poet Nadson and his mother's gentle voice. He dined alone, in a city where people looked shabby and didn't smile much.

The next morning he was covered in bites, because the 1917 revolution, of which he was no supporter, 'had not abolished the fleas'. He left from the Yaroslavsky Rail Terminal, the longest train journey in the world, ten days to Vladivostok, 3,600 miles to the east, sharing a compartment with a Polish couple and their young children. The train made its way past small, dreary Soviet towns, a melancholy grey landscape of snow and slowly passing hours, where only the dining carriage offered a distraction: Lemkin liked to wait until someone who looked Russian took a seat before pouncing into the empty seat opposite to converse in the language of childhood. A sociable creature, he worked out that Russians were 'most gregarious' when eating.

Five days on, the train pulled in to Novosibirsk station, halfway across the Soviet Union, as busy as the Gare du Nord in Paris or London's Victoria Station. Two days later, brilliant sun, deep blue water and mountains introduced Lake Baikal, north of Mongolia, a place of purity and scale, appreciated by Lemkin. Two more days passed before they pulled into a small station with a name written in Russian and Yiddish. He'd reached the Jewish Autonomous Region created by Joseph Stalin, the minorities commissar, in 1928. As Lemkin stretched his legs, two shabbily dressed men were reading *The Voice of Birobidzhan*. 'A handful of displaced persons, cut off from their roots,' Lemkin reflected. Seven decades later, the situation remained difficult, but at least they existed.

Forty-eight hours later the train rolled in to Vladivostok, a city with 'little regard for beauty'. Lemkin spent the night in an ugly hotel, then took a boat to Tsuruga, a thousand kilometres across the ocean, a port on Japan's west coast. In the tired, anxious atmosphere, Lemkin recognized a fellow passenger, a distinguished Polish banker, a senator from a once wealthy family. Dishevelled and unkempt, with a runny nose, he looked like a character from Joseph Roth's *Radetzky March*, a man who failed to notice the constant 'crystalline drop' that resided at the end of his nose.

The ship arrived in Tsuruga in the early days of April 1941, two months after he left Stockholm, a year and a half after a last embrace with Bella and Josef. Lemkin befriended a young couple and travelled with them to Kyoto, Japan's historic capital. Lemkin admired the buildings and kimonos, the old cherry tree on the public square, opposite the large Buddha. They went to a theatre, understanding not a word but appreciating the 'impression of torture and pain' created only by 'expressive facial and bodily tremblings'. The performance was preceded by a tea ceremony, conducted in silence, geisha girls offering service, each one in a uniquely patterned kimono, expressions of individuality. The beauty of the ceremony was not matched by the green tea, too bitter for his taste. He visited the geishas' living quarters, surprised that most of the men present were married.

In Yokohama he bought himself a kimono, sat on the hotel terrace, looked out at the lights of the harbour and thought about Wołkowysk. The next day he boarded the *Heian Maru*, a modern ship, for the last leg to America. Lemkin relaxed, the suitcases and German decrees safe in the hold, and befriended a fellow traveller, Toyohiko Kagawa, the Japanese Christian leader whose arrest a year earlier had generated much publicity. Kagawa's offence was to apologize for Japan's treatment of the Chinese; now he was en route to America to argue against war. Together the two men fretted about the state of the world.

71

After a brief stop in Vancouver, with its lights as an 'augury of security', the *Heian Maru* set off on the last stretch for Seattle. On Friday, 18 April, the ship entered the harbour under snowcapped peaks, Lemkin on deck under a clear blue sky, like the day that Warsaw was bombed. Suitcases were offloaded; passengers stood in line waiting to be processed by a friendly customs officer. He looked at Lemkin's suitcases, then at the Pole. 'How was it in Europe? Very bad?' Lemkin nodded. The officer opened the cases, surprised by the mass of paper, but asked no questions. 'I'm from over there myself. My mother still lives in Shannon,' he said, putting his hand on Lemkin's shoulder. 'Okay, boy – you're in!'

Lemkin spent a day in Seattle, then boarded a night train to Chicago. He sat in the glass-domed observatory car, a new experience, as the horizon changed, passing the Bavarian-themed town of Leavenworth, over the Rocky Mountains, through Glacier National Park, across the plains of Montana, close to Fargo in North Dakota. Compared with frightened Europeans and diffident Japanese, the Americans seemed relaxed. In Chicago he visited the Loop, the business district, like being 'inside the stomach of a huge industrial whale'. Efforts at conversation failed. 'The one on my right only grunted "Huh" very loudly, and the man on the other side paid no attention to me whatever, keeping his nose in his soup.' A night train took him through the dreamy Appalachians, as though descending from the heavens. On a short stop in Lynchburg, Virginia, Lemkin was surprised to see two entrances to the station restroom, one marked 'For Whites', the other 'For Coloureds'.

He asked a black porter whether a 'coloured' person had to use a special toilet? In Warsaw, he recalled, there was 'one Negro in the entire city', a dancer at a popular nightclub, who was not required to use a separate toilet. The porter was taken aback by the question.

The train pulled in to Durham station on 21 April, a warm spring day, a smell of tobacco and human perspiration in the air. Lemkin spotted McDermott. Five years had passed, yet the conversation carried on where it had left off, talk of journeys, articles, governments, commerce, minorities. McDermott was bemused by the extent of Lemkin's luggage and the contents. Lemkin wept on arriving at the campus, the first time he permitted himself such a display of emotion. So different from a European university, without suspicion or angst, the smell of fresh-cut grass, boys wearing open white shirts, girls in light summer dresses, books being carried, everyone smiling. A sense of idyll regained.

There was no time for rest, because the university president asked him to address a dinner, to talk about the world he had left behind. He talked about a faraway place where a man called Hitler acquired territories and destroyed groups. He spoke of history, Armenians and oppression, constantly focusing on an elderly lady near the front, a woman with shining eyes and a benign smile. 'If women, children and old people would be murdered a hundred miles from here, wouldn't you run to help?' he asked, looking at her. The question generated thunderous, unexpected applause.

Because the semester had ended, there was no opportunity to teach. He returned to the suitcases and decrees, keeping his office door open to welcome a constant flow of talkative visitors. Faculty members, students, librarians came and went, curious about the square-headed, courteous man from Poland. He sat in on classes, struck by the difference between an American law school – focused on cases, debate and disagreement – and the European tradition, with the emphasis on codes and deference. American students were encouraged to challenge, not expecting to be spoon-fed. How remarkable that a professor might care what a student thinks, Lemkin reflected, so different from Lemberg.

Lemkin appreciated the generosity of Dean H. Claude Thorack, who offered assistance with the German decrees. The library staff helped, as did the faculty members he befriended, who had unlikely connections to home. Judge Thaddeus Bryson told him he was named after a Polish military hero – Tadeusz Kościuszko – who fought for American independence. Amazing, Lemkin told him, in Wołkowysk his brother Elias lived on a street named in honour of the same man.

72

The university arranged speaking engagements across North Carolina at about the time that Lauterpacht was on his own lecture tour. Lemkin bought himself a fine white suit, which he wore with white shoes and socks, and a silk tie that had a hint of colour. In this natty outfit – I found one photograph – he became a familiar sight on campus and on travels around the state. He talked of Europe, speaking with care and emotion. The passion was evident, as was the heavy middle European accent.

McDermott invited Lemkin on a trip to Washington, offering an opportunity to reacquaint himself with colleagues from League of Nations days and to create a constituency of supporters for his work on the decrees. He liked Washington, the 'subdued elegance'

Lemkin in white suit, Washington DC, undated

of Sixteenth Street and the extravagance of Massachusetts Avenue, the simplicity of the monuments, the lack of pretension. He visited the Polish embassy and the Library of Congress. There he met with the law librarian John Vance, whom he knew from a conference held in The Hague four years earlier. The slender, friendly librarian sported a generous moustache and sideburns and had a voice with a timbre that accommodated all the world's concerns. Vance offered Lemkin access to the resources of the Library of Congress and his own address book. One important introduction followed, to Colonel Archibald King, head of the War Plans Division in the US army's Office of the Judge Advocate General, a senior military lawyer.

Lemkin shared his ideas on barbarity and vandalism with Colonel King, who listened patiently before revealing his belief that Germany's lawyers would surely respect the laws of war. Lemkin explained the measures being taken in Germany and the occupied territories, with documents in proof. King asked to see them. Germany's war was directed 'against peoples', Lemkin explained, in violation of international laws. Did Germany officially reject the Hague regulations? 'Not officially,' Lemkin replied, 'but unofficially.' He told Colonel King about Alfred Rosenberg, Hitler's principal theorist, but King hadn't heard of him.

Germany wanted 'to change the whole population structure of Europe for a thousand years', Lemkin explained, to make 'certain nations and races' disappear completely. King was taken aback and said he'd look into the matter.

73

Back in North Carolina, as Lemkin continued to work on the decrees, a letter arrived from Bella and Josef. Slow to travel, the tired envelope contained a tiny scrap of paper, dated 25 May 1941. Josef thanked Lemkin for letters sent, said he was feeling better, that the potato season was over so he could spend more time at home. 'For the time being, we are lacking nothing.' He sent his son a few names and addresses in America, and Bella offered reassurance that all was 'perfectly well' and they had everything they needed. It was a message of survival. Write more often, Bella asked, 'be healthy and happy'.

A few days later, on 24 June, as Lemkin listened to music on the wireless, the programme was interrupted. 'The German army has invaded eastern Poland.' The Germans broke the pact with Stalin, sending troops eastward, to Lvov and Żółkiew, to Wołkowysk and beyond. Lemkin knew what would follow.

'Have you heard the news,' someone asked as he entered the Law School, 'about Operation Barbarossa?' He heard 'sorry' many times that day and those that followed, because sombre and silent colleagues and students understood the implications. Overwhelmed with foreboding, he carried on with work. 'Keep your chin up, be strong,' McDermott encouraged him.

The Wehrmacht headed east, accompanied by the SS, extending Governor Frank's empire. Żółkiew was taken within a week, then a day or two later Lvov was occupied and Professor Roman Long-champs de Bérier murdered with his three sons. That same day, farther north, Wołkowysk was taken by the Germans, just beyond Frank's General Government. Lemkin's family was now subject to German decrees of the kind with which he was familiar.

That same day brought another announcement: Ignacy Pader-ewski, the founder of modern Poland, the man who objected to the Minorities Treaty of 1919, had died in New York while on a concert tour (buried in Arlington National Cemetery, his remains were transferred half a century later to St John's Cathedral in Warsaw). Shortly before he fell ill, Paderewski gave a public address to remind listeners of the distinction between good and evil and the role of the one and the many. 'It certainly is important to individuals as well as to groups of individuals to keep on this path', to avoid unnecessary suffering and aimless destruction.

In September, five months after arriving in America, Lemkin taught his first class at Duke Law School. That same month he trav-elled to Indianapolis to attend the annual conference of the American Bar Association, where he delivered a lecture on totalitarian control and added his name to a resolution prepared by John Vance, con-demning German atrocities. The US Supreme Court justice Robert Jackson gave the after-dinner speech, titled 'The Challenge of In-ternational Lawlessness'. The talk was threaded with ideas drawn from Lauterpacht, a man whose work Lemkin was coming to know. Lemkin would not have been aware, however, that another former student from Lwów had played a role in writing Jackson's words.

'Germany went to war in breach of its treaty obligations,' Jackson told the attendees, discharging America from an obligation to treat the belligerents equally. He ended his speech with words of hope that there would be a 'reign of law to which sovereign nations will defer, designed to protect the peace of the society of nations'. The talk must have resonated with Lemkin.

74

A year after arriving in Durham, Lemkin gave an address of his own to the annual meeting of the North Carolina Bar Association. Norman Birkett, an English judge, joined him on the platform. It took a little time to uncover the full report of the meeting, but eventually I found it.

The dean of the Law School, Thorack, introduced Lemkin with a brief account of his escape from Poland. The Pole had recently learned that his country house had been appropriated by the Germans, the dean explained, and his fine collection of paintings on the administration of justice, one that 'ran clear back to the Middle Ages', had been expropriated and sent to Berlin. The dean read out a short biography. 'Dr Lemkin's University' was founded as long ago as 1661 and was called 'the University of Lvov, and that is spelled L-v-o-v'. Anyone who could suggest a better pronunciation was invited to meet Thorack and Lemkin at the end of the evening.

Lemkin spoke on 'law and lawyers in the European subjugated countries'. He talked of the 'dark picture' that Nazi decrees painted of life in Europe, acts that undermined the courts, imprisoned lawyers and violated international laws. He mentioned Hans Frank, in whose hands he believed the fate of his parents and millions of Poles to rest. Would Frank protect the rights of civilians in occupied Poland? The question answered itself. He referred to a paper Frank had given at the Academy for German Law in December 1939, when he said that law was nothing more than 'that which is useful and necessary for the German nation'. Such words were 'a cynical denial of international law', Lemkin declared, provoking the 'deepest aversion'. Frank's conception subordinated the individual to the state and was designed 'to subordinate all the world under Germany'.

Lemkin also used the occasion to restate his ideas on barbarity and vandalism, recalling his own role at the Madrid conference in October 1933. The conference president told him he should not speak of Germany, he explained, but he ignored the advice: 'When I was reading this proposal [on the need for new laws], the German delegation, consisting of the President of the Supreme Court of Germany, and the President of Berlin University, Professor Kohlrausch, left the room of the proceedings.'

The account surprised me. The official records of the Madrid meeting confirmed that those present included Kohlrausch and the president of the German Supreme Court (Erwin Bumke, who presided over the court whose judgement Lauterpacht had reported earlier that year, the one ruling that the *Reich*'s ban on sexual relations between a German and a Jew covered acts outside Germany). Lemkin's colleagues Vespasian Pella and Judge Schlyter were in Madrid, as was Judge Rappaport, who headed the Polish delegation. Lemkin was not listed as present.

He wasn't in Madrid, hadn't read out the paper, didn't observe the two Germans leave the room. It was a slight embellishment, without material consequence, but an embellishment nonetheless.

75

As word spread about Lemkin's work on the decrees, he was offered a consultancy in Washington DC, at the Board of Economic Warfare. It was the spring of 1942, and the board's role was to coordinate America's war efforts following the attack on Pearl Harbor and its entry into the war. Work at the board, which was chaired by Vice President Henry Wallace, gave Lemkin a direct entrée to the upper echelons of American political life.

He decamped to Washington, a city engrossed by the war effort, teeming with energy and populated with military uniforms. Work at the board was challenging; no one there seemed to know much about what was happening in occupied Europe or exactly what the Germans were up to. Colleagues weren't much concerned about the information he tried to share, absorbed as they were in their own assignments, uninterested in the worries of a somewhat emotional Pole who cut a lonely figure. His concerns were seen as 'theoretical' and 'fantastic'. 'Have the Nazis really begun to implement these plans?' one colleague asked. Everyone knew the stories of German atrocities during the First World War, yet most turned out to be wrong. Why was the situation different now?

Dispirited, Lemkin found the time to socialize and enjoyed the cocktail circuit. He gathered a few kindred souls, including Katherine Littell, the wife of Assistant Attorney General Norman Littell (the number of married women with whom he associated was a notable feature of the archival material). The Littells introduced Lemkin to Vice President Wallace, with whom they were close (Norman Littell noted in his diary that the vice president appeared to be 'greatly interested in Ralph Lemkin's collection of Nazi decrees'). Lemkin was asked to help the vice president prepare a draft of a speech to be delivered at Madison Square Garden in New York (an early text argued that America would only be a true democracy if it contemplated 'a coloured man elected President of the United States'; the precocious line was removed when Littell suggested to Wallace that the words would haunt him if he ever ran for the presidency).

Occasionally, Lemkin would meet Wallace in his large office in the US Senate Building, hoping to engage him in his work on the decrees. The vice president was more interested in the cornfields of Ohio, he concluded. 'We have a debt to the farmers of the world,' Wallace told him, that's what they should be focusing on. Lemkin was unimpressed by Wallace, unable to penetrate the vice president's 'lonely dreams', so he decided to aim higher, encouraged by the Littells, at President Roosevelt. That, at least, was Lemkin's interpretation.

He prepared a memorandum, but it was far too lengthy. Reduce it to one page, he was told, if you want Roosevelt to read it. How could the atrocities be so compressed? He revised his approach, deciding to put a different idea to Roosevelt: outlaw mass killing, he wrote, make it a crime, the 'crime of crimes'. Lemkin proposed a treaty to make the protection of groups an aim of the war and to issue a clear warning to Hitler. The memo went off, weeks passed, a negative answer arrived. The president recognized the danger, but this was not the time to act. Be patient, Lemkin was informed, a warning would come, but not quite yet.

Like a mourner at his own funeral, without news from Wołkowysk, Lemkin was brushed by melancholy. Yet once again he picked himself up and decided to forget about politicians and statesmen. He would write a book and appeal directly to the American people.

76

Documents from Stockholm, the Library of Congress and friends across Europe continued to arrive in North Carolina. On German actions, they offered detail (food rations and the number of calories allocated to individuals depending on the group of which they were a member) and rumour, of mass executions and deportations. The gathering decrees were part of a larger framework, a system for killing. Lemkin used the materials to teach a course at the School of Military Government in Charlottesville. Students were impressed.

The idea for a book was intended to make such materials more widely available. 'I am from Missouri, show it to me' was the reaction he hoped for, ever optimistic. He wanted to persuade the people of America, by advocacy and evidence, in a tone that was objective and scholarly. He sent a proposal to the Carnegie Endowment for International Peace in Washington, where it ended up on the desk of George Finch, who gave a green light. Finish the manuscript, Lemkin was told, and Carnegie would put the material into a publishable form. They agreed on a length of two hundred pages, an honorarium (five hundred dollars) and modest expenses. The timing was perfect, with war crimes on the international agenda, following the Declaration of St James's Palace. In October 1942, President Roosevelt spoke about 'barbaric crimes' committed in occupied countries, calling for perpetrators to answer 'before courts of law'. He declared that 'war criminals' would be made to surrender, that individual responsibility would be established by means of 'all available evidence', and that a United Nations commission for the investigation of war crimes was being created.

Lemkin had valuable raw materials to support these efforts. He agreed to make the decrees available to the board but insisted on a condition: the provenance of each document must be acknowledged. The first page of each document carried a brief note to the effect that the collection had been compiled by Rafael Lemkin when serving on the faculties at Stockholm and Duke Universities and as a consultant with the Board of Economic Warfare.

If Lemkin's mood lifted, he nevertheless remained anxious about the family and was troubled by health problems. Forty-two years old, with dangerously high blood pressure, he ignored medical advice to slow down and rest as ever more information arrived in Washington about mass killings in Europe. In December, the Polish foreign minister in exile published a pamphlet titled 'The Mass Extermination of Jews in German Occupied Poland'. This was based on material provided by Jan Karski (another graduate of Lwów's law faculty), who worked with the Polish resistance in Warsaw.

A full year was devoted to the manuscript, although Lemkin allowed himself some breaks. In April 1943, he attended the dedication of the Jefferson Memorial in Washington with the Littells, where they chatted with the actors Edward G. Robinson and Paul Muni. President Roosevelt arrived, to a cheering crowd, and stood in a black cape just a few paces from Lemkin, Eleanor Roosevelt close by. 'Ralph's impressions were the best,' Littell noted in his diary, 'as he had not seen the President before.' Lemkin was struck by the Roosevelts' 'rare spiritual quality'. 'How lucky you are,' he told the Littells, 'to have two people of such unmistakable capacity for spiritual leadership in the nation.'

Lemkin completed the manuscript in November. Even with material omitted, it ran to more than seven hundred pages, well beyond the length agreed on with Carnegie, which irritated Finch. They settled on a title – *Axis Rule in Occupied Europe* – that was unlikely to produce a bestseller in Missouri or anywhere else. Lemkin's preface explained that he wanted decent men and women across the Anglo-Saxon world to know about the ruthless cruelty of the Germans against certain groups, based on 'objective information and evidence'. His focus was mainly on the treatment of 'Jews, Poles, Slovenes and Russians', but of at least one group – homosexuals – Lemkin made no mention. He wrote of the misdemeanours of the 'Germans', rather than the Nazis, making but one reference to the 'National Socialists', and argued that 'the German people' had 'accepted freely' what was planned, participating voluntarily in the measures and profiting greatly from their implementation. The desire to protect groups did not prevent him from singling out the Germans as a group. Lemkin acknowledged the help of a small coterie of friends, offered no dedication, and signed off on 15 November 1943.

Axis Rule was not a light read. Organized to cover 'each phase of life' under occupation, the book was divided into three sections. The first eight chapters dealt with 'German techniques of occupation', addressing administrative matters, the role of law and the courts, and diverse matters such as finance, labour and property. A short chapter addressed 'the legal status of the Jews'.

Chapter 9 followed. Lemkin had discarded 'barbarity' and 'vandalism' and created a new word, an amalgam of the Greek word *genos* (tribe or race) and the Latin word *cide* (killing).

To this chapter he gave the title 'Genocide'.

In the archives at Columbia University, I found a few remnants of his papers. Among them was a single sheet of lined yellow paper, with Lemkin's scribblings in pencil. On it, he wrote the word 'genocide' more than twenty-five times, before crossing them out and interspersing a few other words. 'Extermination'. 'Cultural'. 'Physical'. He was toying with other possibilities, like 'met-enocide'.

In the middle of the page, hidden among the thicket, was another word, crossed out, with a line pointing away from it, like an arrow. The word appears to be 'Frank'.

Genocide concerned acts 'directed against individuals, not in their individual capacity, but as members of national groups,' Lemkin wrote in chapter 9. 'New conceptions require new terms.' The evolution that led to his choice is unclear. A year earlier, he'd made a proposal to the Polish government in exile in London, using the Polish word *ludobójstwo*, a literal translation of the German word *Völkermord* (murder of peoples), a formulation used by the poet August Graf von Platen (in 1831), then by Friedrich Nietzsche in *The Birth of Tragedy* (1872). He dropped the word for 'genocide', without offering an explanation. The chosen word offered a reaction against Germany's 'gigantic scheme' of effecting a permanent change to the biology of the occupied territories. The 'extermination of nations and ethnic groups' required the intelligentsia to be killed off, culture to be destroyed, wealth transferred. Entire territories would be depopulated, by starvation or other forms of mass killing. Lemkin described the stages of destruction, with examples, like a prosecutor who sets out his case.

The second part of the book addresses the measures taken in seventeen occupied countries, from A (Albania) to Y (Yugoslavia). For each territory, the book detailed the stages in which groups were

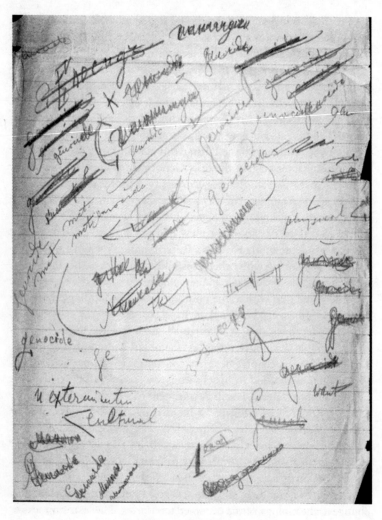

Lemkin's scribbles, c. 1945

oppressed, including Jews, Poles and gypsies. Disabled people got a passing mention. His earlier analysis was refined. Once the country was occupied, the targeted group was given a defined status, and then each member of the group was to define himself, in the case of Jews by an armband with a Star of David 'at least ten centimetres wide'. A ban on activities followed, then sequestration of property, then a prohibition on free movement and the use of public transport. Then ghettos were created into which the groups were moved, threatened with death if they left. Then came mass transportation from the occupied territories into a central, designated area – the General Government of Hans Frank. That was a liquidation area, initially achieved by reducing food rations to starvation levels, then by gunshot in the ghetto, then by other means. Lemkin knew of the transports, of the use of 'special trains' headed to destinations 'unknown'. He estimated that nearly two million people had already been murdered.

The analysis was detailed and original, supported by evidence set out in the final section of the book, four hundred pages of decrees, translated into English. Here were the minutiae, instruments of death recorded, accessible, irrefutable. Many of the documents originated in Poland, signed by Frank, including his first proclamation. 'With the establishment of the General Government,' Frank decreed, 'the Polish territories have been brought safely within the German sphere of interest.' Lemkin seemed to have Frank in his sights, a lawyer whose views were the antithesis of everything he believed in.

Physically and emotionally exhausted, Lemkin retained a practical perspective. The existing rules were inadequate; something new was needed. A new word was accompanied by a new idea, a global treaty to protect against the extermination of groups, to punish perpetrators before any court in the world. Countries would no longer be free to treat citizens as they wished.

77

Lemkin spent the first few months of 1944 in Washington, writing articles and consulting, and sought to improve himself with courses at Georgetown Law School (he performed better in criminal law than in constitutional law, for which he obtained a dismal D grade). That summer, waiting for the book to be published, he was buoyed by a decisive turn in the war. Moving westward at speed, at the end of July the Red Army had taken Lemberg, Żółkiew and Wołkowysk. En route, it uncovered terrible atrocities. In August, the Russian journalist Vasily Grossman, writing for the Red Army magazine, described what they came across in an article titled 'The Hell of Treblinka'. How could this happen? Grossman asked. 'Was it something organic? Was it a matter of heredity, upbringing, environment or external conditions? Was it a matter of historical fate, or the criminality of the German leaders?'

Such questions and accounts began to have an effect in America, softened up by the warnings of Jan Karski and, less widely, of Lemkin. President Roosevelt commissioned a report from Henry Morgenthau Jr., the son of the man who in November 1918 reported on the Lemberg pogrom against Jews that caused Lauterpacht to take to the barricades. Unlike his father, the younger Morgenthau, joining with others, called for immediate measures to prevent 'the complete extermination of the Jews in German-controlled Europe'. Inaction would cause the administration to be accused of sharing responsibility. The *New York Times* ran the first articles on death camps in Poland, including one that focused on murders in Lwów at the Janowska camp. The War Refugee Board, created by Roosevelt a few months earlier, published a more detailed report titled *The German Extermination Camps of Auschwitz and Birkenau*.

This was the fertile context in which Lemkin's book was finally published in November 1944. A first review appeared in the *Washington Post* on 3 December, and a month later the *New York Times* devoted the front page of its book review section to a positive article that came with a sting. 'A most valuable guide,' wrote Otto Tolischus, the paper's Pulitzer Prize-winning former Berlin correspondent, who nevertheless fretted that the book deserved a larger audience than its 'dry legalism' would allow. He had more serious concerns, objecting to Lemkin's tirade against Germans and the claim that the terrible acts reflected a 'militarism born of the innate viciousness of the German racial character'. He challenged Lemkin's claim that the 'vast majority of the German people put Hitler into power through free elections', noting the irony that Lemkin sought to protect some groups by blaming another.

Generally, the reviews were favourable, but not everyone appreciated the focus on groups. In an archive, I came across an irate letter sent to Lemkin by Leopold Kohr, an Austrian academic refugee (a remarkable individual, he originated the idea 'small is beautiful', which was given greater prominence by one of his pupils, E.F. Schumacher). Attached to the letter was a review that Kohr decided not to publish. *Axis Rule* was 'extremely valuable', Kohr wrote in the draft review, but 'dangerous'. Lemkin had selectively used the facts, and his attack should have been on the Nazis, not the Germans ('Dr Lemkin does not mention *National Socialism* once,' Kohr complained, not entirely accurately, because the genocide chapter uses the term, but only once).

Kohr complained that the book felt like political journalism, not scholarship, because Lemkin focused on facts that confirmed his preconceptions, presenting only a partial account. This was a 'Prussian method of writing history'. Yet the strongest criticism was reserved for chapter 9, which may be the 'most interesting' but was deeply flawed. By making groups the 'prime beneficiary' of protection and international law, Lemkin had fallen into a trap, adopting 'biological thinking' of the kind that led to anti-Semitism and anti-Germanism. Kohr told Lemkin he was wrong to focus on the responsibility of groups rather than individuals and should have adopted an approach that made 'the individual, not the group, the object of prime concern'. The road he'd taken, 'even if it does not always end in Hitler, leads to him'.

The brutal critique was offered in private. I do not delight in 'attacking friends', Kohr wrote, unaware that his concerns would have resonated in Cambridge, England, where Lauterpacht was finishing a book that focused on the rights of individuals.

78

Six months after *Axis Rule* was published, the war in Europe was over, Roosevelt was dead and Wołkowysk was back under Soviet control. Lemkin, without news of his family, immersed himself in the practicalities of President Truman's desire for a war crimes trial for the leading Germans, with Robert Jackson as chief prosecutor.

Lemkin contacted Jackson around the time that Hans Frank was arrested by the US army in Bavaria, 4 May. He informed Jackson that his book was available in the library of the Supreme Court and enclosed a copy of his article 'Genocide: A Modern Crime' (with a byline describing Lemkin as a Pole with an international 'viewpoint'). The article retraced Lemkin's dogged efforts, from his Madrid pamphlet to the book, with the aim that any Nazi who 'put his foot abroad' would be caught.

Jackson read the article and marked it up. He highlighted a quotation that Lemkin attributed to Field Marshal Gerd von Rundstedt, deeply engaged in Operation Barbarossa. Heading eastward, von Rundstedt was said to have noted that one of Germany's great mistakes in 1918 was 'to spare the civil life of the enemy countries', that one-third of the inhabitants should have been killed by 'organized underfeeding'. These words alone justified criminal charges against the field marshal, Lemkin suggested.

On 6 May, the *Washington Post* ran an editorial on retribution, citing Lemkin's book. By then, *Axis Rule* had been borrowed from the Supreme Court library and taken to Jackson's office, where it would remain for more than a year, to be returned in October 1946. Jackson thanked Lemkin for writing as he recruited a legal team for the trials, including lawyers from the War Department, where Lemkin had worked as a consultant. Jackson's principal lawyer was Sidney Alderman, a genial and brilliant general counsel of the Southern Railway system, who spent a weekend immersed in Lemkin's book.

By 14 May, Jackson's team had finalized a planning memo. It summarized the evidence needed to prosecute individuals for the 'decimation of racial minorities' but made no mention of 'genocide'. Two days later, with the draft memo in hand, Jackson met his legal team at the Supreme Court and personally added the word 'genocide' to the list of possible crimes. The detailed report he sent to delegations at the London Conference set out that list, which included 'genocide', described by Jackson as the 'destruction of racial minorities and subjugated populations'.

Lemkin worked hard to get himself hired. On Friday, 18 May, he was introduced to Alderman, an alumnus of Duke University. Alderman told Lemkin (whom he erroneously believed to be German) that *Axis Rule* was 'comprehensive' and 'very interesting' and might serve as a 'basic text' for Jackson's team. Discussing how 'genocide' might be used in the trial, Alderman understood that Lemkin was 'very proud' of the word and his role as its inventor. At the end of the month, Lemkin attended a meeting at the Department of Justice. This was a contentious affair, concerned with the role to be played by the Office of Strategic Services (OSS) – the forerunner to the Central Intelligence Agency (CIA) – in collecting evidence against the defendants. Jackson's thirty-six-year-old son Bill, a member of the team, attended the gathering, at which he first encountered Lemkin (Bill Jackson was one of the few people to work with both Lemkin and Lauterpacht, present at the meeting at Cranmer Road a few weeks later, when 'crimes against humanity' made its way into the Nuremberg Charter). Bill wasn't overly impressed by Lemkin, a passionate man and a 'scholar of parts' but impractical and without any sense of the kind of case the team was preparing. Nevertheless, the younger Jackson and Alderman must have thought Lemkin to be knowledgeable enough to justify an invitation to join the team, if only to keep an eye on the OSS.

On 28 May, Lemkin started work with the War Crimes Office, an official member of Jackson's team. Disappointment came quickly, because his ideas were rebuffed. Although he was recognized to be knowledgeable about the facts of German atrocities, the problem concerned style and temperament. Some in Jackson's group thought he wasn't a team player, others that he lacked the instinct of a litigator, without a sense of how to run a case. Concluding that Lemkin wasn't up to the task, Alderman approached Telford Taylor, another lawyer on the team, with a view to getting Lemkin removed from the core staff.

They agreed to 'eliminate him' from the inner circle and use him for background tasks, an 'encyclopedia' to be available in preparing the trial. Despite being rated as 'top of the refugees' and the reliance placed on his materials, he was shifted to the periphery. When Jackson's team left for London in July, it didn't include Lemkin. He remained in Washington, disappointed, working with a 'rear echelon Task Force' to develop ideas on the crimes for which the Germans would be indicted.

79

On the Internet, I found a reference to a signed first edition of *Axis Rule*. Sold, the bookseller informed me, but when I told him I was interested in Lemkin's inscription, he introduced me to the buyer. A few days later, a kind note arrived from a lawyer at the Department of Justice in Washington DC: Eli Rosenbaum, legendary hunter of fugitive Nazis, sent a photograph of the words 'To Dr Robert M. Kempner, with compliments, R. Lemkin, Washington DC, 5 June 1945.'

The name was familiar: Kempner, a colleague of Lemkin's at the War Crimes Office, spent a part of the summer of 1921 as a young law student sitting in the public gallery of a Berlin courtroom watching the trial of Tehlirian. He had been expelled from the *Reich* in 1933 because of his involvement in court proceedings against Hitler, and his connection with Lemkin in Washington offered a direct link to the trial that inspired Lemkin. The date of 5 June stood out too: it was the day the Allies gathered in Berlin to carve up Germany and agree on the punishment of the 'principal Nazi leaders'. They implemented an agreement reached three months earlier at Yalta, a commitment to 'bring all war criminals to just and swift punishment'.

Jackson's team gathered in London in July, with British, French and Soviet colleagues to work on the list of crimes to be included in the Nuremberg Charter. Agreement was reached and signed on 8 August. The list of crimes in Article 6 included crimes against humanity – at Lauterpacht's suggestion – but not genocide. Lemkin was bitterly disappointed and suspected the British of having played a devious role. 'You know how they are,' Bob Silvers recalled Lemkin saying of the British during a class at Yale a decade later.

Genocide having been left out of the Nuremberg Charter, Lemkin knew that the crimes listed in Article 6 still had to be elaborated into specific charges against the defendants. This offered a further opportunity to introduce the charge of genocide. I wasn't able to ascertain exactly how he procured an invitation to London to work with Jackson's team to prepare the indictments, but it appears to have been at the instigation of Colonel Murray Bernays, who ran Jackson's office and thought Lemkin's encyclopedic knowledge might be useful. Bernays was one of Lemkin's few supporters, believing that he could help on the crimes that occurred in occupied Poland.

Bernays met resistance. Commander James Donovan, general counsel to the OSS, objected and sent a secret memorandum to Jackson's inner team, complaining that Lemkin's work was 'inadequate', that better Polish scholars were available. Donovan thought Lemkin too passionate, driven by an 'emotional approach' that wasn't appropriate for such complex legal matters. He also thought him to have 'personality difficulties', a view that was supported but ultimately didn't prevail. Colonel Bernays offered to take responsibility for the Pole but returned to Washington shortly after Lemkin arrived in London. No one else was willing to take him under his wing, yet somehow he managed to stay on, a loose cannon, largely unsupervised, without his own assigned office or telephone number.

80

In London, Lemkin spoke to anyone who'd listen, which eventually proved to be his undoing. Complaints multiplied that he was unmanageable and went off on unauthorized frolics. Rumours swirled that he'd arranged informal sessions with members of the UN War Crimes Commission, that he had unauthorized meetings with prominent individuals associated with the World Zionist Organization. The complaints reached Commander Donovan's office in Washington, word that Lemkin was pursuing his own agenda and claiming credit for the work of others. The final straw was the news that Lemkin had privately briefed the press, then embarrassed Jackson's staff by complaining that members of the UN War Crimes Commission hadn't been provided with copies of *Axis Rule*.

'The sooner Lemkin is out of London,' Donovan told Telford Taylor, the better. Lemkin fought his corner, long enough to make a difference. A persistent 'bugger', Bill Jackson later observed, Lemkin somehow hung on, through September and into October, as work continued on the draft indictments. He somehow turned Sidney Alderman into an ally on genocide, in the face of considerable opposition from others on Jackson's team, under pressure from politicians in states that required whites and blacks to use different toilets. The British too were firmly opposed to the inclusion of the charge of genocide, the opposition led by Geoffrey Dorling 'Khaki' Roberts, a huge, beetle-browed barrister and King's Counsel who was close to Hartley Shawcross. The Americans liked Roberts, admiring the fact he played rugby at Oxford and for England, but didn't think much of him as a lawyer.

Khaki Roberts's opposition might have helped Lemkin. Alderman took up the cause so that 'genocide' made its way into an early draft of the indictment. British opposition firmed up against a word that was 'too fancy' and 'outlandish' to put into a serious legal document. The graduates of Oxford University 'couldn't understand what the word meant', Alderman told a colleague. Lemkin was 'greatly pleased' that the British failed to get rid of the offending word.

On 6 October, the Four Powers reached agreement on an indictment that contained four counts, the last of which was crimes against humanity. Yet genocide wasn't introduced under this head, as Lemkin had hoped, but in count 3, on war crimes. This included ill-treatment and murder of civilians in occupied territories and the allegation that the defendants 'conducted deliberate and systematic genocide'.

Lemkin's awkward persistence paid off. This was the first time the word was used in any international instrument, along with a definition, lifted more or less directly from Lemkin's book. Genocide was

> extermination of racial and religious groups, against the civilian populations of certain occupied territories in order to destroy particular races and classes of people and national, racial, or religious groups, particularly Jews, Poles, Gypsies and others.

The destruction of groups would be in the Nuremberg trial, a moment of personal triumph for Lemkin. Years of lugging documents around the world paid off, but at a price. Three days before the indictment was agreed to, the US army doctor Captain Stanley Vogel diagnosed Lemkin with nasopharyngitis, a common cold. This offered a perfect excuse to return him to Washington, just as Lauterpacht was preparing to travel in the opposite direction, from Cambridge to Nuremberg. By the time the indictment was laid before the tribunal, on 18 October, Lemkin was back in the United States, exhausted but satisfied. 'I went to London and succeeded in having inscribed the charge of Genocide against the Nazi war criminals in Nuremberg,' he later wrote. 'I included genocide in the indictment at the Nuremberg trials.'

Crimes against humanity and genocide were both in the trial.

THE MAN IN A BOW TIE

Among my grandfather's papers, I had found a small black-and-white photograph, taken in 1949, not quite square. It showed a middle-aged man staring intently into the camera. A faint smile across the lips, he wears a pin-striped suit, with a white handkerchief neatly folded into the breast pocket, and a white shirt. His polka-dot bow tie emphasizes a slightly mischievous air.

For two years, a photocopy of the photograph remained on the wall above my desk, competing with Miss Tilney. Her role now resolved, I looked at him daily, taunted and frustrated. 'If you're any good, you'll find me,' he seemed to say. Occasionally prompted, I tried what I could to rise to the challenge, half-hearted efforts, inevitably fruitless without a name. I scanned the photograph, tried facial recognition on the Web. Nothing.

Time and again I returned to the modest information on the back of the photograph. 'Herzlichste Grüsse aus Wien, September 1949', it said, 'Warmest wishes from Vienna'. The signature was firm and indecipherable.

I tried to squeeze what I could from these words, the small red stamp, the name and address of the photographic studio where the photograph had been taken. 'Foto F. Kintschel, Mariahilferstrasse 53, Wien VI'. The street still existed, but the studio was long gone. I spent hours trying to decipher the signature, without success, and closely examined the two other photographs of the same man. That dated 'London, 8 August 1951' was the same size, with a stamp from the Kintschel photo studio, but in blue. On that summer day, he wore a regular tie with diagonal stripes, a handkerchief again in the breast pocket. Was he slightly cross-eyed?

The third photograph was larger than the others, postcard-size. It bore no studio mark or signature. He wore a dark tie with diamond pattern and a handkerchief. The handwritten note on the back says 'Wien-London, Oktober 1954'. He'd put on a little weight, the outlines of a double chin now visible. He *was* cross-eyed. In blue ink he wrote, 'Zur freundlichen Erinnerung an einen Grossvater' – 'In kind memory of a grandfather'. Had a grandfather died? Had he become a grandfather?

When I first asked my mother about the man, she said she didn't really know who he was. I persisted. Well, she said, she did once ask Leon who the man was. 'He said it wasn't important, that was all.' So she let the matter lie, with doubts of her own.

'Warmest wishes from Vienna, September 1949'

So Leon knew who he was, and he kept two more photographs of the same man, one taken in August 1951, the other in October 1954. Why did Leon keep the three photographs if the man wasn't important?

In fact, my mother later clarified, she found them among Rita's papers after she died in 1986. She then moved them over to Leon's papers, where they remained for a decade. With a little more pushing, my mother shared a fleeting memory from childhood, obscure but real. Perhaps she recalled a visit by this man to the apartment in Paris, on the rue Brongniart, after the war. An argument ensued between Leon and Rita, voices were raised, there was anger, then reconciliation. 'My parents had many arguments like that.' Intense, then forgotten.

The information percolated slowly. Perhaps the man in the bow tie was connected to Leon's solitary departure from Vienna in January 1939. The general circumstances – the arrival of the Germans, banishment from the *Reich* – were clear enough, but Leon's decision to leave alone, without his wife or young child, was less easily explicable. Maybe the man in the bow tie was involved in some way in Rita's life in Vienna after Leon left. Maybe he was a Nazi. Rita spent three years separated from husband and child, fleeing Vienna only in October 1941, a day before Eichmann locked the doors shut.

82

Time passed without any progress. I put the three photographs to one side, ready to give up. I concentrated on Lemberg, Lwów, Lvov, Lviv, Lauterpacht, Lemkin. Then, out of the blue, I got an unexpected break.

Soon after the first visit to Lviv, I attended a friend's ninetieth birthday celebration, a party at London's Wigmore Hall, the classical music venue. Milein Cosman was the centre of the festivities, a diminutive painter of distinction and unbounded intelligence and warmth, the widow of Hans Keller, a distinguished musicologist. She and her husband arrived in Britain before the war, separately as refugees, she from Germany, he from Austria. In the 1950s, they moved into a small house on Willow Road in north London, close to Hampstead Heath. Forty years later my wife and I bought the house, where we live today (opposite Willow Cottages, home to the nephew of Sofka Skipwith).

Hans Keller worked with the Third Programme on BBC radio, allowing him and Milein to meet many of the great musicians and conductors of the twentieth century. They knew Furtwängler ('most definitely not a Nazi,' Milein told me, with passion) and Karajan ('a Nazi sympathizer and opportunist,' her views rather clear). In 1947 she drew Richard Strauss, shortly before he died, a portrait that hung in Wigmore Hall, along with an extended family of her other drawings, where a hundred or more friends and family gathered to celebrate her.

Milein directed me towards a friend, a relative of her late husband's. Inge Trott was ninety-one years old, fiercely intelligent and, it turned out, amiably mischievous. She was born in Vienna, arriving in London in 1938 at the age of seventeen. After the war, she got a job as a laboratory assistant with Professor Maurice Wilkins at King's College London, who would later share a Nobel Prize with Francis Crick and James Watson, to whom Inge would deliver samples of sperm in Cambridge. Inge felt pride in her contribution, a transporter of the materials that unlocked the secrets of DNA.

Our conversation touched on Vienna, the character of Austrians, the *Anschluss*. She recalled the arrival of the Germans, the parades, humiliations, the family home being requisitioned by a German soldier in a grey uniform. I mentioned the photograph of the man in a bow tie, the handwriting, the indecipherable signature.

'Send me a copy,' Inge instructed. 'I will see if I can read the signature.' Probably you can't decipher it because it's in old German, she added.

'I'll pop it in the mail.'

'No,' Inge said firmly. 'Scan it, e-mail it, that will be quicker.'

That evening I followed her instructions, and the next day a reply arrived. 'I could read all the writing on the back of the photo except the signature, because it was upside down.' Scan it again, 'the right way up this time'.

83

A day passed, the phone rang.

'The name is Lindenfeld,' Inge said with certainty before a quiet note of doubt intruded. 'Well, it could be Lindenfels, with an *s,* but I don't think so.'

She scolded Herr L. 'I really don't know why people purposely make their signatures unreadable.'

The moment felt oddly dramatic. With a name, new avenues for exploration would be unveiled. I would be able to check all the Lindenfelds (or Lindenfelses) who lived in Vienna in 1949 and then cross-check with those of that name who were there in 1939. Simple enough, I thought, with a set of telephone directories from those years. A doctoral student at the University of Vienna helped with my initial research, and then I obtained the assistance of a private investigator. Frau Katja-Maria Chladek, a specialist in Viennese genealogy based in Vienna, was jolly, courteous and fabulously efficient.

The law student found the 1939 telephone directory for Vienna. No Lindenfelses, ten Lindenfelds. Nine of those entries were men, with good Wagnerian names: Bela, Emil, Erwin, Kurt, Max, Mendel, Rudolf and Siegfried.

The next task was to find a phone directory for 1949 to cross-refer the names. This proved to be more of a challenge, but eventually Frau Chladek, the private investigator, found a copy, then reported on the findings. By 1949, the ten Lindenfelds who lived in Vienna in 1939 were reduced to just one. His name was Emil, Frau Chladek explained, in her view not a Jewish name. The implication she let hang was that something was amiss.

Emil Lindenfeld lived at Gumpendorferstrasse 87, in Vienna's 6th District, close to Foto Kintschel on Mariahilferstrasse. A ten-minute walk from his apartment to the studio to collect the images, Frau Chladek explained. The phone directory, which listed him as 'a member of the public administration', included him until 1969, when his name disappeared. 'I think he died in 1968 or 1969,' Frau Chladek said.

She continued her research in the library at Vienna City Hall, which revealed that Emil Lindenfeld lived at the same address for two decades after 1949. 'I think the chances are good that he is the searched person.' She was hopeful, encouraging even, but it didn't mean that the man in the bow tie was Emil Lindenfeld. The next step was to find the date of his death. With this information, Frau Chladek thought she could obtain his *Verlassenschaftsabhandlung,* the estate file that would contain details about his family, maybe a photograph. Was I willing to instruct her to carry out the search? I was.

I enjoyed her communications, lively and enthusiastic. A couple of weeks after that exchange, she sent another e-mail with new information, some of which was, in her words, 'very surprising'. Emil Lindenfeld was a merchant, born on 2 February 1896, in the town of Kopyczynce in Poland. In the file, the reference to Poland is crossed out and replaced with 'USSR'. He died on 5 June 1969, in Vienna.

'Now to my very surprising news.'

Frau Chladek had located Herr Lindenfeld's *Totenbeschauprotokoll*, the official document that recorded his personal circumstances at the time of death. 'The first name Emil was written but then cancelled,' she said. In its place, an 'unknown person' had inserted a different first name, Mendel. It was exceptional for a name to be changed, something she had come across only rarely in her work. Her interpretation? 'He was Jewish,' but the fact was not public. Frau Chladek thought he was 'a secret Jew'.

The *Protokoll* threw up other information, so Frau Chladek thought we should obtain Herr Lindenfeld's complete estate file. This she did, and it was indeed helpful. 'His mother was Sara Lindenfeld, who had her last residence in London, GB,' Frau Chladek wrote. That might have explained the references to London on the back of the 1951 and 1954 photographs, perhaps to visit his mother.

Frau Chladek had other information. When the war broke out in 1939, Emil Lindenfeld was married to Lydia Sturm, a Jew. They had one child, a daughter named Alice. At some point in 1939, Lindenfeld's wife, Lydia, and his daughter, Alice, left Vienna for London. This offered a direct parallel with Rita's life: by the end of 1939, Emil and Rita were both living alone in Vienna, their children and spouses having left, coping with war, the Nazis and loneliness.

Frau Chladek had yet more. When Emil Lindenfeld died, his daughter, Alice, was living in Flushing, New York, married to Alfred Seiler. Alfred and Alice had two children, Sandra and Howard, born in the 1950s. The points of connection were coming together. The birth of Sandra, in 1952, could explain the reference in the 1954 photograph to becoming a grandfather.

What I needed was a photograph of Emil Lindenfeld, but Frau

Chladek said there were none in the files. I had other leads, however, with the names of his grandchildren, so the search shifted to New York.

84

I couldn't find an Alice Seiler listed in Flushing, New York. Nor was any local information available on Sandra and Howard Seiler, the grandchildren, in Flushing or anywhere in the New York area.

Facebook offered a way forward. Among its hundreds of millions of users was a Howard Seiler in Florida. The clue was that he was a high school student in Flushing. The Facebook photograph showed a man in his early fifties, consistent with the date of birth that Frau Chladek had offered. Among Howard's 'friends' was a Sandra, with the surname of Garfinkel.

I sent a message to Howard; no reply came. So I searched for a Sandra Seiler Garfinkel and found an address in Massapequa, Long Island, not far from Flushing. The phone number wasn't publicly available, but the payment of a small sum produced a ten-digit number. On a warm summer evening in London, I dialled the number, with some trepidation.

A woman with a heavy New York accent answered. I told her I was looking for Sandra Seiler, granddaughter of Emil Lindenfeld of Vienna. This was followed by a long silence and then 'This is she.' More silence, then 'This is pretty weird. What do you want?'

I told her the story, in truncated form, that my grandmother might have known her grandfather in Vienna before the war. 'My grandfather was Emil Lindenfeld; he lived in Vienna,' Sandra said. She was sceptical, not hostile or friendly, or unfriendly. She did offer a short history of her family.

'Emil was married to Lydia, my grandmother. After the Nazis arrived in Vienna, in March 1938 but before the war began, Lydia left Vienna with her daughter, my mother, Alice, who was fourteen years old. They went to London, where my grandmother worked as a maid. After the war, Alice and Lydia came to America, but Emil stayed in Vienna. We were told that he could not travel to America because he had tuberculosis. In 1958, my grandmother Lydia died, and Emil came to America. I was six years old. He stayed for six weeks, taught me German, then left. That was the only time I ever saw him.'

Did she have any photographs of Emil? 'Yes, of course.' There might even be one on the Web, she added. Her mother died in 1986, but her father had lived on, until quite recently. 'He wrote a book about his wartime experiences; it's on the Web, with photographs.' She gave me the details, and as we spoke I searched for her father's book. It came up instantly, with the cheery title *From Hitler's Death Camps to Stalin's Gulags*. The reader was invited to 'Look Inside', and as we chatted away, I did so. The book was short, fewer than two hundred pages. I scrolled down, at speed, checking out the photographs. At page 125, a familiar face peered out from the screen, a man in a dark suit with a white handkerchief in the breast pocket and a dark, regular tie. Under the photograph was a name, Emil. The next page had a picture of Emil's wife, Lydia, with photographs of Sandra and Howard, Emil's grandchildren.

I apologized to Sandra for my silence. The three photographs of Emil had been in my grandfather's papers for decades, and for several years I had been trying to find out who the man was. Sandra understood; she was generous. Could I read out the words around the photograph in her father's memoir, she asked. She hadn't been able to bring herself to read the book, published only after her father's death.

I read out the text. Emil Lindenfeld-Sommerstein was a childhood friend of Alfred's father. He married Lydia Sturm, the daughter of a man with a 'Posamentrie' factory in Jägerndorf in the Sudetenland, which made 'fancy table cloths, coverlets and such'. The marriage produced one child, a daughter, Alice, sent to England in 1939 on 'one of the famous Kinder Transports'. Lydia followed soon after, having obtained a permit to work as a domestic. A single sentence hinted at Emil's life in Vienna after his wife and daughter left: 'Emil was able to stay in Vienna during the Nazi occupation as a "U-Boat", hiding out with non-Jewish relatives and friends. Alice's parents never reunited and the father continued living in Vienna.'

Emil Lindenfeld remained alone in Vienna, like Rita, then went into hiding 'with non-Jewish relatives'. This suggested he might not have been fully Jewish or that he stayed in Vienna as a non-Jew. After the war, Emil and Lydia separated, unlike Leon and Rita, who were reunited in Paris.

Reading this account by Emil's son-in-law reminded me of my mother's recollection, that the man I now knew to be Emil Linden-feld had visited Rita and Leon in Paris after the war. When he left their apartment, her parents had argued. An obvious inference – but not the only one – is that Rita and Emil were lovers, that he had come to Paris after the war to find her, to persuade her to return to Vienna. I said nothing of this to Sandra at the time, although later, as we became better acquainted, such thoughts were shared.

I thanked Sandra for taking my phone call. She asked me to send her a copy of the photograph of her grandfather, the one pinned to the wall above my desk, which I did. A couple of days later, she wrote back. Our telephone conversation had prompted her to dig up Emil's papers, which were sent from Vienna to New York after he died. She had his photograph albums, some of which might date back to the period before the war. If my grandparents had photographs of Emil, perhaps Emil had photographs of Leon and Rita?

'Send a picture of your grandparents,' Sandra suggested. I sent the photographs of Leon and Rita from their Nazi-era passports. Rita's must have been taken around 1941, the one in which she looked sad. I had long believed this to have been because of the separation from husband and child; now I began to wonder if it might be connected to something else, maybe to do with Emil.

85

The following day, a batch of e-mails arrived from Sandra. She had gone through Emil's albums and found several photographs of Rita, she wrote, but only one of Leon (an image of him with Rita and my mother taken on a Paris street in the 1950s, a photograph that my mother has in her album).

I opened Sandra's e-mails with trepidation. The photographs might help explain the silence that had fallen over this period. The photographs were black-and-white, eight of them, undimmed by the passage of time. I'd never seen any of the photographs of Rita, the ones that Sandra had sent. Each was unexpected.

The first was a studio portrait of Rita, in soft focus. She smiled, glamorous in a way that I'd not previously noticed. She was beautiful, her face carefully made up, with strong and striking lipstick.

The next photograph offered a greater surprise. Taken on a date unknown, it was an image of Rita with Leon's mother, Malke, which must have been one of the last photographs ever taken of my great-grandmother. It seemed familiar. Malke was elegant, eyelids long, sloping, slanted like Leon's. She wore a dark shirt with simple buttons, silver hair brushed back. Her face had a faded dignity and calm, before she knew what was to come.

Rita and Malke, Vienna, c. 1938

Yet there was something strange about the photograph, which I half recognized. Then I realized that I had seen it, but only a half of it, the side that showed Malke. My mother has a copy of that half, torn down the middle, so the other side, with the smiling Rita, has been removed. Only now, with this more complete version, did I see that in the original Malke was not alone, that Rita was with her.

The next photograph, the third, showed Rita lounging in a deck-chair in a garden, in spring, or maybe summer. A fourth had her standing in a striped jumper, in formal shoes, alone in a garden. Perhaps the same garden.

The final photographs came in a group of four. They seemed to have been taken on the same day, again in a tranquil garden. The leaves on the trees and bushes were filled with life, young and vibrant. It felt like spring. The individuals looked peaceful and relaxed. In one, Rita sat alone on a bench; three women and Emil Lindenfeld lay on the grass behind her. They were smiling and laughing, talking. Each looked towards the camera and the unknown photographer, carefree.

The next photograph showed Rita on the same bench, wearing a hat. A third showed an unknown woman on that bench, with a man in a hat and in lederhosen, wearing the 'Weißstrümpfe' (white socks) that were a sign, as I have learned, of sympathy towards the Nazis. Context was everything, and that knowledge gave the socks a sinister feel.

The last image showed Rita, standing between two men. I did not recognize the one to her right, but on her left was Emil, in lederhosen and white stockings, his arm entwined with Rita's. She smiled, elegant and peaceful, more beautiful than I had ever seen her. (Later I would show the photograph to my aunt, who had the same reaction: 'I never saw her looking like that, not ever.') Emil stood with his hands in his pockets. He had a mischievous air, head tilted back, a faint smile as though caught out unexpectedly.

Rita wore a dark flowery dress. Looking closely, but the image was not too clear, I could see a wedding ring on her right hand, presumably the one I wear today.

When were the photographs taken? Perhaps they were innocent images taken before 1937, before Rita and Leon married. Or they could have been taken after January 1939, when Leon left Vienna for Paris. I had often imagined that period, Rita alone in Vienna, without daughter or husband, looking after her mother. That was the reason she stayed behind, we were told, a time of darkness, of overwhelming unhappiness. Yet the photographs conveyed a serenity, not consonant with the times, as war raged and the Jews of Vienna found themselves on the rack, in ghettos, or on the road to extermination.

Did the four photographs have a date? Sandra said they were stuck onto the pages of the album. She could peel them off but worried she might damage them. Come and visit, she said, next time you are in New York.

'We can peel them off together.'

Rita and Emil (right), with unknown man, Vienna

86

Several weeks later, I took a train from Manhattan's Penn Station to Massapequa, on the coast of Long Island, to spend a day with Sandra Seiler, granddaughter of Emil Lindenfeld.

It was less than an hour on the Long Island Rail Road. Sandra waited at the train station, sitting in her car, blonde, black sunglasses. She invited me to lunch by the sea, a seafood restaurant. After lunch we drove to her home, and I met her husband and a daughter. Emil's photograph albums were there, ready to be examined. She pulled out the volume that held the images of Rita. We wanted dates.

The photographs were small, stuck close and hard to the album's dark pages, just as Sandra said, as firm as the day they were fixed to the pages. We peeled one off as carefully as possible, not wanting to cause damage. I hoped the photographs had been taken in the mid-1930s, before Rita and Leon were married. That would be simpler.

The first four photographs – including the one of Malke alongside Rita – came off the pages to reveal no date. Then the second set, the 'garden quartet', as Sandra called them. Even more careful, not wanting to damage the backs, I peeled each of the four photographs from its page.

The back of each photograph bore the mark of a studio, Foto-Kutschera, in Vienna's 4th District. On the back there was only a barely discernible pencil mark, in the top right-hand corner, four numbers: 1941.

Within a few weeks, I had found the address where Emil Lindenfeld lived in 1941, a prosperous address at the centre of Vienna, outside the Jewish area, a location where Emil could not have been living as a Jew. The address was 4 Brahmsplatz, a magnificent building, constructed in the late nineteenth century, a few houses down from a home once owned by the Wittgensteins.

I visited. To the side of No. 4 was a large garden, a bench, grass, like the scene in the four photographs. Might this be the garden where Rita and Emil were photographed in 1941? I remembered how relaxed they appeared, an air of intimacy that transcended the photograph.

Emil Lindenfeld and Rita were together in 1941, maybe in this very garden. No month was given, but Rita left in October, and the garden photographs offered the appearance of spring. I plumped for April 1941. Did Rita stay in Vienna to be with Emil? It was impossible to know, and maybe it didn't matter. By November, she had left Vienna.

Leon had left precipitously in January 1939, alone. A few months later he sent for his daughter, benefiting from the assistance of Miss Tilney. Rita remained in Vienna. Why Leon would have left his daughter behind, and why he then sent for her, I did not know. But the new photographs suggested that Leon's departure had something to do with Emil Lindenfeld.

VI

FRANK

*Community takes precedence over the individualistic liberalistic
atomizing tendencies of the egoism of the individual*

Hans Frank, 1935

87

In May 1945, a few days after Hitler committed suicide, as Lauter-pacht worked with British lawyers on the investigation of crimes and Lemkin lobbied to get himself onto Robert Jackson's prosecution team, Governor-General Hans Frank awaited the arrival of the Americans. He did so in the front room of his chancellery, now located in the old Café Bergfrieden in the small Bavarian town of Neuhaus am Schliersee. He was accompanied by a staff that was reduced to just three, including Herr Schamper, the chauffeur. After a brutal reign in occupied Poland, Frank had returned to the vicinity of the family home, thirty-five miles south of Munich.

As Frank waited, the Allies prepared the prosecution of the main Nazi leaders, including Frank. He had been Hitler's lawyer and one of the leading jurists of National Socialism, acting against the rights of individuals and groups, motivated by an ideology that put the love of the Führer, and the idea of national community, first. For five years he was the king of occupied Poland, with a wife and mistress, five children, thirty-eight volumes of detailed daily diaries, and a collection of paintings that included a famous portrait by Leonardo da Vinci. He had even brought *The Lady with an Ermine* home with him to Schliersee, and she now rested in the *Andachtsraum,* a faux chapel.

On Friday, 4 May, an American military jeep pulled up. Lieuten-ant Walter Stein jumped out, walked up to the building, entered by the front door, and asked, 'Which of you is Hans Frank?'

88

Frank was born in Karlsruhe on 23 May 1900, near the Black Forest, to a Protestant father and a Catholic mother. Like Lauterpacht and Lemkin, he was the second of three children. The family soon moved to Munich, where Frank attended school. In June 1916, his older brother, Karl, died of an unexpected illnesss. After his parents separated, he spent a year in Prague with his mother, but mostly lived in Munich with his father, who worked as a lawyer before he was disbarred for defrauding his clients.

As the First World War ended, Frank was conscripted into the Wehrmacht and then associated himself with a private right-wing militia. He joined an organization of anti-Communist and anti-Semitic conservatives, the Thule Society, which allowed him to attend meetings to vent a strongly held distaste for the Versailles Treaty. In January 1920, at Munich's Mathäser-Bräu, Frank saw Adolf Hitler speak, as one of the first members of the German Workers' Party (Deutsche Arbeiterpartei, or DAP), a forerunner to the NSDAP. The following month, he attended a meeting with Hitler at the Hofbräuhaus, present at the proclamation of a political programme for the NSDAP, the Nazi Party that he eventually joined.

In 1923, as a student, he joined the Sturmabteilung, the Storm Troopers known as the SA. That same year he enthusiastically supported Hitler's putsch, an attempt to overthrow the Weimar government, joining a march into the centre of Munich, where he set up a machine-gun emplacement on the east side of the city's Museum Bridge. The failure of the putsch and Hitler's arrest ignited Frank's interest in *völkisch* politics. He fled to Italy, fearing legal difficulties. Two years later, in 1925, he met Hitler on a Munich street, a harbinger of future possibilities.

After completing legal studies at the University of Kiel and graduating in 1924, he worked as a lawyer in private practice and taught in the law department of Munich's Technical University. Solid and opportunistic, not an intellectual or a high-flyer, he experienced a sudden change of trajectory in October 1927 when he saw an advertisement in the *Völkischer Beobachter* newspaper seeking a lawyer to represent Nazi defendants in a Berlin trial. Frank applied, was hired, and eventually entered into a world of high-profile political trials.

He became one of the Nazis' legal luminaries, defending the party in dozens of trials. One of the more notorious was a treason trial in Leipzig, in September 1930, involving three military officers accused of creating a Nazi cell in the Reichswehr. Defending the three, he called Hitler as a witness. With Frank's help, Hitler used the courtroom to generate media attention with the claim that he would only seek political power by legal means, in effect a public commitment to the Oath of Legality (*Legalitätseid*). The publicity cemented the relationship between the two men, although Hitler would never have much time for lawyers or legal niceties, even of Frank's flexible brand.

Frank's career ascendant, he was elected a member of the Reichstag having married Brigitte Herbst in 1925, five years his senior and a secretary at the Bavarian parliament. His true love and sweetheart, however, was Lilly Weidert (later Grau), the daughter of a Munich banker, but the relationship was terminated by Lilly's family, deeming Frank unsuitable. Brigitte was a nondescript but strong-willed woman, who soon bore him two children. Three more followed, the last being Niklas, born in 1939.

As large parts of Germany embraced Hitler, Frank made the most of his connections to the leadership, positioning himself as a legal 'theorist'. In 1931, he published a long article on the Jewish 'jurisprudence of decadence', an approach to the law, he argued, that alienated Germans from understanding the difference between right and wrong. Now an insider, after Hitler was appointed chancellor, in April 1933 Frank became the state minister of justice in Bavaria.

89

Four months after Hitler took power, on the morning of Saturday, 13 May, Hans Frank flew in a tri-motored German government plane to the Aspern Airfield to the east of Vienna, not far from Leon's liquor store in Leopoldstadt. A newspaper described the opening of the plane's door and the descent onto Austrian soil of seven German ministers, led by a beaming Frank, the first visit by representatives of the new Nazi government of Germany. The Reichstag had recently been destroyed by fire, federal elections held (at which the Nazis won the largest share of the vote) and new legislation adopted, allowing Hitler's new government to pass laws that deviated from the constitution. These measures were viewed with anxiety by many in Austria, including its diminutive chancellor, Engelbert Dollfuss.

Frank was known to have a close relationship with the Führer, for service as his lawyer. Hitler's numerous court appearances before 1933 were widely reported, and at least one media photograph showed Hitler on the steps of the courthouse, with Frank at his side in black legal robes.

Such images helped Frank. Years of loyal service to the National Socialists made him a familiar – and feared – figure. Within weeks of being appointed minister of justice, he signed a raft of measures to clean up Bavaria's legal system. These specifically targeted Jews,

Hitler with Hans Frank outside a German court, 1928

forbidding them to enter courts of law and removing all Jewish judges and state's attorneys from office. Frank's direct involvement in such measures, coupled with his connection to Hitler, made the visit to Austria unwelcome, opposed by Chancellor Dollfuss as an unfriendly act. Frank didn't help with a speech given shortly before the visit, threatening violent intervention if Austria didn't align itself with Germany's new direction.

Two thousand sympathizers greeted Frank at the Vienna airfield, singing 'Deutschland über Alles' and the 'Horst Wessel Song', the Nazi anthem. Frank's entourage was driven to the Vienna Brown House, the streets lined with citizens who cheered or whistled, depending on political affiliation. Many of Frank's supporters wore white socks, the symbol of support for the Nazi cause. In the evening, Frank addressed a large crowd of supporters to mark the 250th anniversary of Vienna's liberation from the Turks (a victory delivered by Jan Sobieski III, king of Poland, celebrated with the construction of the castle in Żółkiew, on a wall of which I had found the photographs placed there by a courageous Ukrainian curator). Frank delivered a personal greeting from Hitler. The Führer would soon be with them 'to visit the grave of his parents.'

Later, Frank met privately with journalists. The *New York Times* correspondent noted the Bavarian minister's style, treating the group of twenty 'as if it had been 20,000'. He continually raised his voice, screaming out objections to any negative views expressed towards him or Hitler. 'It is only a question of *what* measures shall be taken,' he threatened, if Austria didn't come into line with Germany.

From Vienna Frank travelled to Graz, where he told a large crowd that an insult to him was an insult to Hitler, and then on to Salzburg. The visit caused a commotion in Austria, the Dollfuss government declaring him to be unwelcome. The visit was widely reported around the world, most likely picked up by Lauterpacht in London and Lemkin in Warsaw. Word would also have spread to the well-informed citizens of Lemberg and Żółkiew, many of whom followed developments in Austria.

A week after Frank's departure, Chancellor Dollfuss delivered an address to reassure his citizens, words transmitted in translation to the United States. Austria would not emulate the German government by taking measures against Jews; it was a country inspired by modern conceptions in which 'all citizens have equal rights'. He was referring to the Austrian constitution crafted by Lauterpacht's teacher Hans Kelsen, one that offered individual rights for all.

Frank's visit left a mark, giving encouragement to many in Austria inclined to the Nazi approach. A year later, Dollfuss was dead, assassinated by a group of Nazi sympathizers, led by thirty-three-year-old

Otto von Wächter, Lauterpacht's classmate at the University of Vienna, who fled to Germany.

90

Nineteen thirty-five was a good year for Frank. He bought a large country house in Bavaria (the Schoberhof, near Schliersee), which I visited eighty years later, shortly before it was torn down, Frank's crest and initials still visible in his office under the rafters. He assisted in the preparation of the Nuremberg decrees, anti-Semitic laws that stripped Jews of citizenship rights and banned extramarital intercourse between Germans and Jews. In August, he presided over a joint meeting of the Akademie für Deutsches Recht (the Academy for German Law, which he had founded a couple of years earlier) and the eleventh International Penal and Penitentiary Congress, held at the Kroll Opera House (which served as the Reichstag after the fire).

Frank had founded the academy to offer an intellectual and ideological vision for German lawyers. As president, he delivered the keynote address to the congress, choosing 'international penal policy' as his subject, an opportunity to set out some thoughts on the future direction of the criminal law. He offered a riposte to Lemkin and his ilk, those who pushed for a new list of international crimes and an international criminal court. A fine orator, Frank captivated the crowd, even if (like the Führer) he spoke with a curiously high pitch, a product of excitement, intensity and power.

Frank's speech focused on issues of keen interest to Lauterpacht and Lemkin, although neither was in the audience. Vespasian Pella, the Romanian professor who wrote on barbarity and vandalism, was present. Judge Emil Rappaport, Lemkin's mentor and a member of the congress's organizing committee, failed to show. Frank expressed strong objections to universal jurisdiction, an idea he opposed on the grounds it would destroy international criminal law, not strengthen it. No laws or international organizations would resolve the differences between Bolshevism and National Socialism, and there would be no common policies for states that didn't share 'the same moral principles'. He attacked the ideas of Professor Henri Donnedieu de Vabres, another of Lemkin's colleagues, singled out by name, although not in attendance. A few weeks earlier, Frank had invited Donnedieu to address the academy on the subject of international crimes and 'aggressive war'.

Frank brushed aside Donnedieu's ideas, because they would require the creation of a superstate. What about the Frenchman's proposal for 'an international court of criminal justice'? A myth. World law? 'An idle dream.' Expand the list of international crimes? Never. One idea that Frank did like, however, was to criminalize the global Jewish boycott against Germany.

What did Frank want? 'Non-interference in the internal affairs of foreign states' was a fine idea supported by Frank to cover any criticism of Germany. So were independent judges, but only up to a point. He wanted strong government based on values that protected the vision of 'national community', a legal system that was informed by the 'idea of community', which should prevail over all else. There would be no individual rights in the new Germany, so he announced a total opposition to the 'individualistic, liberalistic atomizing tendencies of the egoism of the individual' ('Complete equality, absolute submission, absolute loss of individuality,' the writer Friedrich Reck recorded in his diary, citing Dostoevesky's *The Possessed* as reflecting ideas of the kind expressed by Frank).

Frank listed all the positive developments since 1933, including Hitler's new approach to criminal policy, one from which the world should learn. Innovations included 'eugenic prophylactics', the 'castration of dangerous moral criminals' and the 'preventive detention' of anyone who threatened the nation or 'national community'. Those who should not have children would be sterilized (he described this as a 'natural process of elimination'), undesirables deported, new racial laws adopted to prevent 'the mixing of absolutely incompatible races'. To this international audience he made no explicit mention of the Jews or the gypsies, but those present knew of whom he spoke. He was silent too about the scourge of homosexuality, a subject addressed earlier in the year by the *Reich* penal code (which he helped draft), which criminalized all homosexual acts. The new Germany would be 'racially intact', he declared, allowing Germany to 'get rid of the criminal as a healthy body gets rid of the germs of disease'. The images had been lifted from the writings of Julius Streicher, publisher of the anti-Semitic newspaper *Der Stürmer*, with whom he and Donnedieu had dined in February.

It was easy to imagine his voice at its highest pitch. 'National Socialism has abandoned the false principle of humanity,' he shrilly proclaimed, against all 'excessively humane' behaviour. Suitable punishments were on their way, to be handed down to expiate violations of the duty of loyalty to community. The Nazis were waging a 'war on crime for all time'.

Audience reaction was mixed. The majority of the 463 delegates present were Germans, who cheered loudly. Others were less supportive. Geoffrey Bing, a young English barrister who later became a Labour MP (and the first attorney general of independent Ghana), wrote an account expressing horror at the sight of foreign officials, criminologists and reformers who cheered Frank's 'monstrous proposals'. Bing gave a clear warning: be aware of the new breed of lawyers taking over Germany, men like Dr Frank, 'a fanatical exponent of the principle of reprisal and intimidation'.

91

Four years later, as Germany marched into Poland and divided the country with the Soviet Union, Frank was summoned to Silesia for a personal meeting with Hitler. Following the audience, Frank was appointed governor-general of German-occupied Poland, the Führer's personal representative in an area known as the General Government for the Occupied Polish Territories, a population of 11.5 million people in a territory that encompassed Warsaw in the north and Kraków in the west. He took up the post on 25 October 1939: Hitler's decree stated that Frank reported personally to the Führer – a point noted by Lemkin – and ordered that the entire administration 'be directed by the Governor General'. Frank was now personally in charge; his wife, Brigitte, became queen.

In an early interview, Frank explained that Poland was now a 'colony', its inhabitants the 'slaves of the Greater German World Empire' (lawyers in Berlin sought to ensure that the international laws that governed occupied territories did not apply – the General Government was effectively treated as an annexed part of the *Reich*, so German law applied, supposedly unconstrained by international law). In a singular humiliation for Poland, Frank installed himself and his government at the Wawel Castle in Kraków, the former home of Polish kings. Brigitte and their five children would later spend time with him there, including the youngest, Niklas, born a few months earlier in Munich. Otto von Wächter, fresh from Vienna, was appointed governor of Kraków, one of Frank's five deputies.

Frank acted like a sovereign, the Polish people being told they were fully subject to his power: this was not a 'constitutional state' in which people had rights, and there was to be no protection for minority groups. Warsaw was badly damaged in the short war, but Frank decided not to rebuild. Instead he signed a raft of decrees, many of which would make their way into the luggage that Lemkin would cart around the world. Frank's writ covered a large territory and many subjects, from wildlife (protected) to Jews (not protected). From 1 December, all Jews more than twelve years old were required to wear a white stripe at least ten centimetres wide on the right sleeve, with a blue Star of David on it, on indoor and outdoor clothing. To save public funds, the Jews were required to produce their own armbands.

From the start of his reign, Frank kept a daily diary (*Diensttagebuch*), a record of activity and accomplishment. By the time he left Kraków, there were at least thirty-eight incriminating volumes that had been preserved, eleven thousand foolscap pages of daily entries typed up by two male secretaries. The earliest entries reflected the sense of permanence that characterized the regime's actions, noting that the territory would be a place to give effect to Himmler's desire that 'all Jews be evacuated from the newly gained Reich territories'. Poles would be treated with brutality: concerned that they might wish to celebrate the country's independence, on 11 November Frank passed a decree to prohibit the display of any celebratory poster, with the penalty of death for any breach. Frank assumed total control over life and death and intended to exercise it, putting into effect ideas expressed at the 1935 Berlin Congress: in his General Government, the 'community of the people' would be the only legal standard, so individuals would be subjugated to the will of the sovereign, the führer.

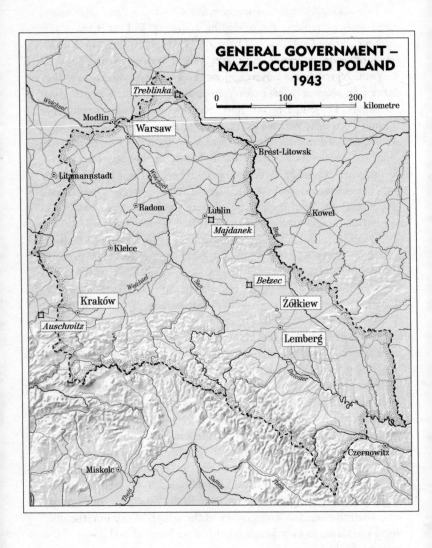

GENERAL GOVERNMENT –
NAZI-OCCUPIED POLAND
1943

0   100   200
kilometre

Treblinka

Modlin

Warsaw

Brest-Litowsk

Weichsel

Litzmannstadt

Radom

Lublin

Kowel

Majdanek

Weichsel

Klelce

San

Bug

Belzec

Żółkiew

Kraków

Weichsel

Lemberg

Auschvitz

Dniester

Miskolc

Czernowitz

Theis

Samos

Theis

92

In October 1940, Frank travelled to Berlin to dine with Hitler in his private apartment and to discuss the future of his territory. The other guests were Baldur von Schirach, the new *Reich* governor of Vienna, and Martin Bormann, Hitler's private secretary. Frank offered a personal account of progress in the General Government. Bormann's note of the meeting recorded the early successes: 'Reich Minister Dr Frank informed the Führer that the activities in the Government General could be termed very successful. The Jews in Warsaw and other cities were now locked up in the ghettos and Kraków would very shortly be cleared of them.'

Frank's efforts were celebrated. What about the Jews – like Rita and Malke – who remained in Germany or Austria? The four men discussed Frank's role and that of his government, in particular the welcome offer of assistance for 'transportations' of these Jews towards the east. Frank initially raised concerns but quickly capitulated:

> Reichsleiter Von Schirach, who had taken his seat at the Führer's other side, remarked that he still had more than 50,000 Jews in Vienna whom Dr Frank would have to take over. Party Member Dr Frank said this was impossible. Gauleiter Koch then pointed out that he, too, had up to now not transferred either Poles or Jews from the District of Ziechenau, but that these Jews and Poles would now, of course, have to be accepted by the Government General.

Frank was overruled. The decision was taken to transfer the Viennese Jews into his territory. Frank returned to Kraków knowing that his population was about to gain a large influx of new inhabitants. He would do what he was told.

93

Frank's territory soon expanded. Following Hitler's attack on the Soviets in June 1941 with Operation Barbarossa, the German army

overran the Soviet-controlled territory of Poland (and the former
Austro-Hungarian province of Galicia), which was incorporated
into the General Government on 1 August. Frank took control of
Lemberg, which became the capital of Distrikt Galizien, with its
own governor, Karl Lasch. Frank had used his powers to save a few
intellectuals from detention in Kraków, but not Professor Longchamps de Berier in Lemberg, teacher of Lauterpacht and Lemkin.
For him, there was no mercy.

The expansion brought new challenges. The easy success of the
Wehrmacht, marching eastward into lands that were rich with
Jews, gave Frank control over more than 2.5 million Jews across the
General Government. The numbers were even greater – 3.5 million
– if Jewish 'mixtures' were included. Frank worked on their future
with Himmler, and even if the two men didn't always see eye to eye,
Frank, who was keen to accommodate, ultimately chose not to cause
difficulties. Himmler decided, and Frank followed.

In December, Frank informed a cabinet meeting at the Wawel
Castle about a conference to be held in Berlin on the future of the
Jews. Held at Wannsee under the direction of SS-Obergruppenführer
Reinhard Heydrich, it would inaugurate a 'great Jewish migration'.
State Secretary Dr Josef Bühler would attend as his representative,
he told the cabinet, warning colleagues to eliminate 'all feeling of
pity' and leaving no doubt as to the meaning of the term 'migration'.
'We must annihilate the Jews, wherever we find them and wherever
it is possible,' he explained, to maintain the structure of the *Reich*.
Reading this diary entry, so faithfully entered, I wondered whether
his secretaries ever questioned the wisdom of committing such pro-
nouncements to writing.

The Wannsee Conference met in January 1942, as Lauterpacht
dined with Robert Jackson at the Waldorf Astoria in New York and
as Lemkin pored over Frank's decrees in a small university office in
Durham, North Carolina. The conference minutes were taken by
Adolf Eichmann, recording an agreement 'to purge German living
space of Jews by legal means', a technique referred to as 'forced
emigration'. A list of Jews was prepared, eleven million in total,
20 per cent of whom were under Frank's control. 'Europe will be
combed through from West to East,' Bühler told Frank on his return
from Berlin. The 'evacuated Jews' from Austria – a mere 43,700 remained – would be taken to 'transit ghettos', then transported east

to the territory of Frank's General Government. The elderly living in Austria or Germany would first be sent to an old people's ghetto in Theresienstadt. My great-grandmothers Malke Buchholz and Rosa Landes were among them.

Keen to play a useful role, Frank communicated his enthusiasm to Bühler, who expressed his leader's support to Heydrich and the others present at Wannsee. The General Government would be absolutely delighted, Bühler told the conference, 'if the final solution of this question would begin in the *General-Gouvernement*'. The territory offered numerous advantages, with good transport and plenty of labour, so the removal of the Jews could be implemented 'speedily'. The administrative agencies of the General Government would provide all necessary assistance, Bühler said, ending his Wannsee presentation with a request.

Roughly translated, Eichmann's minute recorded the unambiguous offer: please allow the Jewish question to be resolved as quickly as possible, and allow us the honour to begin.

94

Bühler returned to Kraków, reporting to Frank that the offer of full assistance from the General Government had been accepted with keen gratitude. This coincided with the arrival in Kraków of the Italian journalist Curzio Malaparte, sent by the newspaper *Corriere della Sera* to interview Frank. With a soft spot for Italy and Mussolini (a personal friend), Frank was delighted to receive Malaparte at the Wawel, offering a private dinner to which senior officials were invited, with their wives. Among the guests was Otto von Wächter, the governor of Kraków, and Josef Bühler, recently returned from the Wannsee Conference.

Malaparte was impressed by the detail, the tight-fitting grey uniforms, red armlets and swastikas. A host with fine wines, Frank sat at the head of the table on a high, stiff-backed chair, close to Bühler. Malaparte noticed Frank's black glossy hair and high ivory-white forehead, the prominent eyes with their thick, heavy eyelids, and Bühler's flushed cheeks, perspiring temples, eyes that glistened with deference to Frank. Each time Frank asked a question, Bühler was the first with an answer, shouting and fawning. '*Ja, ja!*'

Frank (centre) hosts a dinner party at the Wawel Castle, undated

Did Malaparte know that Bühler had recently returned from the Wannsee Conference in Berlin? Did Bühler talk of Heydrich, of the measures agreed on, of the 'total solution of the Jewish question in Europe'? The Italian didn't report on such matters in the article he filed with *Corriere della Sera,* which was published on 22 March 1942. He said little about the Jews – a passing reference to the confiscation of property, which caused difficulties – but did shower adulation on Frank. 'He is a man of great stature, strong, agile,' the Italian wrote, 'with a subtle mouth, a slim and aquiline nose, large eyes, an ample forehead, illuminated by a premature baldness.'

Frank, who spoke fluent Italian, would have been pleased with such a description of him, a leader 'sitting on the throne of the Jagellions and Sobieski'. A revival of the great Polish tradition of royalty and chivalry was under way.

'My one ambition,' Frank was quoted as saying, 'is to elevate the Polish people to the honour of European civilization.' After dinner, they retired to Frank's private apartment. Sprawled across deep Viennese settees and large armchairs upholstered in soft leather, the men talked, smoked, drank. Two valets dressed in blue livery moved around the room, offering coffee, liqueurs and sweets. The opulence was great: green-and-gold-lacquered Venetian tables laden with bottles of old French brandy, boxes of Havana cigars, silver trays heaped with candied fruit, the celebrated Wedel chocolates.

Frank invited Malaparte to his private study, with its rare double loggias: one on the outside, overlooking the city, the other internal, facing the castle's laddered Renaissance courtyard. At the centre of the study was a vast mahogany table, bare and polished in the candlelight, long gone by the time I visited the room seven decades later.

'Here I think about Poland's future,' Frank told Malaparte.

The two men walked onto the external loggia, to admire the city that lay below.

'This is the German Burg,' Frank explained, pointing a raised arm to a shadow of the Wawel, sharply cut into the blinding reflection of the snow. Malaparte reported the sound of barking dogs, a troop that guarded Marshal Piłsudski in his tomb, deep below the castle.

That night was bitterly cold, so much so that tears came to Malaparte's eyes. They returned to the study and were joined by Frau Brigitte Frank. She came to the Italian and put her hand on his arm gently. 'Come with me,' she said. 'I want to reveal his secret to you.' They passed through a door at one end of the study, entering a small room with bare, whitewashed walls. His own 'Eagle's Nest', Brigitte announced, a place of reflection and decision, empty save for a Pleyel piano and a wooden music stool.

Frau Frank opened the piano and stroked the keyboard. Malaparte noticed the fat fingers that so disgusted her husband.

'Before taking a crucial decision, or when he is very weary or depressed, sometimes in the very midst of an important meeting,' she told the Italian, 'he shuts himself up in this cell, sits before the piano and seeks rest or inspiration from Schumann, Brahms, Chopin or Beethoven.'

Malaparte was silent. 'He is an extraordinary man, isn't he?' Frau Frank whispered, a look of pride and affection crossing her harsh, greedy, adoring face. 'He is an artist, a great artist, with a pure and delicate soul,' she added. 'Only such an artist as he can rule over Poland.'

Frank didn't perform that evening in Kraków. A few days later, Malaparte was able to listen to him perform in Warsaw, when the governor-general visited the city to meet Himmler to discuss set-backs on the Russian front and changes of personnel on his territory. Himmler and Frank agreed that Otto von Wächter, the governor of Kraków, would move to Lemberg, 180 miles to the south, to be governor of Distrikt Galizien. He would replace Karl Lasch, accused of corruption, rumoured to be having an affair with Frau Frank, and said by some to be the father of the infant Niklas Frank.

95

In our first meeting, Niklas Frank and I sat on the terrace of the Hotel Jacob on the outskirts of Hamburg, overlooking the river Elbe. It was early spring, and after a full day of hearings in court – Hamburg was home to the International Tribunal for the Law of the Sea – we were under the canopy of a sweet-smelling tree, with a bottle of Riesling and a generous plate of German cheeses.

Niklas was seventy-three, with a bearded, vulnerable face, recognizable from the childhood photographs. He had the air of an academic, kindly, gentle but also steely, with his own temperament and agenda. Niklas was three when Malaparte visited the Wawel in the spring of 1942, so he didn't remember the Italian but knew what he wrote of his father. I learned this from the book Niklas wrote in the 1980s, the catalyst for our meeting. For many years a journalist with *Stern* magazine, in 1987 he published *Der Vater* (The Father), an unforgiving, merciless attack on his father, a work that broke a taboo that directed the children of senior Nazis to honour their parents (and not spill too many beans). An abridged version was published in English with the title *In the Shadow of the Reich,* although Niklas told me he was unhappy with the translation and certain sections that were left out. I found a copy on the Web – ten pence, plus postage – and read it over a weekend. Later I located the translator – Arthur Wensinger, Professor Emeritus of German Language and Literature at Wesleyan University – who introduced me to Niklas. In yet another odd coincidence, it turned out that Niklas Frank's translator had spent the war years at Phillips Academy in Andover, where he was a classmate of Eli Lauterpacht.

Niklas and I met a few weeks later in Hamburg. I liked him from the outset, a generous man with a good sense of humour and a sharp tongue. He spoke of a childhood in Kraków and Warsaw, of life at the Wawel Castle, of the challenges of having had a father like Hans Frank. When, as a journalist in the early 1990s, he travelled to Warsaw to interview Lech Walesa, newly elected as president of Poland, they met at the Belvedere Palace, in the same room where Malaparte had watched Frank play the piano.

Niklas Frank with parents, the Wawel, 1941

'I remembered running around the table, my father on the opposite side. My only wish was to be embraced by him. I was crying, because he kept on calling me *fremdi*' – stranger – 'as though I was not a member of the family. "You don't belong to this family," my father told me, and I wept.' I must have looked puzzled, so Niklas offered an explanation.

'Only later did I learn that my father believed I was not his son but the son of his best friend, Karl Lasch, the governor of Galicia; he was, for a short time, my mother's lover.' Niklas eventually learned what had happened from his mother's letters and diaries. 'She was a true writer,' he explained, 'always writing down conversations, including the one she had with my father when Lasch was shot.'

(Accused of corruption, Lasch was removed from his position as governor of Galicia in the spring of 1942, to be succeeded by Otto von Wächter, and was executed or committed suicide.)

In fact, Brigitte Frank's letters made clear that Frank was Niklas's father. Years later, the truth was confirmed when Niklas visited Helene Winter (née Kraffczyk), who was Frank's personal secretary in the Wawel years. 'As I approached her house, I noticed a tiny movement of the curtain. Later I asked, "Frau Winter, do I look like Mr Lasch?"' Frau Winter's face turned pale. It was true; she wondered whether he would resemble Frank or Lasch, relieved that the likeness was to Frank.

'She loved my father; she was in love with him.' Niklas paused, then said with a blunt finality that I had come to enjoy, 'She was his last mistress, a very nice woman.'

Niklas's feelings towards his father and members of his family had not warmed over the years. Frank's sister Lily traded off the family connections. 'She liked to go to the Płaszów concentration camp,' Niklas explained, close to Kraków, where they lived. 'After the Kraków ghetto was demolished, thousands of the Jews went to Auschwitz, others to Płaszów. Our aunt Lily went to them at Płaszów and said, "I am the sister of the governor-general; if you have some precious thing to give me, maybe I can save your life."' How did he know? I asked. 'My mother's letters,' he replied.

Niklas said that Brigitte Frank had good relations with Jews until 1933. Even after the Nazis took over, she continued to trade with them, buying and selling furs and baubles of the kind that her new status required. 'The first months after they took power she was still dealing with the Jews.' This upset his father. 'You can't do this,' he would say. 'I am minister of justice and you are dealing with Jews, and I will throw them all out.'

What of his relationship with his father? Niklas recalled but a single moment of affection, which occurred at the Wawel Castle, in his father's bathroom, near the sunken bath.

'I was standing beside him; he was shaving. Suddenly he put some foam on my nose.' Niklas said this wistfully. 'It was the only private, *intime* moment I remember.'

Later Niklas and I visited the Wawel Castle, toured Frank's private apartments, the family rooms, the bathroom. We stood before the mirror as Niklas showed me how his father bent over towards him, putting a spot of shaving foam on the tip of his nose.

'It hasn't changed,' Niklas says, admiring the sunken bath next to his father's bedroom. Above the door, carved into the sixteenth-century stone lintel, we read the words inscribed into the stone, *tendit in ardua virtus*. 'Courage in hard times.'

96

Malaparte had another dinner with Frank, this time in Warsaw at the Brühl Palace, which he'd previously visited in 1919, when the new Polish premier, Ignacy Paderewski, performed Chopin preludes. Now Malaparte sat on a sofa in one of the palace's private rooms, recalling Paderewski's ghostly face, bathed in tears. What a difference a quarter of a century made! Frank now played, seated at a piano, face bowed, forehead pale and damp with sweat. Malaparte observed the expression of suffering on the governor-general's 'proud' features, heard his laboured breath, saw him bite his lip. Frank's eyes were closed, eyelids trembling with emotion. 'A sick man,' Malaparte thought. On this occasion the pure, seditious notes of a Chopin prelude flowed from the hands of the German. Malaparte claimed to feel a sense of shame, of rebellion.

This account did not appear in the articles Malaparte wrote for *Corriere della Sera* in 1942. Rather, it was taken from his novel *Kaputt*, published in 1944, by which time Frank's fortunes had turned. In this version, which might or might not have been accurate, Malaparte observed Frau Brigitte Frank seated close to her husband, a ball of knitting wool in her lap.

'Oh, he plays like an angel!' the queen of Poland whispered.

The music ceased; Frank came over to them. Brigitte tossed away the ball of wool and made for her husband's side, took his hand and kissed it. Malaparte expected Frau Brigitte to kneel in worship, but instead she raised Frank's hands and turned towards the guests.

'Look!' she said in triumph. 'Look at the way the hands of angels are made!'

Malaparte saw Frank's hands, small, delicate and white, quite unlike his wife's.

'I was surprised and relieved not to see a single drop of blood on them,' he wrote in the pages of the novel, at a time when it was safe to put such thoughts on paper.

At the Belvedere Palace, Frank's Warsaw home, Malaparte attended a lunch in honour of Max Schmeling, the German boxer who knocked out Joe Louis in the twelfth round of their June 1936 fight in Yankee Stadium. Frank wanted to get things off his chest.

'*Mein lieber* Malaparte,' Malaparte's novel reported Frank as stating, 'the German people are the victim of an abominable slander. We are not a race of murderers . . . Your duty, as an honest and impartial man, is to tell the truth. You will be able to say with a clear conscience that the Germans in Poland are a great, peaceful and active family . . . That's what Poland is – an honest German home.'

What of the Jews? Malaparte asked.

'Just think!' exclaimed Ludwig Fischer, the governor of Warsaw. 'More than one and a half million Jews are now living in the same space where three hundred thousand people lived before the war.'

'Jews like to live like that,' Frank's press chief, Emil Gassner, exclaimed, laughing.

'We cannot force them to live differently,' Frank explained.

'It would be contrary to the Law of Nations,' Malaparte suggested, with a smile.

Frank recognized that the space in Warsaw where the Jews were housed might be a little confined, yet the 'filth' in which they lived was a natural habitat.

'It's sad that they die like rats,' he added, realizing such words were apt to be misunderstood. He clarified that that was 'merely a statement of fact'.

The conversation turned to the subject of children.

'What is the children's death rate in the Warsaw ghetto?' Governor Fischer was asked.

'Fifty-four per cent,' Frank interrupted, with notable precision. The Jews were degenerates; they didn't know how to care for children, not like the Germans. Still, a bad impression existed outside Poland, and it needed to be addressed.

'If one believed British and American newspapers, the Germans would appear to do nothing else in Poland but kill Jews from morning till night,' he continued. 'In spite of this, you have been in Poland for over a month, and you cannot say that you have seen a single hair pulled out of a Jewish head.'

Malaparte did not record a response as Frank raised a Bohemian crystal glass of deep-red *Türkischblut*.

'You may drink without fear, my dear Malaparte, this is not Jewish blood. *Prosit!*'

Talk turned to the nearby Warsaw ghetto.

'Inside the ghettos they enjoy the most complete freedom,' Frank explained. 'I persecute no one.'

Nor did he kill anyone.

'To kill Jews is not the German method.' Such actions would be a waste of time and strength. 'We deport them to Poland and shut them up in ghettos. There they are free to do what they like. Within the Polish ghettos, they live as in a free republic.'

Then Frank had an idea.

'Have you been to see the ghetto, my dear Malaparte?'

97

I bought a copy of the first edition of *Kaputt* in Italian, which made clear that the English translation followed the original text, where Malaparte offered a full account of his visit to the Warsaw ghetto. Although I had come to learn that the words of Curzio Malaparte were not to be taken at face value, the account of the outing is worth recounting. Malaparte records his departure from the Belvedere Palace, sitting in the first car with Frau Wächter and Governor-General Frank, followed by a second car occupied by Frau Frank and Max Schmeling, with other guests in two more cars. At the entrance to the 'Forbidden City', in front of a gate in the red-brick wall the Germans had built around the ghetto, the cars stopped and they all got out.

'See this wall?' said Frank to me. 'Does it look to you like the terrible concrete wall bristling with machine guns that the British and American papers write about?' And he added, smiling, 'The wretched Jews all have weak chests. At any rate this wall protects them against the wind' . . .

'And still,' said Frank laughing, 'although leaving the ghetto is punishable by death, the Jews go in and out as they please.'

'Over the wall?'

'Oh, no,' replied Frank, 'they go out through rat holes that they dig by night under the wall and that they cover up by day with a little earth and leaves. They crawl through those holes and go into the city to purchase food and clothing. The black market in the ghetto is carried on mainly through such holes. From time to time one of the rats is caught in a trap; they are children not over eight or nine years old. They risk their lives in a true sporting spirit, that is cricket too, *nicht wahr*?'

'They risk their lives?' I shouted.

'Basically,' replied Frank, 'they risk nothing else.'

'And you call that cricket?'

'Certainly. Every game has its set of rules.'

'In Cracow,' said Frau Wächter, 'my husband has built a wall of an Eastern design with elegant curves and graceful battlements. The Cracow Jews certainly have nothing to complain about. An elegant wall in the Jewish style.'

They all laughed as they stamped their feet on the frozen snow.

'*Ruhe* – Silence!' called a soldier who was kneeling concealed behind a mound of snow a few feet away from us with his rifle against his shoulder. Another soldier, kneeling behind him, peered over the shoulder of his companion who suddenly fired. The bullet hit the wall just at the edge of a hole. 'Missed!' remarked the soldier gaily, slipping another cartridge into the barrel.

Frank walked over to the two soldiers and asked them what they were firing at.

'At a rat,' they replied, laughing loudly.

'At a rat? *Ach, so!*' said Frank, kneeling and looking over the men's shoulders.

We also came closer, and the ladies laughed and squealed lifting their skirts up to the knees as women do when they hear anything about mice.

'Where is it? Where is the rat?' asked Frau Brigitte Frank.

'It is in the trap,' said Frank laughing.

'*Achtung!* Look out!' said the soldier, aiming. A black tuft of tangled hair popped out of the hole dug under the wall; then two hands appeared and rested on the snow.

It was a child.

Another shot and again the bullet missed its mark by a few inches. The child's head disappeared.

'Hand me the rifle,' said Frank in an impatient voice. 'You don't know how to handle it.' He grabbed the rifle out of the soldier's hand and took aim. It snowed silently.

This was a ghetto visit as social occasion, accompanied by wives and friends and maybe children. I thought of Sasha Krawec, the young man who spent six months hidden in Elsie Tilney's room in Vittel, one of Frank's escaped rats. I asked Niklas about Malaparte's account, the supposed visit to the Warsaw ghetto. Could Frank have taken a gun and aimed it at a Jew?

His mother did read *Kaputt*. 'I have this memory of her on the sofa, very angry about Malaparte's book. He wrote that my father had very long fingers; they were really long. Or was he writing about my mother's fingers?'

'Your father's fingers,' I said. Malaparte described Brigitte's fingers as fat. Niklas nodded, then smiled his toothy smile. 'My mother was agitated, moving around, really upset. "It's not true," she said, "lies, nothing but lies."'

Did the visit to the ghetto take place?

'We all visited the ghettos,' Niklas said quietly. He remembered a visit, maybe to the Kraków ghetto, the one built by Wächter. 'My brother Norman visited the Warsaw ghetto, my sister Sigrid visited the Kraków ghetto. I visited the Kraków ghetto with my mother.' Later he shared with me a copy of clippings from a home movie kept by his father, with the title 'Kraków'. Interspersed into the family scenes and images of Frank at work were a few moments in the ghetto. In one short scene, the camera lingers on a girl in a red dress.

Looking straight into the camera, she smiles, a beautiful long, hopeful smile that has remained with me. So did the red dress, an image picked up by the director Steven Spielberg in the film *Schindler's List*. Same ghetto, same dress, fiction, fact. Could Spielberg have seen this film, which Niklas told me was not in the public domain, or was it just another coincidence?

I asked Niklas whether his father and Malaparte might have visited the Warsaw ghetto together.

'It could be,' Niklas said. 'I don't believe that he personally killed any Jews, and my mother certainly didn't believe that.'

Yet within the family a difference emerged on this important matter. Niklas's older brother Norman, now dead, had a different recollection.

'Norman visited the ghetto with Schamper,' Niklas added, referring to his father's chauffeur. 'He told me he could imagine that our father took a gun from a soldier.'

Girl in red dress

98

By the summer of 1942, Frank had enemies in high places and needed to be on his guard. In June and July, he delivered four big speeches on legal matters, the rule of law and its importance. Directed against Himmler, who was by now actively engaged in leading the plans to exterminate the Jews and with whom he was in open conflict on the exercise of power on occupied Polish territory, he stressed the need for a legal system that recognized a rule of law, with proper courts and independent judges. Speaking at the great universities in Berlin, Vienna, Heidelberg and Munich, he was responding to pressure from senior judges, concerned that justice in the *Reich* was being undermined. Frank wanted a *Reich* under the law.

'The legal mind will always recognize that war takes precedence over everything else,' he told the audience in Berlin on 9 June. Nevertheless, even in times of war there must be legal security, because people needed a 'sense of justice'. There was a striking absence of irony, given the actions he was overseeing in Poland. He had his own ideas about justice, organized around two distinct themes, 'authoritarian governance' on the one hand, and 'judicial independence' on the other. The law must be authoritarian, but it had to be applied by independent judges.

The four speeches were not well received by Himmler, who complained to Hitler. Perhaps Frank should have been more judicious in his choice of words. A strong reaction against the speeches was not long in coming. First he was questioned by the Gestapo, then, on a visit to the Schoberhof, he learned that he was stripped of all his roles, bar one.

'Brigitte, the Führer has left me the Government General,' he told his wife. Frau Frank was relieved he kept his position, according to Niklas.

If Frank had real concerns about the direction of the *Reich,* which Niklas doubted, they were as nothing compared with the other problem in his life. Politics took second place to matters of the heart: Lilly Grau re-emerged unexpectedly from the past, the childhood sweetheart he had wanted to marry. She arrived in the form of a letter, telling Frank that her only son was missing on the Russian Front. Could he help? The request provoked a strong reaction and an overwhelming desire. He visited Lilly at her home in Bad Aibling in Bavaria, the first time they'd seen each other in nearly two decades. 'Immediately we burst into uncontrollable flame,' he recorded in his diary. 'We were reunited once more, so passionately that now there is no turning back.' A week later they met in Munich, Frank managing to escape from Kraków for long enough to give her a day and a night of personal attention. 'A solemn and transfigured reunion of two human beings who ignited one another and whom nothing could restrain for long,' he wrote. The passage made me laugh out loud when I first read it.

Frank decided to extricate himself from a loveless marriage with Brigitte to be with Lilly. A week after the Munich conflagration, he concocted the most original and terrible of plans to free himself from Brigitte, invoking the decisions taken at the Wannsee Conference to get himself a divorce. As Malke Buchholz prepared to be transported to Treblinka, as the Lauterpachts were rounded up in Lemberg and the Lemkins herded out of the Wołkowysk ghetto, Hans Frank invoked matters of that kind to tell his wife that he was deeply implicated in criminal actions – 'the most gruesome things' – and that she should distance herself from him to protect herself. He gave her the details of a matter that was secret and terrible, to be known as the Final Solution. The horror offered a path to personal happiness, a way out of daily life with an overbearing, greedy wife. To save herself from association with the governor-general, he was willing to offer her 'the greatest sacrifice', a divorce, so she could avoid being tainted by the Final Solution. Mass extermination offered a path to Lilly and happiness.

Brigitte Frank did not take the bait, any more than Hitler or Himmler were willing to accept the ideas Frank had set out in his four speeches. The queen of Poland enjoyed an opulent lifestyle of castles and guards, and she wasn't about to throw it away. She preferred to take the risk, pay the price, hang on. 'I prefer to be the widow of a Reichsminister than a divorced wife!' she told friends. Niklas shared the details, set out in black and white in her diary. Hans has told me the 'most gruesome things', Brigitte wrote, matters not to be talked about openly. One day she might share them, 'details later but only in private'.

A few days later, Frank changed direction. He summoned Brigitte into the music room at the Wawel Castle to tell her that Karl Lasch had shot himself. She was surprised by her husband's reaction. 'He declares that the divorce is now no longer necessary,' she recorded. The evening was 'harmonious', the change of direction 'totally incomprehensible'.

The roller-coaster summer wasn't over. Two weeks later, Frank again asked to end the relationship, blaming Brigitte for his unhappiness. 'Someone had told him I was not a good National Socialist,' she wrote, 'and he made it look as if they had advised him to get divorced.'

The next day all was fine again. Frank bought her an item of jewellery, a talisman to compensate for the suffering he'd caused. But within a month he had changed direction again, renewing the demand for an immediate divorce.

'There is nothing physical left between us,' he told Brigitte. His needs were being taken care of by Lilly (and apparently also by another lady, named Gertrud).

Brigitte maintained an admirable composure through this difficult period, perhaps because her control over Frank was total. According to Niklas, she wrote to Hitler, begging him to intercede to prevent a divorce. She sent the Führer a photograph of the happy family, a matriarch protective of her three sons and two daughters, a true and model Nazi family.

The photograph must have helped. Hitler intervened to forbid Frank to divorce. Brigitte Frank had quite a hold over her husband. 'My father loved the Führer more than he loved his family,' Niklas said to me on another occasion.

99

This was the personal turmoil that engulfed Frank as he travelled to Lemberg in the summer of 1942. He controlled the territory of Galicia but not his wife or emotions, and certainly not his physical impulses.

It was the anniversary of Lemberg's incorporation into the General Government as the capital of a newly Germanized Distrikt Galizien. He arrived on the morning of Friday, 31 July, following a three-day tour that began in Tarnopol, looped southward to Chortkiv and Zalischyky, then east to Kosiv and Yaremche. The final leg,

Photograph sent by Brigitte Frank to Adolf Hitler, 1942

a short north-easterly hop, was to the City of Lions. Frank travelled by armoured car and train, in the face of constant rumours about attacks. The *Gazeta Lwowska* reported that in his presence the faces of his new subjects 'shine with happiness' and many of his subjects voiced gratitude: children offered flowers; women passed bouquets of roses, baskets of bread, salt and fruit.

Lemberg was now firmly under German control. Frank's main task was to restore civilian rule under the firm hand of Governor Otto von Wächter, who had replaced Lasch a few weeks earlier. Frank had plans for the city, following the eviction of the Soviets. Embroiled in major policy differences with Himmler, Frank wanted to be fully involved in all the key decisions. The more oversight and responsibility he had, the more he would be recognized as leader. To this end, he applied a principle of 'unity in administration', as he had explained to party leaders in Kraków. Astride this pyramid of power, he described himself as 'fanatic'. 'The Higher SS and Police Leader is subordinated to me, the Police is a component of the Government, the SS and Police Leader in the district is subordinated to the Governor.' Frank was at the pinnacle, Wächter one stone down.

The point was simple. Within the General Government, Frank was deemed to know everything, to be responsible for all actions. He received reports on all activities, including those of the Einsatzgruppen of the Security Police and of the SD. He was copied in on all key documents. Knowing all, he was responsible for all, believing that power would last for ever without accountability.

His train pulled into the main railway station in Lemberg, from which Lauterpacht and Lemkin had departed. It was nine o'clock in the morning when he joined his colleague Otto von Wächter, governor of Galicia, tall and blond, with a military bearing, an impeccably good-looking Nazi compared with Frank. Church bells rang; a military orchestra played. The two men travelled together, from station to city centre, through streets decorated with flags of the *Reich,* past Leon's first home, past Lemkin's student accommodations, close to where Lauterpacht lived. Schoolchildren lined Opern Strasse (Operowa Street), waving little flags as Frank entered the main square in front of the opera house, now renamed Adolf-Hitler-Platz.

Lemberg Opera House, on Frank's visit, August 1942

That evening, Frank inaugurated a newly refurbished theatre, the 'sanctuary of art' that was the Skarbek Theatre. He stood proudly before an audience of dignitaries, introducing them to Beethoven and Fritz Weidlich, a little-known conductor who would fade into Austrian obscurity after the war. Frank had wanted von Karajan to conduct, or Furtwängler, a reminder of a marvellous evening in February 1937 when he attended the Philharmonic Hall in Berlin in the presence of a radiant Führer. The Berlin concert produced moments of indescribable emotion, a memory that caused him to 'shiver in the ecstasy of youth, strength, hope and gratitude', he wrote in his diary.

This evening he spoke with equal passion, standing in the middle of the orchestra. 'We, the Germans, do not go to foreign lands with opium and similar measures like the English,' he declared. 'We bring art and culture to other nations', and music that reflected the immortal nation of the German *Volk*. They made do with Weidlich, who opened with Beethoven's Leonore Overture no. 3, opus 72, followed by the Ninth Symphony, to which the Lviv Opera choir added their voices.

100

The following morning, Saturday, 1 August, Frank attended events to mark the anniversary of the incorporation of Distrikt Galizien into the General Government, held at the Opera House and in the Great Hall of the former parliament of Galicia. Seven decades later, when the university invited me to give a lecture about that ceremony, I spoke in the same room, standing before a photograph of Frank as he delivered one of his speeches, celebrating the transfer of power from military to civilian government, now under the control of Wächter.

When Frank spoke the university building was draped in red, white and black flags. To get to the Great Hall, Frank ascended the central staircase and walked to a seat at the centre of the stage. He was introduced, moved to a wooden lectern garlanded in leaves, under an eagle astride a swastika. The room was packed, the speech praised in the *Gazeta Lwowska* as announcing the return of civilization to the city. 'European rules of social order' were coming home to Lemberg. Frank thanked Governor Wächter for 'superb leadership' after two years as governor of Kraków. 'I came here to thank you and express gratitude on behalf of the Führer and the Reich,' Frank told Wächter, who sat on the raised platform, to his right.

Frank told the audience of party leaders that Hitler's anti-Semitism was justified, that Galicia was the 'primeval source of the Jewish world'. Control of Lemberg and its environs allowed him to deal with the core of the Jewish problem.

'We appreciate what the Führer has given us with his gift of the district of Galicia, and I am not talking here about its Jews,' he shouted, once more too loudly. 'Yes, we still have some of them around but will take care of that.' He was a fine orator, no doubt about that, able to keep the audience's attention.

'Incidentally,' he said, pausing for dramatic effect, addressing his words to Otto von Wächter, 'I don't seem to have any of that trash hanging around here today. What's going on? They tell me that there were thousands and thousands of those flat-footed primitives in this city once upon a time – but there hasn't been a single one to be seen since I arrived.' The audience erupted into applause. Frank had the answer to the question. The entrance to the Lemberg ghetto

Frank, Great Hall, 1 August 1942

was no more than a few hundred metres from the lectern at which he spoke. That he knew, because his administration had prepared the map 'Umsiedlung der Juden' (Resettlement of the Jews) just a year earlier, with the ghetto's seven districts, in which all the city's Jews lived. His decree meant that to set foot outside the ghetto without permission was punishable by death.

He didn't know exactly who was in that ghetto, although he knew how to whip up the audience.

'Don't tell me that you've been treating them badly?' he said. Have people finally got outraged by them? Frank told the audience that he was solving the Jewish question. No more would they be able to travel to Germany. The message was clear, his words met by 'lively applause'.

Later that evening he spent time with Frau Charlotte von Wächter, the wife of the governor. She spent a considerable part of the day with Frank, as she recorded in her diary:

> Frank came for breakfast at nine o'clock and went away
> immediately with Otto. [I] should have come but didn't. I am
> home with Miss Wickl. Afterward, I slept deeply. Very tired. At
> four o'clock . . . [I was sent] to Frank, who wanted to play chess
> again. I won two times. After that he angrily went to bed. Then
> he came back and drove away immediately.

The diary made no mention of the day's other developments, the decisions taken by her husband under the watchful eye of Governor-General Frank and soon implemented.

101

A week after Frank's visit, the great Lemberg round-up began. *Die Grosse Aktion* began early in the morning of Monday, 10 August, gathering up many of the remaining Jews in the ghetto and outside, holding them in a school playground before they were taken to the Janowska camp in the city centre. 'A lot had to be done in Lemberg,' Governor Wächter wrote to his wife on 16 August, referring in one line to the '*grosse Aktion* against the Jews' and in another to games of Ping-Pong played 'with great enthusiasm'. Heinrich

Himmler arrived in Lemberg on 17 August to confer with Governor Wächter and Odilo Globocnik, responsible for the construction of the death camp at Bełzec, fifty miles to the north-west. Over dinner at Wächter's home, conversation addressed the future of the Jews of Lemberg and surrounding areas, including Żółkiew. Within two weeks, more than fifty thousand people were on the railway line heading to Bełzec.

Among the thousands caught up in *die Grosse Aktion* was Lauterpacht's family, when his young niece Inka watched from a window as her mother was taken, a moment recalled years later, the clarity of a dress and high-heeled shoes. Lauterpacht's parents and the rest of his extended family were also taken. Most likely this was when my grandfather's Lemberg family was extinguished, among them Uncle Leibus, along with his wife and children. All that remained was a congratulatory wedding telegram sent to Leon and Rita in 1937.

As these events unfolded, the *Krakauer Zeitung* reported another speech by Frank, announcing the 'real success' of his administration. 'One now sees hardly any Jews,' Frank declared, in Lemberg or in Kraków or in any of the other cities or towns or villages or hamlets under his control.

102

Knowing my interest in Lemberg, Niklas Frank mentioned that he was acquainted with the son of Otto von Wächter, the governor of Distrikt Galizien who had been a classmate of Lauterpacht's at the University of Vienna in 1919. Horst took 'a rather different attitude to mine,' Niklas explained, on matters of paternal responsibility. Niklas added that the approach wasn't unusual, that Himmler's daughter 'never did want to speak with me after I wrote my book'.

Niklas procured an invitation from Horst von Wächter to visit him at Schloss Hagenberg, the imposing seventeenth-century castle where he lives, an hour north of Vienna. Built around an enclosed courtyard, the Baroque *Schloss* stood four storeys high, a foreboding and impenetrable stone structure that has seen better days. Horst and his wife, Jacqueline, occupied a few sparsely furnished rooms. I liked amicable, gentle Horst, a generously proportioned man in a pink shirt and sandals, bespectacled, grey hair and, judging by a photograph of his father, the same broad smile. He was engaging and friendly, captured (or maybe imprisoned?) by the faded glory of the *Schloss* bought a quarter of a century earlier with a small inheritance. Without central heating, the bitter cold of midwinter was barely kept at bay by a wood-burning fire under crumbling Baroque cornice work and the fading paint of its walls.

In one room, under the rafters that support the towering roof, Horst kept his father's library, the 'National Socialist department' of the family's history. He invited me to look around. I picked a book at random from the tightly stacked shelf. The first page contained a handwritten dedication in a small, neat German script. To SS-Gruppenführer Dr Otto Wächter, 'with my best wishes on your birthday'. The deep-blue signature, slightly smudged, was unforgiving. 'H. Himmler, 8 July 1944.'

My shock at the signature was heightened by the context: this book was a family heirloom, not a museum artefact, offered to Horst's father as a token of appreciation. For services rendered. It was a direct line between Horst's family and the Nazi leadership of Germany. (On a later visit, I picked out a copy of *Mein Kampf,* a gift from his mother to his father while they were courting. 'I didn't know that was there,' Horst said with obvious pleasure.)

In the room he used as a study, Horst had gathered a few family albums. He was equally comfortable with these pages, which held the stuff of normal family life: images of children and grandparents, ski holidays, boating trips, birthday parties. But interspersed among these unsurprising images were other photographs. August 1931, an unknown man chiselled at a swastika carved into a wall; an undated photograph of a man departing a building under a line of arms raised in Nazi salute, with the caption 'Dr Goebbels'; three men in conversation in a covered railway yard, undated, with the initials 'A. H.' I looked more closely. The man at the centre was Hitler; next to him the photographer Heinrich Hoffmann, who introduced Hitler to Eva Braun. The third man I didn't recognize. Horst said, 'It may be Baldur von Schirach; it's not my father.' I was less sure.

I turned the pages. Vienna, autumn 1938. Wächter in uniform at his desk in the Hofburg Palace, pensive, examining papers. A date was written on the page, 9 November 1938. *Kristallnacht* began a few hours later.

Another page: Poland, late 1939 or early 1940, images of burned-out buildings and refugees. At the centre of the page, a small, square photograph shows an anxious group. They might be in a ghetto. According to Malaparte's account, Wächter's wife, Charlotte, appreciated the wall of the Kraków ghetto, with its Eastern design of 'elegant curves and graceful battlements', offered to the Jews, according to Frau Wächter, as a place of comfort (the photograph turned out to have been taken in the Warsaw ghetto, near 35 Nowolipie Street, close to a small passage that led towards a marketplace).

The group includes a young boy and an old woman, dressed against the cold. A white armband draws my eye, identifying its bearer, an old lady in a headscarf, as a Jew. A few feet behind her, at the centre of the image, a boy looks directly into the camera, towards the photographer, most likely Wächter's wife, Charlotte, on a visit to the ghetto of the kind reported by Malaparte. She studied

*A. H. with Heinrich Hoffmann and unknown man, c. 1932
(from Otto von Wächter's album)*

Street scene, Warsaw ghetto, c. 1940 (from Otto von Wächter's album)

with the architect Josef Hoffmann's Wiener Werkstätte and had a good eye for a line.

The pages of these family albums held other notable images. The Wächters with Hans Frank. Wächter with his Waffen-SS Galician Division. Wächter with Himmler in Lemberg. They placed Otto von Wächter at the heart of German operations, personal mementoes of international crime committed on a great scale. Their implications were inescapable, although Horst seemed unwilling to recognize them.

Horst was born in 1939, like Niklas, with only a limited recollection of his father, who was often away. The attitude he adopted to his father, a political leader indicted for war crimes by the Polish government in exile, differed from that taken by Niklas, as he struggled to come to terms with Otto's legacy.

'I must find the good in my father,' he said in one of our first conversations. He was on a mission of rehabilitation, against the odds and the facts. Our tentative exchanges grew more comfortable. 'My father was a good man, a liberal who did his best,' Horst said, digging deep for belief. 'Others would have been worse.'

He gave me a detailed biographical record of his father, with many footnotes. I'll study it. 'Of course,' Horst said quickly, 'then you will come back.'

103

In the midst of the killing, and still worrying about his marriage, Frank found the time to implement another bright idea: he invited the famous Baedeker publishing company to produce a travel guide for the General Government to encourage visitors. In October 1942 Frank wrote a short introduction, which I read in a copy obtained from an antiquarian bookseller in Berlin. The familiar red cover of a book that contained a large pullout map showing the outer limits of Frank's territory, etched in light blue. Within that border, Lemberg was on the east, Kraków to the west, Warsaw to the north. The borders enclose the camps of Treblinka, Bełzec, Majdanek and Sobibor.

'For those coming to the *Reich* from the East,' Frank wrote in the introduction, 'the General Government is the first glimpse of a structure offering a strong impression of home.' For visitors arriving from the west, travelling out of the *Reich,* his lands offered a 'first greeting from an Eastern world'.

Karl Baedeker added a few personal words to thank Frank, the inspiration behind this happy new addition to the Baedeker collection. Preparation was overseen by Oskar Steinheil, who visited the area in the autumn of 1942, with the personal support of the governor-general. What did Herr Steinheil see but decide to leave out as he travelled around by car and rail? Baedeker hoped the book might 'convey' an impression of the tremendous work of organization and construction accomplished by Frank 'in the difficult wartime conditions of the past 3½ years'.

The visitor would benefit from great improvements, the province and cities having 'acquired a different appearance', German culture and architecture once more accessible. Maps and city plans were modernized, names Germanized, all in accordance with Frank's decrees. The reader learned that the General Government had an area of 142,000 square kilometres (37 per cent of the former Polish territory) and was home to eighteen million people (72 per cent Polish, 17 per cent Ukrainian [Ruthenian] and 0.7 per cent German). A million or more Jews had been erased ('free of Jews' was the formulation used for various towns and cities). The attentive reader might have noted the odd error, including the reference to the fact that Warsaw's population used to comprise 400,000 Jews, now disappeared.

Lemberg got eight pages (and a two-page map), Żółkiew just one, although it was a town 'worth seeing', for its Germanic seventeenth-century heritage. The Ringplatz (Ring Square) was 'characteristically German'; the Baroque Dominican church (dating to 1655) and the Roman Catholic church (rebuilt in 1677) had paintings by a German artist. German tourists would be reassured by the presence of nearby German settlements. The only place of worship in Żółkiew not mentioned in the guide was the seventeenth-century synagogue, gutted by the fire of June 1941. Nor did the guide make any mention of the Żółkiew Jews or the ghetto in which they lived when it was published. Within six months of publication, almost all of them had been murdered.

The volume offered no hint as to the uses to which the 'densely wooded' areas around Żółkiew were put or any information on the myriad concentration camps dotted around Frank's territory. The editors offered a passing mention of the connections that Bełzec's train station offers to the rest of Galicia and a fleeting reference to the small town of Auschwitz, located on Reichsstrasse No. 391, the main route which then connected Warsaw to Kraków.

104

The publication of the Baedeker guide coincided with a different kind of account, one that appeared in the *New York Times* under the headline 'Poland Indicts 10 in 400,000 Deaths'. The piece identified a group described as the 'unholy ten', leading members of the General Government indicted as war criminals by the Polish government in exile. 'German Governor is No. 1.'

This was a reference to Frank, whose crimes were said to include the execution of 200,000 Poles, the transfer of hundreds of thousands more to Germany and the creation of the ghettos. Otto von Wächter came in at No. 7, although wrongly identified as 'J. Waechter', the governor of Kraków (a position he'd left in March 1942, when he was transferred to Lemberg). Wächter's speciality was described as 'the extermination of the Polish intelligentsia'.

I sent a copy of the article to Horst von Wächter, who asked to see anything I came across that mentioned his father's activities in Poland. His first reaction was to point out the errors. The article treated all of Frank's deputy governors 'as criminals evenly', Horst complained, as did the Poles. He invited me to return to Hagenberg without Niklas, accompanied by a photographer. We talked about events in Lemberg in August 1942. One account was written by the Nazi hunter Simon Wiesenthal, who claims to have seen Wächter in the Lemberg ghetto early in 1942 and asserts that the governor was 'personally in charge' when his mother was separated from him and sent to her death on 15 August 1942. Horst was sceptical, saying that his father wasn't in Lemberg on the day in question. Later I found a photograph of Wächter with Frank at Wawel Castle, taken on 16 August, the day after Wiesenthal claimed to have seen Wächter in the Lemberg ghetto.

These events continued to have consequences, much later and at great distances. I told Horst about a judgement handed down in March 2007 by a US federal judge, stripping one John Kalymon, a resident of Michigan, of his US citizenship. The judge ruled that Kalymon was serving as a Ukrainian auxiliary policeman in August 1942, in *die Grosse Aktion*, that he was directly involved in the killing of Jews. The judgement relies on an expert report prepared by a German academic, Professor Dieter Pohl, which made a few references to Wächter. Pohl's report led me to other documents at the US Department of Justice in Washington, three of which implicated Wächter directly in the events of 1942. I showed them to Horst, as he had requested.

The first was a note of a meeting held in Lemberg in January 1942, just before Wächter arrived, titled 'Deportation of Jews from Lemberg'. It heralded a one-way trip to Bełzec and the gas chambers in March. 'If feasible, the term "resettlement" is to be avoided,' the document noted, attentive to the nuances of language and truth. Wächter must have known of their fate.

*Wawel Castle, Kraków, 16 August 1942: Frank (at the front)
and Wächter (fourth from left)*

The second document was an order of March 1942 signed by Wächter. Intended to restrict the employment of Jews throughout Galicia, it was issued two days before the first ghetto operation (15 March), taking effect the day after the transfers to Bełzec (1 April). The order severed access to the gentile world for most working Jews, a step Lemkin identified as a necessary precursor to genocide.

Damaging as these two documents are, the third was devastating. It was a short memorandum from Heinrich Himmler to Dr Wilhelm Stuckart, the *Reich* minister of the interior in Berlin. Dated 25 August, it was sent as *die Grosse Aktion* was under way. 'I recently was in Lemberg,' Himmler wrote to Stuckart, 'and had a very plain talk with the governor, SS-Brigadeführer Dr Wächter. I openly asked him whether he wants to go to Vienna, because I would have considered it a mistake, while there, not to have asked this question that I am well aware of. Wächter does not want to go to Vienna.'

A frank conversation, evoking the possibility of departure and alternative career options, a way out, a return to Vienna. Wächter declined; he chose to remain. To accept would have killed his career. He did so in full knowledge of *die Grosse Aktion*, as was made clear by a letter Horst showed me, sent by his father to his mother on 16 August. It noted that after Frau Wächter left 'a lot had to be done in Lviv ... recording the harvest, providing workers (now already 250,000 from the district!), and the current *grosse Aktion* against the Jews'.

Himmler ended his own letter of that period with an additional thought: 'It now remains to be seen how Wächter will conduct himself in the General Government as governor of Galicia, following our talk.'

Wächter must have conducted himself to Himmler's full satisfaction because he got on with the job and remained in Lemberg for two more years. As civilian leader, he had a role in *die Grosse Aktion* of August 1942.

Himmler's letter offered no ambiguity or escape. When I showed it to Horst, he stared at it, without expression. If his father stood before him now, what would he say?

'I don't really know,' Horst said. 'It's very difficult ... maybe I wouldn't ask him anything at all.'

A silence hung around the desolate room. After a while, Horst punctured it with an exonerating thought: his father was overwhelmed by the situation, its inevitability and catastrophic proportion, by the orders and their immediacy. Nothing was inevitable, I suggested to Horst, not the signature, not the oversight he exercised. Wächter could have left.

This prompted another long silence, space for the sound of snow and the crackle of burning logs. Faced with such a document, could Horst not condemn the father? Was this a father to love, or was it something else?

'I cannot say I love my father,' Horst said. 'I love my grandfather.' He looked towards the portrait of the old military man that hangs above his bed.

'I have a responsibility for my father in some way, to see what really happened, to tell the truth, and to do what I can do for him.'

He reflected out loud, 'I have to find some positive aspect.'

He had somehow constructed a distinction between his father and the system, between the individual and the group of which he was a leader.

'I know that the whole system was criminal and that he was part of it, but I don't think he was a criminal. He didn't act like a criminal.'

Could his father have walked away from Lemberg and the murderous operations his administration oversaw?

'There was no chance to leave the system,' Horst whispered. The US Justice Department documents said otherwise. Yet Horst managed to find a way to sanitize the material, able to describe it only as 'unpleasant' or 'tragic'.

It was difficult to comprehend his reaction, yet I felt sadness rather than anger. By failing to condemn, was he not perpetuating the wrongs of the father?

'No.' Friendly, warm, talkative, Horst offered nothing more, unable to condemn. It was the fault of Frank's General Government, of the SS, of Himmler. Everyone else in the group was responsible, but not Otto. Finally, he said, 'I agree with you that he was completely in the system.'

A crack.

'Indirectly, he was responsible for everything that happened in Lemberg.'

Indirectly?

Horst was silent for a long moment. His eyes moist, I wondered if he had wept.

105

Frank was proud to be identified as a war criminal by the *New York Times*. Early in 1943, he announced at an official meeting, 'I have the honour of being number one.' The words were recorded in the daily diary, without embarrassment. Even as the war turned against the Germans, he still believed the Third Reich would last a thousand years, with no need to show restraint in relation to the treatment of the Poles and the Jews or the words he had spoken of them. 'They must go,' he had told his cabinet. 'I will therefore, on principle, approach Jewish affairs in the expectation that the Jews will disappear.'

'To disappear.' The words generated applause, encouraging him to go further, because he never did know quite when to stop. They will be obliterated wherever they are found, he went on, whenever the opportunity was afforded. In this way, the unity and integrity of the *Reich* would be upheld. How exactly would his government proceed? 'We cannot shoot these three and a half million Jews; we cannot kill them with poison,' he explained. 'But we can proceed with the necessary steps that somehow or other will lead to their successful extermination.' These words too were recorded in his diary.

On 2 August, Frank hosted a reception in the grounds of the Wawel Castle. This was an opportunity for party officials to reflect on developments. There had been setbacks on the Russian Front, but good progress elsewhere. In March, the Kraków ghetto had been emptied, in a single weekend, under the efficient leadership of SS-Untersturmführer Amon Göth (later portrayed by the British actor Ralph Fiennes in the film *Schindler's List*). This was because Frank no longer wished to see it from the Wawel. In May, an uprising in the Warsaw ghetto had finally been crushed, the final act being the destruction of the Great Synagogue. This was implemented by SS-Gruppenführer Jürgen Stroop, who described the details with pride in a report prepared for Himmler. A million fewer people lived in Warsaw, causing Frank to hope the population could be reduced 'even further' if the ghetto was 'totally demolished'.

Yet the war was turning. In Italy, Mussolini had been deposed, arrested on the orders of the Italian king, and Polish intellectuals spoke increasingly openly of atrocities at the nearby camps at Auschwitz and Majdanek. Frank had hoped that the discovery of the bodies of thousands of Polish officers in mass graves at Katyn, along with members of the Polish intelligentsia murdered by the Soviets in 1940, might improve relations between the Germans and the Poles. It didn't. Polish opinion compared Katyn to 'the mass death rate in the German concentration camps', he noted with dismay, or the 'shooting of men, women and even of children and old people, during the infliction of collective punishment'.

The party at the Wawel offered a refuge. On this bright August day, Frank's diary recorded new lines of combat in crisp and clear words. 'On the one hand, the swastika, and on the other, the Jews.' He described the progress on his territory: having 'started out with 3,500,000 Jews', his territory now contained just 'a few workers' companies'. What had happened to the rest? 'All the others have, let us say, emigrated.' Frank knew his role and his responsibility. 'We are all, as it were, accomplices', he recorded with careless abandon.

His relationship with Hitler and Himmler seemed to have

improved, because the Führer offered him a new appointment, without irony, as president of an international centre for legal studies. His position as governor secure, he had work and friends, and a ceasefire had becalmed his marriage. Lilly Grau wasn't far away, and there was music, a new piece composed in his honour by Richard Strauss after he intervened to prevent the composer's driver from being conscripted to the east:

Who enters the room, so slender, so swank?
Behold our friend, our Minister Frank.

The words were available, and I searched for the score, without success. 'Disappeared,' I was told, no doubt for good reasons of reputation.

Frank appreciated the music and art with which he surrounded himself. As governor-general, he adopted a selfless policy of taking into custody important Polish art treasures, signing decrees that allowed famous works of art to be confiscated for 'protective' reasons. They became a part of Germany's artistic heritage. It was all rather straightforward. Some pieces went to Germany, like the thirty-one sketches by Albrecht Dürer, lifted from the Lubomirski collection in Lemberg and personally handed to Göring. Other pieces were held at the Wawel Castle, some in Frank's private rooms. He produced a finely bound catalogue, listing all the major works of art protectively plundered in the first six months. The catalogue revealed an extraordinary range of exquisite and valuable items: paintings by German, Italian, Dutch, French and Spanish masters; illustrated books; Indian and Persian miniatures and woodcuts; the renowned fifteenth-century Veit Stoss altarpiece installed at St Mary's Basilica in Kraków, dismantled on Frank's orders and sent to Germany; gold and silver handicrafts, antique crystal, glass and porcelain; tapestries and antique weapons; rare coins and medals. All plundered from the museums of Kraków and Warsaw, taken from cathedrals, monasteries, universities, libraries, private collections.

Frank kept some of the best for his own rooms. Not everyone shared his taste. Niklas rarely entered his father's office suite but recalled a particularly 'ugly painting', a woman with 'a bandage around her head', her hair 'smooth and perfectly combed' with a straight parting. Frank used the painting as an example to his son. 'This is how you should comb your hair,' he told Niklas of the woman who carried 'a little white animal' in her arms, the creature that resembled a rat. She petted it with one hand, looking not at the animal but into the void. 'Adopt the same parting,' Niklas was told. The picture, painted in the fifteenth century by Leonardo da Vinci, was a portrait of Cecilia Gallerani, *The Lady with an Ermine*. He last saw it in the summer of 1944.

106

Niklas told me this story as Cecilia Gallerani visited London, the centrepiece of a major Leonardo da Vinci exhibit at the National Gallery. I visited her on a grey December morning, the celebrated beauty, mistress to Ludovico Sforza, Duke of Milan, to whom she bore a son. She sat for the portrait in about 1490, the ermine a symbol of purity. In 1800, the painting joined the collection of Princess Czartoryska, in Russian-controlled Poland, hanging from 1876 at the Czartoryski Museum in Kraków. There it remained for sixty-three years (with a brief interlude in Dresden, during the First World War), until Frank purloined it. Mesmerized by the beauty and symbolism of the painting, he kept her close by for five years.

Niklas recalls the painting with dread and a smile. As a small boy, he feared the ratlike creature, objecting to his father's efforts to make him wear his hair like Cecilia. He and his brother Norman remembered it in different rooms, 'one of those little spots in my memory', like the shaving foam in the bathroom.

On my first visit to the Wawel, the curators were preparing for the return of Cecilia Gallerani. After a tour of Frank's private apartments, the photography director took me to her office to show me a large flat box, bound in faded velvet. The title on the cover was 'The Castle in Kraków', the lining a fine red crushed velvet. 'It was forgotten when the Nazis left; we found it in the basement.'

Inside, printed on a large card, was a happy message: 'To Herr Governor General Reich Minister Dr Frank, on the occasion of his birthday on 23 May 1944, offered by his Court Office with gratitude.' The words were presented with eight signatures, loyal servants who commissioned a series of fine black-and-white photographs even as the Soviets approached. They showed the splendour of the Wawel, rooms and artefacts. Among them was a black-and-white

The Lady with an Ermine *by Leonardo da Vinci*

photograph of *The Lady with an Ermine,* framed in the 'red-white-black' imagery of the Nazi period.

107

I visited the Wawel in the company of Niklas, by which time Cecilia Gallerani had returned. The museum director and the owners of the painting allowed us to spend a little time with her, on our own, early in the morning, before the museum was open. Seventy years had passed since Niklas last stood before her. He now did so once more, made small before the power of the painting.

That evening, Niklas and I dined at a local restaurant in Kraków's old town. We talked of writing, of words and time, of responsibility. Towards the end of the meal, three people left an adjoining table. As they passed, an older lady among them said, 'We couldn't help but overhear your conversation; your book sounds interesting.' We talked; they joined us, a mother with her daughter and son-in-law.

Niklas Frank and Cecilia, 2014

The mother was an academic, serene and distinguished, a Brazilian professor of chemistry. She had returned to the city of her birth, forced out in 1939 as a ten-year-old Jew. To return wasn't easy. How much of our conversation had she actually overheard? I wondered. Not much, it emerged.

The daughter was born well after the war in Brazil. She took a stronger line than her mother. She said, 'I enjoy being in Kraków, but I will never forget what the Germans have done. I don't ever want to talk to a German.'

Niklas and I glanced at each other.

The mother looked at Niklas and asked, 'And you are a Jew from Israel!?'

Niklas answered immediately: 'Quite the opposite. I am a German; I am the son of Hans Frank, the governor-general of Poland.'

There was a fleeting moment of silence.

Then Niklas stood and rushed away, out of the restaurant.

Later that evening, I found him.

'They were right to have such strong views,' he said. 'I feel a horror for the wrong that the Germans have done to them, to the mother, to their family.'

I comforted him.

108

Nineteen forty-four was a challenging year for Niklas's father. There were attempts on his life, including one as he travelled by train from Kraków to Lemberg. In the summer the Allies liberated Paris; the Germans retreated from the west and from the east, gathering inward.

The news from the east and the speed of the Red Army's advance were particularly worrisome. Yet Frank still found time to turn his mind to the remaining Jews on his territory, no more than a hundred thousand. They must be dealt with, he told a Kraków meeting of Nazi Party members, 'a race which must be eradicated'.

Two days after the speech, delivered in early spring, the Soviets entered the territory of the General Government, rapidly approaching Kraków and the Wawel. In May, Frank celebrated his forty-fourth birthday. Trusted colleagues offered a gift, the fifty photographs in a velvet box, including the photograph of *The Lady with an Ermine*.

On 11 July, the head of the German police in Kraków was the subject of an audacious assassination attempt by Polish resistance. Frank retaliated with the execution of Polish prisoners. On 27 July, Lemberg fell, taken by the Soviets. As Wächter fled towards Yugoslavia, Lauterpacht's niece Inka Gelbard could once again walk freely on the streets. Zółkiew too was liberated, allowing Clara Kramer to leave the cellar in which she had spent nearly two years. On 1 August, an uprising began in Warsaw. With no intention of backing down, Frank ordered new measures, harsher than ever before.

In September, Frank turned his mind to concentration camps located in his territory. His diary recorded a conversation with Josef Bühler about the Majdanek camp, the first mention of any such place of death. After liberating the camp two months earlier, the Soviets had circulated a documentary film about the terrible situation they discovered, focusing on the plight of the fifteen hundred prisoners who remained.

109

As the Soviets advanced towards Kraków, Frank decided to take the painting of Cecilia Gallerani with him when he fled the city. Early in 1945, as the Soviets closed in from the east, near enough for gunfire to be heard, Frank ordered his staff to prepare *The Lady with an Ermine* to travel with him to Bavaria.

In those last weeks, Frank tidied up loose ends. He completed two essays, one titled 'On Justice', the other 'The Orchestra Conductor'. He managed a final visit to the Kraków opera house, a performance of *Orpheus and Eurydice*. He watched films, including *Seven Years of Bad Luck* with Hans Moser, the renowned Austrian actor who had once played the lead in the film version of *The City Without Jews*. Prospects were so bright back then, although Frank was oblivious to the fact that Moser had refused to divorce his Jewish wife, Blanca Hirschler.

January 17 1945 was chosen as the day of departure. The sky over Kraków was a deep blue, not a cloud in sight, a city bathed in sunshine. Frank left the Wawel Castle at 1.25 p.m. in a black Mercedes (licence plate EAST 23) driven by his chauffeur, Herr Schamper, in a convoy that carried his closest associates and at least thirty-eight volumes of his daily diary back to Bavaria. *The Lady with an Ermine* was with them, a form of preventive action, Frank would later claim, so it 'could not be plundered in my absence'.

The convoy headed north-west for Oppeln, then on to Schloss Seichau (Sichów), where Frank holed up for a few days with Count von Richthofen, an old acquaintance. Much of the art stolen from Kraków had already been moved there. Brigitte and most of the children, including Niklas, were back at the Schoberhof. Four days after leaving the Wawel, Frank and the stenographers Mohr and von Fenske, who faithfully wrote up his diary each day from October 1939, destroyed most of the official documents taken from Wawel. The diaries, however, were not harmed, preserving the evidence of accomplishment.

Frank headed south-east to Agnetendorf (now Jagniątków) to visit another of his friends, the Nobel Prize-winning novelist Gerhart Hauptmann. After taking tea with the Nazi-sympathizing writer, Frank continued to Bad Aibling, a visit with Lilly Grau, the need for affection. It was only a short trip from Bad Aibling to the village of Neuhaus am Schliersee, the Frank family home.

On 2 February, Frank established a chancellery in exile for the General Government, maintaining the illusion of authority. He set up office at 12 Joseftalerstrasse, the former Café Bergfrieden, where he would spend twelve weeks. Occasionally, he visited Brigitte and the children at the Schoberhof but also spent time with Lilly in Bad Aibling (according to Niklas, a photograph of Frank was found on her bedside table, following her death many years later). In April President Roosevelt died, succeeded by the vice president, Harry Truman. Three weeks later, German radio announced the death of the Führer.

It was the end of the war and the Nazi *Reich*. On Wednesday, 2 May, Frank observed American tanks making their way towards Schliersee. Two days later, on Friday, 4 May, he gave Brigitte a final gift, a bundle of bills amounting to fifty thousand reichsmarks in cash. Niklas's brother Norman, present at the moment that Frank offered a farewell to his wife, noted that it came without a final kiss or any affectionate exchange of words. Frank became more fearful than ever of Brigitte as his authority declined. Niklas believed that Brigitte bore a share of the responsibility, encouraging her husband, profiting from his positions of power, refusing him a divorce in the summer of 1942. 'If my mother had said, "Hans, stay out of it, I order it," he would have stayed out of it.' This was offered as an explanation, not an excuse.

Niklas has his own understanding of Brigitte's powerful hold over her husband, despite the cruelty of his behaviour towards her. 'He was cruel, to hide the secret of his homosexuality,' Niklas told me. How did he know? From the letters of his father and the diary of his mother. 'Every time it seemed as if my Hans was desperately struggling, again and again,' Brigitte confided, 'to free himself from his youthful involvement with men,' a reference to time spent in Italy. This was the same Frank who welcomed the adoption in 1935 of paragraph 175a of the *Reich* penal code, extending the prohibition on homosexuality. Such behaviour was 'expressive of a disposition opposed to the normal national community,' Frank had declared, to be punished without mercy 'if the race is not to perish'. 'I think he was gay,' Niklas said.

After the farewells between Frank and Brigitte, the former governor-general headed back to the faux chancellery. He sat in the front room of the old café, waiting with his adjutant, chauffeur and secretary, all three loyal to the end. They drank coffee.

A vehicle pulled up, a US army jeep, outside the front door. The engine was switched off. Lieutenant Walter Stein of the US Seventh Army hauled himself out, looked around, made his way to the café, entered, scanned the room and asked which one was Hans Frank.

'I am,' said the *Reich* minister and former governor-general of occupied Poland.

'You're coming with me, you're under arrest.'

Stein sat Frank in the back of the jeep. The diaries were placed on the front seat, then the jeep left. At some point, Stein returned to Joseftalerstrasse to pick up some film, which remained in the Stein family until it made its way back to Niklas decades later. He allowed me to watch it, footage of Frank being kind to a dog, of passing trains, of a visit to the Kraków ghetto, of the girl in a red dress.

The Lady with an Ermine lingered at Joseftalerstrasse, to be collected a few weeks later, with a couple of Rembrandts. Another painting, *Portrait of a Young Man* by Raphael, disappeared, one of the most famous missing paintings in the world. Niklas thought Brigitte might have traded it for milk and eggs with a local farmer.

'Perhaps it hangs above a fireplace in Bavaria,' Niklas suggested, with a twinkle.

110

In June, Frank's name appeared on a list of possible defendants for a criminal trial of leading German officials. The inclusion of the 'Butcher of Warsaw', as he had come to be known, was approved by Robert Jackson, with the support of the Polish government in exile. Frank was moved to a prison near Miesbach, beaten up by the US army soldiers who'd liberated Dachau. He attempted suicide, first slitting his left wrist and then taking a rusty nail to his throat. He failed and was taken to Mondorf-les-Bains, a spa town in Luxembourg, housed at the requisitioned Palace Hotel with other leading Nazis. There he was interrogated.

One visitor to the hotel was the economist John Kenneth Galbraith, on leave of absence from the US War Department. He wrote an article about the Palace Hotel, published in *Life* magazine alongside an advertisement for vitamin B capsules featuring an impossibly glamorous Dorothy Lamour. Galbraith was unimpressed by Frank's group, which spent most of its time walking along the veranda, looking out at the view. Galbraith observed the traits of individual prisoners, noting the habit of Julius Streicher, founder of *Der Stürmer* newspaper, who would break his stroll and, without warning, turn to the railing, where he would 'stiffen to attention and throw out his arm in a Nazi salute'. Robert Ley, head of Hitler's German Labour Front, looked like 'a Bowery bum'; Hermann Göring gave the impression of being a 'not very intelligent shyster'.

In such distinguished company, an unkempt, distraught Frank filled the hours weeping or in prayer. In early August, he was interviewed by a US army officer. His words reflected a troubled state of mind, feeble efforts to extricate himself from the accounting that was to come. In this first period of captivity, Frank sought to sanitize the role he'd played. The position in Kraków was 'unbelievably difficult', he told the interrogator. 'Special powers' were granted to the SS; it was they who carried out 'all those dreadful atrocities'. They, not he, had acted against the Polish resistance movement and the Jews. Yet inadvertently he confirmed knowledge of the facts, claiming to have put up 'a constant fight' to avert 'the worst'. Sometimes he wept as he spoke.

Frank explained that he had never been politically active, that his early role was confined to legal matters (as though this might be a defence), that he fell out with Hitler in 1942, after the four big speeches delivered at universities around Germany. He denied knowledge of concentration camps in Poland, even in the area he controlled. He learned of them only from the newspapers after the Soviets took over. Auschwitz? It was outside his territory. The diaries would exonerate him; that's why he kept them. 'If Jackson gets my diaries I shall be able to stand there as a fighter for law and justice in Poland.'

Who was responsible? The 'German leaders'. The SS. The Himmler and Bormann 'clique'. Not the 'German people'. The Poles? 'A brave people, a good people.' The paintings he took to Germany? Preserved 'for the Polish people'.

Did he feel a sense of responsibility? Yes, he was 'conscience-stricken' because he hadn't had the courage to kill Hitler. The Führer feared him, he told the interrogator, because he was 'a man possessed with the passion of a Matthew'. This was the first of several references I would come across in which Frank touched on the central character in Johann Sebastian Bach's work about passion and solace, forgiveness and mercy. It reminded me that Frank was a deeply cultured man, widely read, greatly interested in classical music and well connected to leading writers and composers.

On 12 August 1945, he was transferred to prison cell 14 at the Palace of Justice in Nuremberg, behind the courtroom. At the end of the month the prosecutors announced a list of defendants, twenty-four 'war criminals' to be tried before the International Military Tribunal. Frank was near the top of the list.

A few days later he was subjected to more interrogation in the presence of a twenty-year-old US army interpreter. Today Siegfried Ramler lives in Hawaii, with no great recollection of the questions that were asked, but with a clear memory of the man. 'Oh yes,' Siegfried told me, 'Frank's eyes were strong and penetrating; there was strong eye contact with me.' He thought Frank to be 'interesting and impressive', articulate, cultured, a man with a 'clear mind', one 'overtaken by fanaticism' who recognized 'collective guilt but not his own'. The responsibility of the group, not the individual? Yes. 'The deeds he did were committed with a clear mind,' Ramler added, 'he knew he had done wrong, that I saw.'

On 18 October, shortly after Lemkin had finished his work on the indictment and prepared to return to Washington, Frank was formally charged. His circumstances had been transformed in the decade since he had railed against the idea of an international criminal court, in the summer of 1935. That court was now a reality in which he was ensnared, and one of the eight men who would judge him was none other than Professor Henri Donnedieu de Vabres, the man with a walrus moustache who'd addressed his Akademie für Deutsches Recht in 1935 and with whom he had dined.

The connection between the two men troubled the Soviets, who were no more impressed by Frank's newly discovered religious devotion: at the end of October, in an empty cell behind the Palace of Justice, Frank was baptized into the Catholic Church. In this way he would face up to the crimes with which he was charged, including crimes against humanity and genocide in occupied Poland.

The coming together of the lives of Frank, Lauterpacht and Lemkin was formalized in Nuremberg's Palace of Justice, in the words of the indictment.

VII

THE CHILD WHO STANDS ALONE

1.

Wien am 6. Feber 1939

Diese Niederschrift ist seitens eines gutgesinnten Freundes, für die Familie Buchholz angesichts einer überstandenen Gefahr, ihrer zum Erlöschen bedrohte junge Liebesche, verfaßt worden.

Da dieselbe nunmehr glücklicherweise, der vollständigen Genesung entgegen geht, eben in Form eines Glückwunsches gedacht ist zum Andenken gewidmet.

Steuer

In October 1945, as *Le Monde* reported Frank's conversion to Catholicism, Leon worked at the Lutetia Hotel on the boulevard Raspail. Previously occupied by the Gestapo, the hotel served as home to a number of relief organizations, including the Comité Juif d'Action Sociale et de Reconstruction, with Leon working as a *chef de service*. At the end of each day, he returned from his work with displaced individuals to the small apartment on the fourth floor of the rue Brongniart, to be with Rita and their daughter.

There was no news from Vienna, Lemberg, or Żółkiew. As more details emerged about what had transpired, he feared the worst for his mother in Vienna, for his sisters, for the family in Poland. In July his daughter celebrated her seventh birthday – the first one to be spent in the company of both her parents. My mother had no recollection of those days, beyond a sense of upheaval and anxiety, not a time of tranquillity. I shared with her all that I had learned: the circumstances of Leon's departure, Miss Tilney's journey to Vienna, Rita's relationship with Emil Lindenfeld, her departure from Vienna in October 1941, the closing of Vienna's doors.

Only now did she tell me about another document, one that was tucked away, kept apart from the other papers. It was new to me, a handwritten letter sent to Leon shortly after he left Vienna for Paris. Dated 6 February 1939, received in Paris, it offered another view on the life he left behind in Vienna.

The twelve-page, elegantly handwritten document was signed by a man named Leon Steiner. He styled himself a *Seelenarzt*, a 'doctor of the soul', a shrink who signed off the letter as a *Psycho-graphologe* (psycho-graphologist). I was able to find no record or trace of this man, or anyone of this name with any medical qualifications.

The writing was in an old German script. In need of assistance, I returned to Inge Trott, who sent me a complete English translation, which was then reviewed by another German-speaking friend. A first reading suggested why the letter might have been kept apart.

Herr Steiner included a brief foreword:

> The present manuscript has been written by a well-meaning friend
> for the Buchholz family in view of the danger that threatened
> their young love marriage. Because fortunately this marriage is
> now looking forward to a full recovery, my manuscript is designed
> to be in the form of a congratulation and as a memory.

Then to the substance. 'Dear Herr Buchholz,' he began.

The author described the efforts he had undertaken to restore the marriage and offered a firm riposte to Leon's critique that 'the soul doctor Steiner has not done his job well'. I could have done without your unjustified remarks, Herr Steiner added. He referred to Rita's 'behaviour', in the face of which Leon had 'heaped punishing accusations onto' his wife, with the consequence that Steiner was only able to commence his psychological work after Leon's 'successful departure' from Vienna, which was but a few days earlier. Steiner had assumed – 'because of a misunderstanding' – that Leon was 'full of anger and antagonism', that he left Vienna 'with the firm intention of leaving the only recently established home for good'. The decision to leave was taken in the face of 'disharmony' and 'lamentable conflicts' in the young marriage. These were a result of Rita's 'trying excesses' (no explanation is offered) and of her 'shortcomings' (no details are given).

The letter thus made clear that Leon's departure occurred at a time of great conflict with Rita, and perhaps because of it. The nature of the conflict was not set out. With this background, Herr Steiner described his efforts to apply to the situation 'every psychoanalytical method' at his disposal, reflecting a desire to leave 'nothing undone'. He explained that he too, like Leon, heaped accusations onto Rita ('she honestly deserved them!') and that eventually his labours were 'crowned with success'. Despite Leon's slurs, Rita had finally 'acknowledged her shortcomings', which opened the door to 'a full recovery'.

To reach even that point was not without its considerable difficulties, Steiner added, given the 'prevailing bad situation' in the family. He continued, 'External and potentially damaging influences – admitted by both parties – created lamentable conflicts', a situation of 'disharmony' that threatened to become 'antagonistic'.

Lieber Herr Buchholz!

Gelegentlich meines letzten Besuches, bei Ihrer mir lieb gewordenen Familie hat mir Ihre Frau Gemahlin einen an mich gerichteten freundlichen Gruß übermittelt, wofür ich mich bestens bedanke.

Ferner haben Sie auch, eine mich peinlich berührende Bemerkung, folgenden Inhaltes hinzugefügt:

„Der Seelenarzt Steiner, hat diesmal nicht gut gearbeitet."

Falls Sie lieber Buchholz blos einmal Ohrenzeuge sein könnten wie ich mich bemühe, d.h. wie energisch

Letter from Leon Steiner to Leon Buchholz, 6 February 1939

Steiner reported that success was premised on what he was able to uncover, that which was concealed, namely Leon's 'deep love' for his wife and also 'for the delightful child who stands alone'. This seemed to be a reference to my mother, who was then just a few months old. Leon would begin to miss the two beings, Steiner predicted, individuals he loved 'so utterly'. Rita 'will be longing for your company', he foresaw, having sensed the 'reawakened feelings of love' reflected in a single sentence of a recent letter from Leon. Armed with this expression of affection, Steiner attempted to prepare Rita – 'likewise filled with reawakened love' – for a happily married future. He signed off optimistically, expressing the hope that Leon's 'firm belief in God' would help both overcome the obstacles that would surely confront them in 'the new world'. Of life in Vienna beyond the family, of the German takeover, of the new laws, Herr Steiner had nothing to say.

112

Something had happened, there were 'lamentable conflicts', so Leon left. What that might have been was unclear from this peculiar, tortuous, defensive letter. Steiner's fawning words were coded, laden with ambiguity, open to interpretation. Inge Trott asked whether I wanted to know what she thought the letter meant. Yes, I would. She offered the thought that the letter might be taken to indicate that a question had been raised as to the paternity of the child, the 'child who stands alone'. It was a curious expression, Inge said. The choice of words caused a thought to enter her mind, because she was conscious that in those days information of such a nature – that the child may have a different father – was not a matter that could have been communicated explicitly.

I reviewed the letter with our German neighbour, who tidied up the translation. She agreed with Inge that the reference to the 'child who stands alone' is 'tricky', certainly ambiguous. She didn't accept, however, that it necessarily referred to an issue of paternity. A German teacher at my son's school offered to read the letter. He tended towards the view of my neighbour, rather than that of Inge, but was not willing to offer an interpretation of his own.

Another neighbour, a writer of novels who had recently been

awarded the Goethe Prize for his facility with German, indicated another view. 'Rum indeed,' he wrote in a handwritten letter posted through our front door. The term *Seelenarzt* might be 'pejorative', or perhaps 'self-ironic'. From the style of the letter, he concluded that Herr Steiner was most likely 'a semi-intellectual' or just a 'dismal and tortuous writer'. What the writer might have actually been saying – with a sort of vindictive triumphalism – was unclear. 'I have a feeling he is shoving it to Herr Buchholz in a big way, but with Herr B. not with us, what is he shoving?' This neighbour suggested the letter be shown to a specialist in German linguistics. I found two and, unable to decide which to opt for, I sent the letter to both.

Linguist No. 1 said that the letter was 'strange', with its grammatical errors, incomplete sentences, numerous mistakes of punctuation. Herr Steiner seemed to have a 'language deficit', he said, and went a step further, offering a specific prognosis. 'It reads like the text of someone with a milder form of Wernicke's aphasia,' a language disorder caused by damage to the left side of the brain. Or it might be that Herr Steiner had simply been compelled to write under enormous pressure – the times were difficult in Vienna, after all – so that great chunks of thought were churned out and 'hastily thrown onto paper'. 'I do not see any implications about the child's origin,' this linguist concluded, beyond the presence of 'family trouble during which the child's father left the family'.

Linguist No. 2 was a little more generous to Herr Steiner. At first, he thought that the references to the wife and child might refer to a single person, one 'with two personas'. Then he showed the letter to his wife, who disagreed (she tends to have more experience in the comprehension of subtle meanings, he explained). The wife shared the instinct of Inge Trott, that the reference to 'the child who stands alone' was intentionally subtle, that it might mean that the father was a person 'unknown', or that Herr Steiner simply didn't 'want to declare himself'.

The views were inconclusive. They offered hints, but no more, that Leon left Vienna in circumstances of considerable tension and conflict. These might (or might not) have been occasioned by questions as to the child's paternity.

That Leon might not be my biological grandfather was not a thought that had ever occurred to me. It seemed a most unlikely possibility. At one level, it wasn't disturbing; because he acted and felt like my grandfather, he *was* my grandfather, irrespective of any biological consideration. Yet the implications for others, for my mother in particular, were more difficult to countenance. This was unexpectedly delicate.

113

I pondered the matter for several weeks, wondering what to do next. That process was interrupted by an e-mail from Sandra Seiler on Long Island. She too had been thinking about her grandfather Emil Lindenfeld, thinking about the Viennese photographs of Rita and Emil Lindenfeld, taken in a garden in 1941. She'd spoken with a friend; a thought had emerged.

'The idea that something might have been going on between them made perfect sense,' she wrote. Like Rita, Emil Lindenfeld chose to remain in Vienna, after his wife and a daughter left, in 1939. The two of them were alone in Vienna, without spouse or child. Three years passed, then Rita left. After the war Emil was alone; he went in search of Rita.

'I dwelled on that thought all day,' Sandra wrote.

Sitting in Sandra's living room a few months earlier, peeling photographs off the pages of Emil's album, we had touched on the possibility of a DNA test, 'to be sure'. It seemed a disloyal idea, so we pushed it away. Yet it lingered.

Sandra and I continued to exchange e-mails, and the subject of a DNA test returned. I'd explored the possibility, I told her. It turned out to be complicated: learning whether two people shared a grandparent was not an altogether straightforward exercise; it was much easier if you were trying to establish whether the two shared a grandmother. A shared grandfather was a more complex matter, in the technical sense.

I was referred to an academic at the Department of Genetics at the University of Leicester, a specialist in the exhumation of mass graves. She introduced me to a company that specialized in these matters. A test was available to assess the likelihood that two individuals of different gender – Sandra and I – might share the same grandfather. It worked by comparing matches among segments of

DNA (in units known as centimorgans). The test took the number of matching segments and then the sizes, as well as the overall total size of the matching segments (or blocks) between two or more individuals. From these centimorgans and blocks, it was possible to estimate whether two individuals are related. The test was not definitive, only an estimate, merely the assessment of a probability. It required nothing more than a swab of saliva.

After some reflection, Sandra Seiler and I agreed to proceed. The materials arrived from the company. Having paid a fee, you received a kit, scraped the inside of your cheek with a cotton swab, placed the scraper in a sealed plastic container, posted the packet off to America, then waited. Sandra was braver than I. 'I scraped rather vigorously last night and put it into today's outgoing mail,' she wrote cheerily.

I waited two months before scraping, not sure whether I really wanted to know. Eventually, I scraped, posted, waited.

A month passed.

114

An e-mail arrived from Sandra. The results of the DNA test were available on the website. I took a look at the site, but the information was so complicated that I was unable to work out what it meant, so I e-mailed the company for assistance. My contact there, Max, responded promptly, taking me through the results.

Max explained that I had 'about 77% Jewish ancestry and 23% European ancestry'. This was subject to a large margin of error (25 per cent), due to the historic mixing between Ashkenazi Jews and Europeans. Some might find this material to be 'interesting', he added, in the sense that such results tended, as he put it, to 'endorse the idea that Jews, in addition to being bound by their religion, are a people-nation bound by, among other things (culture, language, etc. . . .) a common genetic background'. I offered no comment to Max on the observation, which struck me as raising all sorts of issues, on identity, on the individual and the group.

Max got to the point. I may be 'very distantly' related to Sandra, he said, but was actually more closely related to Max. In both cases, the connection was likely to be no more than a single common ancestor, a single individual who would have been shared 'many generations ago'. There was 'zero possibility' that Sandra and I shared a grandfather.

This was a relief. I suppose I never really doubted the conclusion. That's what I told myself.

Leon left Vienna alone. Perhaps he did so because of doubts about paternity, or because he and Rita weren't getting on, or because he was banished, or because he was sick of the Nazis, or feared them, or because he was able to leave, or because of Herr Lindenfeld, or for myriad other possible reasons. That he was the father of 'the child who stands alone' was not in doubt.

There were, however, other uncertainties. Leon left on his own. A few months later, Elsie Tilney travelled to Vienna to collect the child. Rita allowed this, then she was alone. They married in 1937, a child arrived a year later, then there was 'disharmony' in the marriage, 'lamentable conflicts' in the relationship. They reached out to the 'soul doctor'. Something else was going on, and I still didn't know what it was.

VIII

NUREMBERG

115

The first time I visited courtroom 600 in Nuremberg's Palace of Justice, I was struck by its intimacy and a warmth created by the wood panelling. It was strangely familiar, not the brutal space I'd expected and not nearly as large. I noticed a wooden door directly behind the seats where the defendants had sat but didn't make much of it on that first visit.

Now I was back, accompanied by Niklas Frank, and keen to pass through the door. As Niklas wandered around the room I stood below the windows, behind the place once occupied by the long judges' table. The flags of the four victorious Allies were long gone as I made my way around the outer edge of the room, along the wall with the large white screen, behind the witness box, around the wall on the left, to the place behind the seats where the defendants sat on two rows of wooden benches.

Niklas slid the door open, walked in, shut the door. A little time passed, then the door opened, he came out and ambled over to the place where his father had sat for nearly a year. In this room, prosecutors had given their all to obtain convictions as the defendants sought to justify their actions and save themselves from the rope. Lawyers argued obscure points, witnesses offered testimony, judges listened. Questions were posed and sometimes answered. Evidence was examined and pored over, documents, photographs, moving images, skin. There was commotion, tears, drama and much tedium. In this way, it was an ordinary courtroom experience, yet in reality there had never been one quite like it; this was the first time in human history that the leaders of a state were put on trial before an international court for crimes against humanity and genocide, two new crimes.

116

Early on the morning of the first day of the trial, 20 November 1945, Hans Frank awoke in a small cell with an open toilet in the prison behind the courtroom. At about nine o'clock, he was escorted by a white-helmeted guard along a series of corridors to the small lift that took him up to the courtroom. He entered through the sliding wooden door and was then led to the front bench of the dock. Five along from Hermann Göring, he was seated next to Alfred Rosenberg, Hitler's principal racial theorist. The prosecutors were seated to Frank's right, around four long, wooden tables, divided by nationality. In military garb, the Russians were closest to the defendants, then the French, then the British. The Americans were farthest away. Behind the prosecutors sat members of the press corps, chatting noisily. Above them, a lucky few were allowed to sit in the public gallery. Directly opposite Frank was the judges' bench, still empty, behind a row of female stenographers.

Frank wore a grey suit and the dark glasses that would distinguish him through the trial. He kept his gloved left hand out of sight, evidence of the failed suicide attempt. He was composed and showed no obvious emotion. Fourteen more defendants followed Frank into the courtroom, seated to his left and on a second bench. Arthur Seyss-Inquart, former deputy to Frank and Reichskommissar in the Netherlands, sat immediately behind him. Three defendants were absent: Ley had killed himself, Ernst Kaltenbrunner felt unwell, and Martin Bormann was yet to be apprehended.

Lauterpacht was in the courtroom that morning, observing the defendants, but Lemkin was back in Washington. Neither man knew what had happened to his family, unaccounted for somewhere in Poland. Nor did they have any information as to the role Frank might have played in their fate.

At exactly ten o'clock, a clerk entered the courtroom through another door, this one near the judges' table. 'The Tribunal will now enter,' he said, the words translated into German, Russian and French, through six overhead microphones and ungainly headphones, another novelty. A heavy wooden door opened across from Frank, on the left. Eight elderly men trundled in, six in black gowns, the two Soviets in military uniform, making their way to the judges' table. Frank knew one of them, although ten years had passed since they were last together in Berlin: Henri Donnedieu de Vabres, the French judge.

The man in charge of the courtroom, Sir Geoffrey Lawrence, an English court of appeal judge, sat at the centre of the judges' bench. Bald and Dickensian, he'd been appointed just a few weeks earlier by Clement Attlee, the British prime minister. He was chosen to preside over the case by the other seven judges because they couldn't agree on anyone else. He and his wife, Marjorie, occupied a house on Stielerstrasse, at No. 15, on the outskirts of the city, a grand house that once belonged to a Jewish toy manufacturer, later used as an SS mess.

Each of the four Allied powers nominated two judges, and the defendants did what they could to glean a little information on each. On the far left – from the defendants' vantage point – sat Lieutenant-Colonel Alexander Volchkov, a former Soviet diplomat, alongside Major-General Iona Nikitchenko, a dour-faced, hard-line military lawyer who once served as a judge in Stalin's show trials. Then came the two British judges, possibly offering some hope to Frank. Norman Birkett – who had shared a lecture platform with Lemkin at Duke University in the spring of 1942 – had been a Methodist preacher, then a parliamentarian and next a judge. To his right, Sir Geoffrey Lawrence, a career barrister, then the senior American, Francis Biddle, who succeeded Robert Jackson as Roosevelt's attorney general and once worked with Lauterpacht. Then John Parker, a judge from Richmond, Virginia, still embittered by the failed effort to get to the US Supreme Court. The French were seated on the far right: Henri Donnedieu de Vabres, professor of criminal law at the Sorbonne, and Robert Falco, a judge of the Paris Court of Appeal, removed from judicial office in late 1940 for being a Jew. Behind the judges hung the four Allied flags, a reminder of the victors. There was no German flag.

Lord Justice Lawrence opened the proceedings. The trial was 'unique in the history of the jurisprudence of the world', he began, offering a brief introduction before the indictment was read out. Frank and the other defendants, well-behaved men, listened politely. Each of the charges was addressed by a prosecutor from the four Allied powers. The Americans opened with the first count, the conspiracy to commit international crimes. The baton was passed to the British and the round figure of Sir David Maxwell Fyfe, who addressed the second count, crimes against peace.

The third count was allocated to the French: war crimes, including the charge of 'genocide'. Frank must have wondered about this word and how it made its way into the proceedings, as prosecutor Pierre Mounier became the first person to use it in a court of law. The fourth and final count, 'crimes against humanity', was addressed by a Soviet prosecutor, another new term for Frank to ponder, addressed for the first time in open court.

The charges having been set out, the prosecutors proceeded to address the litany of terrible facts, the killings and other acts of horror of which the defendants were accused. Dealing with the atrocities against Jews and Poles, the Soviet team soon homed in on the atrocities in Lvov, touching on the *Aktionen* of August 1942, matters of personal knowledge for Frank, but only of imagination for Lauterpacht. The Soviet prosecutor was strikingly precise with the dates and numbers. Between 7 September 1941 and 6 July 1943, he told the judges, the Germans killed more than eight thousand children in the Janowska camp, in the heart of Lemberg. Reading the transcript, I wondered whether Frank would have recalled the speech he gave in the auditorium of the university on 1 August or the game of chess he played and lost with Frau Wächter. On the newsreel, Frank showed no discernible reaction.

The first day ran long. Having set out the general facts, prosecutors then turned to the actions of the individual defendants. First Hermann Göring, then Joachim von Ribbentrop, Rudolf Hess, Ernst Kaltenbrunner, Alfred Rosenberg. Then Hans Frank, his role being summarized by the American prosecutor Sidney Alderman, the man who supported Lemkin on genocide. He needed but a few sentences to encapsulate Frank's role. The former governor-general would have known what to expect because the details had been shared with his lawyer, Dr Alfred Seidl. Alderman described Frank's role in the years to 1939, then his appointment by the Führer as governor-general. He had a personal influence with Hitler, it was said, and he 'authorized, directed, and participated' in war crimes and crimes against humanity. The events in Poland and Lemberg were placed at the heart of the trial.

117

Lauterpacht wrote to Rachel, who was visiting her parents in Palestine, to offer an account of a day 'packed with emotion', one he never forgot but of which he rarely spoke. 'It was an unforgettable experience to see, for the first time in history, a sovereign State in the dock.'

As Lauterpacht listened to the Soviets addressing the killings in Lemberg, he was entirely in the dark about the whereabouts of his family. The press noted his presence, an important part of the team led by the dashing Sir Hartley Shawcross. The young group of British barristers was 'strongly reinforced by Professor Lauterpacht, of Cambridge University,' *The Times* reported, describing him as 'an eminent authority on international law'. He'd travelled from Cambridge to Nuremberg a day earlier and was lodged at the Grand Hotel, an establishment with a fine bar that is unchanged today. He was issued pass No. 146, which allowed him general access around the building ('This pass admits owner into security area and courtroom').

With the Soviets addressing crimes against humanity, the protection of individuals was brought to centre stage. Lauterpacht would have heard the references to 'genocide', an impractical concept of which he did not approve, a term he feared would undermine the protection of individuals. He worried that emphasis on genocide would reinforce latent instincts of tribalism, perhaps enhancing the sense of 'us' and 'them', pitting one group against another.

The proximity of the defendants, including Frank, left a deep impression. 'My table was at a distance of about 15 yards from the accused,' he explained to Rachel, allowing close observation. It was a 'great satisfaction' to watch the faces of the defendants as the list of their crimes was read out in public. Yet he said nothing to Rachel about the terrible facts described on the opening day, of events in Lemberg in the summer of 1942. Did he look at Frank with particular attention? Did Frank notice Lauterpacht? I asked Eli if he knew where his father sat, in the public gallery or with the British prosecutors or elsewhere. Eli told me he had no information. 'My father never spoke of the matter to me,' he explained, 'and there is no photograph of my father in the courtroom.' All that remained was a single photograph published in the *Illustrated London News,* showing the British prosecution team outside the courtroom.

A team of twelve unsmiling men in suits. Shawcross sits at the centre, legs crossed, hands on knees. To his right, looking at the photographer, sits a sombre David Maxwell Fyfe, and next to him, at the beginning of the front row, Lauterpacht looks into the camera with arms folded. He seems confident, satisfied even.

I wondered where Lauterpacht had sat in courtroom 600. On a warm September afternoon, I took myself to the archive of Getty Images, tucked into a west London suburb. There I found many photographs from the trial, including an invaluable collection commissioned by the *Picture Post,* a defunct newspaper that had several photographers present in the courtroom. There were contact sheets – 'shot by a German photographer', the archivist said with an ironic smile – and many negatives, each imprinted on a fragile rectangle of thin glass, requiring the use of a special viewer. This was a time-consuming exercise, because each glass plate had to be removed from a protective translucent paper envelope, then placed onto the viewer, which had to be brought into focus. Over the course of an afternoon, hundreds of small envelopes and their glass plates passed through my hands, a laborious search for Lauterpacht. Many hours passed and then I spotted him, walking into court on the opening day of the trial, looking apprehensive, wearing a dark suit and white shirt, his familiar round spectacle frames perched across the bridge of his nose. He walked in behind Hartley Shawcross, who stared into the camera with an air of mild disdain. Both men were about to see the defendants.

I worked my way through each of the many small glass plates, scanning the tiny faces, hoping to find another of Lauterpacht. There were so many people in court that day the exercise was like a search for a familiar face in a painting by Bruegel. Eventually I spotted him, just a short distance from Frank.

The photograph was taken on the opening day, from the loft above the courtroom, looking down. The defendants were in the bottom right-hand corner, the dominant figure of Hermann Göring visible as he leaned forward in an oversized, light-coloured suit. Along the bench, five defendants to Göring's left, just before the image was interrupted by the sill of the opening that allowed the image to be taken, I could see the semi-bowed head of Frank. He was seated

*Nuremberg, 20 November 1945: Shawcross (looking into the camera)
enters the courtroom, followed by Lauterpacht*

next to Alfred Rosenberg, who seemed to be looking at something
in Frank's lap.

In the middle of the photograph, I counted five long wooden
tables, each with nine or ten seats around it. The British prosecution team was seated at the second table from the left. There was
David Maxwell Fyfe, seated to the left of the Soviet prosecutor at
the lectern addressing the judges, who were out of image to the left.
Lauterpacht was visible at the end of the same table, hands clenched
under his chin, intent, reflective. Looking towards the defendants,
he was separated from Frank by only a few tables and chairs.

Frank must have had many concerns that day. Brigitte had written, he told Alfred Rosenberg and Baldur von Schirach, the former
gauleiter of Vienna who oversaw the deportation of Malke Buchholz
and more than fifteen thousand other Viennese Jews to Theresienstadt. She told her husband that Niklas and the other children had
been sent out on the streets to beg for bread.

'Tell me, Rosenberg, was all this destruction and misery necessary?' Frank asked. 'What was the sense in all that racial politics?'

Baldur von Schirach heard Rosenberg explain that he hadn't expected his brand of racial politics to lead to mass murder and war. 'I
was only looking for a peaceful solution.'

British prosecution team, Nuremberg, Illustrated London News,
*December 1945 (front row, from left: Lauterpacht, Maxwell Fyfe,
Shawcross, Khaki Roberts, Patrick Dean)*

118

Frank pleaded on the second day, in the presence of Lauterpacht.
Like the other defendants, he was given two options, 'guilty' or 'not
guilty'. The five who spoke before him opted for 'not guilty'.

'Hans Frank,' Lord Justice Lawrence said in a rounded, gravelly
voice, directing the German jurist to take the stand. Martha Gellhorn, the American war correspondent who was in court that day,
was struck by Frank's 'small cheap face', the pink cheeks framing
a 'little sharp nose' and the 'black sleek hair'. A patient air, she
thought, like a waiter in an empty restaurant, quietly composed as
compared with twitching, mad Rudolf Hess.

Frank's dark glasses kept the world away from his eyes, which
might have revealed something akin to emotion. He'd had much time
to weigh the pros and cons between the two options, to think through
the opportunities offered to the prosecution by the thirty-eight incriminating volumes of diaries. If he thought about expressing some

degree of responsibility, perhaps just the little needed to distinguish him from the other defendants, he wasn't going to show it.

'I declare myself not guilty.' He spoke with purpose, then sat down on the unforgiving bench. I found a picture, his gloved left hand on the railing of the dock and his jacket tightly buttoned as he stood upright and proud, looking firmly ahead at the judges, observed by a curious defence lawyer.

None of the defendants chose the 'guilty' option. Although they were generally well behaved, the only incident was prompted by Göring, who suddenly stood up to address the tribunal, only for Lord Justice Lawrence to intervene immediately and firmly. Sit down, say nothing. Göring offered no resistance, a moment to illuminate the silent shift of power. Instead, Robert Jackson was invited to open the case for the prosecution.

Over the next hour, Jackson spoke words that made him famous around the world. Lauterpacht sat close behind a colleague he admired, watching him walk the few steps to the wooden lectern on which Jackson neatly arranged his papers and a pen. From a different angle, behind the ranks of the German defence counsel staring

'I declare myself not guilty,' Hans Frank, 21 November 1945

Palace of Justice, Nuremberg, 20 November 1945

intently at the American, Frank could study the features of the prosecution's principal architect.

'The privilege of opening the first trial in history for crimes against the peace of the world imposes a grave responsibility.' Jackson crafted each word with care, signalling its significance. He spoke of the victors' generosity and the responsibility of the vanquished, of the calculated, malignant, devastating wrongs that were to be condemned and punished. Civilization would not tolerate their being ignored, and they must not be repeated. 'That four great nations, flushed with victory and stung with injury, stay the hand of vengeance and voluntarily submit their captive enemies to the judgement of the law is one of the most significant tributes that Power has ever paid to reason.'

Speaking with calm deliberation, Jackson captured the unique intensity of that long moment in the courtroom, reinforced it and offered a practical way forward. Yes, the tribunal was 'novel and experimental', he recognized, created 'to utilize international law to meet the greatest menace'. Yet it was intended to be practical, not to vindicate obscure legal theories, and it was certainly not concerned with 'the punishment of petty crimes by little people'. The defendants were men who had possessed great power, using it 'to set in motion evils which leave no home in the world untouched'.

Jackson spoke of the defendants' 'Teutonic passion for thoroughness', their propensity to record their actions in writing. He described the treatment of national groups and Jews, the 'mass killings of countless human beings in cold blood', the commission of 'crimes against humanity'. These were ideas discussed with Lauterpacht in New York in 1941 and then again four years later in the garden at Cranmer Road. They were the themes he'd raised in Indianapolis in September 1941, when Lemkin heard him call for a 'reign of law' against international lawlessness.

Jackson alighted on the person of Hans Frank, who seemed to perk up at the mention of his name. 'A lawyer by profession, I say with shame,' and one who helped to craft the Nuremberg decrees. Jackson introduced Frank's diaries, drawing easily from the daily record of private musings and public speeches, an early indication of the central role that the diaries would play in the proceedings. 'I cannot eliminate all lice and Jews in only a year,' Frank said in 1940. A year later, he spoke with pride of the million and more Polish he'd sent to the *Reich*. And as late as 1944, even as the Soviets approached Kraków, Frank was on the case, proclaiming the Jews to be 'a race which has to be eliminated'. The diaries were a gold seam to be mined. If Frank had a sense of foreboding as to the use to which his words would be put, he didn't show it.

Such rich evidence allowed Jackson to end his submissions with a simple plea. The trial was an 'effort to apply the discipline of the law to statesmen', and its usefulness would be measured by its ability to end lawlessness, just as the new United Nations organization offered the prospect of a step towards peace and the rule of law. Yet the 'real complaining party', Jackson told the judges, was not the Allies but 'civilization' itself. Because the defendants had brought the German people to so low a 'pitch of wretchedness', stirring hatreds and violence on every continent, their only hope was that international law would lag far behind morality. The judges must make clear that 'the forces of international law' were 'on the side of peace, so that men and women of good will, in all countries, may have "leave to live by no man's leave, underneath the Law"'. Lauterpacht recognized the words, taken from Rudyard Kipling's poem 'The Old Issue', evoking events in England in 1689, the struggle to subject an all-powerful English sovereign to the constraints of the law.

As Jackson spoke, Lauterpacht showed no hint of emotion. He was pragmatic, stoical, patient. Jackson's performance was magnificent and historic, he would tell Rachel, a 'great personal triumph'. He found satisfaction too in watching the faces of Frank and the other accused, forced to hear the stories of their atrocities. As soon as Jackson finished, Lauterpacht went up to him and shook his hand, contact that lasted 'a long minute'. He would have registered at least one notable omission in Jackson's words: despite the support offered to Lemkin back in May, and then again in October, when the indictment was finalized, Jackson did not use the word 'genocide'.

119

Lauterpacht left Nuremberg on the third day of the trial to return to Cambridge and the classroom. He travelled with Shawcross, who was needed in London on government business, which pushed back the British opening speech to 4 December. Shawcross didn't want his deputy, Maxwell Fyfe, to be the first British speaker.

Lauterpacht's journey home was slow because of bad weather. By the time the small plane landed at Croydon Airport, he felt ill. Always a poor sleeper, he experienced nights that were ever more difficult, haunted by details heard in the courtroom. The words set out in Frank's diaries, fears and uncertainties about the family in Lwów, the sense of failure and of responsibility that he'd failed to persuade them to move to England. Such personal concerns were compounded by professional doubts, about the poor quality of Shawcross's opening speech, which was badly structured and weak on the law.

With Jackson's strong opening, the British would have to up their game, he told Rachel first and then Shawcross himself, which was not an easy task because the attorney general had written large parts of the draft speech. Shawcross asked him to improve the draft, not an invitation to be declined. Ignoring his doctor's instruction to rest, Lauterpacht dedicated a full week to the task, an opportunity to promote his own ideas about the protection of individuals and crimes against humanity. He wrote the draft in his own hand, then passed the pages over to Mrs Lyons, his loyal secretary, who prepared a typescript for his review. The final typed manuscript ran to thirty pages, sent by train from Cambridge to Liverpool Street Station in London for collection by Shawcross's office.

Eli had his father's original handwritten draft. I was able to read Lauterpacht's treatment of the main subject allocated to him by Shawcross, Germany's recourse to war, which Lauterpacht put in better order. He then introduced arguments on the subject for which he felt a greater passion, the rights of the individual. The text he crafted drew rather obviously from ideas he'd set out in *An International Bill of the Rights of Man,* published just a few months earlier. The gist of his thinking was captured in a single sentence: 'The community of nations has in the past claimed and successfully asserted the right to intercede on behalf of the violated rights of man trampled upon by the State in a manner calculated to shock the moral sense of mankind.'

These words invited the tribunal to rule that the Allies were entitled to use military force to protect the 'rights of man'. The argument was contentious then and it remains so today, sometimes referred to as 'humanitarian intervention'. Indeed, on the very day I first saw Lauterpacht's original handwritten draft, President Obama and the British prime minister, David Cameron, were trying to persuade the US Congress and the British Parliament that military intervention in Syria was justified in law, to protect the human rights of hundreds of thousands of individuals. The arguments they made – without success – drew on ideas expressed by Lauterpacht, reflected in the concept of crimes against humanity, acts so egregious that others were entitled to act in a protective capacity. Lauterpacht argued that he was doing no more than developing existing, well-established rules. The argument – an ambitious one in 1945 – was now made as an advocate, not as a scholar.

Lauterpacht's draft made no reference to genocide, or to the Nazis, or Germans as a group, or crimes against Jews or Poles, or indeed crimes against any other groups. Lauterpacht set his back against group identity in the law, whether as victim or perpetrator. Why this approach? He never fully explained it, but it struck me as being connected to what he experienced in Lemberg, on the barricades, observing for himself how one group turned against another. Later he saw first-hand how the law's desire to protect some groups – as reflected in the Polish Minorities Treaty – could create a sharp backlash. Poorly crafted laws could have unintended consequences, provoking the very wrongs they sought to prevent. I was instinctively sympathetic to Lauterpacht's view, which was motivated by a desire to reinforce the protection of each individual, irrespective of which group he or she happened to belong to, to limit the potent force of tribalism, not reinforce it. By focusing on the individual, not the group, Lauterpacht wanted to diminish the force of inter-group conflict. It was a rational, enlightened view, and also an idealistic one.

The counter-argument was put most strongly by Lemkin. Not opposed to individual rights, he nevertheless believed that an excessive focus on individuals was naive, that it ignored the reality of conflict and violence: individuals were targeted *because* they were members of a particular group, not because of their individual qualities. For Lemkin, the law must reflect true motive and real intent, the forces that explained why certain individuals – from certain targeted groups – were killed. For Lemkin, the focus on groups was the practical approach.

Despite their common origins, and the shared desire for an effective approach, Lauterpacht and Lemkin were sharply divided as to
the solutions they proposed to a big question: How could the law
help to prevent mass killing? Protect the individual, says Lauterpacht. Protect the group, says Lemkin.

120

Lauterpacht completed the draft speech for Shawcross and sent it
off to London on 29 November, silent as to genocide and groups.
He allowed himself a modest celebration, a walk in the dark to the
Fellows Parlour at Trinity College and a single glass of port. The
following day, Shawcross sent a courteous note of thanks.

Shawcross returned to Nuremberg without Lauterpacht to deliver
the British opening speech. On 4 December, the attorney general
addressed the tribunal shortly after the screening of a first, grim
film about concentration camps, which left many in a state of considerable distress. The grainy black-and-white film's brutal contents
heightened the aura of methodical calm adopted by Shawcross
in his delivery as he traced the acts of Nazi aggression across
Europe. Starting with Poland in 1939, he moved on to 1940 and
Belgium, Holland, France and Luxembourg, then to Greece and
Yugoslavia in early 1941, and finally to Russia in June 1941, Operation Barbarossa.

Shawcross's legal arguments drew largely from Lauterpacht's
draft. A great swathe of the speech used the Cambridge academic's
words to argue that the idea of crimes against humanity was well
established, that the 'community of nations' had long asserted 'the
right to intercede on behalf of the violated rights of man trampled
upon by the State in a manner calculated to shock the moral sense
of mankind'. This part of the speech ran to fifteen printed pages,
twelve of which were written by Lauterpacht. On crimes against humanity and the rights of individuals, Shawcross spoke Lauterpacht's
exact words, arguing forcefully that the tribunal should sweep aside
the tradition that sovereigns could act as they wished, free to kill,
maim and torture their own people.

Lauterpacht prompted Shawcross to pre-empt the arguments of
the defendants, the prospect that they'd assert that because states

couldn't commit crimes under international law, it followed that the individuals who served them also couldn't be guilty of crime. A state could be criminal, Shawcross told the tribunal, and so it was imperative to repress its crimes by means 'more drastic and more effective than in the case of individuals'. Individuals who acted on behalf of such a state were 'directly responsible' and should have punishments heaped upon them. Göring, Speer and Frank were in his sights.

The core of the Shawcross argument belonged to Lauterpacht. 'The state is not an abstract entity,' the British attorney general proclaimed, using a formulation that would be repeated frequently before the tribunal and long after. 'Its rights and duties are the rights and duties of men', its actions those of politicians who should 'not be able to seek immunity behind the intangible personality of the state'. These were radical words, embracing the ideas of individual responsibility, placing 'fundamental human rights' and 'fundamental human duties' at the heart of a new international system. If this was an innovation, Shawcross concluded, it was one to be defended.

Following Lauterpacht's lead, Shawcross had made no mention of genocide. As the attorney spoke in Nuremberg, Lauterpacht delivered a lecture in Cambridge on the trial's role in emphasizing the protection of individuals. After the lecture, T. Ellis Lewis, a fellow of Trinity Hall, sent a note of appreciation on a 'capital performance'. 'You spoke with conviction, from your head and your heart, and with the fairness one expects from a lawyer who knows his subject.'

121

In the course of the opening weeks of the trial, the judges were presented with novel legal arguments and unparalleled, ghastly evidence. Beyond documents such as Frank's diaries, grotesque artefacts were placed before them – tattooed human skin, a shrunken head – and films were projected onto the great white screen that hung at the back of the courtroom. Hitler's appearance in one short film provoked a commotion among the defendants. 'Can't you feel the terrific strength of his personality,' Ribbentrop was heard to observe, 'how he swept people off their feet?' A force of personality, it was 'erschütternd'. Staggering.

Other films prompted more subdued reactions, notably the scenes shot in camps and ghettos across Europe. One private film – made by a German soldier who participated in a pogrom in Lemberg – offered an accompaniment of sorts, according to the *New Yorker* magazine, 'to texts read aloud from the diary of Nazi Governor General Frank of Poland'. Did the interplay of words and images cause Frank to reflect on the wisdom of his actions in Warsaw or the decision not to destroy his diaries? Did he recall Hitler's order that Warsaw be razed 'to the ground'? Or the self-congratulatory telegram he sent to the Führer – later found by the Soviets – evoking the wonder of a Warsaw 'wreathed in flames'? Or the finely bound report prepared by the SS general Jürgen Stroop on the destruction of the ghetto? Or his own visit to the Warsaw ghetto, in the company of Curzio Malaparte? Or the girl in the red dress, the one who smiled in the home movie that he kept with him to the end of his reign?

If there was any such reflection, Frank's face failed to reveal it. He showed no emotion beyond an occasional reflex of 'strained attentiveness', the eyes hidden behind dark glasses. This was not because he felt shame, it seems, but because he was concentrating on the legal arguments, busily preparing notes of protest and reaction to such films. The Warsaw film offered only one side of a more complicated story, his lawyer, Seidl, told the judges and asked that Frank be given the right to respond immediately. The application was refused. Frank would have a chance to address the tribunal, but not yet.

The films were watched by journalists as well as observers in the public gallery. Over the course of the trial, notable visitors included the likes of Fiorello La Guardia, the former mayor of New York, writers such as Evelyn Waugh and John Dos Passos, academics, military officials, even actors. Visitors were attracted by the daily media articles, the prospect of seeing the 'theatrical energy' of Hermann Göring, so resplendent in his 'fancy clothes'. A few family members of the judges and prosecutors sat in the public gallery, and one among them was Enid Lawrence, the twenty-one-year-old daughter of Lord Justice Lawrence, who was presiding over the proceedings.

122

Enid Lawrence, who became Lady Dundas, known as Robby, invited me to tea at her calm and orderly flat in Kensington. She was one of the few people around who could offer a first-hand account of the early days of the hearing. The widow of a Battle of Britain hero, she spoke with a resigned energy and clarity about her first visit to Nuremberg, in December 1945, when she lodged with her parents. She had kept a small pocket diary into which entries were written in pencil, and now she used it to refresh her memory.

She travelled to Nuremberg on official business, she explained, because she worked for the Allies during the war and after it ended on the use of double agents. She went to Nuremberg to interview the defendant Alfred Jodl, a chief of operations for the Wehrmacht. 'A nice enough little man,' she said, and quite cooperative. He had no idea the young woman who interviewed him was the daughter of the presiding judge or that she spent her free time visiting the sites of Nuremberg.

She admired her father, a 'straightforward man' untainted by ambition or ideology, with little interest in theological debates about genocide or crimes against humanity or fine distinctions between the protection of groups or individuals. He was appointed at the insistence of Winston Churchill, a fellow member of a private dining group, the Other Club. The job, as her father saw it, was simply to apply the law to the facts and to do so fairly and speedily. He expected to be home within six months.

The presidency came to him by chance, Robby added, because he was the only judge acceptable to all: 'The Russians didn't want the Americans, the Americans didn't want the Russians or the French, the French didn't want the Russians.' Her father never wrote of the trial, not in any detail, unlike Biddle, the American judge who wrote a book, or Falco, the French judge who kept a diary that was published only seventy years after the trial.

'My father disapproved of Biddle's diary,' Robby said sharply. Decisions made in private between the judges should remain private.

She came to know the other judges. General Nikitchenko? 'Under the control of Moscow.' His alternate, Lieutenant Colonel Volchkov, with whom she occasionally danced, was 'more human'. He taught her how to say 'I love you' in Russian (her father stayed in touch with Volchkov after the trial, but one day the letters stopped, and he was advised by the Foreign Office to keep a distance). Donnedieu was old and 'pretty much unapproachable'. Her father was much closer to Falco, the French alternate, and they became good friends after the trial. He liked Biddle too, an educated 'Ivy League-type American'.

Of the prosecutors, the one Robby most admired was Maxwell Fyfe, because he was 'on top of everything', a committed lawyer who was present in the courtroom throughout the trial. I took this to be a dig at Shawcross, who dropped in on the hearings at key moments but wasn't generally around, unlike Jackson, who remained in Nuremberg for a full year. Robby was reluctant to say more, but she wasn't the first to express a firm dislike of Shawcross, seen by many as haughty and self-important, even if a fine advocate.

In early December, Robby spent five days in courtroom 600. It was bigger than the English courtrooms, and translation through headphones offered a novelty. The scene was intensely male – every judge, every defendant, every prosecutor. The only women were the stenographers and translators (one, with a great stack of blonde hair, was known to the judges as 'the passionate haystack') and a few journalists and writers.

She recalled the accused as 'a memorable bunch'. Göring stood out, because 'he intended to', very much the leader. Hess was 'very visible', with 'most peculiar' behaviour that included odd and constant facial movements. Kaltenbrunner had a 'long thin face, looked very cruel'. Jodl was 'nice looking'; his boss Wilhelm Keitel 'looked like a general, a soldier'. Franz von Papen was 'very good-looking'. Ribbentrop got much press in London because of his name recognition. Hjalmar Schacht was 'distinguished and tidy'. Albert Speer? 'Simply extraordinary', because of his bearing and control. Streicher? 'Absolutely horrible.' Robby Dundas smiled as she said, 'He looked horrible; everything about him was horrible.'

Frank? Yes, she remembered Hans Frank, with his dark glasses. He seemed insignificant, closed in on himself. The British papers published a vicious image of him about that time, she reminds me, drawn by the cartoonist David Low. 'Opinions might differ about the award of "nastiest-person-present",' Low wrote, but he was compelled to vote without hesitation for Frank, 'the butcher of Warsaw'. The combination of the fixed sneer and quiet mutterings got him the cartoonist's vote.

'Was he the one who cried the whole time?' she asked suddenly, which reminded me that others had spoken of Frank's tears. Yes, I said. She was in court on the day a film about Hitler was projected, causing Ribbentrop and others to weep uncontrollably.

Moments of horror remained vivid. She recalled the evidence of a woman commandant from Dachau, the one who 'made lamp shades out of human skin'. She shook her head gently as she spoke, as though trying to evict the memory, and her voice dropped until it was barely perceptible.

'Much of the time it was very boring, then something would happen, and my reaction was horror.'

She stopped herself.

'It was horrific . . .'

She heard extracts from Stroop's report, titled *The Warsaw Ghetto Is No More*.

Sitting in the public gallery, she listened as extracts from Frank's diary were read out. 'That we sentence 1,200,000 Jews to die of hunger should be noted only marginally,' those words she heard.

She saw human skin said to have been taken from bodies at Buchenwald. She remembered the talk of tattoos inked into living flesh.

The evidence had a profound effect on Robby Dundas, one that had persisted over seven decades. 'I loathe the Germans,' she said suddenly and most unexpectedly. 'I always have.' Then a hint of regret passed across her demure face. 'I am so sorry,' she said so quietly I almost missed the words. 'I just haven't forgiven them.'

123

What of Lemkin? Two months into a trial that had started well enough for the ideas he was espousing, all his efforts seemed to have evaporated into nothingness. Genocide was referred to on the first day by the French and Soviet prosecutors, much to his satisfaction. The Americans and the British followed, but they avoided any mention of the word. To Lemkin's dismay, the rest of November and all of December – thirty-one days of hearings – passed without the word being spoken in court.

Lemkin followed developments from Washington, kept far away from Nuremberg by Jackson's team. It was frustrating to read the daily transcripts as they reached the War Crimes Office, where he worked as a consultant, to read news reports that made no mention of genocide. Maybe it was the Southern senators who got to Jackson and his team, fearful about the implications that the charge of genocide might have in local politics, with the American Indians and the blacks.

Jackson's team took active steps to keep Lemkin away from the trial. After the difficulties he'd caused in London back in October, with his wayward behaviour, this was no surprise. Instead his talents were directed to the preparation of another war crimes trial, which was expected to open in April 1946 in Tokyo. He was, however, tasked with investigating the activities of Karl Haushofer, a First World War German general who later became a Munich academic, an acquaintance of the writer Stefan Zweig. It was said that Haushofer laid the intellectual foundations for the idea of *Lebensraum*, the need for greater living space for Germans by the appropriation of the territory of others, and that Rudolf Hess had been his research assistant. Lemkin recommended that Haushofer be prosecuted, but Jackson resisted on the grounds that his activity was limited to 'teaching and writing'. In due course, the matter became moot after Haushofer and his wife committed suicide.

On 20 December, the tribunal broke for the Christmas break. Donnedieu returned to his flat on the boulevard St Michel in Paris, where he found a letter from Lemkin waiting, along with a copy of *Axis Rule*. The reply, received by Lemkin in January 1946, must have ignited the Polish lawyer's desire to find some way to reinsert himself into the trial. 'Maybe I will have the pleasure of seeing you in Nuremberg,' the French judge wrote enticingly. The two men had known each other since the 1930s from League of Nations meetings. 'I am so pleased to have received your letter and its news,' Donnedieu added, in a thin handwriting, surprised that Lemkin's letter took so long to arrive. 'I am a judge at the International Military Tribunal,' he went on, as though Lemkin might not have known.

The Frenchman appreciated Lemkin's book as an 'important' work. He hadn't read every page, he admitted, because his responsibilities only allowed time for a 'skim' read. But he did read chapter 9 and believed the word 'genocide' to be 'very correct', as a term that 'expressively' designated 'the terrible crime that occupies our Tribunal's attention'. Lemkin would have been buoyed by the words yet astute enough to recognize their ambiguity. After all, Donnedieu was a man who felt able to accept Frank's invitation to visit him in Berlin in 1935.

'Alas, Poland has been the principal victim,' the French judge continued. The formulation was curious, because the judge had seen the evidence. Of course Poland was a victim, but *the* principal victim? Perhaps he was being polite to Lemkin, a Pole. Perhaps he didn't know that Lemkin was Jewish. Have you heard anything about 'our friend Rappaport'? the judge asked, referring to the Polish Supreme Court judge, the man who warned Lemkin he wouldn't be travelling to Madrid in October 1933. (Rappaport survived the war and was appointed president of Poland's Supreme National Tribunal, which conducted the criminal trials of Amon Göth, made more famous by the film *Schindler's List,* Frank's colleague Josef Bühler and the Auschwitz commandant Rudolf Höss – all sentenced to death.)

Donnedieu mentioned that he'd lost a son-in-law in the war, killed a year earlier, 'in the Resistance', and that he was in touch with Vespasian Pella, who was in Geneva writing a book about war crimes. Donnedieu's letter went to the address in London from which Lemkin had written a few months earlier and from there was forwarded to Washington. It reached Lemkin at the small apartment he kept at the Wardman Park Hotel. If genocide was to get any traction in the case, Lemkin knew he needed to get himself to Nuremberg.

124

When I first raised the subject of how or when his father learned what happened to his parents and other members of the family in Lemberg and Żółkiew, Eli said rather brusquely that he didn't know. The subject was never mentioned at home. 'I suppose he wanted to protect me, so I never asked.' It was a familiar silence, the one chosen by Leon and many others, respected by those around them.

The unlikely chain of events that led to the reunion between

Lauterpacht and his niece Inka emerged only from a conversation I had with Clara Kramer, who had been a neighbour of the Lauterpachts' in Zółkiew. One of her companions when she was in hiding in Zółkiew was Mr Melman, who travelled to Lemberg after being freed, to find out who might have survived. He visited a Jewish welfare committee, where he left a list of names, the few Jews who'd survived in Zółkiew, who included some Lauterpachts. This list was pinned to a wall of the committee's office, which Inka happened to visit after leaving the convent that offered refuge during the German occupation. She saw the Zółkiew names, made contact with Mr Melman, then went to Zółkiew. There she was introduced to Clara Kramer.

'Melman came back with this beautiful beauty,' Clara told me with emotion. 'She was gorgeous, like a Madonna, my first friend when I came out of hiding.' Inka, three years younger than Clara, became her best friend, and they remained close over many years, 'like sisters'. Inka told Clara about her uncle, a famous professor at Cambridge, a man called Hersch Lauterpacht. They would try to find him with the help of the Melmans and Mr Patrontasch, another Zółkiew survivor who was a classmate of Lauterpacht's at school in Lemberg back in 1913. The Melmans and Inka left Soviet-occupied Poland for Austria, where they ended up in a refugee camp near Vienna. At some point – Clara didn't recall the exact circumstances – Mr Patrontasch learned that Lauterpacht was involved in the Nuremberg trial. Perhaps from a newspaper, Clara said. 'Inka's uncle is at Nuremberg, and I will try to see him,' Mr Patrontasch told Mr Melman.

Because he lived outside the camp, Patrontasch was able to travel freely. 'He agreed to look for the famous professor Lauterpacht,' Clara explained. He travelled to Nuremberg, where he stood outside the entrance of the Palace of Justice, guarded by tanks. He waited, unable to gain entry, not wishing to make a fuss.

'They wouldn't let him in,' Clara added, 'so he just stood there, day after day, for three weeks. Every time a civilian came out, he whispered, "Hersch Lauterpacht", "Hersch Lauterpacht".' Clara used her body to describe the actions of Artur Patrontasch, cupping her soft hands. She spoke so quietly I could barely hear. 'Hersch Lauterpacht, Hersch Lauterpacht, Hersch Lauterpacht.'

At some point a passer-by heard the whispers and, recognizing the name, stopped to tell Patrontasch he knew Lauterpacht. 'That was how Inka found her uncle.' From this initial connection, direct contact followed several weeks later. Clara couldn't remember the month, but it was during the opening days of the trial. Just before the end of the year, in December 1945, Lauterpacht received a telegram with information about the family. There were no details, but enough information to offer hope. 'I hope that at least the child is alive,' Lauterpacht wrote on New Year's Eve to Rachel in Palestine. Early in 1946, he learned that Inka was the only family member to survive. A few weeks passed, then in the spring letters began to pass directly between Inka and Lauterpacht.

Clara asked whether she might share another thought with me. She was reluctant, she said, because she was talking to an Englishman.

'To tell you the truth, there was a moment I hated the British worse than the Germans.' She apologized. Why? I enquired.

'The Germans said they would kill me, and they tried. Then, much later, I was sitting in a displaced persons camp and wanted to go to Palestine, and the British wouldn't let me. For a time, I hated them as much as I hated the Germans.'

She smiled, adding that her views had changed since then. 'I was seventeen; you were allowed such feelings.'

125

Early in 1946, Frank found himself a confidant. In the absence of his wife, Brigitte, or his mistress, Lilly Grau, his new interlocutor was Dr Gustave Gilbert, the US army psychologist charged with keeping an eye on Frank's mental and spiritual health. Gilbert kept a diary in which he described many conversations, publishing long extracts after the trial was over (*Nuremberg Diary*, published in 1947).

Frank trusted the psychologist, feeling comfortable enough to discuss many of the matters that occupied his thoughts, both personal and professional. He talked about his wife and mistress, of suicide and Catholicism, of the Führer ('Can you imagine a man cold-bloodedly planning the whole thing?'). He shared vivid dreams, including inexplicable, violent sexual fantasies that occasionally led to 'nocturnal emissions' (this was how Dr Gilbert referred to them). Gilbert was not averse to sharing the confidences he picked up with

others; at a dinner party at Robert Jackson's home, he told Judge
Biddle that there were three 'homos' among the defendants, one of
whom was Frank.

During the Christmas recess, Dr Gilbert paid a routine visit to
Frank in his small cell. The former governor-general was busily
preparing his defence, apparently bothered by his decision not to
destroy the diaries, which were being used to great effect by the
prosecutors. So why didn't you destroy them? Dr Gilbert enquired.

'I listened to . . . the Bach Oratorio, "The Passion of St Matthew,"'
Frank told the American. 'When I heard the voice of Christ, something seemed to say to me: "What? Face the enemy with a false face?
You cannot hide the truth from God!" No, the truth must come
out, once and for all.' Bach's monumental work was quite frequently
evoked by Frank, offering solace with its message of mercy and
forgiveness.

The reference prompted me to attend a number of performances
of the *St Matthew Passion* in London and New York, and even a
performance at the St Thomas Church in Leipzig, where Bach had
written the work. I wanted to understand which parts of the work
Frank might have had in mind, how he had drawn solace in the
prison cell. The most familiar aria was 'Erbarme dich, Mein Gott,
um meiner Zähren willen', 'Have mercy, my God, for my tears'
sake'. Dr Gilbert might have understood the weeping for the weak-
ness of the individual, expressing a contrition that begged for mercy,
speaking on behalf of humanity as a whole. Did Frank appreciate
Bach's intent? If he had, he would surely have chosen another work.
A decade earlier, he'd railed in Berlin against the idea of individuals
having rights; now he took refuge in a musical work that famously
embraced the individual's right to redemption.

Dr Gilbert raised the subject of Frank's conversion to Catholicism
in his cell in the days before the trial began. Frank mumbled about
feelings of responsibility, the need to be truthful. Might it not be
more of a hysterical symptom, a reaction to the feelings of guilt?
Frank didn't respond to the suggestion. The American psychologist
sensed a residue of positive feelings towards the Nazi regime, yet
also a feeling of enmity towards Hitler. In early January, Frank's
lawyer asked if the Vatican was helping the prosecution and whether
Frank should leave the Church. The issue caused Frank to reflect.

'It is as though I am two people,' Frank said as Dr Gilbert listened.

'Me, myself, Frank here – and the other Frank, the Nazi leader.'
Was Frank playing a game or being truthful? Dr Gilbert wondered
silently.

'Sometimes I wonder how that man Frank could have done those
things. This Frank looks at the other Frank and says, "Hmm, what
a louse you are Frank! – How could you do such things? – You certainly let your emotions run away with you, didn't you?"'

Dr Gilbert said nothing.

'I am sure as a psychologist you must find that very interesting.
– Just as if I were two different people. I am here, myself – and that
other Frank of the big Nazi speeches over there on trial.'

Still Gilbert remained silent. The less he spoke, the more Frank
talked.

'Fascinating, isn't it?' Frank said, slightly desperately.

Fascinating and schizoid, Gilbert thought, and no doubt designed
to save Frank from the rope.

126

Over the next month, the trial moved from matters of general
evidence to individual accounts as witnesses appeared to offer personal, first-hand testimony. One such witness was Samuel Rajzman,
a Polish-speaking accountant, a lone survivor from Treblinka.

I found Rajzman's account to be especially compelling and personal, because Treblinka was where Malke was murdered. Leon
learned of the details only at the end of his life, when my mother
showed him a book that contained a long list of the names of those
detained at Theresienstadt. Among the thousands was the name
of Malke Buchholz, with the detail that she was transported from
Theresienstadt to Treblinka on 23 September 1942. Leon retired to
the privacy of his room, along with the volume, where my mother
heard him weep. The next day he said nothing more about the book.
Of Treblinka, he never spoke, not in my presence.

Samuel Rajzman appeared in the witness box on the morning of
27 February, introduced to the judges as a man who had 'returned
from the other world'. He wore a dark suit and tie, peered through
spectacles. His angular, lined face offered a sense of astonishment
and bemusement that he was alive, seated just a few feet from Frank,

in whose territory Treblinka was located. To look at the man, one would not know the path he travelled or the horrors he witnessed.

He spoke in a measured and calm voice of the journey from the Warsaw ghetto in August 1942, transportation by rail in inhumane conditions, eight thousand people in overcrowded cattle cars. He was the only survivor. When the Russian prosecutor asked about the moment of arrival, Rajzman told him how they were made to undress and walk along *Himmelfahrtstrasse,* the 'street to heaven', a short walk to the gas chamber, when suddenly a friend from Warsaw singled him out and led him away. The Germans needed an interpreter, but before that he loaded the clothes of the dead onto empty trains that departed Treblinka. Two days passed, then a transport arrived from the small town of Vinegrova, bringing his mother, sister and brothers. He watched them walk to the gas chambers, unable to intervene. Several days later he was handed his wife's papers, with a photograph of his wife and child.

'That is all I have left of my family,' he said in the courtroom, a public act of revelation. 'A photograph.'

He offered a graphic account of killing on an industrial scale, individual acts of horror and inhumanity. A ten-year-old girl was brought to the '*Lazarett*' (infirmary) with her two-year-old sister, guarded by a German called Willi Mentz, a milkman with a small black moustache (Mentz later returned to the job, which he held until sentenced to life imprisonment at the Treblinka trial, held in Germany in 1965). The older girl threw herself onto Mentz as he removed his gun. Why did he want to kill the little girl? Rajzman described how he watched Mentz pick up the two-year-old, walk the short distance to a crematorium, and throw her into an oven. Then he killed the sister.

The defendants listened in silence, two rows of shamed faces. Did Frank seem to slump?

Rajzman continued in a flat monotone. An aged woman was brought to the '*Lazarett*' with her daughter, who was in labour, made to lie on a plot of grass. Guards watched her give birth. Mentz asked the grandmother which one she'd prefer to see killed first. The older woman begged to be the first.

'Of course, they did the opposite,' Rajzman told the courtroom, speaking very quietly. 'The newborn baby was killed first, then the child's mother, and finally the grandmother.'

Rajzman talked of conditions at the camp, of the fake railway station. The deputy commander, Kurt Franz, built a first-class railroad station with false signs. Later an imaginary restaurant was added, and schedules were listed with times of departures and arrivals. Grodno, Suwałki, Vienna, Berlin. It was like a film set. To calm people, Rajzman explained, 'so there should not be any incidents'.

The purpose was psychological, to offer reassurance as the end approached?

'Yes.' Rajzman's voice remained calm, flat.

How many were exterminated each day? Between ten and twelve thousand.

How was it done?

Initially, by three gas chambers, then ten more.

Rajzman described how he was on the platform when Sigmund Freud's three sisters arrived. It was 23 September 1942. He saw Commander Kurt Franz deal with one of the sisters' request for special treatment.

After reading this transcript of the trial, with the details of the arrival of the Freud sisters from Theresienstadt, I searched for the details of the transport on which the Freud sisters arrived. When I found them, I looked at the other names on the list, a thousand of them, and eventually I found the name of Malke Buchholz. Rajzman must have been on the platform when she arrived.

127

I decided to visit Treblinka, or what remained. The opportunity came with an invitation to give two lectures in Poland, one in Kraków, the other in Warsaw, which was only an hour from the Treblinka site. The Kraków lecture was at the Allerhand Institute, named in honour of the professor who taught Lauterpacht and Lemkin, murdered in Lemberg for the crime of enquiring of a guard whether he had a soul. In Warsaw, I gave a lecture at the Polish Institute of International Affairs. Both events were well attended, with numerous questions about Lauterpacht and Lemkin. Issues of identity dominated. Would I say they are Poles or Jews, or both? Did it matter? I answered.

In Warsaw, I met a Polish legal historian, Adam Redzik, who talked to me of Stanislaw Starzynski, the Lemberg professor who taught Lauterpacht and Lemkin. He believed Starzynski should be credited for inadvertently saving Lauterpacht, because he'd supported another candidate for appointment to the chair of international law in Lwów in 1923. It was Professor Redzik who gave me the photograph of the Lemberg professors, an image taken in 1912, eighteen men, each with moustache or beard, Makarewicz included, along with Allerhand and Longchamps de Berier, who would be murdered by the Germans in Lemberg.

At the Warsaw lecture, a former Polish foreign minister sat in the audience. Later Adam Rotfeld and I talked about Lwów, near the town of Przemyślany, where he was born. We touched on minority rights, the 1919 treaty, pogroms against Jews, Nuremberg. Yes, he told me, Makarewicz probably was the teacher who inspired Lauterpacht and Lemkin. How ironic, he mused, that a man with such strong nationalist sympathies should be the person to catalyse the conflict between Lauterpacht and Lemkin, between individuals and groups.

Later my son and I visited the new Warsaw Uprising Museum. One room was dominated by a large black-and-white photograph of the Frank family, spread across an entire wall. I knew the image, which had been sent to me a few months earlier by Niklas Frank. He was three years old then, dressed in a checkered black-and-white outfit and shiny black shoes, holding his mother's hand. He stood with his back to his father; he looked sad, as though he wanted to be somewhere else.

From Warsaw, my son and I travelled by car to Treblinka. The landscape was dull, flat, grey. Turning off the main highway, we passed thickening woods, villages and churches. A single wooden structure, a house or a barn, occasionally broke the monotony. We stopped at a marketplace to buy dry biscuits and a pot of flowers, blood red. In the car was a map that showed Treblinka to be on the route to Wołkowysk.

Nothing tangible remained of the camp at Treblinka, hastily destroyed by the Germans as they departed. There was a modest museum that held a few photographs and documents, tired and grainy, a cheap model of the camp, reconstructed from the memories of the few survivors. A handful of government decrees floated behind protective glass, some with Frank's signature, one authorizing the penalty of death in October 1941.

Another document was signed by Franz Stangl, the commander, the subject of a disquieting book by the writer Gitta Sereny. Alongside Stangl's signature was the familiar round stamp of the General Government. Treblinka, 26 September 1943. Here was irrefutable evidence that Frank's authority encompassed the camp. A black sign, indelible and definitive as to the matter of responsibility.

When the camp was discovered by the Soviets, Vasily Grossman's article 'The Hell of Treblinka' offered another account, immediate and brutal. 'We tread the earth of Treblinka,' he wrote, 'casting up fragments of bone, teeth, sheets of paper, clothes, things of all kinds. The earth does not want to keep secrets.' That was September 1944.

The entrance led to a path of earth and flattened grass, with concrete sleepers tracing the railway line along which Rajzman, the Freud sisters and Malke travelled to the terminus point of their lives, a platform. Gone were the half-rotted shirts and penknives of which Grossman wrote, gone were the child's shoes with red pom-poms. The mugs, passports, photographs and ration cards were no longer present, buried in a forest later cleared for symbolic railway sleepers and a platform, taking the imagination on an inner journey.

Under the endless grey sky, a memorial of roughly hewn rocks was laid, hundreds of them, like gravestones, or snowdrops, set into the earth. Each marked a hamlet, a village or town, a city or region from which a million individuals were brought. It was a place of reflection, dominated by the sky, as it was then, framed by green firs that reached upward. The forest was silent, a keeper of secrets.

Later we made our way to a nearby town, looking for food. We passed the abandoned Treblinka town train station, a couple of miles from the camp, the one used by Willi Mentz and other German and Ukrainian workers. Nearby was the town of Brok, a place to have lunch in a sad restaurant. A radio played quietly in the background, a familiar tune cutting across the room, a song written in the 1980s during riots in Los Angeles. 'Don't dwell on what has passed away, or what is yet to be.'

Leonard Cohen was popular these days in Poland, with his message. There was a crack in everything; that's how the light got in.

128

The conclusion of Samuel Rajzman's testimony coincided with a
new phase of the trial. Göring was the first of the defendants to set
out his case, in March 1946. As Frank's turn approached, he knew
he faced a real challenge to save himself from the gallows, that it
would be no easy matter. The diaries had been used to 'spike' him,
the *New Yorker* reported, frequently invoked by the Soviets.

On Thursday, 18 April, Frank got his day in court. He followed
Ernst Kaltenbrunner and Alfred Rosenberg, who attempted to persuade the tribunal that the word 'extermination' did not mean what
it literally said, and most certainly it did not refer to mass killing.
Rudolf Höss, the commander of Auschwitz, appeared as a witness
for Kaltenbrunner, offering a detailed account of the gassing and
burning of 'at least 2,500,000 victims' over three years. As Höss
spoke without regret or emotion, Frank listened attentively. Privately, Höss told Dr Gilbert that the dominant attitude at Auschwitz
was of total indifference. Any other sentiment 'never even occurred
to us'.

Against this backdrop, Frank could hope he'd come across as
thoughtful and deliberate, rather less guilty than the neighbour
who sat to his right, if such matters could be measured on a scale.
Up to the moment of his appearance on the stand, he was torn, not
knowing whether to offer a robust defence of his actions or to take
a more subtle approach, one that pleaded ignorance to some of the
horrors. Another option, not to be excluded, would be to express
some degree of responsibility. What had he decided as he made his
way to the stand?

All eyes were on him, without dark glasses, hiding his damaged
left hand. He seemed nervous, slightly self-conscious. Occasionally
he looked towards the other defendants, who now sat to his right,
as though seeking their approval (which was not forthcoming).
Dr Seidl asked a few questions about his career to the moment he
was appointed governor-general. Seidl was tentative. Reading the
transcript, watching what I could find by way of newsreel, I had
the impression – developed from my own courtroom experience –
that Dr Seidl didn't know what surprise his client might spring in
response to questions.

Frank got into his stride. He spoke with increasing confidence in a strong, loud voice. I imagined him on a different kind of platform. Dr Seidl asked about Frank's role in Poland after his appointment by Hitler. 'I bear the responsibility,' Frank responded.

'Do you feel guilty of having committed ... crimes against humanity?'

'That is a question that the Tribunal has got to decide.' Frank explained that five months into the trial he had learned things of which he had not been fully aware, perhaps a reference to Höss. He now had 'a full insight' into the horrible atrocities committed. 'I am possessed by a deep sense of guilt.'

It sounded like an admission of sorts and a warning to Dr Seidl. The other defendants heard his words in that way, so did others in the courtroom.

Did you introduce Jewish ghettos?

Yes.

Did you introduce badges to mark the Jews?

Yes.

Did you yourself introduce forced labour in the General Government?

Yes.

Did you know of the conditions in Treblinka, Auschwitz and other camps?

This was a dangerous question. Frank heard Rajzman give evidence, and the witness testimony of Höss, so terrible. So he sidestepped.

'Auschwitz was not in the area of the Government General.' Strictly speaking, this was correct, although it was close enough to Kraków, where he worked, to be able to smell the place.

'I was never in Majdanek, nor in Treblinka, nor in Auschwitz.'

There was no way of knowing whether that was true. The attentive judges must have noted the brief evasion, that he hadn't answered the question posed.

Did you ever participate in the annihilation of Jews?

Frank reflected, his face quizzical. He offered a carefully crafted response.

'I say "yes", and the reason why I say "yes" is because, having lived through the five months of this trial, and particularly after having heard the testimony of the witness Höss, my conscience does not allow me to throw the responsibility solely on these minor people.'

The words caused a commotion among the defendants, which he must have noticed. He wanted to be clear about what he was saying: he never personally installed an extermination camp or promoted their existence. Nevertheless, Hitler had laid a dreadful responsibility on his people, so it was his responsibility too. One step forward, one step back.

'We have fought against Jewry for years.' These words he was bound to recognize. Yes, he'd made 'the most horrible utterances'; the diaries bore witness against him, no escaping that.

'Therefore, it is no more than my duty to answer your question in this connection with "yes".' The courtroom was silent. Then he said, 'A thousand years will pass and still this guilt of Germany will not have been erased.'

This was too much for some defendants. Göring was seen to shake his head in disgust, whisper to a neighbour, pass a note along the dock. Another defendant expressed displeasure that Frank associated his individual guilt with that of the entire German people. There was a difference between the responsibility of the individual and that of the group. Some who heard this last comment might have noted its irony.

'Did you hear him say that Germany is disgraced for a thousand years?' Fritz Sauckel whispered to Göring.

'Yes, I heard it.' The contempt towards Frank was apparent. He would not have an easy evening.

'I suppose Speer will say the same thing,' Göring added. Frank and Speer were weak-kneed. Cowards.

During the lunch break, Dr Seidl encouraged Frank to refine his expression of guilt, to narrow it down. Frank declined the request. 'I am glad I got it out, and I'll let it go at that.' Later he suggested to Dr Gilbert that he was hopeful that he might have done enough to avoid the gallows. 'I did know what was going on. I think the judges are really impressed when one of us speaks from his heart and doesn't try to dodge the responsibility. Don't you think so? I was really gratified at the way they were impressed by my sincerity.'

Other defendants were contemptuous. Speer doubted Frank's honesty. 'I wonder what he would have said if he hadn't turned in his diary,' he said. Hans Fritzsche was bothered that Frank associated his guilt with that of the German people. 'He is more guilty than any of us,' he told Speer. 'He really knows about those things.'

Rosenberg, who had spent five months sitting alongside Frank, was appalled. '"Germany is disgraced for a thousand years"? That is going pretty far!'

Ribbentrop told Dr Gilbert that no German should say that his country was disgraced for a thousand years.

'I wonder how genuine it was?' Jodl asked.

Admiral Karl Dönitz shared Fritzsche's concerns. Frank should only have spoken as an individual, for himself. It was not for him to speak for the Germans as a whole.

After lunch, Dr Seidl asked a few more questions, then the American prosecutor Thomas Dodd took over, raising the subject of looted art. Frank considered the suggestion that he was involved in any wrongdoing offensive.

'I did not collect pictures and I did not find time during the war to appropriate art treasures.' All the art was registered, remaining in Poland to the end. That wasn't true, Dodd said, reminding him about the Dürer etchings taken from Lemberg. Before my time, Frank retorted. What about the paintings he took to Germany in 1945, what about the Leonardo?

'I was safeguarding them, but not for myself.' They were widely known; no one could appropriate them. 'You cannot steal a *Mona Lisa*.' This was a reference to Cecilia Gallerani. At one end of the dock, Göring was deadpan; at the other end, some defendants were seen to grin.

129

Frank's approach generated a buzz around the Palace of Justice. Yves Beigbeder, who was in court that day, confirmed that to me. Now ninety-one, he was retired and living in Neuchâtel, Switzerland, after a distinguished career at the United Nations and writing several works on international criminal law. He was still affected by Frank's testimony, heard when he was a twenty-two-year-old law graduate, working as legal secretary for his uncle the French judge Donnedieu.

Donnedieu never spoke to his nephew about the trial, not even during the lunch break. 'My uncle was very reserved; I could ask any questions, but he expressed no views to me at all. My aunt was the same; she just kept very quiet.' Beigbeder had no recollection of meeting Lauterpacht or Lemkin but knew both by name and repute, even then, and the arguments each was pursuing. Yet he didn't focus on the battle of ideas that divided the two Lemberg men, the individual and the group. 'I was too young and ignorant!' Now, many years later, he recognized its importance and vitality, a starting point for modern international law. Donnedieu and Falco sometimes talked about Lemkin in a lighthearted way. The man had an 'obsession' with genocide; that he remembered them saying.

Frank presented his defence a month after Beigbeder had arrived in Nuremberg. There were rumours he'd adopt a different approach from the others, so Beigbeder made sure he was in court. On his recollection, Frank was the only defendant to recognize any degree of responsibility. That made an impression, causing Beigbeder to write an article for a French Protestant periodical, *Réforme*, an 'unexpected acknowledgment of guilt'.

'Frank seemed to accept a certain responsibility,' he told me. 'It was not complete, of course, but the fact that he recognized a certain responsibility was important, and different, and we all noticed that.'

I asked about his uncle's connection with Frank. Did Donnedieu ever mention that he'd known Frank in the 1930s, even visited Berlin at Frank's invitation? The questions elicited only a silence, then, 'What do you mean?' I told him of Donnedieu's trip to Berlin to speak at the Akademie für Deutsches Recht. Later I sent a copy of the speech Donnedieu gave that day, ironically enough titled 'The Punishment of International Crimes'. Frank responded to Donnedieu's ideas with an attack, 'a great source of danger and unclearness'. I also sent a photograph, evidently a real surprise to Beigbeder. 'I did not know until you told me that my uncle already knew Hans Frank. That is most surprising.'

Frank and Donnedieu had a mutual interest in keeping their connection under wraps. Judge Falco knew, however, noting in his diary that his French colleague had dined with Frank and had even met Julius Streicher. The Soviets also knew, objecting to the appointment of Donnedieu as a judge. *Le Populaire*, a French socialist newspaper, ran an article with a neat headline: 'A Nazi Judge on the Nuremberg Tribunal'.

130

Frank appeared on the stand on Maundy Thursday, the day after the *St Matthew Passion* was usually performed in Leipzig at the St Thomas Church. Dodd wrote to his wife in America that he'd expected Frank to be 'ornery', given the 'wicked' record in Poland, yet in the end there was no need for much cross-examination. Frank had practically admitted his guilt, one of the more dramatic moments of the trial.

'He has become a Catholic,' Dodd wrote, 'and I guess it took.'

Frank was calm. He'd paid his dues, passed through the black gates, felt optimistic. The French, British and American judges must have appreciated his candour. God was a generous host, he told Dr Gilbert, who asked what had caused him to take the direction he chose.

A newspaper article was 'the last straw', Frank explained.

'A few days ago I read a notice in the newspaper that Dr Jacoby, a Jewish lawyer in Munich, who was one of my father's best friends, had been exterminated in Auschwitz. Then when Höss testified how he exterminated two and a half million Jews, I realized that he was the man who coldly exterminated my father's best friend – a fine, upright, kindly old man – and millions of innocent people like him, and I had done nothing to stop it! True, I didn't kill him myself, but the things I said and the things Rosenberg said made those things possible!'

Like Brigitte Frank, he took comfort in the belief that he'd not killed anyone personally. Perhaps that would save him.

IX

THE GIRL WHO CHOSE
NOT TO REMEMBER

131

Leon chose the path of silence. Nothing was said of Malke, his sisters Laura and Gusta, the family in Lemberg and Żółkiew, or the other family members in Vienna, including his four nieces.

One of the four nieces was Herta, the eleven-year-old daughter of sister Laura, who was to travel to Paris with Miss Tilney and my mother in the summer of 1939, but did not do so. Leon never spoke of her.

He said nothing either of his sister Gusta and her husband, Max, who remained in Vienna until December 1939.

I knew little about Gusta and Max's three daughters – Daisy, the eldest, Edith, the youngest, and the middle child, also called Herta – save that they had managed to leave Vienna in September 1938. The three made their way to Palestine, and in the 1950s my mother was in touch with two of them.

As my mother and I were preparing to make the first trip to Lviv, she evoked the memory of these three sisters, Leon's nieces, 'long gone'. Two of them, Edith and Herta, had children; perhaps they might be worth tracking down. I had a distant memory of that generation, from childhood, but nothing more.

Now I would try to locate them, to hear their stories. Names and old addresses eventually threw up a phone number, which led me to Doron, the son of Herta, the middle child of Gusta and Max. Doron lived in Tel Aviv, and he sprang a surprise: his mother, Leon's niece Herta, was alive and well, living nearby in a retirement home with a fine view over the Mediterranean. She was a lively, active ninety-two-year-old who played bridge every day and completed at least two crosswords each week in German.

There was a difficulty, Doron added. She had steadfastly refused to talk to him about events before the war, declining to say much about life in Vienna before December 1938, when she left. He had little information and knew almost nothing about that period. 'A mystery', he called it. As far as I could tell, she was the only person alive who was in Vienna with Malke and Leon who might have memories. She wouldn't talk, but perhaps her memory could be jogged. Perhaps she recalled the wedding of Leon and Rita in the spring of 1937, or my mother's birth a year later, or the circumstances of her own departure from Vienna. She may be able to shed light on Leon's life in Vienna.

She agreed to meet with me. Whether she would talk about that period was another matter.

Two weeks later, I stood outside Herta Gruber's front door in Tel Aviv, accompanied by her son Doron. It opened to reveal a diminutive, well-preserved lady with a splendid head of dyed red hair. She had prepared herself, dressed in a crisp white shirt, a gash of freshly applied deep red lipstick running across her mouth, under eyebrows arched in brown pencil.

I spent two days in the company of Herta, surrounded by family photographs, documents and pictures of Vienna from the 1930s. I had brought them from London, hoping to jog her memory. She had her own documents, including a small album that held many family photographs that were new to me.

The first was taken in 1926, when she was six, her first day at school, standing outside Max's liquor store. The summer of 1935, a holiday on the Plattensee. Winter 1936, a school holiday in the ski resort of Bad Aussee. A handsome boyfriend, photographed in 1936. The following summer, with friends in a field in the South Tyrol, picking flowers. Holidays in Döbling and on the Dalmatian coast of Yugoslavia, 1937. An image in Vienna, taken in a municipal park, near a boating lake, early 1938, before the *Anschluss*. The life of a comfortable, happy teenager.

Then the Germans arrived and the Nazis took over; life was interrupted. The pages that followed include a family photograph, Herta with her parents and two sisters, just before she left Vienna. Grandmother Malke was in the picture, shortly to be left on her own. Then a page on which Herta had written the date – 29 September 1938 – the day of departure from Vienna. She left with her younger sister, Edith, travelled by train from Vienna to Brindisi in southern Italy. From there, they took a ship to Palestine.

Tucked into these pages was an undated photograph of her cousin, also called Herta, the only child of Leon's sister Laura. A girl I hadn't seen before, in glasses, standing anxiously next to a doll with long braided hair, placed on the street. Both wore a hat. This was the Herta who stayed behind, a last-minute decision, the girl who couldn't bear to be separated from her mother, who decided that Herta would not travel with Miss Tilney. Two years later, she and her mother were dead in the ghetto in Lodz.

There were pictures of Leon. A portrait on his wedding day, without the bride, taken by Simonis, a well-known society studio. Four photographs of my mother, taken in Vienna, during the first year of her life, in the arms of Malke. It was a tender image, new to me. Malke looked weary, with a tired face.

Herta Rosenblum (cousin of Herta Gruber), c. 1938

Malke and Ruth, 1938

132

Herta's comportment could best be described as neutral. She was neither happy nor unhappy to see me. I was simply there. She remembered uncle Leon, pleased to talk about him, warming up, her eyes alive. Yes, she said, I know who you are, his grandson. This was treated as a point of fact, not accompanied by any hint of emotion. Indeed, at no point in the course of the two days we spent together did she indicate sadness or happiness or any other sentiments that lie between the extremes. There was another curiosity: in the many hours we spent together, Herta didn't ask me a single question.

Early in the conversation it emerged that Herta knew nothing about what happened to her parents. She knew they were dead, but not how or when. I asked her if she wanted to know what happened to them.

'Does he know?' The question was put to her son, not to me. She seemed surprised at the prospect of new information.

'He says he knows,' Doron replied. They spoke in Hebrew; I could only infer the gentleness with which he answered.

I broke the silence and asked her son if she wanted to know.

'Ask her,' Doron said, with a shrug of the shoulders.

Yes, she replied, she wanted the details, all of them.

Many years had passed between the events I described and our coming together in Herta's small apartment in Tel Aviv. Your parents were murdered, I told her, seventy years ago, after you and your sisters left Vienna. The circumstances were terribly unlucky. I discovered that Gusta and Max found places on a steamship, the *Uranus,* which was to sail down the Danube towards Bratislava, taking them and several hundred other Jewish émigrés towards the Black Sea. From there, they would take another boat to Palestine.

The *Uranus* left Vienna in December 1939, but the journey was interrupted by a confluence of unfortunate events, natural and unnatural, of ice and occupation. By the end of the year, the boat had reached Kladovo, a town in Yugoslavia (now in Serbia). Further passage was blocked by the ice that came with a freakish, cold winter. Gusta and Max spent a frozen winter on board the crowded boat, not allowed to disembark for several months, until the following spring. They were then taken to a camp near Kladovo, where they remained for several months. In November 1940, they boarded another boat, which returned towards Vienna, back up the Danube, to the town of Šabac, near Belgrade. That was where they happened to be in April 1941, when Germany attacked and occupied Yugoslavia. There they remained, unable to travel on.

In due course, they were detained under the authority of the Germans. The men and women were separated. Max was taken to Zasavica, in Serbia, to a field where he was lined up and shot with the other men from the boat. It was 12 October 1942. Gusta survived a few more weeks, then she was transported to the Sajmište concentration camp, near Belgrade. It was there that she was killed, on a day unknown, in the autumn of 1942.

Herta listened attentively to this account, which I shared with some anxiety. When I had finished, I waited to see if she had any questions, but there were none. She had heard and understood. She chose this moment to offer an explanation of her approach to the past, to silence and remembrance.

'I want you to know that it's not correct that I have forgotten everything.'

That is what she said, her eyes fixed firmly on mine.

'It is just that I decided a very long time ago that this was a period that I did not wish to remember. I have not forgotten. I have chosen not to remember.'

133

Over the course of those two days, photographs from her album and others loaded on my laptop had caused Herta's memory to open up a little. Initially, it was as though there were no light, then a flicker, a glow, intermittent illumination. Herta remembered a few things, but others were buried too deep to emerge.

I showed her a picture of Laura, her aunt, her mother's sister. No memory. Then a wedding photograph, Leon and Rita, a picture of the temple where they married. These images too made no impression. She said she didn't remember, although she must have attended the wedding. Rita's name meant nothing to her. Rita, I say, Regina, but there was no flicker of recognition, nothing. No, I don't remember. It was as though Rita never existed. Herta had no memory of the birth of my mother in July 1938, a couple of months before she left for Brindisi. She knew Leon had a child, but nothing more.

Other memories did return, but hardly a rush.

Herta's face lit up when I showed her a photograph of Malke. My grandmother, she said, 'a very, very kind woman', although 'not so tall'. Herta recognized an image of the building on Klosterneuburger Strasse where they lived, at No. 69. She recalled the interior ('three bedrooms and another for the maid, a large dining room where the family would gather for meals'). The subject of family meals catalysed another memory, one that her son had previously shared with me, of being made to eat with a book lodged under each arm, to keep her arms straight as she ate.

I put a photograph of the building before her, taken a few months earlier, when I visited with my daughter. It hasn't changed, she said. She pointed to a large window on the corner of the first floor.

'From that room, my mother waved to me every morning, when I went off to school.'

Her father's shop was on the ground floor. She pointed to the windows, described the interior in detail. The bottles, the glasses, the smell. The friendly customers.

Now she was almost expansive, remembering summer holidays on Austrian lakes, skiing holidays at Bad Aussee ('wonderful'), trips to the Burgtheater and the Wiener Staatsoper ('glamorous and exciting'). Yet when I showed her a picture of a street near her home that was bedecked in swastikas, she claimed to have no memory of such a scene. It was as though everything from March 1938 had been rubbed out. She was the same age as Inge Trott, who remembered the arrival of the German army and the Nazi takeover. Herta remembered none of that.

Digging deep, with some prompting, she remembered a place called Lemberg and a trip by train to visit Malke's family. Żółkiew rang a bell, but she couldn't recall if she'd visited.

Leon's name produced the most vivid of family memories. She described him as 'beloved', her uncle Leon, like an older brother, only sixteen years older than she. He was always around, a constant presence.

'He was so nice, I loved him.' She stopped herself, surprised by what she had just said. Then she said it again, in case I missed it. 'I really loved him.'

He grew up with her, Herta explained, living in the same apartment after Malke returned to Lemberg in 1919. He was there when she was born in 1920, sixteen years old, a Viennese schoolboy. Her mother, Gusta, was his guardian in Malke's absence.

Over the years, Leon was a constant in her life. When Malke returned from Lemberg, she moved into an apartment in the same building, owned by Gusta and Max (later I found the papers that showed the building was sold by Max and Gusta for a pittance to a local Nazi, a few months after the *Anschluss*). Malke was reassuring, a matronly presence throughout Herta's childhood, especially during the large family gatherings on religious holidays. As far as Herta can recall, there was almost no religion in the family life; they rarely went to synagogue.

'I think Leon loved his mother very much,' Herta said suddenly, without prompting. 'He was very attentive to her,' and she to him, her only son after the death of Emil, killed in the first days of the First World War. There was no father around, Herta reminded me.

As we went through the photo albums, her face visibly softened each time she came across an image of Leon.

She recognized the face of another young man, who appeared in several photographs. The name escaped her. Max Kupferman, I told her, Leon's best friend.

'Yes, of course,' Herta said. 'I remember him, he was my uncle's friend, they were always together. When he came over, he always came with his friend Max.'

This prompted a question from me about women friends. Herta shook her head firmly, then smiled, a warm smile. Her eyes were expressive too. 'Everyone was always saying to Leon, "When will you get married?" He always said he never wanted to get married.'

I asked again about girlfriends. She remembered none.

'He was always with his friend Max.' That is all she said, repeating the words.

Doron asked if she thought Leon might have been gay.

'We didn't know what that was back then,' Herta replied. The tone was flat. She was not surprised or shocked. She didn't confirm; she didn't deny.

134

Back in London, I returned to Leon's papers, gathering up all the photographs I was able to find, which were in no apparent order. I put to one side all the images of Max, arranging them in chronological order as best I could.

The first photograph was a formal portrait, taken by the Central Atelier in Vienna in November 1924. On the back of the little square image, Max wrote an inscription ('To my friend Buchholz, with memories'). The last image of Max in Leon's album was taken twelve years later, in May 1936, the two men lying on a grass field with a leather football. Max signed it 'Mackie'.

Between 1924 and 1936, over a period of twelve years, Leon had several dozen photographs of his friend Max. Not a year passed without a photograph, it seemed, and often there were several.

The two men on a walking holiday. Playing football. At a function. A beach party, with girls, arms entwined. By a car in the countryside, standing together.

Leon (left) and 'Mackie', 1936

Over a dozen years, from the age of twenty until just a few months before he married Rita, when he was thirty-three, the photographs signalled a close relationship. Whether it was intimate in another way was unclear. To view them now, with Herta's recollections in my mind, pointed to a particular kind of intimacy. He said he never wanted to get married.

Max managed to get out of Vienna, although when or how I did not know. He went to America, to New York, then to California. He stayed in touch with Leon, and many years later, when my mother was in Los Angeles, she met him. He married late in life, my mother told me, no children. What was he like? Warm, friendly, funny, she said. 'And flamboyant.' She smiled, a knowing smile.

I went back to the only letter from Max that I found in Leon's papers. It was written in May 1945, on the ninth, the day Germany capitulated to the Soviet Union. It was a reply to a letter sent by Leon from Paris a month earlier.

Max described the loss of family members, the sense of survival, the renewed sense of optimism. The words conveyed a palpable sense of hope. Like Leon, he embraced life, a cup half-full.

The last, typed line caught my eye, as it did when I first read it, although in a different way back then, without the context, without having heard Herta. Did Max linger on the memory of Vienna as he typed out the words, as he offered 'heartfelt kisses', before closing with a question?

'Should I reciprocate the kisses,' Max wrote, 'or are they only for your wife?'

X

JUDGEMENT

135

After Frank finished setting out his case, the remaining defendants set out their defences, and then the prosecutors made closing arguments. The Americans chose not to involve Lemkin in their efforts, but the British turned to Lauterpacht, who worked with Shawcross. Having regard to the 'tremendous help' he'd given with the opening, Shawcross asked Lauterpacht to craft the final legal arguments and apply them to the facts. 'I should in any event be most grateful for your advice.'

Lauterpacht took some time to recover from the first trip to Nuremberg several months earlier. He did so by immersing himself in teaching and writing, including one article that reflected the challenges posed by the trial, the tension between 'realism' and 'principle'. 'Sound realism' and a pragmatic approach were both necessary, he concluded, but in the long run the commitment to 'principle' was more important and should prevail. He didn't address Lemkin's ideas, but if he had, he would have said they were wrong in principle and impractical.

By the spring of 1946, Lauterpacht felt tired and dismal. Rachel was concerned about his health and state of mind and an insomnia that caused him to worry greatly about life's minor challenges, such as the cost of membership at the Athenaeum Club in Pall Mall. The terrible news delivered by Inka about the deaths of his parents and the entire family weighed heavily on him, even without any details. Rachel told Eli that in the privacy of the night his father would 'cry out awfully in his sleep', a reaction to 'the bestialities he had heard described'.

Inka's survival did offer one ray of light. Lauterpacht put time and energy into persuading her to move to England, to be with them in Cambridge. He had the right to bring her over, he explained, as her closest living relative, but he couldn't bring the Melmans, who were caring for her in a displaced persons camp in Austria. Lauterpacht understood that Inka was inclined to stay with the Melmans, the

couple who offered security and continuity after the 'horrible sufferings' she had lived through. 'We know about you a lot,' he wrote to
the fifteen-year-old, 'because your Grandfather Aron loved you very
much and was very often speaking about you.' He wanted to respect
her wishes, up to a point. It *was* for her to decide on her future,
he wrote, yet she should come to England, where conditions of life
would be 'more normal'.

Rachel intervened to end the impasse. I understand your 'fears
and doubts', she told Inka, but Hersch is your closest relative, your
mother's brother. 'I met your mother and I loved her very much,'
Rachel wrote, 'I think it is right that you come to us as your own
home and to your own family.' She added a line that must have influenced: 'You will be our own child, our daughter.' Later that year,
Inka travelled to England to move in with them in Cranmer Road.

During this correspondence with Inka, Lauterpacht returned to
Nuremberg, now armed with the knowledge that his family had been
destroyed by the men he was prosecuting. He travelled on 29 May to
confer with David Maxwell Fyfe and the British legal team charged
with preparing closing arguments. They would be delivered a few
weeks later, at the end of July, so Shawcross proposed a division of
labours: the British lawyers in Nuremberg would deal with the facts
about the individual defendants, and Lauterpacht would address the
'legal and historical part of the case'. His task would be to persuade
the judges that there were no obstacles to finding the defendants
guilty of crimes against humanity or any of the other crimes. Your
part will be 'the main feature of the speech', Shawcross explained.

136

Lemkin remained frustrated in Washington DC, purposely kept
away from the action, an outsider. Only now did he try once more
to find a way to get back to Europe, as 'genocide' fell out of the trial,
his word unspoken. He believed that only he could bring genocide
back into the case, and for that he needed to be in Nuremberg.

Working part-time as an adviser in the US War Department (on
a daily fee of twenty-five dollars), he lived alone, worried about the
fate of his family – still no news – and followed the trial through the
news reports and transcripts. He had access to some of the evidence

and was attentive to the details set out in Frank's diaries. They were 'minute records', he wrote, offering an account of 'every "official" word uttered or deed performed'. Sometimes they read 'like a bad Hollywood script', the words of a cold-blooded, cynical, arrogant man with no pity in his heart or any sense of the immensity of his crimes. The diaries brought Frank into his sights.

Yet life was not all work and worry. He socialized – more actively than Lauterpacht – and became something of a man-about-town. So much so, in fact, that the *Washington Post* included him in a feature about the capital's 'foreign-born' men and their views on American women. Among the seven who agreed to participate, Dr Rafael Lemkin was identified as a 'scholar', the 'serious-minded' Polish international lawyer who wrote *Axis Rule*.

Lemkin didn't forgo the chance to share his views about American women. A confirmed bachelor, he found the ladies of Washington DC, to be 'too frank, too honest' to allure themselves to him, lacking what he thought of as the 'tempting, subtle qualities of the European coquette'. Yes, in America 'practically all women' were 'attractive' because beauty was 'so democratized'. European women were, by contrast, usually 'shapeless and often ugly', which meant one had to visit the 'upper strata of society' to find real beauties. There was another difference: unlike Americans, European women used their intellect to captivate men, to play 'the role of intellectual "geisha girls"'. Still, he told the interviewer, whatever the faults of American women he would happily 'settle for one'.

He never did. When I raised matters of the heart with Nancy Ackerly, the 'Druid princess' Lemkin met in New York's Riverside Park, she recalled him telling her that he had 'no time for married life, or the funds to support it.' A few weeks later, the post delivered a few pages of Lemkin's poetry, thirty poems that Lemkin wrote and shared with Nancy. Most focused on the events that touched on his life's work and did so in fortunate obscurity, yet a number dealt with matters of the heart. None were obviously addressed to a woman, but two appeared to be addressed to men. In 'Frightened Love', he wrote,

> *Will he love me more*
> *If I lock the door*
> *When he knocks tonight?*

Another, which was untitled, opened with the following lines:

> *Sir, don't fight*
> *Let my kiss quite*
> *Your breast with love.*

Quite what these words referred to is a matter of speculation. Yet it was clear that Lemkin experienced a solitary, lonely existence, and there were few people around with whom he could share the frustration at the progress of the trial. Perhaps he was fortified by hope in the spring of 1946, when national criminal trials opened in Poland under the guidance of his old mentor Emil Rappaport, cases in which the German defendants would be charged with genocide. At Nuremberg, however, the word simply disappeared, and after the early salvo of the opening days, 130 days of hearings passed with not one mention of genocide.

So in May he began a new campaign of intensive letter-writing, to influence key individuals who might help change the direction of the trial. The letters I found were wordy and rather desperate, infused with a naive, almost fawning quality. There was nevertheless something endearing about them, a vulnerable but genuine tone. A three-page letter went to Eleanor Roosevelt, chair of a new United Nations committee on human rights, who Lemkin identified as sympathetic because she understood 'the needs of under-privileged groups'. He thanked Mrs Roosevelt for taking up his ideas with her husband – 'our great war leader', he called Roosevelt – and informed her that Justice Jackson had accepted 'my idea of formulating genocide as a crime', a claim that was only partly accurate. The law was 'not the answer to all the world's troubles', he recognized, but it offered a means to develop key principles. Would she help to create a new machinery to prevent and punish genocide? He enclosed a few articles he'd written.

A similar letter went to Anne O'Hare McCormick of the *New York Times* editorial board, and another to the newly elected secretary-general of the United Nations, Trygve Lie, a Norwegian lawyer. More letters went to those with whom he found a point of connection, however tenuous: Gifford Pinchot, for example, a former governor of Pennsylvania whom he had met years earlier through the Littells but with whom he lost touch ('I missed both of you very much,' Lemkin wrote). The head of international organizations at the State Department got a letter that included an apology ('a sudden call to Nuremberg and Berlin' had intervened to prevent continued conversation). Lemkin, the consummate networker, was laying the foundations for a renewed campaign.

The 'sudden call' to Nuremberg was unexplained. He left for Europe at the end of May, armed with an identity card freshly minted by the War Department, one that might open doors in Germany even if it was stamped with the words 'Not a Pass'.

Lemkin's War Department ID card, May 1946

The photograph presents Lemkin as an official man, in white shirt and tie, first seen in the *Washington Post* article published two months earlier. Lemkin stares intently into the camera, lips pursed, brows furrowed, purposeful, distracted. The pass recorded him as having blue eyes and 'black/grey' hair, weighing 176 pounds and standing exactly five feet nine and a half inches tall.

137

Lemkin's first stop was London. There he met Egon Schwelb, head of the United Nations War Crimes Commission, a sympathetic Czechoslovak lawyer who had represented anti-Nazi German refugees in Prague before the war and who was in parallel contact with Lauterpacht. They talked of genocide and accountability, and Lemkin floated the idea of producing a film to track down missing war criminals. Nothing came of it. From London, he made his way to Germany and Nuremberg, where he arrived in early June, missing Lauterpacht by a few hours. Fritz Sauckel was in the dock that day, responding to charges of criminal responsibility for forced labour in Germany, telling the judges of his meeting with Frank in Kraków, just after Frank returned from Lemberg in August 1942. Frank had told Sauckel that he'd already sent 800,000 Polish workers to the *Reich,* but he could easily find him another 140,000. People were treated as cheap commodities.

On Sunday, 2 June, Lemkin was offered a meeting with Robert Jackson to explain the purpose of his European trip, which was to assist the War Department in assessing the impact of releasing SS men from detention camps. More than 25,000 SS men had already been released, Lemkin told Jackson. The prosecutor, who was accompanied by his son, Bill, expressed surprise, because the SS was being prosecuted as a criminal organization. The three men also talked of Lemkin's work on the Tokyo trials, and it would have been surprising if Lemkin didn't weave the word 'genocide' into the conversation. Not formally a member of Jackson's team, Lemkin described his role as 'Legal Adviser' to Jackson, a modest embellishment of the reality. He was given a pass allowing him access to the officers' mess in Nuremberg, with the dining privileges of a colonel. I found no formal pass to the courtroom, and no one could point me to a photograph of him in courtroom 600. Despite many hours spent at the archives of Getty Images, I too found nothing.

Yet it was apparent that he was present in the Palace of Justice, because he spent time chasing prosecution lawyers and also – a greater surprise – talking to defence lawyers. Benjamin Ferencz, a junior lawyer on Jackson's team, described Lemkin as a dishevelled and disoriented figure, constantly trying to catch the attention of prosecutors. 'We were all extremely busy,' Ferencz recalled, not wanting to be bothered with genocide, a subject that was 'not something we had time to think about'. The prosecution lawyers wanted to be left alone to 'convict these guys of mass murder'.

One prosecutor who was more helpful to him was Dr Robert Kempner, to whom he'd given a copy of his book a year earlier, in June 1945. Dismissed by Hermann Göring from his position as a lawyer in Germany and then banished from the *Reich,* Kempner was now an important player on Jackson's team: remarkably, he turned the tables and was prosecuting Göring. Kempner allowed Lemkin to use his office, room 128 at the Palace of Justice, as a poste restante, and a place from which Lemkin could plot the revival of his campaign.

Three days after meeting the Jacksons, Lemkin wrote a lengthy memorandum to plead the case for genocide. It wasn't clear whether the memo was written in response to a request from the American prosecutor, although I doubted it. The paper – titled 'The Necessity to Develop the Concept of Genocide in the Proceedings' – was sent to Kempner on 5 June. It made the point at some length that 'genocide' was the proper term to describe the defendants' intent to destroy nations and racial and religious groups. Lesser terms – like 'mass murder' or 'mass extermination' – were inadequate, because they were incapable of conveying the vital element of racial motivation and the desire to destroy entire cultures. How impoverished we would be, Lemkin wrote,

> if the people doomed by Germany such as the Jews had not been
> permitted to create the Bible or to give birth to an Einstein [or]
> a Spinoza; if the Poles had not had the opportunity to give the
> world a Copernicus, a Chopin, a Curie; the Greeks a Plato and a
> Socrates; the English a Shakespeare; the Russians a Tolstoy and
> a Shostakovich; the Americans an Emerson and a Jefferson; the
> Frenchmen a Renan and a Rodin.

He also made clear that he was concerned with the destruction of any group, not just Jews. He singled out Poles, gypsies, Slovenes and Russians. To stress 'only the Jewish aspect' was something to be avoided, because it would offer an invitation to Göring and other defendants 'to use the court for anti-Semitic propaganda'. The charge of genocide had to be part of a broader trial strategy, to show the defendants as enemies of mankind, a 'specially dangerous crime', one that went beyond crimes against humanity.

Lemkin sent a revised version of the memo to Thomas Dodd, the American lawyer prosecuting Frank. To this version he added new material, tailoring the document to the needs of the recipient, including a couple of Czechoslovak names (Buss and Dvořák) on the list of those whom the Germans had sought to destroy. He also wrote a new section, to make the point that the 'German people' were a 'Kain who killed Abel' who had to be made to understand that the Nazis destroyed individuals not by way of sporadic criminality but for another intentional purpose, 'the killing of brotherly nations'. Lemkin ended the letter with a warning: if the charge of genocide was left out of the judgement, it would leave the impression 'that the prosecution did not prove its case'. I found no evidence that the letter influenced Dodd, one way or another.

Lemkin met again with Jackson at the end of June, this time to persuade him to argue for genocide as a distinct crime. He faced political objections in the United States and in Britain, arising respectively from historic American treatment of blacks and British colonial practices. There were practical difficulties evoked by Lauterpacht: How did one actually prove the intent to destroy a group? And there were objections of principle, of the kind evoked by Leopold Kohr, that Lemkin had fallen into the trap of 'biological thinking', focusing on groups in a manner that gave rise to anti-Semitism and anti-Germanism. The hurdles remained high.

138

Despite these obstacles, Lemkin's efforts did have some success. Within four days of the second meeting with Jackson, the word 'genocide' made its way back into the proceedings. It happened on 25 June, and Lemkin's unexpected white knight was Sir David Maxwell Fyfe, the Scottish cross-examiner of the elegant, distinguished and white-haired diplomat Konstantin von Neurath, Hitler's first foreign minister. A young German diplomat in Constantinople during the massacre of the Armenians, von Neurath later became *Reichsprotektor* for occupied Bohemia and Moravia, and it was on a note written in that capacity that Maxwell Fyfe focused. In August 1940, von Neurath had written about the treatment of the Czech population in the occupied area. One option he aired – described as the 'most radical and theoretically complete solution' – would be to evacuate all Czechs from the territory and simply replace them with Germans, assuming enough Germans could be found. The alternative was to achieve 'Germanization by individual selective breeding' of some Czechs and the expulsion of others. With either approach, the aim was to destroy the Czech intelligentsia.

Maxwell Fyfe read out extracts from von Neurath's memorandum. 'Now, Defendant,' he said, speaking in a clipped tone, did he recognize that he was being charged 'with genocide, which we say is the extermination of racial and national groups'? Lemkin's satisfaction must have been great, and even greater a few moments later when Maxwell Fyfe referred to 'the well-known book of Professor Lemkin' and then read into the record Lemkin's definition of 'genocide'. 'What you wanted to do,' Maxwell Fyfe told von Neurath, 'was to get rid of the teachers and writers and singers of Czechoslovakia, whom you call the intelligentsia, the people who would hand down the history and traditions of the Czech people to other generations.' That was genocide. Von Neurath offered no response. Lemkin's trip to Nuremberg had made an immediate difference.

Lemkin later wrote to Maxwell Fyfe, in an elated tone, to express his 'very warm appreciation' for the British prosecutor's support for the charge of genocide. Maxwell Fyfe's response, if there was one, has been lost. After the trial, the prosecutor did write a foreword to the *Times* journalist R. W. Cooper's fine account of the proceedings, invoking genocide and Lemkin's book. The crime of genocide was 'essential' to the Nazi plan, he wrote, and led to 'terrible' actions. Cooper devoted a full chapter to the 'new crime' of 'genocide', a term whose 'apostle' was Lemkin, a man with 'a voice crying in the wilderness'. Cooper noted that the opponents of the term 'genocide' knew it could be applied to 'the extinction of the Red Indians in North America', recognition that Lemkin's ideas offered 'an imperative warning to the white race'.

The journalist mentioned Haushofer, 'barbarity', 'vandalism' and the Madrid conference from which Lemkin 'was recalled to Poland' (which suggested that Lemkin continued to embellish, as he had done at Duke four years earlier). It was clear that the Polish lawyer used Cooper to obtain access to Maxwell Fyfe, and this was the likely path by which the word 'genocide' returned to the courtroom.

Because Shawcross and Lauterpacht weren't in Nuremberg at the time, Maxwell Fyfe was free to act alone in running with the genocide argument. The consequence was potentially significant: unlike the concept of crimes against humanity, which was concerned with responsibility for acts connected to war, the charge of genocide opened the door to all acts, including those that occurred before the war began.

139

As Lemkin harried and lobbied and persisted, Lauterpacht wrote parts of Shawcross's closing speech. He worked alone on the first floor of 6 Cranmer Road, without pressing the flesh of journalists in the bar of Nuremberg's Grand Hotel. I imagine Bach's *St Matthew Passion* playing in the background, as the ideas flowed and he put pen to paper. Occasionally he might look out of the window, over to the university library and the football field.

Lauterpacht worked on the draft for several weeks. He completed a short introduction and lengthier first and third parts of the attorney's speech, setting out legal arguments (the second part, on facts and evidence, was being written in Nuremberg). I had the typewritten version of Lauterpacht's text but was curious to see the handwritten original, the one Lauterpacht gave Mrs Lyons to type up. Eli had it in Cambridge, so I returned once more to take a look. The handwriting was familiar, as were the arguments, so clearly and logically set out, inviting the tribunal to reject the argument of the defendants that the charges were novel or unprecedented. The opening pages were understated; the emotion and passion had been stripped out. As in so many ways, Lauterpacht was the very opposite of Lemkin.

Yet this draft would have a different conclusion from the one he wrote for the opening of the trial, a finale that was raw, gripping and impassioned. That's not how it began, a nine-page introduction on the purpose of the trial and the need for fairness. The trial wasn't about revenge, Lauterpacht wrote, but about delivering justice according to law, an 'authoritative, thorough and impartial ascertainment' of the crimes. The tribunal's task was to develop the law to protect individuals, to create 'a most valuable precedent for any future International Criminal Court' (the observation was prescient, because five long decades passed before the ICC came into being).

The second part of Lauterpacht's draft ran over forty pages, and wove together many of the ideas he'd spent years thinking about. On war crimes, he focused on murder and prisoners of war, on Polish intellectuals, on Russian political workers. He went out of his way to assert that the charge of 'crimes against humanity' wasn't in any way novel, directly contradicting what he'd told the Foreign Office just a few months earlier. Rather, it was a starting point to vindicate 'the rights of man', to offer protection against the 'cruelty and barbarity of his own State'. Such acts were illegal even if German law allowed them. The draft proclaimed that the fundamental rights of man trumped national laws, a new approach to serve the interests of individuals, not states.

In this way, each individual human being was entitled to protection under the law, a law that could not turn a blind eye to atrocity. Notably, Lauterpacht made only a passing mention of Hitler and a solitary reference to the Jews, five million of whom were murdered 'for no other reason than that they were of Jewish race or faith'. Of the events in Lemberg, addressed by the Soviets on the opening days of the trial, he wrote nothing. Lauterpacht stripped out references to matters that might be seen as personal, writing nothing of the treatment of the Poles, and of course he did not use the word 'genocide'. He remained implacably opposed to Lemkin's ideas.

His focus then turned to the defendants, a 'pathetic' bunch who invoked international law to save themselves. They sought refuge in outmoded ideas, that somehow the individual who acted for the state was immune from criminal liability. Of the twenty-one defendants in the courtroom, he identified five by name, singling out Julius Streicher for his race theories and Hermann Göring for participating in the 'butchery' of the Warsaw ghetto.

The only defendant Lauterpacht mentioned repeatedly was Hans Frank. It was perhaps no coincidence that he was the man in the dock most closely connected to the murder of his own family. Frank was a 'direct agent' of the 'crimes of extermination', Lauterpacht wrote, even if he was not personally involved in the act of execution.

*

Lauterpacht put the emphasis on Frank in the last pages of his draft, the closing bars of a near-symphonic text. The new Charter of the United Nations offered a step towards the enthronement of the rights of man. It heralded a new epoch, one that placed 'the rights and duties of the individual in the very centre of the constitutional law of the world'. This was pure Lauterpacht, the central theme of his life's work. But in these pages he also found a different voice, releasing a well of pent-up emotion and energy. The handwriting changed, words were added and crossed out, a raw anger aimed at defendants who didn't even offer 'a simple admission of guilt'. Yes, there were 'abject confessions', perhaps some with an air of sincerity, but these were false, no more than 'artful evasions'.

Then Lauterpacht homed in on the defendant most closely connected to the fate of his own family, a man who offered a tentative expression of responsibility in April. 'Witness . . . defendant Frank,' he wrote, 'confessing to a sense of deepest guilt because of the terrible words which he had uttered – as if it were his words that mattered and not the terrible deed which accompanied them. What might have become a redeeming claim to a vestige of humanity reveals itself as a crafty device of desperate men. He, like other defendants, have [sic] pleaded, to the very end, full ignorance of that vast organized and most intricate ramification of the foulest crimes that ever sullied the record of a nation.'

This was uncharacteristically emotional. Interesting, Eli said, when I took him to the passage. He hadn't appreciated the significance of the words; 'my father never spoke to me of these matters, not once'. Now, faced with the document in the context I explained, Eli reflected aloud on the connection between his father and the defendants. Nor did he know, until then, that Governor Otto von Wächter, Frank's deputy, a man directly involved in the Lemberg killings, was a classmate of his father's in Vienna. A few months later, a chance arose for him to meet Niklas Frank and Robby Dundas, a reunion of the children of judge, prosecutor and defendant. Eli declined.

Lauterpacht fretted that Shawcross wouldn't use what he'd written. 'I am naturally inclined to think [it] is relevant and necessary,' he told the attorney general, reminding him of the need to reach the audience outside the courtroom. If the speech was overly long, Shawcross could submit the whole text to the tribunal but only read out 'selected portions'.

Witness, 'for instance,' defendant Frank confessing to a ~~sense~~ deepest sense of ~~terrible~~ guilt because of the terrible words which he had uttered — as if it were his words, that ~~mattered~~ and not the terrible

28

deed which ~~followed~~ accompanied them. What might have become a redeeming ~~hope~~ decision to a vestige of ~~humanity to the~~ vestige of humanity in this and ~~other defendants~~ ~~They have all pleaded~~ ~~ignorance~~ reveals itself as a crafty device of desperate men. He, like other defendants, have ~~Yet this trial is~~ pleaded, to the very end, full ignorance of that ~~vast~~ vastest, organized and most intricate ramification of the foulest crimes that ~~was~~ ever sullied the record of a nation. (These crimes transcend any conceivable measure of individual retribution. They have raised

'Witness . . . defendant Frank', Lauterpacht's draft, 10 July 1946

On 10 July, Lauterpacht's secretary placed these covering thoughts and the typewritten draft into a large envelope and sent it off.

140

As Lauterpacht's draft made its way by train to London, Lemkin redoubled his efforts. Help came from an unlikely source, Alfred Rosenberg. I am no *génocidaire,* Frank's neighbour on the defendants' front bench told the judges, speaking through his lawyer. Dr Alfred Thoma sought to persuade the tribunal that Rosenberg's contribution to Nazi policy was merely a 'scientific' exercise, that there was no connection with 'genocide' in the sense evoked by Lemkin. On the contrary, Rosenberg had been motivated by a 'struggle between psychologies', the lawyer added, without desire to kill or destroy. The unexpected argument was prompted by a line in Lemkin's book that quoted from Rosenberg's magnum opus, *Der Mythus des 20. Jahrhunderts* (The Myth of the Twentieth Century), published in 1930. The book claimed to offer an intellectual foundation for racist ideas. Rosenberg was aggrieved that Lemkin had misused his words, asserting that Lemkin omitted a crucial sentence from the original work and that Rosenberg had not argued for one race to extinguish another. The argument was contorted and hopeless.

Wondering how Lemkin's ideas reached Rosenberg, I came across the answer without looking for it, in the archives of Columbia University. Tucked in among the few remnants of Lemkin's papers was a copy of a lengthy pleading written by Dr Thoma for Rosenberg. Thoma had given it to Lemkin with a handwritten note of personal appreciation. 'Ehrerbietig überreicht,' Thoma wrote. 'Presented with all due respect.' The document pointed to Lemkin's unstinting efforts, willing even to engage with the defendants through their lawyers. In the days that followed, other defence lawyers also invoked his ideas, if only to disagree with them.

Perhaps because he was burdened by the absence of news on his family, Lemkin's health took a further turn for the worse. Three days after Rosenberg's anti-genocidal outburst, Lemkin took to bed, where he remained for six days under sedation. On 19 July, a US military doctor found he was suffering from acute hypertension, nausea and vomiting. Further examination was followed by admission to a hospital. He spent a few days in the US army 385th Station Hospital; another doctor recommended that he return without delay to America. He ignored the advice.

141

Lemkin was in Nuremberg on 11 July when Dr Seidl presented Frank's closing arguments in court. Confronted with Frank's virtual admission of collective guilt in April, and the evidence that seeped from his diaries, the lawyer had a challenging task. It didn't help that the tribunal was irritated with Dr Seidl, who also represented Rudolf Hess (Seidl annoyed the judges by not giving them an English translation of the defence speech he delivered for Hess, and going on endlessly about the Versailles Treaty being the cause of the terrible acts for which his clients were charged).

Dr Seidl sought to minimize Frank's earlier testimony and the many unhelpful passages in the diaries. 'With one exception', Seidl told the judges, the diary entries were merely secretarial transcripts, not words actually dictated by Frank. No one could know their accuracy because Frank hadn't personally checked the entries made by the stenographers. They were only words, not proof of actions or facts. Yet Seidl had to concede that Frank's speeches tended towards a certain 'point of view' on the Jewish question and made 'no secret of his anti-Semitic views', which was something of an understatement. The prosecution had established no 'causal connection' between Frank's words and the measures perpetrated by the Security Police, Seidl argued, and the police weren't under his client's control.

Moreover, Dr Seidl continued, the record showed that Frank had objected to the worst excesses. Terrible crimes were committed on the territory of the General Government, not least in the concentration camps. Frank denied none of this, but he wasn't responsible. To the contrary, he'd waged a '5 year struggle against all violent measures', complaining to the Führer but without success. Seidl tendered numerous documents in support.

Frank sat quietly through these optmistic arguments without showing any expression. Occasionally, he was seen to wiggle, and some observed his head to have been a little more bowed than earlier in the trial. Frank couldn't investigate the rumours about Auschwitz,

Dr Seidl continued, because the camp was outside his territory. As to Treblinka, which was on his territory, the lawyer adopted a different line of argument. Could the mere construction and administration of a concentration camp on Frank's territory amount to a crime against humanity? 'No', Dr Seidl retorted. As an occupying power, Germany was entitled to take 'necessary steps' to maintain public order and security. Treblinka was one such step, and not one for which Frank was responsible. Dr Seidl had nothing to say about the testimony of Samuel Rajzman.

This approach prompted an intervention from the prosecutor Robert Kempner, visibly irritated. Seidl's arguments were 'completely irrelevant', he told the judges, and made without any supporting evidence. Lord Justice Lawrence accepted the point, but Dr Seidl simply continued in the same vein.

The judges sat impassively. Three months earlier, in April, Frank had spoken words that appeared to reflect some degree of collective responsibility, if not personal or individual responsibility. Now his lawyer was adopting a different tack. The other defendants had got to him, impressing upon him the need for solidarity with the group.

142

The defence lawyers completed their arguments at the end of July. All that remained for each of the twenty-one defendants was to present a short, closing personal statement. Before that, the prosecution would speak.

The four prosecution teams took the floor in the same order as the opening statements. The Americans first, focusing on count one and the conspiracy claim. Then the British, on crimes against peace in count two, together with an overview of the legal aspects of the case as a whole, prepared by Lauterpacht. Then the French and the Russians, on war crimes and crimes against humanity.

Robert Jackson opened for the prosecution on a Friday morning, 26 July. Lemkin was still in Nuremberg, eager to hear what might be said about genocide; Lauterpacht stayed in Cambridge. Jackson took the tribunal back to the facts, the war, its conduct, and the enslavement of occupied populations. The 'most far-flung and terrible' of the acts was the persecution and extermination of Jews, a 'final solution' that led to the killing of six million. The defendants offered a 'chorus', claiming to be oblivious to the terrible facts. A 'ridiculous' argument, Jackson told the judges. Göring said he 'knew nothing' of any excesses, not suspecting an extermination programme despite having signed a 'score of decrees'. Hess was merely an 'innocent middleman', transmitting Hitler's orders without reading them. Von Neurath? A foreign minister 'who knew little of foreign affairs and nothing of foreign policy'. Rosenberg? A party philosopher with 'no idea of the violence' that his philosophy incited.

And Frank? A governor-general in Poland who 'reigned but did not rule'. Among the upper echelons of government, he was 'fanatical', a lawyer who solidified Nazi power, brought lawlessness to Poland and reduced the population to 'sorrowing remnants'. Remember Frank's words, Jackson told the judges, that 'a thousand years will pass and this guilt of Germany will still not be erased.'

Jackson spoke for half a day. It was powerful, incisive and elegant, but the speech had one big hole at its heart, at least from Lemkin's perspective: Jackson said nothing of genocide. Lemkin recognized the danger: if the chief prosecutor wasn't on board, there was little prospect that the American judges on the tribunal, Biddle and Parker, would be. This made the British even more important, yet Lemkin couldn't know that the draft Lauterpacht had already written for Shawcross made no mention of genocide.

143

Shawcross walked to the lectern after lunch and spoke through the afternoon and into the next day. He addressed the facts, 'crimes against peace' and the sanctity of the individual.

As Shawcross prepared to speak, Lauterpacht knew his draft would have been drastically edited by the British lawyers in Nuremberg, who were worried about the direction the trial was taking. 'We are very apprehensive over the way the Judges are talking about conviction and sentence,' Colonel Harry Phillimore had told Shawcross. 'Informally at dinner, etc., they have indicated that they may acquit two or three and that quite a number may not get the death sentence.' Shawcross was deeply concerned. We can imagine 'one or two escaping the death penalty', Phillimore added, 'but the acquittal of any of the accused, and any low sentences for some of the others, would reduce the trial to a farce'.

Shawcross had told Lauterpacht that his lengthy draft presented 'some considerable difficulty'. To address the difficulties, and also by way of self-protection, the attorney general would devote more time to the facts, which meant cutting back on Lauterpacht's legal arguments. 'If I failed to be guided by Fyfe's advice and anything went wrong, it would obviously be said that it was my fault.' And he was not prepared to submit in written form a longer speech, for the record, but read out only parts of it. He would use what he could from Lauterpacht's draft. In the end, three-quarters of Shawcross's seventy-seven-page text was devoted to the facts and supporting evidence. That left sixteen pages for legal arguments, of which twelve were fully written by Lauterpacht. There was cutting but, as Lauterpacht was soon to discover, also some addition.

Shawcross started with a chronology, from the prewar period of the defendants' conspiracy to commit crimes through to the war. He traced events across Europe, following along the trail of decrees and papers gathered by Lemkin, beginning in the Rhineland and Czechoslovakia, working his way through Poland, then westward to Holland, Belgium and France, up north to Norway and Denmark, south-east through Yugoslavia and Greece, and finally east into Soviet Russia. The war crimes he laid out were both 'the object and the parent of the other crimes', Shawcross told the judges. Crimes against humanity were committed, but only in the course of the war. He made the connection that Lemkin most feared, silent about all the crimes committed before 1939.

Yet this speech also offered a single, brilliant, defining moment of courtroom advocacy. Shawcross took the judges to a single act of killing, one that allowed ten years of horror to be reflected in one powerful moment. He read out the witness statement prepared by Hermann Graebe, the German manager of a factory near Dubno on Frank's territory, which was close to the home of the baker where Lemkin had taken refuge for a few days in September 1939. Shawcross adopted a timbre that squeezed all emotion out of the words, speaking slowly and articulating each word with crystalline precision:

Without screaming or weeping these people undressed, stood
around in family groups, kissed each other, said farewells, and
waited for a sign from another SS man, who stood near the pit,
also with a whip in his hand.

A silence descended over the courtroom as time slowed and the
words worked their effect. As Shawcross spoke, the writer Rebecca
West, who sat in the press gallery, noticed Frank wriggling in his
seat, like a small child being berated by a schoolmaster.

During the 15 minutes that I stood near I heard no complaint or
plea for mercy. I watched a family of about eight persons, a man
and a woman both about 50 with their children of about 1, 8,
and 10, and two grown-up daughters of about 20 to 24. An old
woman with snow-white hair was holding the one-year-old child
in her arms and singing to it and tickling it. The child was cooing
with delight. The couple were looking on with tears in their eyes.
The father was holding the hand of a boy about 10 years old and
speaking to him softly; the boy was fighting his tears.

Shawcross paused to look around the courtroom, towards the
defendants. Did he notice Frank, head down, looking at the courtroom's wooden floor?

'The father pointed to the sky, stroked his head, and seemed to
explain something to him.'

A moment of 'living pity', as Rebecca West described it.

144

Shawcross turned his attention to Frank. These acts occurred
on his territory, a fact sufficient to convict him, then he pressed
deeper.

Hans Frank, the minister of justice for Bavaria, who'd received
reports on murders in Dachau as early as 1933.

Hans Frank, the leading jurist of the Nazi Party, a member of the
Central Committee that ordered the boycott of the Jews.

Hans Frank, a minister who took to the airwaves in March 1934
to justify racial legislation.

Hans Frank, a defendant who asked the judges to believe that the words in his diaries were written in ignorance of the facts.

'That damn Englishman,' Frank said of Shawcross, a curse that was loud enough to be heard across the courtroom.

Hans Frank, a lawyer who spoke and wrote in support of a 'horrible policy of genocide'.

The word came out of the blue, not written into the text drafted by Lauterpacht. Shawcross must have added it, and then he repeated it. 'Genocide' as a broad aim. 'Genocide' applied to gypsies, to Polish intelligentsia, to Jews. 'Genocide' pursued 'in different forms' against other groups, in Yugoslavia, in Alsace-Lorraine, in the Low Countries, even in Norway.

Shawcross was on a roll, turning to the techniques of genocide. He described the pattern of action that ended with the deliberate murder of groups, in gas chambers, by mass shootings, by working the victims to death. He spoke of 'biological devices' to decrease the birthrate, of sterilization, of castration, of abortion, of the separation of man and woman. The evidence was overwhelming, he continued, each defendant knew about the 'policy of genocide', each was guilty of the crime, each was a murderer. The only proper sentence was 'the supreme penalty'. This caused a commotion in the dock.

Shawcross used Lemkin's word but held back from embracing the fullness of its meaning. Lemkin wanted to criminalize all group killings, from 1933 onward, before the war began. Shawcross used the term in a more limited sense, as he made clear. 'Genocide' was an aggravated 'crime against humanity', but only if committed in connection with the war. The restriction was imposed by Article 6(c) of the charter, by the infamous comma introduced into the text in August 1945. For an act to be a crime, it had to be connected to the war. This was 'a very important qualification', Shawcross told the judges, and took away with one hand what he had given with the other, the full expression of the concept of genocide. Reading his words, I understood the consequence, the carving-out from the trial of all the acts that occurred in Germany and Austria before September 1939. The acts of impoverishment and banishment taken against individuals like Leon, in November 1938, and against millions of others – of confiscation, expulsion, detention, killing – would be outside the jurisdiction of the tribunal.

Nevertheless, Shawcross drew much from Lauterpacht. There was no question of retroactivity, because all the acts involved – extermination, enslavement, persecution – were crimes under most national laws. The fact that they were lawful under German law offered no defence because the acts affected the international community. They were 'crimes against the law of nations', not mere matters of domestic concern. In the past, international law had allowed each state to decide how it would treat its nationals, but that was now replaced by a new approach:

> International law has in the past made some claim that there is a limit to the omnipotence of the state and that the individual human being, the ultimate unit of all law, is not disentitled to the protection of mankind when the state tramples upon his rights in a manner which outrages the conscience of mankind.

War was just and lawful to prevent 'atrocities committed by tyrants against their subjects'. If humanitarian intervention by war was allowed under international law, how could it be said that 'intervention by judicial process' was illegal? Shawcross found his stride. He rejected the argument of the defendants that 'only the state and not the individual' could commit a crime under international law. There was no such principle of international law, so those who helped a state commit a crime against humanity would not be immune from responsibility; they couldn't shelter behind the state. 'The individual must transcend the state.'

This took the essence of Lauterpacht's ideas, with a passing nod to Lemkin's ideas on genocide and groups. Yet Shawcross ended exactly where Lauterpacht had wanted him to be, in a place that emphasized the individual as the 'ultimate unit of all law'. He had departed from Lauterpacht on genocide, and I noticed another change: Shawcross had removed all the references to Frank that Lauterpacht entered into the last pages of his draft. No doubt they were too personal and too passionate.

145

Shawcross was followed by the elderly, frail French chief prosecutor, Auguste Champetier de Ribes, who managed a brief introduction before handing over to his deputy. The tone of Charles Dubost's arguments was less harsh, but the French were still clear that the defendants were criminally culpable; they were *accomplices* in Germany's actions. Frank's words were once more thrown back at him: He had admitted, had he not, that the responsibility of those in government was heavier than that of those who carried out the orders?

The French joined with Shawcross in seeking a conviction for genocide. The exterminations that occurred were 'scientific and systematic', millions killed simply because they happened to be members of a national or religious group, men and women who stood in the way of the 'hegemony of the Germanic race'. Genocide was 'almost totally achieved', in the camps and elsewhere, at the instance of the Gestapo, with the support of the defendants, one way or another.

The French prosecutor rejected Dr Seidl's argument that individuals who acted for the state could not be liable for its wrongs. 'Not one of the defendants was an "isolated individual",' Dubost told the judges. Each demonstrated cooperation and solidarity in the actions. 'Hit hard, without pity,' he implored, hit Frank and all the others who were content to decree the terrible acts. They are guilty, convict them, sentence them to hang.

The Soviets followed, as though part of a coordinated assault. General Roman Rudenko, as stocky and tough in argument as in physique, turned on the individual defendants. He had no time for nuance, intricate theory, or irony. He denounced the Germans for the invasion of Poland, without a hint of irony as to the parallel Soviet operation from the east. He dissected Frank's brutal rule, reminding the tribunal about Lvov and the events of August 1942. He'd found more evidence, a new Soviet report on crimes in the city of Lvov, the testimony of Ida Vasseau, a Frenchwoman who worked in a children's home. Vasseau described young children being used as target practice, a 'terror' that continued until the very last day of the German occupation in July 1944. The aim was complete annihilation, nothing less.

'How vain,' Rudenko told the judges, to seek to deprive us 'of the right to punish those who made enslavement and genocide their aim'. He brought them back to Frank's diaries, to the gleeful accounts of the manner in which the territory would be emptied of Jews! Frank knew about the camps; he should face the 'supreme

penalty'. Frank had been wrong in 1940 to tell Seyss-Inquart that
the memory of his work in Poland would 'live for ever'. There was
no positive legacy, none.

I remembered an image of Otto von Wächter that his son Horst
had placed alongside a photograph of Seyss-Inquart, tucked into the
frame. 'Seyss-Inquart was my godfather,' Horst once told me, 'my
middle name is Arthur'.

146

Around the time I first read Rudenko's speech, with its focus on
events in Lvov, a small package arrived from Warsaw. It contained
the photocopied pages of a slim and long-forgotten volume written
by Gerszon Taffet, a schoolteacher who lived in Zółkiew. It was
published in July 1946, as Rudenko was addressing the tribunal.

Taffet wrote vividly of the town's history, of the destruction
of its Jewish inhabitants, of the catastrophic events of 25 March
1943, described to me by Clara Kramer. On that day, Taffet wrote,
thirty-five hundred residents of the ghetto were marched along the
town's east-west street to the *borek,* the small wood where Lauterpacht and Leon once played. The occupiers left that street lined with
corpses and hats, sheets of paper and photographs. Taffet offered a
first-hand account of the acts of execution:

> Once they were stripped naked and thoroughly searched
> (especially the women), they were lined up above the open graves.
> One by one, they had to step onto the plank which hung over
> the ditch, so that when they were shot they fell straight into the
> open grave . . . After the operation the graves were covered up . . .
> for several days after the operation the earth covering the graves
> moved; it seemed to ripple.

Some chose to refuse other options:

> The conduct of Symcha Turk, a respected citizen of Zółkiew,
> can be cited as an example of the commitment of a father and
> husband. The Germans told him that he, as a professional, can
> be saved if he abandons his family. In response, he ostentatiously

Portrait of Otto von Wächter (main), with image of Arthur Seyss-Inquart (below right), Schloss Hagenberg, December 2012

took his wife's arm on one side and his child's on the other and thus united they walked to their deaths with their heads held high.

Taffet described the destruction of an entire group, descended from the inhabitants of Żółkiew dating back to the sixteenth century. Of the five thousand Jews in Żółkiew in 1941, he wrote, only 'about seventy people survived'. He offered a list of survivors, which included Clara Kramer, Mr and Mrs Melman, Gedalo Lauterpacht. Mr Patrontasch was on the list too, the schoolmate who went to Nuremberg to find Lauterpacht for Inka. I learned that Mr Patrontasch, the whisperer, was called Artur. The names on the list didn't include Leibus Flaschner, Leon's uncle, or any of the other fifty or more Flaschners in town.

Taffet found the means to offer hope for the future. He singled out for mention two notable contemporaries of Żółkiew. One was murdered in Lemberg in *die Grosse Aktion* of August 1942. The other was 'Dr Henryk Lauterpacht, a renowned expert in international law, presently a professor at Cambridge University'.

147

The Nuremberg prosecutors brought their final submissions to a close with a call for the death penalty to be imposed on all the defendants. What remained for the judges was a month of arguments on largely technical issues relating to the criminality of various organizations of the Third Reich. Importantly, this invoked the collective responsibility of the SS, the Gestapo and the cabinet, but more controversial still was the inclusion of the General Staff and the High Command of the German armed forces. Each defendant would then make a brief closing statement, the hearings would adjourn and the judges would retire to deliberate. Judgement was expected at the end of September.

The rift between Lauterpacht and Lemkin was now wide. Lauterpacht's ideas on crimes against humanity and the rights of the individual were firmly entrenched in the proceedings, colouring the entire case. There seemed to be a growing support for the idea that the tribunal's jurisdiction would be limited to wartime acts, excluding the Nuremberg laws, murders committed after January 1933, and *Kristallnacht*.

Lemkin was distressed by this prospect. He still hoped that the tide might be turned, that genocide arguments would obtain traction so the tribunal could judge the earlier acts. He had some grounds for optimism: after months of silence, the charge of genocide had made it back into the hearings, thanks to David Maxwell Fyfe, who brushed aside the sceptics, Lauterpacht included. The holdouts were the Americans, yet even here there seemed to be an opening, as I discovered in the archives of Columbia University.

Among Lemkin's papers, I found a press release from Jackson's office on 27 July, issued a day after he addressed the tribunal but which made no mention of genocide. The document, with the title 'Special Release No. 1', noted that the British had referred to 'genocide' in questioning von Neurath, that the term had been invoked by Shawcross ('several times'), and that it would 'be employed in the French and Russian presentations'.

The press release stated that if the tribunal convicted the defendants for genocide, a precedent would be set 'for protecting such groups of people internationally – even if the crime is committed by a government against its own citizens'. Someone in the American delegation supported Lemkin. He kept a copy of the document, which encouraged him to press on.

The opportunity to pursue his case came unexpectedly at an international conference to be held in August in Cambridge, England. Lemkin was given to understand that his efforts for the genocide case would be strengthened if he persuaded the conference to adopt a resolution expressing support for his ideas.

148

The International Law Association is a venerable institution. Founded in 1873, it is based in London but with roots in America. Its regular conferences had been suspended after 1938, resuming seven years later with the Forty-First Conference, which opened in Cambridge on 19 August 1946. Three hundred international lawyers descended on the city from across the whole of Europe, except Germany, from which no participants were listed.

Those present offered a roll call of the great and the good, including many names I had come across on the road that started in Lemberg in 1919. Arthur Goodhart was there, down from the hill that overlooked Lwów. So was Lauterpacht's mentor Sir Arnold McNair, and Egon Schwelb, whom Lemkin met with in London. Sir Hartley Shawcross was due to attend, but inclement weather prevented his trip from the west of England. Lauterpacht was present, his name listed in the alphabetically ordered official record, five lawyers up from Lemkin (who gave his address as the 'International Military Tribunal, Nuremberg', without mention of a room number). This was the first time I could place Lauterpacht and Lemkin in the same town and building at the same time.

Lemkin's failing health almost prevented his attendance. He collapsed after his flight from Nuremberg landed at Croydon Airport in south London. Dangerously high blood pressure required immediate attention, but he ignored advice to rest, hastening up to Cambridge to be present at the conference opening. He was listed as the third speaker on the opening day, speaking after introductory remarks from Lord Porter, a judge and the chair of the conference. Porter implored the lawyers present to be 'practicable' in their work and to 'restrain their enthusiasms' in dealing with the many challenges ahead. Unsuccessful advocacy was 'apt to antagonize', he reminded everyone present. This was British pragmatism of the kind that Lemkin abhorred.

Lemkin ignored Lord Porter. He spoke with his usual passion about genocide, the evidence from the Nuremberg trial, the need for practical responses, the vital role of the criminal law. He argued against general declarations about human rights of the kind that would be raised at the first General Assembly of the United Nations, to be held later that year. How could piracy and forgery be international crimes, he asked rhetorically, but not the extermination of millions? He made a pitch for genocide to be 'declared an international crime', reminding those in the room about *Axis Rule*. Anyone involved in 'the criminal philosophy of genocide' should be treated as a criminal, he told those present.

Politely listened to, Lemkin awaited the response. A couple of speakers offered general support, but none endorsed his plea for hard action. If Lauterpacht was there (he was preparing for a trip to Copenhagen), the record made clear that he felt no need to intervene against Lemkin. Perhaps he sensed the mood in the room, and he was right. The draft resolutions prepared that week made no reference to genocide or any other international crimes.

Disappointed, Lemkin returned to London and sent thanks to Maxwell Fyfe, for 'moral and professional inspiration'. The Cambridge conference gave his ideas no more than a 'cool reception', he wrote, but he wouldn't give up:

> We cannot keep telling the world in endless sentences: Don't murder members of national, racial and religious groups; don't sterilize them; don't impose abortions on them; don't steal children from them; don't compel their women to bear children for your country; and so on. But we must tell the world now, at this unique occasion, don't practise Genocide.

The failure prompted a renewed bout of frantic letter-writing. Lemkin wrote to Judge Parker, the junior American judge, with a vaguely optimistic tone. 'I think I succeeded in convincing the audience as to the usefulness of such a concept of law,' he explained, ever hopeful.

Lemkin was unaware that his earlier advocacy efforts had persuaded some to his view. On 26 August, the day he wrote to Maxwell Fyfe, the *New York Times* published an editorial that commended Lemkin, recognizing genocide to be a crime of 'distinct technique and distinct consequences'. What remained, the newspaper informed its readers, was for the term to be incorporated into international law, a task that 'Professor Lemkin has already half accomplished'.

149

Lemkin returned to Nuremberg in time to hear the defendants' brief closing statements. Dr Gilbert observed the group of twenty-one as tense and somewhat depressed, after a month of horror stories about the SS and its associate organizations, with an air of 'hurt surprise that the prosecution still considered them criminals'. Maxwell Fyfe's closing speech offered a full-blooded condemnation of the Nazis' 'demonic' plans. Pushing aside the restraint of Shawcross, he brimmed with vitriol at the 'awful crime of genocide' reflected in

Hitler's ideology and *Mein Kampf*'s message of group struggle.

Lemkin believed the British to have been won over, leaving the Americans isolated. Despite Jackson's press release in July, his fellow American prosecutor Telford Taylor made no mention of genocide when he spoke after Maxwell Fyfe. The French, by contrast, invoked 'genocide' as a catch-all to cover all the crimes, from concentration camps to enslavement. The Soviet prosecutor Rudenko characterized the SS as a genocidal entity, so that anyone associated with the organization was complicit in genocide. The claim had potentially far-reaching consequences.

Finally, on the last day of the month, 31 August, the defendants had their chance to address the judges. Göring spoke first, defending the German people as free from guilt and denying his own knowledge as to the terrible facts. Hess fell into customary incoherence, recovering sufficiently to reassure the judges that if he had to start again he 'would act just as I have acted'. Ribbentrop, Keitel and Kaltenbrunner spoke next, then Rosenberg, who surprised Lemkin and many others by recognizing genocide as a crime, but one that also protected German people as a group. At the same time, he denied his own guilt for genocide or for any other crimes.

Frank was the seventh to speak. Many in courtroom 600 wondered what he might say, what direction he would take given his earlier admission of partial responsibility. This time he began by recognizing that all the defendants had turned away from God without imagining the consequences. In this way, he became 'more and more deeply involved in guilt', something he felt as the spirits of the dead passed through the courtroom, millions who perished 'unquestioned and unheard'. He sought to obtain assistance from the decision he had taken not to destroy the diaries and to voluntarily 'surrender' them at the end, in the hour in which he lost his liberty.

He returned to the sense of collective responsibility articulated a few months earlier. He did not wish to 'leave any hidden guilt which I have not accounted for behind me in this world', he told the judges. Yes, he was responsible for the matters for which he had to answer. Yes, he acknowledged a 'degree of guilt'. Yes, he was 'a champion of Adolf Hitler, his movement, and his Reich'.

Then came the 'but', which was broad and all-encompassing.

He felt the need to bring the judges back to something he'd said in April, words that now bothered him and required rectification. He was referring to his 'thousand years' admission, words that Jackson and Shawcross and other prosecutors seized upon but he realized had been misunderstood. On reflection, he hadn't been careful enough and had fallen into error in speaking those words. With the passage of time, he observed a different reality, one in which Germany had already paid a sufficient price. So he said, 'Every possible guilt incurred by our nation has already been completely wiped out.'

All in the courtroom listened attentively as he continued. Germany's guilt had been erased 'by the conduct of our war-time enemies towards our nation and its soldiers'. Such conduct had been entirely excluded from the trial, he was saying, a lopsided justice. Mass crimes 'of the most frightful sort' had been committed against Germans by Russians, Poles and Czechs. Unconsciously perhaps, he evoked the view once again of one group against another.

Looking towards his fellow defendants, he then posed a question: 'Who shall ever judge these crimes *against* the German people?' The question was left hanging. At a stroke, the earlier admission of partial guilt was retracted.

After Frank, the fourteen other defendants took their turns. None offered an admission of responsibility.

After the last had spoken, Lord Justice Lawrence announced that the tribunal would adjourn until 23 September. Judgement would be given on that day.

150

By the time the hearings ended, Lemkin still had no news about his family. Only in the middle of September, during the adjournment, did he learn what had befallen Bella and Josef. The information came from his brother Elias in the course of a reunion that took place in Munich. He learned that his own family was a part of 'the files of the Nuremberg trials'.

Elias had survived by a stroke of good fortune, in circumstances described to me by his son Saul Lemkin. Saul was twelve in June 1941, living with his parents in Wołkowysk, when the family decided to take a Soviet holiday. 'We were sitting in the dacha when my aunty said something happened with the war, so we turned on the radio.' They learned that Hitler had broken the pact with Stalin, launching

Operation Barbarossa, that the Germans occupied Wołkowysk a week later, and that Bella and Josef were trapped along with the rest of the family left at home.

A short vacation became three years in the heartland of the Soviet Union. They knew that 'Uncle Rafael' was safe in North Carolina, but the murder of Bella and Josef, and the decision not to bring them on the vacation due to ill health, became a source of acute tension between the brothers Rafael and Elias. 'My uncle was quite mad that we left them, but alas we didn't know what was going to happen.' Saul seemed dejected, seventy years after the events, and apologetic. 'We just went for a visit; nobody knew the war would start, not even Stalin.'

Saul and his family remained in Moscow until July 1942. When their visas ran out, they took a train east to Ufa, the capital of Bash-kortostan, a small Soviet republic. They returned to Moscow in February 1944. After the war, they returned to Poland, ending up in a displaced persons camp in Berlin, which was where Lemkin found them. 'My uncle called us in Berlin in August 1946. He was at Nuremberg; he spoke to me,' Saul explains. 'He told my father not to stay in Berlin too long, the Russians might blockade the city.'

With Lemkin's help, the Americans arranged for the family to travel from Berlin to Munich, to another camp. Saul was in the hospital recovering from an operation on his appendix when Lemkin joined them in mid-September.

'He came to visit me in the hospital with his secretary Madame Charlet, an American, in the US army. She spoke a little Russian, a very nice woman. My uncle looked very well, nice clothes; we embraced. He told me, "You must come to America."'

They shared what little information they had about events in Wołkowysk. 'My father, Elias, found out there were only a few Jews remaining when the Soviets came in the summer of 1944, maybe no more than fifty or sixty.' A repetition of events in Żółkiew and Dubno and tens of thousands of other places small and large across central Europe, reflected in the stones of Treblinka. Saul spoke gently about this subject, but the light in his eyes was dimmed. 'The rest, we knew what happened to them. A Jew sent us a letter. My grandparents were taken to an unknown destination. They were dead.'

Did Saul have a photograph of Bella and Josef? No. He learned that the last transport from Wołkowysk was in January 1943 to Auschwitz, but it was an earlier transport that took his grandparents to another place, not far away. 'Bella and Josef went to Treblinka, because it wasn't far away.'

He spoke these words with much sadness, a weary and deep sadness, and then he perked up.

'What's the name of that famous journalist, the one who wrote *Life and Fate*?' he asked.

Vasily Grossman.

'That's it; he's the one who wrote about Treblinka. I read it and thought of my grandparents.'

Saul believed that Uncle Rafael never knew they went to Treblinka. 'That information came only later, long after he was gone.'

Saul's account offered a frame of sorts for another story. In this way did I learn that my grandmother Malke Flaschner, who lived in Żółkiew on the same street as the Lauterpachts, had died in Treblinka on the same street as the Lemkins.

'There is one thing I must say about that time,' Saul said with a sudden sense of cheer. 'The Germans in the clinic were *very* nice to me, very polite. Compared to life in Poland, Germany was a paradise for the Jews.' If Saul harboured ill feelings, he kept them under wraps.

'Of course, Uncle Rafael had a different view,' he continued. 'There were many Germans in the clinic, but my uncle would not look at them.' Saul fixed his eyes on mine. 'He hated them. For him, they were poison. He hated them.'

151

Lauterpacht spent September in Cambridge, awaiting a judgement he hoped might offer protection for individuals and support for an international bill of rights. Less voluble than Lemkin, without displaying visible emotion, he was no less passionate or caring. The trial had affected him deeply, but he didn't like to show it, even to his son, who spent time with him that month, preparing to enter his second year as an undergraduate at Trinity.

Looking back, Eli now wondered if something changed in his

father around that time. The trial and news of the family took a toll and must have influenced the direction of his work. Eli felt this to be the time when he developed a better – or at least more conscious – understanding of his father's work.

'It's not just that there was a greater intellectual involvement on my part; it's that I was aware of something else, that this was a particularly difficult period.' Inka's imminent arrival in Cambridge underscored the sense of loss but also offered hope.

'Emotionally, he was so deeply involved in the trial,' Eli added. He didn't talk much about those matters and 'never said anything to me about his parents, not once'. This was a source of recent reflection for Eli, who recognized he'd never asked himself the questions I had been exploring. He had accepted the situation for what it was, adopting his father's approach. The difficulties and the pain were reflected in other ways, not articulated in words.

I asked about his father's views on the term 'genocide'. He wouldn't have liked it, because it was too 'impractical', Eli replied, and he might even have thought it to be dangerous. One of Lauterpacht's contacts at that time was Egon Schwelb, the same man who met and encouraged Lemkin in May 1946. Eli thought Schwelb to have been a strong supporter of his father's approach to individual rights, an admirer of his intellect and work. In one letter Schwelb noted Lauterpacht's belief in the 'close connection' between 'crimes against humanity' in the Nuremberg trial and 'the idea of fundamental Human Rights and their protection in criminal law'. The letter from Schwelb also confirmed that Lauterpacht was 'not too much in favour' of 'the so-called crime of Genocide', and offered an explanation: Lauterpacht thought that 'if one emphasises too much that it is a crime to kill a whole people, it may weaken the conviction that it is already a crime to kill one individual.'

Schwelb also knew that Lauterpacht wasn't too well-disposed towards Lemkin, in a personal sense. There wasn't antagonism, certainly, and no doubt Lauterpacht appreciated 'the drive, idealism and candour of Dr Lemkin'. These were words of faint praise. However, the former Cambridge professor didn't recognize the former Polish prosecutor as a real scholar or a man with serious intellectual abilities, and that mattered. Lauterpacht and Schwelb agreed that it was 'advisable' to 'put right' the relationship between crimes against humanity and genocide, in favour of the former. Putting things right meant silence. The best would be for the tribunal to say nothing about genocide.

152

Niklas Frank was seven years old in September 1946, old enough to recollect the air of anxiety that hung around the family home in the weeks leading up to the judgement. That month, he took a trip to Nuremberg and saw his father, the first time in more than a year. The visit evoked a memory without sentiment.

By then, the Frank family was pretty much impecunious, gathering food and information about the trial as best it could. More or less estranged from Frank, Brigitte maintained contact with a journalist in Bavaria, a man who offered a summary of the trial each evening on German radio. 'My mother listened every night, at seven o'clock,' Niklas recalled. Occasionally the journalist paid a visit, and sometimes he brought chocolate, a rare treat for the children. He was looking for snippets of information to use on his radio programme. Niklas remembered one detail, that the journalist was Jewish: 'My mother wrote to my father in the prison, "I like this Mr Gaston Oulman, and would like that you meet each other in the prison."'

Niklas chuckled at the crazy idea.

'My mother's letter went on. "He is a Jew, but I think he has some heart."' Niklas paused. 'She wrote that,' Niklas exclaimed, 'can you imagine, that "he has some heart"? The end of the Nuremberg process, from the radio my mother knew all the crimes the Germans had done, yet she was still able to write such a sentence.'

He shook his head.

'Unbelievable,' he said, before pausing.

'It was right that my father should be put on trial.' He was consistent in this view. Yes, when his father took the stand in April, he'd offered an expression of guilt, of sorts.

'That was a good thing, but was it genuine?' Niklas had his doubts, confirmed by the change of direction in August. 'His true character emerged with that second statement,' Niklas said bluntly; his father was a weak man.

In September, the whole family travelled to Nuremberg. Niklas showed me a photograph, his mother in a large black hat, black coat and skirt, sparrow legs, smiling, hurrying him along with his sister.

'It was on 24 September, I think. I went with my mother; we were five children. We entered the Palace of Justice, into a big room, maybe twenty metres long. On the right side were windows; on the opposite side of the room, I recognized Göring, there with his family. I was sitting on the lap of my mother; we talked to my father through a glass window, with little holes.'

How was his father?

'He was smiling, trying to be happy. I remember too that my father lied to me.'

Meaning?

'He said, "In two or three months' time, we will celebrate Christmas in Schliersee, at home, and we will be very happy all together."'

Brigitte Frank with Niklas (left), Nuremberg, September 1946

I was thinking, why are you lying? I knew from school, from what my friends were saying, what was going to happen. You must never lie to a seven-year-old child; it is never forgotten.'

This was a week before the judgement. As far as Niklas was able to recall, he spoke not a word to his father. Nothing.

'I didn't say goodbye. The whole thing lasted not more than six or seven minutes. There were no tears. I was really sad, not that he's going to be hanged, sad that he lied to me.'

153

The judgement came down a little later than expected, a week after the Franks visited, over the course of two glorious, golden autumn days, on 30 September and 1 October. The city was apprehensive, with security and tanks around the Palace of Justice more visible than usual. Entry to the courtroom, which was packed, was subject to severe restrictions.

Frank didn't have far to travel from his cell in the old brick building behind the Palace of Justice, since torn down. Military police in white helmets escorted him along a covered corridor, up in the lift, through the sliding door, into the middle of the front row of the defendants' dock. He wore the usual dark glasses, his left hand gloved and purposely kept out of sight.

Lauterpacht had flown in from England, arriving two days before the judgement. He travelled with a group of British VIPs, including Lord Wright, the head of the British War Crimes Executive. Khaki Roberts was with them, the barrister who had led the fight against Lemkin and the charge of genocide a year earlier. They all stayed at the Grand Hotel, to be collected at the hotel reception at 9.15 in the morning on the day of the judgement, from there to be driven to the Palace of Justice.

Lemkin was in Paris on 30 September, attending the Peace Conference. He hoped to persuade the delegates to insert a few words on genocide in the final text. His health hadn't improved; once more he was benefiting from the services of an American military hospital. It was there he learned of the judgement, on a radio next to his bed.

Leon was also in Paris, not far away, at work with returning deportees and refugees. Many in the Lutetia Hotel had a great interest in the outcome of the trial.

The judgement was divided into two parts. The first day, Monday, 30 September, would be devoted to the overall facts and findings on the law; the guilt of the individual defendants would only be addressed on the second day. As to the facts, the judges separated them into neat little sections, artificial but authoritative, in a way that makes lawyers comfortable. The complexities of history and human interaction would be simplified into a narrative that neatly described the Nazi seizure of power, acts of aggression across Europe, the conduct of war. Twelve years of mayhem and horror and killing had been aired over the course of 453 open hearings in the courtroom. Ninety-four witnesses had appeared, thirty-three for the prosecution and sixty-one for the defence.

The judges dealt expeditiously with the organizations. The Nazi leadership, Gestapo, SD and SS were all found to be culpable, along with the Waffen-SS army and the half a million men under its command. This created a very large pool of criminals. The SA, *Reich* cabinet, and General Staff and High Command of the Wehrmacht were let off the hook, an act of judicial compromise.

The judges then turned to the acts of conspiracy, aggression and war crimes. Crimes against humanity got a central place in the judgement and, for the first time in history, it was recognized to be an established part of international law. The courtroom listened in silence to the narrative: murder, ill-treatment, pillage, slave labour, persecutions, all giving rise to international criminality.

It must have been excruciating for Frank and the other defendants, listening carefully for any hint about their prospects. The acquittal of the three organizations distressed the prosecution but offered some hope to the defendants, the swing of a pendulum. On which side would it turn for Frank? Had he done enough to save himself from the gallows? Was the initial admission of collective guilt sufficient, or was it undone by the later retraction? Frank's anxiety would not have been assuaged by the words of the Soviet judge Nikitchenko, who invoked once more words taken from Frank's diary to describe the final chapter of Nazi history and crimes against humanity. A 'thousand years', again and again.

The tribunal adopted the essence of the words written by Lauterpacht but spoken by Shawcross, of international crimes 'committed by men, not abstract entities'. Only by punishing the individuals who committed such crimes, the judges said, could the provisions of international law be enforced. Individuals had international duties that 'transcend the national obligations of obedience imposed by the individual state'.

By contrast, genocide got no mention on the first day. This was despite the support of the British, French and Soviet prosecutors and Jackson's press release. Not one of the eight judges who spoke on that first day used Lemkin's word, and none evoked the function of the law to protect groups. Lemkin would have been bereft, lying in bed in a faraway Paris hospital, hoping for what might come on the second day.

There was no real explanation for the omission, just a few bare words from Judge Nikitchenko. The Soviet judge said that the only acts that could constitute crimes against humanity were those committed *after* the war began in September 1939. No war, no crime against humanity. In this way, the tribunal excluded from its judgement everything that happened before September 1939, however terrible the acts. Lemkin's effort to outlaw atrocity at all times, whether committed during peace or war, was cast aside because of the comma inserted late into Article 6(c) of the charter, the afterthought that Lemkin feared. Leon's expulsion from Vienna in January 1939, together with all the actions taken against his family and hundreds of thousands of others before September 1939, was not treated as a crime.

The judges recognized the difficulty this would cause. Political opponents were murdered in Germany before the war, Judge Nikitchenko reminded those present. Many individuals were kept in concentration camps, in circumstances of horror and cruelty, and a great number were killed. A policy of terror was carried out on a vast scale, organized and systematic, and the persecution, repression and murder of civilians in Germany before the war of 1939 were ruthless. The actions against the Jews before the war were established 'beyond all doubt'. Yet 'revolting and horrible' as these acts were, the comma inserted into the text of the charter excluded them from the tribunal's jurisdiction. We were powerless to do anything else, the judges said.

Thus did the first day of judgement deal a crushing blow to Lemkin. Lauterpacht, sitting in the courtroom, would not have been troubled. The curtain that divided September 1939 from that which came before was impermeable, the consequence of rules agreed to in the Nuremberg Charter, the logic of the law. Practical Lauterpacht had argued for this result in the drafts he prepared for Shawcross in July. Passionate Lemkin had argued against it in Cambridge the following month.

After the first day's hearing, those present dispersed to offices, homes, prison cells and hotels to dissect what was said, to predict what might follow the next day. Rebecca West left the Palace of Justice to pay a visit to a small village not far from Nuremberg. There she encountered a German woman who, having learned that the English writer was attending the trial, launched into a litany of complaints about the Nazis. They had posted foreign workers near her village, 'two thousand wretched cannibals, scum of the earth, Russians, Balks, Balts, Slavs'. This woman was interested in the trial, didn't object to it, but she did so wish they hadn't appointed a Jew as chief prosecutor. Pressed to explain, the woman identified David Maxwell Fyfe as the offending individual. When Rebecca West protested the error, the woman responded curtly, 'Who would call his son David, but a Jew?'

154

Lord Justice Lawrence entered the courtroom at 9.30 precisely on the second day of judgement to deliver a separate judgement for each of the twenty-one defendants present. He carried with him a note that he'd written out on the letterhead of the British War Crimes Executive, a crib sheet that listed the judgement and sentence for each defendant. Marjorie Lawrence would later paste it into the family scrapbook.

The judges would begin by setting out their reasons for declaring the guilt or innocence of each defendant. Lord Justice Lawrence adopted a grave tone.

Frank sat in the middle of the front row, eyes hidden behind dark glasses. Lauterpacht sat at the British table, just a short distance from the defendant most directly responsible for the murders of his parents, siblings, uncle and aunt. Lemkin waited in Paris, a wireless close by.

Lawrence began with Göring, who at times during the trial 're-called the madam of a brothel', Rebecca West observed from the press gallery, entered through the sliding door and 'looked sur-prised'. Guilty on all counts.

Sir Geoffrey Lawrence then dealt with the next five defendants. All guilty. Judge Nikitchenko convicted Rosenberg. The attempt to explain the true purpose of his racial politics was entirely without any merit. Guilty.

Now it was Frank's turn. He sat without motion, looked at the floor. Judge Biddle, embroiled in a messy love affair with Rebecca West, read from the prepared text. The decision was reached three weeks earlier, although Frank didn't know that. Biddle summarized the lawyer's role, from the time he joined the Nazi Party in 1927, through the presidency of the Academy for German Law, to his ap-pointment as governor-general. In the absence of evidence, Frank escaped conviction on count one, no proven involvement in the deci-sion to wage aggressive war. A brief respite.

Biddle turned to count three (war crimes) and count four (crimes against humanity). Both concerned events in Poland after the war began, within the jurisdiction of the tribunal. Frank was involved in the destruction of Poland as a national entity. He ex-ploited its resources to support the German war effort, crushing opposition with utmost harshness. He unleashed a reign of terror. Concentration camps were introduced on his territory, including 'notorious Treblinka and Majdanek'. Thousands of Poles were liquidated, including 'leading representatives' of the intelligent-sia. Slave labour was deported to Germany. Jews were persecuted by being forced into ghettos, discriminated against, starved, exterminated.

The judges recognized Frank's expression of 'terrible guilt' for atrocities committed on the territory over which he reigned. Yet ultimately his defence was largely an attempt to prove that he wasn't responsible, because the activities were not under his control or be-cause he didn't know of them.

'It . . . may well be true that some of the crimes committed in the Government General were committed without the knowledge of Frank,' Biddle concluded, 'and even occasionally despite his op-position.' Perhaps, too, not all the criminal policies originated with him. Nevertheless, he was 'a willing and knowing' participant in the terror, the economic exploitation of Poland, the acts that led to death by starvation of vast numbers of people. He was involved in the deportation to Germany of over a million Poles. He was implicated in a programme that involved the murder of at least three million Jews.

For these reasons, he was guilty of war crimes and of crimes against humanity.

Biddle did not use the word 'genocide'.

Frank listened attentively, seated quietly as the remaining judgements were handed down. Of the twenty-one defendants present, three were acquitted. Hjalmar Schacht, the former president of the Reichsbank, got off because it wasn't proven that he knew of the aggressive plans for war. Franz von Papen, Hitler's vice-chancellor for eighteen months, was acquitted for the same reason. Hans Fritzsche, small fry in Goebbels's Ministry of Propaganda and an inadequate substitute for his absent boss, was acquitted for lack of evidence that he intended to incite the German people to commit atrocities. Several of the others were found to have committed crimes against humanity, but none were found guilty of genocide. The word was unspoken.

The tribunal adjourned for lunch. Sentences would be pronounced after the break. Frank joined in offering congratulations to the three who were acquitted.

155

After lunch, all eyes were turned towards the small wooden door at the back of the dock, waiting for each defendant to enter and face judgement. 'Open, shut, open, shut,' once again, the correspondent R. W. Cooper told the readers of *The Times*.

The tribunal reconvened at ten to three. For the first time in the year-long trial, the eighteen defendants who were found guilty and awaited only the details of their punishment were treated as individuals, not brought into the courtroom as a group. Each awaited his turn outside courtroom 600 at the foot of the lift. They entered the courtroom one at a time to listen to the sentence, then leave.

Those who weren't present in courtroom 600 that afternoon

would not see this most dramatic moment of the trial. Handing down the punishment of each individual defendant was not filmed for public viewing to protect the dignity of each defendant. Frank came in at number seven. Of the first six, five were sentenced to death: Göring, Ribbentrop, Keitel, Kaltenbrunner and Rosenberg. Rudolf Hess escaped the gallows and was sentenced to life imprisonment.

As his turn came, Frank was the seventh to travel up in the lift and pass through the sliding door. On entering, he lost all sense of direction and stood with his back to the judges. The guards had to spin him around to face the judges. Rebecca West noticed the moment. A form of protest? No. She interpreted it as 'odd proof' of Frank's disturbed state. Facing the judges, he listened in silence, and not without courage, as some noted. Lord Justice Lawrence declared the sentence in just a few words.

'On the Counts of the Indictment on which you have been convicted, the Tribunal sentences you to death by hanging.' Through the headphones, Frank heard, 'Tod durch den Strang' (Death by the rope).

Frank would never know that his acquaintance with Henri Donnedieu de Vabres offered a glimmer of hope, that the Frenchman tried to help him. Right to the end, Donnedieu argued for a sentence of life imprisonment, not death, but he was alone, overruled by the others, all seven of them. Judge Biddle was surprised by his French colleague, 'curiously tender' towards the German jurist, now characterized as an international criminal. Perhaps the American judge, like Yves Beigbeder, didn't know of Frank's invitation to Donnedieu to visit Berlin in 1935.

After hearing the verdict, Frank returned to his cell. Dr Gilbert met him, as he did each defendant. Frank smiled politely, unable to look the psychologist in the eye. Such confidence as remained had evaporated.

'Death by hanging.'

Frank spoke the words softly. He nodded his head as he spoke, as though in acquiescence. 'I deserved it and I expected it.' He said no more, offering no explanation to Dr Gilbert or, later, to any member of his family of why he acted as he had.

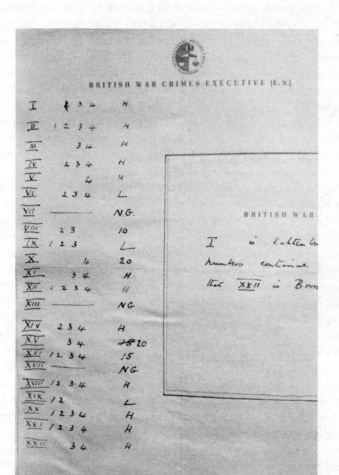

Sir Geoffrey Lawrence's crib sheet, 1 October 1946

156

The judgement came as a relief to Lauterpacht. His arguments on crimes against humanity, endorsed by the tribunal, were now a part of international law. The protection of the individual, and the idea of individual criminal responsibility for the worst crimes, would be a part of the new legal order. The sovereignty of the state would no longer provide absolute refuge for crimes on such a scale, in theory at least.

Shortly after the judgement, he received a note from Shawcross. 'I hope you will always feel some satisfaction in having had this leading hand in something which may have a real influence on the future conduct of international relations.' If Lauterpacht felt any such satisfaction, he never mentioned it publicly or even privately. Not to his son, not to Inka.

Lemkin's reaction was different. He was devastated by the silence on genocide, compounding his earlier sense of the 'Nuremberg nightmare'. There was no mention in the judgement even that it had been argued, or that it was supported by three of the four prosecuting powers. (My own experience before international courts is that the summary of the arguments made, even if without success, offers some comfort; it also opens the door to future arguments in other cases.) Lemkin was equally horrified that the crimes committed before the war were entirely ignored.

Later Lemkin met Henry King, a junior American prosecutor, who described the Pole as 'unshaven' and 'dishevelled', his clothing in tatters. Lemkin confided that the verdict was 'the blackest day' of his life. It was worse even than the moment he learned, a month earlier, that Bella and Josef had perished.

Leon received news of the judgement in Paris. The following morning Lucette, a young girl who lived nearby, collected my mother, Leon's eight-year-old daughter, and walked her to school. Lucette observed Leon in prayer, a ritual he went through every morning, to offer a sense of connection, he would tell my mother, a sense of 'belonging to a group that had disappeared'.

Leon never told me what he thought of the trial or the judgement, whether such a thing could ever be adequate as a means of accountability. He was delighted, however, by my choice of career.

157

Twelve defendants were sentenced to death with no right of appeal. They included Frank, Rosenberg and Seyss-Inquart, who didn't have long to wait for the act of execution by hanging. The pope made a plea for mercy for Frank, which was rejected. The penalty posed no moral dilemma for Lord Justice Lawrence; his daughter Robby told me that her father had condemned several criminals to the gallows in England.

'He considered it to be the just punishment for people who had done very evil things,' she explained. 'He was glad when the death penalty ended in Britain, but I don't think he ever doubted that it was proper in this case, for these defendants.'

Between the day of judgement and the day of execution, President Truman wrote to Lord Justice Lawrence. He expressed appreciation for the 'faithful services' the judge had rendered to 'the strengthening of international law and justice'.

Two weeks later, on the morning of 16 October, a headline appeared in the *Daily Express*. 'Göring is executed first at 1 a.m.', it reported, followed by ten other defendants. The article was famously wrong. Göring escaped the noose, having committed suicide shortly before the scheduled hour of execution.

Ribbentrop was the first to hang; Frank moved up the pecking order to number five. The execution took place in the gym of the Palace of Justice, to which he was accompanied by the US army priest Sixtus O'Connor. He walked across the courtyard and into the gym, closing his eyes, swallowing repeatedly as a black hood was placed over his head. He said a few final words.

The *Times* correspondent R. W. Cooper was in France when news of the hangings emerged later that day. 'The end came in a little Paris restaurant,' he wrote in his memoir. The musicians were strumming a composition called 'Insensiblement', later to become Django Reinhardt's favourite tune. The photographs of the hanged, including Frank, were posted on the back of the evening paper, available in the restaurant for all to see.

'Ça, c'est beau à voir,' a patron murmured. 'Ça, c'est beau.' Then he idly turned the page.

158

Several hundred miles away, at some distance from the small village of Neuhaus am Schliersee in Bavaria, the younger children of Hans Frank were at kindergarten. Brigitte Frank later collected them.

'My mother came in flowery spring clothes to tell us that Father was now in heaven,' Niklas recalled. 'My sisters and brother started to cry, and I was quiet, because I knew now it had happened. I think this was when a big hurt began, when my cold reaction from this family began.'

Years later, Niklas met Sixtus O'Connor, the chaplain who accompanied Frank to the gym. Your father went to the gallows smiling, the chaplain told him. 'Even in the prison cell in Nuremberg,' he added, 'your father was afraid of your mother.'

Niklas had not forgotten that day, one that he often thought about. Together we visited the empty prison wing of Nuremberg's Palace of Justice and sat in a cell like the one in which his father was held. 'The funny thing is,' Niklas said, 'when they came to take my father to the gallows, they opened the door, my father was kneeling.' Niklas got down on his knees to show me. 'He said to the priest, "Father, my mother when I was a little boy, my mother used to give me the cross every morning when I was leaving for school."' Niklas made the mark of the cross on his forehead. 'Please do this also now,' Frank asked the priest.

Niklas wondered whether it was a show. 'Maybe it was one of those moments, very near to the gallows, to the death . . . he knew he will not survive the night of the sixteenth of October, maybe it was really an honest thing, the only and last honest thing he did.'

Niklas was silent for a moment. 'He wanted to go back to being an innocent child again, what he was when his mother made the sign on him.' He paused again, then said, 'It's the first time I think about it. I think he wanted to be a little boy again who had done nothing of all those crimes.'

Yet Niklas had no doubts about the lack of sincerity in his father's partial expression of guilt in the courtroom and no reservations about the hanging of his father. 'I am opposed to the death penalty,' he said without emotion, 'except for my father.' During one of our conversations, he recalled the letter his father wrote to Dr Seidl, his lawyer, the evening before the execution. 'He wrote, "I am not a criminal."' Niklas spoke the words with disgust. 'So really, he took back everything he confessed during the trial.'

As we talked of their last meeting, the conversation with the chaplain, the silent fortitude of his mother, Niklas put his hand into the breast pocket of his jacket and took out a few papers. 'He was a criminal,' he said quietly, removing from them a small black-and-white photograph, worn and faded. He handed it over. An image of his father's body, laid out on a cot, lifeless, taken a few minutes after the hanging, a label across his chest.

'Every day I look at this,' Niklas said. 'To remind me, to make sure, that he is dead.'

Hans Frank, hanged, 16 October 1946

EPILOGUE
To the Woods

The trial at Nuremberg had consequences.

A few weeks after its end, the United Nations General Assembly gathered in upstate New York. On the agenda for 11 December 1946, were a raft of draft resolutions to create a new world order. Two related to the trial.

Desiring to lay the path for an international bill of rights, the General Assembly affirmed that the principles of international law recognized by the Charter of the Nuremberg Tribunal – including crimes against humanity – were a part of international law. By resolution 95, the General Assembly endorsed Lauterpacht's ideas and decided to find a place for the individual in the new international order.

The General Assembly then adopted resolution 96. This went beyond what the judges at Nuremberg had decided: noting that genocide denied the 'right of existence of entire human groups', the Assembly decided to override the ruling and affirm that 'genocide *is* a crime under international law'. Where judges feared to tread, governments legislated into existence a rule to reflect Lemkin's work.

The resolution helped Lemkin to recover from 'the blackest day' of his life. His energies revived, he prepared a draft convention on genocide and sought to persuade governments across the world to support his instrument. It was a hard slog over two years. On 9 December 1948, the General Assembly adopted the Convention on the Prevention and Punishment of the Crime of Genocide, the first human rights treaty of the modern era. The treaty came into force a little more than two years later, allowing Lemkin to devote the final decade of his life to encouraging countries to join the convention. By the time he died of a heart attack in New York in 1959, France and the Soviet Union had signed up. The United Kingdom joined in 1970, and the United States became a party in 1988, after the controversy that followed President Reagan's visit to the graves of SS officers at the Bitburg cemetery in West Germany. Lemkin died without children. It was said that few people attended his funeral, but Nancy Ackerly recalled it differently. 'There were several people there, not the five or six reported by some, maybe for dramatic effect,' she told me, and among them were 'quite a few women in veils'. He is buried in Flushing, New York.

Hersch Lauterpacht returned to Cambridge a day after the judgement to devote himself to academic endeavours and his family and to be with Inka. His work *An International Bill of the Rights of Man* inspired the Universal Declaration of Human Rights, adopted by the UN General Assembly on 10 December 1948, one day after the Genocide Convention. Disappointed that the declaration was not legally binding, Lauterpacht hoped it might open the door to a more forceful development. This came with agreement on the European Convention on Human Rights, which was signed in 1950. The Nuremburg prosecutor David Maxwell Fyfe played a key role in the elaboration of the text that created the first international human rights court to which individuals would have access. Other regional and global human rights instruments followed, but no treaty on crimes against humanity has yet been adopted to parallel Lemkin's Genocide Convention. In 1955, Lauterpacht was elected the British judge at the International Court of Justice in The Hague, despite the opposition of some who thought him insufficiently British. He died in 1960, before completing his term of office, and is buried in Cambridge.

Lauterpacht and Lemkin were two young men in Lemberg and Lwów. Their ideas have had global resonance, the legacies reaching far and wide. The concepts of genocide and crimes against humanity have developed side by side, a relationship that connects the individual and the group.

Fifty summers passed before the idea of an international criminal court became a reality, as states pushed and pulled in different directions, unable to find a consensus on the punishment of international crimes. Change finally came in July 1998, catalysed by atrocities in the former Yugoslavia and Rwanda. That summer, more than 150 states agreed to a statute for an international criminal court at a meeting in Rome. I enjoyed a peripheral role in the negotiations, working with a colleague on the preamble, the introductory words of the treaty, intended to inspire. Working in the shadows, we inserted a simple line into the preamble, one that stated 'the duty of every State to exercise its criminal jurisdiction over those responsible for international crimes'. Seemingly innocuous, the line survived the negotiating process to become the first occasion on which states had recognized any such duty under international law. Three generations after the idea of an international court was debated by Henri Donnedieu de Vabres and Hans Frank in Berlin in 1935, a new international court was finally created, with the power to rule on genocide and crimes against humanity.

Two months after agreement was reached on the ICC, in September 1998 Jean-Paul Akayesu became the first person ever to be convicted for the crime of genocide by an international court. This followed a trial held at the International Criminal Tribunal for Rwanda.

A few weeks later, in November 1998, the House of Lords in London ruled that Senator Augusto Pinochet, former president of Chile, was not entitled to claim immunity from the jurisdiction of the English courts because the acts of torture for which he was said to be responsible were a crime against humanity. This was the first time any national court had ever handed down such a ruling.

In May 1999, the Serbian president Slobodan Milošević became the first serving head of state to be indicted for crimes against humanity, for alleged acts in Kosovo. In November 2001, after he left office, genocide charges were added to his indictment, in relation to atrocities in Bosnia, at Srebrenica.

Six years passed. In March 2007 an American District Court judge stripped John Kalymon of his American nationality. Why? Because in August 1942 he served in the Ukrainian Auxiliary Police, rounding up Jews in *die Grosse Aktion*. He assisted in the persecution of civilian populations in a crime against humanity.

In September 2007, the International Court of Justice in The Hague ruled that Serbia violated its obligation to Bosnia and Herzegovina by failing to prevent a genocide in Srebrenica. This was the first occasion on which any state had been condemned by an international court for violating the Genocide Convention.

In July 2010, President Omar al-Bashir of Sudan became the first serving head of state to be indicted for genocide by the International Criminal Court.

Two years later, in May 2012, Charles Taylor became the first head of state to be convicted of crimes against humanity. He was sentenced to fifty years in prison.

In 2015, the United Nations International Law Commission started to work actively on the subject of crimes against humanity, opening the way to a possible companion to the convention on the prevention and punishment of genocide.

The cases go on, as do the crimes. Today, I work on cases involving genocide or crimes against humanity in relation to Serbia, Croatia, Libya, the United States, Rwanda, Argentina, Chile, Israel and Palestine, the United Kingdom, Saudi Arabia and Yemen, Iran, Iraq and Syria. Allegations of genocide and crimes against humanity abound across the globe, even as the ideas that inspired Lauterpacht and Lemkin resonate along different paths.

An informal hierarchy has emerged. In the years after the Nuremberg judgement, the word genocide gained traction in political circles and in public discussion as the 'crime of crimes', elevating the protection of groups above that of individuals. Perhaps it was the power of Lemkin's word, but as Lauterpacht feared there emerged a race between victims, one in which a crime against humanity came to be seen as the lesser evil. That was not the only unintended consequence of the parallel efforts of Lauterpacht and Lemkin. Proving the crime of genocide is difficult, and in litigating cases I have seen for myself how the need to prove the intent to destroy a group in whole or in part, as the Genocide Convention requires, can have unhappy psychological consequences. It enhances the sense of solidarity among the members of the victim group while reinforcing negative feelings towards the perpetrator group. The term 'genocide', with its focus on the group, tends to heighten a sense of 'them' and 'us', burnishes feelings of group identity and may unwittingly give rise to the very conditions that it seeks to address: by pitting one group against another, it makes reconciliation less likely. I fear that the crime of genocide has distorted the prosecution of war crimes and crimes against humanity, because the desire to be labelled a victim of genocide brings pressure on prosecutors to indict for that crime. For some, to be labelled a victim of genocide becomes 'an essential component of national identity' without contributing to the resolution of historical disputes or making mass killings less frequent. It was no surprise that an editorial in a leading newspaper, on the occasion of the centenary of Turkish atrocities against Armenians, suggested that the word 'genocide' may be unhelpful, because it 'stirs up national outrage rather than the sort of ruthless examination of the record the country needs'.

Yet against these arguments, I am bound to accept that the sense of group identity is a fact. As long ago as 1893, the sociologist Ludwig Gumplowicz, in his book *La lutte des races* (The struggle between the races), noted that 'the individual, when he comes into the world, is a member of a group'. The view persists. 'Our bloody nature', the biologist Edward O. Wilson wrote a century later, 'is ingrained because group-versus-group was a principal driving force that made us what we are.' It seems that a basic element of human nature is that 'people feel compelled to belong to groups and, having joined, consider them superior to competing groups.'

This poses a serious challenge for our system of international law confronted with a tangible tension: on the one hand, people are killed because they happen to be members of a certain group; on the other, the recognition of that fact by the law tends to make more likely the possibility of conflict between groups, by reinforcing the sense of group identity. Perhaps Leopold Kohr got it right, in the strong but private letter he wrote to his friend Lemkin, that the crime of genocide will end up giving rise to the very conditions it seeks to ameliorate.

What of the other main characters in the story?

After being liberated from Vittel, Miss Tilney worked for the US army before returning to Paris. She lived there for two more years, then returned to England. In the 1950s she travelled once more, this time as a missionary to South Africa, and in 1964 she emigrated to the United States. Her last home was in Coconut Grove, Miami, close to her brother Fred, the retired bodybuilder and seller of quack medicines. I was told that her circle of acquaintances included Charles Atlas. She died in 1974. In 2013, I sent the material I had uncovered about her to the Yad Vashem memorial to the Holocaust in Jerusalem, along with two affidavits, one provided by my mother, the other by Shula Troman. On 29 September 2013, Miss Tilney was recognized as a Righteous Among the Nations.

Sasha Krawec, who was saved by Miss Tilney from deportation to Auschwitz, emigrated to the United States after he was freed from Vittel. He travelled by ship from Bremen to New York in 1946. I have been unable to find any trace of what happened to him next.

Emil Lindenfeld remained in Vienna. He spent the last two years of the war hiding with non-Jewish friends and family as a 'U-boat'. He remarried in 1961 and died in 1969 in Vienna, where he is buried.

Otto von Wächter went into hiding after the war, eventually being taken in by the Vatican. In 1949, he played a role as an extra in the film *La Forza del Destino,* made in Rome. He died there in mysterious circumstances, later that year, under the protection of the Austrian bishop Alois Hudal, still on the run, indicted by the Polish government for crimes of mass murder of more than 100,000 Poles in Lwów. His son Horst lives at Schloss Hagenberg with his wife, convinced that his father was a good man with a decent character, not a criminal, even as new evidence of wrongdoing emerges, including the apparent taking of a Bruegel painting and other artworks from the National Museum in Kraków, in December 1939.

Niklas Frank grew up to become a distinguished journalist, eventually serving as foreign editor of *Stern* magazine. In 1992, he returned to Warsaw and the building he lived in as a child to interview Lech Walesa, newly elected president of Poland. He didn't tell Walesa that the room in which the interview took place, and the table at which they sat, were the ones around which his father had once chased him. He lives in a small village north-west of Hamburg with his wife and has a daughter and two grandchildren.

In the summer of 2014, I travelled to Lviv with Niklas Frank and Horst von Wächter. In the making of our film – *My Nazi Legacy: What Our Fathers Did* – we visited the destroyed synagogue in Zółkiew, a nearby mass grave, and the university auditorium where Hans Frank had delivered a big speech on 1 August 1942, in the presence of Otto von Wächter. Niklas surprised us when he produced a copy of the speech from his back pocket and read it out. The following day, the three of us attended a ceremony of remembrance to honour the dead of the Waffen-SS Galician Division, created by Otto von Wächter in the spring of 1943, still venerated by the nationalistic, fringe, Ukrainian group that organized the event. Horst told me that this was the best part of the trip, because men old and young came up to him to celebrate his father. Did he mind, I asked, that many of those men wore SS uniforms with swastikas? 'Why, should I?' Horst replied.

Leon and Rita Buchholz lived together in Paris for the remainder of their lives, in the apartment that I remember from my childhood, near the Gare du Nord. Leon lived until 1997, almost completing the full span of the century. Their daughter, Ruth, married an Englishman in 1956 and moved to London. She had two sons, of whom I was the first, and later ran an antiquarian bookshop in central London, specializing in illustrated books for children. I studied law at Cambridge University, and it was there in 1982 that I took a course on international law taught by Eli Lauterpacht, Hersch's grown-up son. In the summer of 1983, after my graduation, Leon and Rita visited Cambridge, and together we attended a garden party at Eli's home. His mother, Rachel, Lauterpacht's widow, was there, and I distinctly recall the bob in her hair. Whether she and Leon spoke I do not know, but if they did, and the family connections to Vienna, Lemberg and Żółkiew were discussed, then Leon didn't feel any need to share that conversation with me.

In the autumn of 1983, I travelled to America, where I spent a year as a visiting scholar at Harvard Law School. Eli Lauterpacht wrote to me in the spring of 1984, inviting me to apply for an academic position at Cambridge University as a research fellow at a new research centre he was setting up on international law. Back then, and for the quarter of a century that ensued, as collegiality blossomed into friendship, we were unaware that our forebears had lived on the same street, more than a century earlier. Thirty years passed before Eli and I learned that his father and my great-grandmother lived in Żółkiew at opposite ends of the town, on east-west street.

This we learned as a consequence of the invitation from Lviv.

And what of Lviv? My first visit was in 2010, and I have returned each year since. A century after its heyday it remains a wondrous city, yet with a dark and secret past, where its inhabitants occupy spaces made by others. The sweep of the buildings, the hiss of trams, the scent of coffee and cherry, all are still there. The communities that contested the city streets in November 1918 are largely gone, and Ukrainians have emerged as dominant. Still, the presence of others does linger. You feel it in the bricks, helped by Wittlin, and observe it if you look very carefully: you see it in the wings of the lion, the one that 'looks down so challengingly' from its perch above the entrance to 14 Rynok Square, astride the pages of an open book on which the words 'Pax Tibi Marce Evangelista Meus' may be seen

('Peace to you, Mark, my evangelist!'); you see it in the fading Polish street signs and in the angled, empty indents in which a mezuzah once hung; you see it in the window of the old Hungarian Crown pharmacy on Bernardyński Square, once the most beautiful in all Galicia and Lodomeria, and still today at night, when it is alight and busy as ever.

After these visits, I can better understand the words of that young student who approached me on that first trip to explain in hushed tones how personally important my lecture had been. In today's Lviv, where Lemkin and Lauterpacht are forgotten, identity and ancestry are complex, dangerous matters. The city remains a 'cup of gall', as it was for so many in times past.

The conversation with the young woman who enquired about ancestry was not the only time such a message was communicated to me in Lviv. In a restaurant, on the street, after a talk, at the university, in a coffee shop, I heard matters of identity and background alluded to, in subtle ways. I recall being introduced to Professor Rabinovich, the remarkable teacher of law at the Lviv faculty who taught human rights law during the darkest of times. 'He's the one you should talk to,' several people told me. The meaning was clear, a gentle reference to ancestry.

Someone suggested I might want to eat at the Golden Rose, in the old medieval centre, between the town hall and the city archives, in the shadow of the ruins of a synagogue constructed in 1582 and destroyed on the orders of the Germans in the summer of 1941. It presented itself as a Jewish restaurant, a curiosity given the absence of Jewish residents in the city nowadays. The first time I passed the Golden Rose, in the company of my son, we peered through a window and observed a clientele that gave the impression, superficially at least, of having been transported from the 1920s, a number of people dressed in the large black hats and other paraphernalia associated with the Orthodox Jewish community. We were horrified, a place for tourists to dress up, collecting trademark black garments and hats from pegs just inside the front entrance. The restaurant offered traditional Jewish fare – along with pork sausages – from a menu without prices. At the end of the meal, the waiter invited diners to negotiate a deal on the price.

Sitting in this restaurant, having finally summoned up the courage to enter (an effort that stretched over five years), I wondered again whether I was closer to the ideas of Lauterpacht or Lemkin, or stood equidistant between them, or sat with them both. Lemkin would probably have been the more entertaining dinner companion, and Lauterpacht the more intellectually rigorous conversationalist. The two men shared an optimistic belief in the power of law to do good and protect people and the need to change the law to achieve that objective. Both agreed on the value of a single human life and on the importance of being part of a community. They disagreed fundamentally, however, on the most effective way to achieve the protection of those values, whether by focusing on the individual or the group.

Lauterpacht never embraced the idea of genocide. To the end of his life he was dismissive, both of the subject and, perhaps more politely, of the man who concocted it, even if he recognized the aspirational quality. Lemkin feared that the separate projects of protecting individual human rights, on the one hand, and protecting groups and preventing genocide, on the other, were in contradiction. It might be said that the two men have cancelled each other out.

I saw the merits of both arguments, oscillating between the two poles, caught in an intellectual limbo. So I parked the matter and directed my energy into persuading the mayor of Lviv to take a few steps to mark the accomplishments of both men, along with the city's contribution to international law and justice. Tell me where we should put plaques, the mayor told me, and he would arrange for it to be done. Show me the way; show me the route.

I would take Wittlin, the poet of hopeful idylls, infused with the idea of a harmony among friends that cut across the divide of groups, of the myth of Galicia and the city of my grandfather's lost childhood. I might start on Castle Hill, then head where everything began, at the centre on Rynok Square, with its winged lion. Past the warring factions I might breeze, across from the Lauterpacht home on Teatralna Street, with its gated iron door, along May the Third Street towards the home of Inka Katz and the window from which she watched her mother being taken, past the offices of the International Law Department at the university, newly adorned with portraits of Lauterpacht and Lemkin, and then on to the old law faculty building, up past the home of Julius Makarewicz, up the winding streets in the direction of the great Cathedral of St George, to stand in the square where Otto von Wächter gathered his SS Galicia Division. A little beyond that, no more than a stone's throw, up on the hill, I might linger for a moment before the house where Leon was born on Szeptyckich Street.

Then back down the street to the building where Lemkin lived in the year he debated with a professor about matters Armenian and the right of states to kill their own citizens, then on to the old Galician parliament where in August 1942 Frank delivered his murderous lecture, down to the opera house before which children had stood with flags and swastikas, to the playground of the Sobieski high school where the Jews were rounded up, under the railway bridge to the ghetto and Lemkin's first home, to a room in a tenement building in the poorest part of the city. From there it's just a short hop to Janowska, where Maurycy Allerhand had the impudence to enquire of a camp guard whether he had a soul, a few words spoken for which he paid with his life, and on to the great railway station, from which I could take the train to Żółkiew and, if I wanted, beyond to Bełzec and the end of the world.

I did take that train to Żółkiew, where I was met by Lyudmyla, historian of that sad, depleted town. She was the one who accompanied me to a place on the outskirts, ignored by the authorities and all but a few of the inhabitants. From her office in the old Żółkiewski fort, we travelled along the east-west street, on a straight line that would lead to a clearing in the woods. We started at the patch of grass on the western end of that long street, where my great-grandmother Malke's house once stood, past the fine Catholic and Ukrainian churches and the dilapidated, soulful seventeenth-century synagogue, on to the house with the floorboards where Clara Kramer had hidden, just across from the old wooden church, past the crossroads that marked what I now knew to be Hersch Lauterpacht's place of birth. On we went, for one kilometre and then another, across fields, through a gate, onto a path of fine, crushed sand, by trees of oak and the sound of cicadas and frogs and the smell of earth and then into a bright autumn wood, to an area where Leon and Lauterpacht might once have played. We left the sandy path, onto the grass and the bushes, and we reached a clearing in the wood.

'We have arrived.' Lyudmyla spoke quietly. Here were the ponds, two great sandpits filled with an expanse of dark water, mud and reeds that bent in the wind, a site marked by a single white stone, erected not by the town in expression of grief or regret, but as a private act of remembrance. There we sat, on grass, watching the sun fall onto dark, still water that stretched tight across the openings of the earth. Deep down, untouched for half a century and more, lay the remains of the thirty-five hundred people of whom the long-forgotten Gerszon Taffet wrote in the summer of 1946, individuals each, together a group.

Among the bones that lay beneath was a commingling, Leon's uncle Leibus, Lauterpacht's uncle David, resting near each other in this place because they happened to be a member of the wrong group.

The sun warmed the water; the trees lifted me upward and away from the reeds, towards an indigo sky. Right there, for a brief moment, I understood.

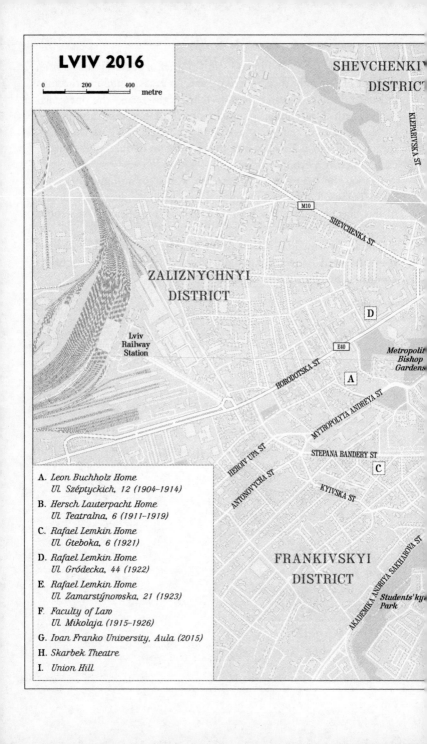

LVIV 2016

0   200   400   metre

SHEVCHENKI DISTRICT

KLEPARIVSKA ST

M10

SHEVCHENKA ST

ZALIZNYCHNYI DISTRICT

D

E40

Lviv Railway Station

Metropolit Bishop Gardens

HORODOTSKA ST

A

MYTROPOLYTA ANDREYA ST

HEROIV UPA ST

STEPANA BANDERY ST

C

ANTONOVYCHA ST

KYIVSKA ST

A. *Leon Buchholz Home*
   Ul. Széptyckich, 12 (1904–1914)

B. *Hersch Lauterpacht Home*
   Ul. Teatralna, 6 (1911–1919)

C. *Rafael Lemkin Home*
   Ul. Gteboka, 6 (1921)

D. *Rafael Lemkin Home*
   Ul. Gródecka, 44 (1922)

E. *Rafael Lemkin Home*
   Ul. Zamarstýnowska, 21 (1923)

F. *Faculty of Law*
   Ul. Mikolaja (1915–1926)

G. *Ivan Franko University, Aula (2015)*

H. *Skarbek Theatre*

I. *Union Hill*

FRANKIVSKYI DISTRICT

AKADEMIKA ANDRIYA SAKHAROVA ST

Students'kyi Park

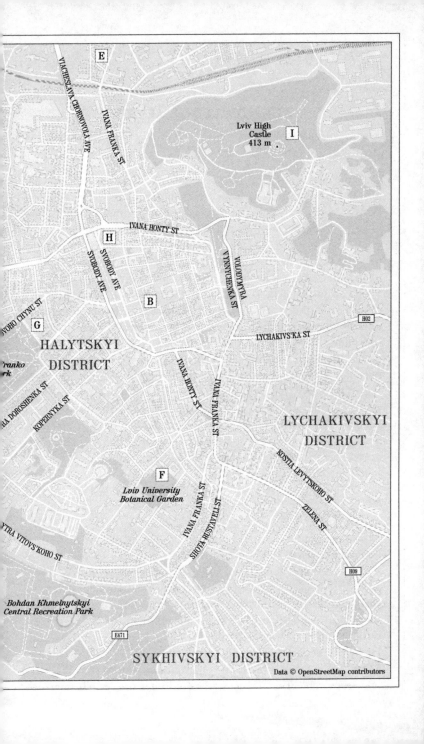

ACKNOWLEDGEMENTS

Over the past six years, I have relied on the assistance of many individuals and institutions from across the world. In some cases, the assistance was substantial and sustained over time; in others, the input was informal and limited to the provision of a single reminiscence or, in one case, the use of a single word. I am deeply grateful to everyone who has contributed to a project that grew beyond what I had expected when I was initially invited to Lviv.

I owe a special debt to members of the families of the four central characters in this story. My mother, Ruth Sands, has been extraordinarily and wonderfully supportive in the face of painful events that cut deep. My aunt, Annie Buchholz, who was very close to my grandfather over two decades, was equally generous in the act of recollection, as was my brother Marc, the finest. Other family members – my father, Allan Sands, his childhood friend Emil Landes, who was my grandfather's nephew, and others such as Doron Peleg and Aldo and Jeannette Naouri – helped add detail to a blurry picture. The opportunity to spend so many hours with Sir Elihu Lauterpacht, my teacher and mentor, has been joyous. Saul Lemkin, the last living family member who knew Rafael, has been unceasingly generous, as has Niklas Frank, a new and most unlikely of friends. I am grateful too to Horst von Wächter for his generosity in making available so much material and time.

In some respects, it could be said that the city of Lviv is the fifth main character in the book, or maybe the first. Two people have served as the most generous of guides to the city's secrets, its archives and coffee houses, and they have become close friends: at Lviv University, Dr Ivan Horodosykyy has been miraculous, a smart, savvy, thoughtful young lawyer of the kind who will surely bring great credit to the city; Dr Sofia Dyak, director of Lviv's Centre for Urban History, has opened up the city's historical riches and complexities in a way that is subtle, honest and entertaining. Among the others too numerous to mention, I must single out Professors Petro Rabinovich and Oksana Holovko, who have been supportive throughout; Dr Ihor Leman, who was drawn to military service against Russia even as he completed his own work on Lemkin and Lauterpacht; Alex Dunai; Professor Zoya Baran; and Lyudmyla Baybula, the courageous and generous archivist of Zhovkva, without whom I would never have known about the *borek* and its secrets.

Colleagues at University College London – led by my dean, Professor Hazel Genn, and Professor Cheryl Thomas, head of research – have been unstintingly supportive of an overextended writing project, and I have benefited greatly from the intelligence and labour of a stream of fine, bright research assistants from UCL: Remi Reichhold, for whom the idea of the unfindable document is unknown; Mariam Kizilbash and Luis Viveros, who helped see off the endnotes; David Schweizer, who assisted with German culture and language; Daria Zygmunt, who conquered matters Polish and uncovered the original copy of Wittlin's *Moy Lwów;* and Hejaaz Hizbullah, who found gold in the League of Nations materials. Elsewhere I have been assisted by Tessa Barsac (Paris), Noa Amirav (Jerusalem), Melissa Gohlke and Shaun Lyons (Georgetown), Eric Sigmund (Syracuse) and Aseem Mehta (Yale).

I have relied on generous assistance across the world. In France, Lucette Fingercwaig opened a wider and more personal door to l'Armée du Crime, as Pastor Richard Gelin opened the archives of the Église Évangélique Baptiste in the 14th arrondissement. Catherine Trouiller of the Fondation Charles de Gaulle explained a single photograph taken in 1944; Danielle Greuillet allowed me access to the archives of Meudon; and Jean-Michel Petit and Raymond Bétrémieux educated me on the history of Courrières.

In Poland, Marek Kornat of the Instytut Historii Polskiej Akademii Nauk told me about Lemkin's short time at Kraków's Jagiellonian University; Dr Janusz Fiolka offered endless assistance in and around Kraków; Arkadiusz Radwan, Jan Fotek, Grzegorz Pizoń and Aleksandra Polak of the Instytut Allerhanda offered a direct connection with the family of Maurycy Allerhand, who taught Lemkin and Lauterpacht; and Dr Adam Redzik of Warsaw University is the foremost historian of Lwów University from the era of which I write. Ewa Salkiewicz-Munnerlyn provided valuable insights into the Polish international law community in the interwar years, and Anna Michta and Joanna Winiewicz-Wolska were my guides at the Wawel Royal Castle. Agnieszka Bieńczyk-Missala reviewed parts of the manuscript, and Antonia Lloyd-Jones offered assistance with translation from Polish.

In Austria, I lucked out with a genial genealogical private eye in the person of Mag. Katja-Maria Chladek. Insight and information were offered by Mag.a Margaret Witek, the current director of the Brigittenauer Gymnasium attended by my grandfather; Ambassadors Helmut Tichy, Emil Brix and Elisabeth Tichy-Fisslberger; and Karin Höfler at the Third Man Museum. Max Wälde was my University of Vienna research assistant.

In Germany, too, archival doors were opened with the help of Dirk Roland Haupt (Ministry of Foreign Affairs) and Rainer Huhle (Nuremberg Human Rights Centre). I came to know the Nuremberg courtroom with the support of Dr Anne Rubesame, Michaela Lissowsky and Ambassador Bernd Borchardt (of the International Nuremberg Principles Academy) and Henrike Zentgraf (of the Memorium Nuremberg Trials). Dr Norbert Kampe offered a personal introduction to the House of the Wannsee Conference. Knots in my understanding of German were partly untied with the help of Daniel Alexander, QC, Professor Josef Bayer (Konstanz University), Sabine Bhose, David Cornwell, Professor Dr Klaus von Heusinger (Cologne), Dr Geoffrey Plow and Eddie Reynolds.

As to the trials, I benefited greatly from the first-hand accounts of Dr Yves Beigbeder, Enid, the Hon Lady Dundas, Benjamin Ferencz and Siegfried Ramler. The private papers of Sir Geoffrey Lawrence, diarized by his wife, Marjorie, were made available to me by Lord and Lady Oaksey and Patrick Lawrence, QC.

In Washington DC, I benefited greatly from the knowledge and experience available at the United States Holocaust Memorial Museum, not least from Raye Farr, Anatol Steck and Leslie Swift. At the US Department of Justice, Eli M. Rosenbaum and Dr David Rich, the last Nazi hunters, found most valuable documentary evidence.

Elsie Tilney became a more distinct and defined character with the help of Rosamunde Codling of the Surrey Chapel, who is the model archivist, and Pastor Tom Chapman. I was greatly assisted on points of detail by Susan Meister; Chris Hill; Elinor Brecher, the obituarist at the *Miami Herald;* Jeanette Winterson and Susie Orbach; Sylvia Whitman and Germaine Tilney.

The complexities of testing for DNA were explained to me by Max Blankfeld of Family Tree and Dr Turi King of the University of Leicester.

The maps were prepared by Scott Edmonds, Tim Montenyohl, Alex Tait and Vickie Taylor of International Mapping, the sultans of cartography. Photographic assistance was provided by my dear friend Jonathan Klein, the master of the pixel, and Matthew Butson, both of Getty Images, and by Diana Matar, who is able to capture almost any moment.

The international community of writers, scholars, librarians, archivists and museum keepers have offered great collegiality. My thanks to Elisabeth Åsbrink Jakobsen (Stockholm); Professor John Q. Barrett (St John's University); John Cooper (London); Professor David Crane (Syracuse University College of Law); Professor Jonathan Dembo (J. Y. Joyner Library, East Carolina University); Michelle Detroit (Jacob Rader Marcus of the American Jewish Archives); Tanya Elder (American Jewish Historical Society); Kristin Eshelman (Thomas J. Dodd Research Center, University of Connecticut); Professor Donna-Lee Frieze (Deakin University); Dr Joanna Gomula (Cambridge); Professor John-Paul Himka (University of Alberta); Dr Martyn Housden (University of Bradford); Professor Steven Jacobs (University of Alabama); Valentin Jeutner (Cambridge); Dr Yaraslau Kryvoi (University of West London); Kristen La Follette (Columbia Center for Oral History); Professor James Loeffler (University of Virginia); Marguerite Most (Goodson Law Library, Duke Law School); Nicholas Penny (National Gallery); Dr Dan Plesch (SOAS); Professor Dr Dieter Pohl (University of Klagenfurt); Dr Radu Popa (New York University); Andrew Sanger (Cambridge); Sabrina Sondhi (Arthur W. Diamond Law Library, Columbia University); Zofia Sulej (William Cullen Library, University of the Witwatersrand); Francesca Tramma (Fondazione Corriere della Sera); Dr Kerstin von Lingen (University of Heidelberg); Dr Ana Filipa Vrdoljak (University of Technology, Sydney); Professor Emeritus Arthur Wensinger (Wesleyan University).

Friends and colleagues, old and new, were supportive and knowledgeable. Stuart Proffitt helped to set the ball rolling on the ideas that turned into this book. James Cameron and Hisham Matar were there, whenever needed. Adriana Fabra, Sylvia Fano, Amanda Galsworthy, David Kennedy, Sean Murphy, Bruno Simma and

Gerry Simpson reviewed draft chapters. Yuval Shany helped to find long-lost members of my family and a long-forgotten manuscript. James Crawford helped me to see the wood from the trees (again). New and obscure insights tumbled from the minds of David Charap, Finola Dwyer, David Evans, Nick Fraser and Amanda Posey even as we laboured on our film, *What Our Fathers Did: A Nazi Legacy.* Performances of *A Song of Good and Evil* with Laurent Naouri, Guillaume de Chassy, Vanessa Redgrave, Emma Pallantt, Valerie Bezancon and Katja Riemann offered unexpected insights. Eva Hoffman helped me to understand the translation of lives and experiences, while Louis Begley (whose novel *Wartime Lies* offered early inspiration), Robby Dundas, Michael Katz (introduced to me by Alex Ulam), Clara Kramer, Siegfried Ramler, Bob Silvers, Nancy Steinson (Ackerly), Shula Troman and Inge Trott were kind enough to share with me what they had actually lived. Anya Hurlbert helped arrange a meeting with Cecilia Gallerani, while Tom Henry suggested useful readings on her long life; Liz Jobey offered hints on style; Marco De Martino enriched my knowledge of Curzio Malaparte; Christine Jennings offered material on long-ago conferences; Sara Bershtel found linguists; Göran Rosenberg introduced me to Swedes; Dennis Marks and Sally Groves unpicked Richard Strauss; and Jonathan Sklar alerted me to the dangers of a mind on the edge of collapse. At Dartington, Celia Atherton and Vaughan Lindsay offered me a fine space to write. My thanks also to the readers who have taken the trouble to point out minor errors and infelicities that crept into the original edition.

I could not have completed the manuscript without the careful, scholarly typing of Louise Rands, my colleague and dear friend over three decades, who also translated a seemingly endless stream of interviews into intelligible words in black and white that were capable of being used.

My generous, marvellous, comforting agent Gill Coleridge devoted more time than was decent to the presentation of these interweaving stories, before seamlessly passing the baton to Georgia Garrett, under whose guidance I am now delighted to be. To both, and to all the fine staff at Rogers, Coleridge & White, my deepest thanks. These I also hurl across the Atlantic to Melanie Jackson in New York, responsible for the instant identification of the one editor who could get this right. Coincidentally, Melanie has a familial interest in these pages, as her father and grandfather both make appearances (allowing me to obtain a more informed view as to which of two possible meanings her father intended when he referred to Lemkin as 'that bugger', in a letter penned in 1947).

Victoria Wilson at Alfred A. Knopf has been the perfect editor. Fearsome, strategic, attentive, loving and sceptical, she endlessly pressed upon me the merits of time and the slower write, for which I am hugely grateful. Later in the process of writing, I have been fortunate to work with Bea Hemming at Weidenfeld & Nicolson, whose insightful and intelligent thoughts have greatly enhanced the text, even at a late stage. Such faults as remain are my responsibility alone.

Finally there are the deepest of all thanks to my closest family, the core five, now thoroughly (and overly) doused in the joys and darknesses of Lviv. Leo the historian taught me about the Pietists; Lara the social scientist reminded me of my excessive false consciousness; Katya the artist encouraged me to look at places and things with a different eye.

And Natalia, the one who makes our little group so incredibly happy, whilst recognizing and dealing with the quirks that cause us to be so very different, and who has borne the brunt of my obsession, no expression of gratitude or love could be excessive. Thank you, thank you, thank you.

SOURCES

I have drawn upon a wide and varied range of materials. Some are newly discovered and original – from the archives of Lviv, touching the lives of Lauterpacht and Lemkin – but more often I have been able to draw on the work of others, resources available as a result of prodigious efforts. Such material is referenced in the endnotes, but among the many sources a few bear special mention for their interest and quality.

The material that pertains to the life of my grandfather Leon Buchholz is largely held in personal, family archives and in the memories of others, in particular my mother and aunt. I have benefited from access to the Austrian State Archives (Österreichisches Staatsarchiv); the Central Archives of Historical Records in Warsaw (Archiwum Główne Akt Dawnych); the Documentation Centre of Austrian Resistance (Dokumentationsarchiv des österreichischen Widerstandes Vienna); the Vienna City and State Archive (Wiener Stadt- und Landesarchiv); the website of JewishGen; the Yad Vashem Archive, including the Central Database of Shoah Victims' Names; and the collections of the United States Holocaust Memorial Museum.

The city of Lemberg/Lviv/Lwów is the subject of a rich literature, comprising scholarly material of a historical nature and personal memoir. As to the scholarly, I have much appreciated the essays in John Czaplicka's fine edited work *Lviv: A City in the Crosscurrents of Culture* (Harvard University Press, 2005). With regard to memoir, the reader will have noted numerous references to Józef Wittlin's *Moy Lwów* (Czytelnik, 1946), which is to be published for the first time in a fine English translation by Antonia Lloyd-Jones, *City of Lions* (Pushkin Press, 2016), with photographs by Diana Matar. On the events following the German occupation (1941–44), the work of the historian Dieter Pohl has been a primary source, including *Ivan Kalyomon, the Ukrainian Auxiliary Police, and Nazi Anti-Jewish Policy in L'viv, 1941–1944: A Report Prepared for the Office of Special Investigations, US Department of Justice,* 31 May 2005, and

Nationalsozialistische Judenverfolgung in Ostgalizien 1941–1944, 2nd edn (Oldenbourg, 1997). I have been fortunate to rely on Philip Friedman, 'The Destruction of the Jews of Lwów, 1941–1944', in *Roads to Extinction: Essays on the Holocaust*, ed. Ada June Friedman (Jewish Publication Society of America, 1980), 244–321; Christoph Mick, 'Incompatible Experiences: Poles, Ukrainians, and Jews in Lviv Under Soviet and German Occupation, 1939–44', *Journal of Contemporary History* 46, no. 2 (2011), 336–63; Omer Bartov, *Erased* (Princeton University Press, 2007); and Ray Brandon and Wendy Lower, eds., *The Shoah in Ukraine* (Indiana University Press, 2008).

Other memoirs from which I have drawn include Rose Choron, *Family Stories* (Joseph Simon/Pangloss Press, 1988); David Kahane, *Lvov Ghetto Diary* (University of Massachusetts Press, 1990); Voldymyr Melamed, *The Jews in Lviv* (TECOP, 1994); Eliyahu Yones, *Smoke in the Sand: The Jews of Lvov in the War Years, 1939–1944* (Gefen, 2004); Jan Kot, *Chestnut Roulette* (Mazo, 2008); and Jakob Weiss, *The Lemberg Mosaic* (Alderbrook, 2010). The remarkable cartographic and photographic collection held by the Center for Urban History of East Central Europe in Lviv (http://www.lvivcenter.org/en/) is a rich and easily accessible resource, and much is to be found, with some digging, in the Government Archive of Lviv Oblast.

The nearby town of Zhovkva/Żółkiew is not the subject of so abundant a literature, although its long history suggests that it ought to be. For historical material dating to the events of the 1930s and 1940s, I have relied on Gerszon Taffet, *The Holocaust of the Jews of Żółkiew* (Lodz: Central Jewish Historical Committee, 1946); Clara Kramer, *Clara's War: One Girl's Story of Survival*, with Stephen Glantz (Ecco, 2009); and Omer Bartov, 'White Spaces and Black Holes', in Brandon and Lower, *Shoah in Ukraine*, 340–42.

Much has been written about the life of Hersch Lauterpacht. The starting point is the encyclopedic reference work by his son, Elihu, *The Life of Hersch Lauterpacht* (Cambridge University Press, 2010). I have also benefited from a series of essays published as 'The European Tradition in International Law: Hersch Lauterpacht', *European Journal of International Law* 8, no. 2 (1997). Eli Lauterpacht has provided access to his father's personal archive, including notebooks, images, correspondence and other documents, not least the original drafts of the two Nuremberg speeches he wrote for Sir Hartley Shawcross in 1945 and 1946.

More has been written about Rafael Lemkin and the word he coined. I have placed particular reliance on Lemkin's long-unpublished memoir, starting with a copy of the manuscript available at the New York Public Library, but have lately been able to rely on the version edited for publication by Donna-Lee Frieze (Yale University Press, 2013), *Totally Unofficial*. I have benefited from John Cooper's pioneering *Raphael Lemkin and the Struggle for the Genocide Convention* (Palgrave Macmillan, 2008), which was the first full-length biography (recently reissued in paperback), and have drawn on William Korey's *Epitaph for Raphael Lemkin* (Jacob Blaustein Institute, 2001) and an excellent collection of essays edited by Agnieszka Bienczyk-Missala and Slawomir Debski, *Rafal Lemkin: A Hero of Humankind* (Polish Institute of International Affairs, 2010). Equally rich is the wonderful article by John Q. Barrett, 'Raphael Lemkin and "Genocide" at Nuremberg, 1945–1946', in *The Genocide Convention Sixty Years After Its Adoption*, ed. Christoph Safferling and Eckart Conze (Asser, 2010), 35–54. Other sources on which I have relied include Samantha Power, *A Problem from Hell* (Harper, 2003), and two works by Steven Leonard Jacobs, *Raphael Lemkin's Thoughts on Nazi Genocide* (Bloch, 2010) and *Lemkin on Genocide* (Lexington Books, 2012), and I have had sight of the manuscript of Douglas Irvin-Erickson, *Raphaël Lemkin and Genocide: A Political History of 'Genocide' in Theory and Law* (University of Pennsylvania Press, forthcoming), an important contribution. The Lemkin archive, such as it is, is scattered across the United States, to be found in the Raphael Lemkin Collection, P-154, American Jewish Historical Society in New York; the Raphael Lemkin Papers, MC-60, American Jewish Archives in Cleveland; the Lemkin Papers, New York Public Library; the Rare Book and Manuscript Library, Columbia University; and the Thomas J. Dodd Research Center at the University of Connecticut.

The first account of Hans Frank's life that I came across, and the one which left the most vivid impression, is that written by his son Niklas, originally published in 1987 as *Der Vater* (Bertelsmann) and later translated into English in an abridged version (too abridged, according to Niklas) as *In the Shadow of the Reich* (Alfred A. Knopf, 1991). I have relied on Stanislaw Piotrowski, ed., *Hans Frank's*

Diary (PWN, 1961), and, through translated extracts, the manuscript that Frank wrote in his Nuremberg prison cell, *In the Shadow of the Gallows* (published posthumously by his wife in Munich in 1953 and available only in German); Piotrowski claims that the manuscript and typescript authorized by Frank were changed, with some sentences omitted and others, 'directed against the Polish nation'. I have greatly benefited from Martyn Housden's thorough *Hans Frank: Lebensraum and the Holocaust* (Palgrave Macmillan, 2003) and Dieter Schenk's *Hans Frank: Hitlers Kronjurist und Generalgouverneur* (Fischer, 2006), as well as Leon Goldensohn, *The Nuremberg Interviews: Conversations with the Defendants and Witnesses* (Alfred A. Knopf, 2004). A detailed account of Frank's daily life is to be found in his diaries (*Diensttagebuch*), with English translations of extracts to be found in volume 29 of the *Trial of the Major War Criminals Before the International Military Tribunal*.

As to the Nuremberg trial, there can be no substitute for a close reading of the transcript of the proceedings and the documentary evidence that was before the judges, which are available in forty-two volumes of the *Trial of the Major War Criminals Before the International Military Tribunal* (Nuremberg, 1947), available at http://avalon.law.yale.edu/subject_menus/imt.asp. I have made extensive use of Robert H. Jackson's official *Report to the International Conference on Military Trials* (1945); the Robert H. Jackson Papers at the Library of Congress, Manuscript Division, Washington DC; and the four large scrapbooks prepared by Marjorie Lawrence and privately held by the Lawrence family in Wiltshire.

Several contemporaneous accounts of the trial stand out. R. W. Cooper's *Nuremberg Trial* (Penguin, 1946) is a personal memoir by the correspondent of the London *Times,* almost as gripping as the *Nuremberg Diary* by the US army psychologist Gustave Gilbert (Farrar, Straus, 1947). Other must-reads include three articles in the *New Yorker* by Janet Flanner, reproduced in *Janet Flanner's World,* ed. Irving Drutman (Secker & Warburg, 1989); Martha Gellhorn's essay 'The Paths of Glory', in *The Face of War* (Atlantic Monthly Press, 1994); and Rebecca West's 'Greenhouse with Cyclamens I', in *A Train of Powder* (Ivan R. Dee, 1955). I have also made use of the writings of two judges: Robert Falco, *Juge à Nuremberg* (Arbre Bleu, 2012), and Francis Biddle, *In Brief Authority* (Doubleday, 1962). Telford Taylor offers a rich history in *The Anatomy of the Nuremberg*

NOTES

Prologue: An Invitation

xxiii 'Open, shut, open, shut': R. W. Cooper, *The Nuremberg Trial* (Penguin, 1946), 272.

xxiii 'This is a happy room': Niklas and I visited courtroom 600 on 16 October 2014, accompanied by a film crew. The documentary we made, titled *What Our Fathers Did: A Nazi Legacy,* explores a son's relationship with his father.

xxv 'What haunts are not': Nicolas Abraham, 'Notes on the Phantom: A Complement to Freud's Metapsychology' (1975), in Nicolas Abraham and Maria Torok, *The Shell and the Kernel,* ed. Nicholas T. Rand (University of Chicago, 1994), 1:171.

xxv 'blurred borders': Joseph Roth, 'Lemberg, die Stadt', in *Werke,* ed. H. Kesten (Berlin, 1976), 3:840, cited in John Czaplicka, ed., *Lviv: A City in the Crosscurrents of Culture* (Harvard University Press, 2005), 89.

xxv 'red-white, blue-yellow': Ibid.

xxvi The parliament had disappeared: Jan II Kazimierz Waza, born 22 March 1609, died 16 December 1672, King of Poland and Grand Duke of Lithuania.

xxvii 'Where are you now': Józef Wittlin, *Mój Lwów* (Czytelnik, 1946); *Mein Lemberg* (Suhrkamp, 1994) (in German); *Mi Lvov* (Cosmópolis, 2012) (in Spanish).

xxvii Six decades later: Ivan Franko, born 27 August 1856, in Nahuievychi (now the town of Ivan Franko), died 28 May 1916, in Lemberg.

xxvii 'I do not wish to disturb': Wittlin, *Mój Lwów*; translation by Antonia Lloyd-Jones, *City of Lions* (Pushkin Press, 2016), 32, is forthcoming. Page references are to the manuscript of the translation.

xxviii 'Let's play at idylls': Ibid., 7–8.

xxviii 'In early August 1942': David Kahane, *Lvov Ghetto Diary* (University of Massachusetts Press, 1990), 57.

I Leon

7 Georgia, my client: On 1 April 2011, the International Court of Justice ruled that it did not have jurisdiction to hear the case.

8 'soaked up the blood': Wittlin, *City of Lions*, 5.

9 For these efforts: He was imprisoned in 1947, and died in 1950, 'Czuruk Bolesław – The Polish Righteous', http://www.sprawiedliwi.org.pl/en/family/580,czuruk-boleslaw.

9 'Waffen-SS Galician Division': Michael Melnyk, *To Battle: The History and Formation of the 14th Galicien Waffen-SS Division*, 2nd edn (Helion, 2007).

9 'Thou Shalt Not Murder': Andrey Sheptytsky, born 29 July 1865, died 1 November 1944; Philip Friedman, *Roads to Extinction: Essays on the Holocaust*, ed. Ada June Friedman (Jewish Publication Society of America, 1980), 191; John-Paul Himka, 'Metropolitan Andrey Sheptytsky', in *Jews and Ukrainians*, ed. Yohanan Petrovsky-Shtern and Antony Polonsky (Littman Library of Jewish Civilization, 2014), 337–60.

9 From the city archives: Government Archive of Lviv Oblast.

12 Only Leon was born: Central Archives of Historical Records in Warsaw.

12 Stanisław Żółkiewski: Born 1547, died 1620.

12 Alex Dunai gave me: Digital copy on file.

13 'at the far end': Joseph Roth, *The Wandering Jews*, trans. Michael Hofmann (Granta, 2001), 25.

13 It lay at the western: Card file of Żółkiew landowners, 1879, Lviv Historical Archives, fond 186, opys 1, file 1132, vol. B.

14 A peace treaty was signed: Treaty of London, signed 30 May 1913, by Bulgaria, the Ottoman Empire, Serbia, Greece, Montenegro, Italy, Germany, Russia, and Austria-Hungary.

14 Yet just a month later: Treaty of Bucharest, signed 10 August 1913, by Bulgaria, Romania, Serbia, Greece, and Montenegro.

14 'most colossal battle': 'Lemberg Taken, Halicz As Well', *New York Times*, 5 September 1914.

14 'What was a single murder': Stefan Zweig, *Beware of Pity*, trans. Anthea Bell (Pushkin, 2012), 451.

15 'no personal files': Austrian State Archives director to author, 13 May 2011.

15 This was a quirk: Treaty of Saint-Germain-en-Laye, signed 10 September 1919, by inter alia Austria, the British Empire, France, Italy, Japan, and the United States. Article 93 provides the following: 'Austria will hand over without delay to the Allied and Associated Governments concerned archives, registers, plans, title-deeds and documents of every kind belonging to the civil, military, financial, judicial or other forms of administration in the ceded territories.'

15 'where they all arrived': Roth, *Wandering Jews*, 55.

16 Bruno Kreisky: Born 22 January 1911, died 29 July 1990; chancellor of Austria, 1970–83.

17 An obscure treaty signed: See note to 'without distinction of birth' on p. 73.

18 'aromas of patisseries': Wittlin, *City of Lions,* 4, 28.

21 'no harder lot': Roth, *Wandering Jews,* 56–57.

23 It carried seven Nazi ministers: *Neue Freie Presse,* 13 May 1933, 1, http://anno.onb.ac.at/cgi-content/anno?aid=nfp&datum=19330513 &zoom=33.

23 The Austrian chancellor, Engelbert Dollfuss: Howard Sachar, *The Assassination of Europe, 1918–1942: A Political History* (University of Toronto Press, 2014), 202.

26 Hitler denounced various agreements: Otto Tolischus, 'Polish Jews Offer Solution of Plight', *New York Times,* 10 February 1937, 6.

28 The *Anschluss* (linkup): Guido Enderis, 'Reich Is Jubilant, Anschluss Hinted', *New York Times,* 12 March 1938, 4; 'Austria Absorbed into German Reich', *New York Times,* 14 March 1938, 1.

28 'the criminal has been': Friedrich Reck, *Diary of a Man in Despair,* trans. Paul Rubens (*New York Review of Books,* 2012), 51.

28 He stood alongside Arthur Seyss-Inquart: 'Hitler's Talk and Seyss-Inquart Greeting to Him', *New York Times,* 16 March 1938, 3.

28 'solution of the Jewish problem': Doron Rabinovici, *Eichmann's Jews,* trans. Nick Somers (Polity Press, 2011), 51–53.

28 Another commission oversaw: Curriculum vitae of Otto von Wächter prepared by Horst von Wächter, on file, entry for 11 June 1938.

29 I located the form Leon: The Israelitische Kultusgemeinde Wien, thought to have been founded in 1852, continues to function today (http://www.ikg-wien.at).

29 That night, 9 November: Rabinovici, *Eichmann's Jews,* 57–59.

29 The only trace that remained: Yad Vashem Database (Julius Landes, born April 12, 1911), based on information found at the Documentation Centre of Austrian Resistance.

31 He'd lost his Polish nationality: Frederick Birchall, 'Poland Repudiates Minorities' Pact, League Is Shocked', *New York Times,* 14 September 1934, 1; Carole Fink, *Defending the Rights of Others* (Cambridge University Press, 2004), 338–41.

34 They included Spanish Republicans: See generally Jean Brunon and Georges Manue, *Le livre d'or de la Légion Étrangère, 1831–1955,* 2nd ed. (Charles Lavauzelle, 1958).

36 'air of venality': Janet Flanner, 'Paris, Germany', *New Yorker,* 7 December 1940, in *Janet Flanner's World,* ed. Irving Drutman (Secker & Warburg, 1989), 54.

38 The division was agreed to: Augur, 'Stalin Triumph Seen in Nazi Pact; Vast Concessions Made by Hitler', *New York Times,* 15 September 1939, 5; Roger Moorhouse, *The Devils' Alliance: Hitler's Pact with Stalin, 1939–1941* (Basic Books, 2014).

38 In June 1941: Robert Kershaw, *War Without Garlands: Operation Barbarossa, 1941/42* (Ian Allan, 2008).

38 The use of public transportation: Rabinovici, *Eichmann's Jews,* 103.

39 Deportations to the east: Ibid.

39 The archivist directed me: On file, available at http://www.bildindex. de/obj16306871.html#|home.

39 In October 1941: Rabinovici, *Eichmann's Jews,* 104.

39 'the borders of the German Reich': Ibid.

41 We made do with the wall: Third Man Museum, http://www.3mpc. net/englsamml.htm.

41 'They are going to take': Testimony of Anna Ungar (née Schwarz), deportation from Vienna to Theresienstadt in October 1942, USC Shoah Foundation Institute, https://www.youtube.com/watch?v= GBFFlD4G3c8.

42 Escorted to the Aspangbahnhof: Testimony of Henry Starer, deportation from Vienna to Theresienstadt in September 1942, USC Shoah Foundation Institute, https://www.youtube.com/watch?v=HvAj3AeKIlc.

42 It was signed: On file.

42 Among the 1,985 other people: The details of Malke Buchholz's transport are at http://www.holocaust.cz/hledani/43/?fulltext-phrase=-Buchholz&cntnto1origreturnid=1; a list of all names is at http://www. holocaust.cz/transport/25-bq-terezin-treblinka/.

42 The routine that followed: On Franz Stangl, no work is more engrossing than Gitta Sereny's *Into That Darkness* (Pimlico, 1995); on Treblinka, none more authentic than the first-hand account by Chil Rajchman, *Treblinka: A Survivor's Memory,* trans. Solon Beinfeld (MacLehose Press, 2011).

43 Eventually the barber cracked: The scene may be viewed at https:// www.youtube.com/watch?v=JXweT1BgQMk.

43 'I was obsessed': Claude Lanzmann, *The Patagonian Hare,* trans. Frank Wynne (Farrar, Straus & Giroux, 2013), 424.

43 Malke was murdered: http://www.holocaust.cz/hledani/43/?fulltext-phrase=Buchholz&cntnto1origreturnid=1.

45 During one of our conversations: Clara Kramer, *Clara's War: One Girl's Story of Survival,* with Stephen Glantz (Ecco, 2009).

47 They were lined up: Ibid., 124; Gerszon Taffet, *The Holocaust of the Jews of Żółkiew,* trans. Piotr Drozdowski (Central Jewish Historical Committee, Lodz, 1946).

47 A year earlier: Maurice Rajsfus, *La rafle du Vél d'Hiv* (PUF, 2002).

47 Monsieur Louis Bétrémieux: Telephone conversation between the author and M. Bétrémieux, 2 August 2012.

48 The bulk of the papers: The UGIF was established by law on 29 November 1941, by the Vichy government's Office of Jewish Affairs, to consolidate all Jewish organizations in France into a single unit; it was dissolved by law on 9 August 1944.

49 In February 1943: Asher Cohen, *Persécutions et sauvetages: Juifs et Français sous l'occupation et sous Vichy* (Cerf, 1993), 403.

49 Later that summer: Raul Hilberg, *La destruction des Juifs d'Europe* (Gallimard Folio, 2006), 1209–10.

49 It held sheets: The American Joint Distribution Committee was founded in 1914 and continues to operate today (http://www.jdc.org); the Mouvement National des Prisonniers de Guerre et Déportés was created on 12 March 1944 and headed by François Mitterrand, fusing three pre-existing French resistance organizations. See Yves Durand, 'Mouvement national des prisonniers de guerre et déportés', in *Dictionnaire historique de la Résistance,* ed. François Marcot (Robert Laffont, 2006); the Comité d'Unité et de Défense des Juifs de France was created towards the end of 1943 in opposition to the UGIF. See Anne Grynberg, 'Juger l'UGIF (1944–1950)?', in *Terres promises: Mélanges offerts à André Kaspi,* ed. Hélène Harter et al. (Publications de la Sorbonne, 2009), 509n8.

51 Many years later: The brasserie, founded in 1927, was a celebrated meeting place for writers, painters, and singers, including Picasso, Simone de Beauvoir, and Jean-Paul Sartre.

52 'Behind Flouret': Nancy Mitford, *Love in a Cold Climate* (Hamish Hamilton, 1949).

53 Among those executed: The Franc-Tireurs et Partisans de la Main d'Oeuvre Immigrée was created in 1941. See generally Stéphane Courtois, Denis Peschanski, and Adam Rayski, *Le sang de l'étranger: Les immigrés de la MOI dans la Résistance* (Fayard, 1989). The proceedings against the twenty-three members before a German military tribunal opened on 15 February 1944, at the Hotel Continental.

53 'It is always foreigners': The front and back of the poster may be seen at http://fr.wikipedia.org/wiki/Affiche_rouge#/media/File:Affiche_rouge.jpg.

53 'Happiness to all': 'Bonheur à tous, Bonheur à ceux qui vont survivre, Je meurs sans haine en moi pour le peuple allemande, Adieu la peine et le plaisir, Adieu les roses, Adieu la vie adieu la lumière et le vent.'

54 'As long as I': Max Kupferman to Leon Buchholz, 9 May 1945, on file.

55 Leon might have known one: Robert Falco, French lawyer, born

26 February 1882, died 14 January 1960. His doctoral thesis, completed in 1907, was on 'the duties and rights of theatre audiences'.

55 'If in the future': Robert Borel, 'Le crime de genocide principe nouveau de droit international', *Le Monde,* 5 December 1945.

II Lauterpacht

57 'The individual human being': Hersch Lauterpacht, 'The Law of Nations, the Law of Nature, and the Rights of Man' (1943), in *Problems of Peace and War,* ed. British Institute of International and Comparative Law, Transactions of the Grotius Society 29 (Oceana Publications, 1962), 31.

59 'good judgment': Elihu Lauterpacht, *The Life of Hersch Lauterpacht* (Cambridge University Press, 2010), 272.

59 A birth certificate: Central Archives of Historical Records, Warsaw.

61 A photograph of the family: Elihu Lauterpacht, *Life of Hersch Lauterpacht,* opposite p. 372.

63 Lauterpacht left Zółkiew: Ibid., 19.

63 That year, the Epsom Derby: 'Lemberg's Derby', *Wanganui Chronicle,* 14 July 1910, 2.

63 Buffalo Bill Cody: Charles Eldridge Griffen, *Four Years in Europe with Buffalo Bill* (University of Nebraska Press, 2010), xviii.

63 'the appearance of a member': Wittlin, *City of Lions,* 32, 26.

64 'retreating in complete': 'Lemberg Battle Terrific', *New York Times,* 4 September 1914, 3.

64 'little wayside praying centres': 'Russians Grip Galicia', *New York Times,* 18 January 1915.

64 'an outburst of wild joy': 'Great Jubilation over Lemberg's Fall', *New York Times,* 24 June 1915.

64 'oblivious' to the sounds: Elihu Lauterpacht, *Life of Hersch Lauterpacht,* 20.

64 'phenomenally good ear': Ibid., 19.

67 We gathered a near-complete set: Government Archive of Lviv Oblast, fund 26, list 15, case 171, 206 (1915–16, winter); case 170 (1915–16, summer); case 172, p. 151 (1916–17, winter); case 173 (1917–18, winter); case 176, p. 706 (1917–18, summer); case 178, p. 254 (1918–19, winter).

67 Of the early teachers: Manfred Kridl and Olga Scherer-Virski, *A Survey of Polish Literature and Culture* (Columbia University Press, 1956), 3.

68 the highest mark ('good'): Government Archive of Lviv Oblast, fund 26, list 15, case 393.

68 This was in November 1918: Timothy Snyder, *The Red Prince: The Secret Lives of a Habsburg Archduke* (Basic Books, 2010).

68 opting for neutrality: Fink, *Defending the Rights of Others*, 110 (and generally, 101–30).

68 'day and night': Elihu Lauterpacht, *Life of Hersch Lauterpacht*, 21.

68 Within a week: The Treaty of Warsaw (known as the Petliura-Piłsudski Agreement) was signed on 21 April 1920, but had little impact.

69 '1,100 Jews Murdered': '1,100 Jews Murdered in Lemberg Pogroms', *New York Times,* 30 November 1918, 5.

69 'sit on the same benches': Elihu Lauterpacht, *Life of Hersch Lauterpacht,* 23.

70 Others wanted greater autonomy: Antony Polonsky, *The Jews in Poland and Russia, Volume 3: 1914–2008* (Littmann, 2012); Yisrael Gutman et al., eds., *The Jews of Poland Between Two World Wars* (Brandeis University Press, 1989); Joshua Shanes, *Diaspora Nationalism and Jewish Identity in Habsburg Galicia* (Cambridge, 2014).

70 The philosopher Martin Buber: Asher Biermann, *The Martin Buber Reader: Essential Writings* (Palgrave Macmillan, 2002).

70 This was an early fluttering: Elihu Lauterpacht, *Life of Hersch Lauterpacht,* 21.

70 Dr Józef Buzek: Born 16 November 1873, died 22 September 1936.

71 'Would you not like': Israel Zangwill, 'Holy Wedlock', in *Ghetto Comedies* (William Heinemann, 1907), 313.

71 'dissolving like jelly': Stefan Zweig, *The World of Yesterday* (Pushkin, 2009), 316.

71 'yellow, dangerous eyes': Ibid., 313.

71 'autonomous development': Address to the US Congress, 8 January 1918; Margaret MacMillan, *Paris 1919* (Random House, 2003), 495.

72 It was known as the Curzon Line: Elihu Lauterpacht, *Life of Hersch Lauterpacht,* 20.

72 The Curzon Line was drawn: R. F. Leslie and Antony Polonsky, *The History of Poland Since 1863* (Cambridge University Press, 1983).

72 'life, liberty, and the pursuit': 'Rights of National Minorities', 1 April 1919; Fink, *Defending the Rights of Others,* 203–5.

72 'injustice and oppression': Fink, *Defending the Rights of Others,* 154n136.

72 As these matters were being debated: Norman Davies, *White Eagle, Red Star: The Polish-Soviet War, 1919–20* (Pimlico, 2003), 47.

73 'rigid protection': David Steigerwald, *Wilsonian Idealism in America* (Cornell University Press, 1994), 72.

73 Fearful that Warsaw: A fine account is provided by Fink, *Defending the Rights of Others,* 226–31, 237–57.

73 protect 'inhabitants' who differed: Article 93 provided the following: 'Poland accepts and agrees to embody in a Treaty with the Principal Allied and Associated Powers such provisions as may be deemed necessary by the said Powers to protect the interests of inhabitants of Poland who differ from the majority of the population in race, language, or religion.'

73 'without distinction of birth': Minorities Treaty Between the Principal Allied Powers and Poland, Versailles, 28 June 1919, Articles 4 and 12, http://ungarisches-institut.de/dokumente/pdf/19190628-3.pdf.

73 A few days after signing: Fink, *Defending the Rights of Others,* 251.

74 'Every faction within Poland': Henry Morgenthau, *All in a Lifetime* (Doubleday, 1922), 399.

74 'exceedingly pretty and modern': Arthur Goodhart, *Poland and the Minority Races* (George Allen & Unwin, 1920), 141.

74 'unfair to condemn': Morgenthau, *All in a Lifetime,* app.

74 'I was unable to take': Elihu Lauterpacht, *Life of Hersch Lauterpacht,* 16.

75 'dark, cunning faces': Karl Emil Franzos, *Aus Halb-Asien: Land und Leute des ostlichen Europas,* vol. 2 (Berlin, 1901), in Alois Woldan, 'The Imagery of Lviv in Ukrainian, Polish, and Austrian Literature', in Czaplicka, *Lviv,* 85.

75 Two years later: Bruce Pauley, *From Prejudice to Persecution: A History of Austrian Anti-Semitism* (University of North Carolina Press, 1992), 82.

75 'If I was able to get out': Hugo Bettauer, *The City Without Jews* (Bloch, 1926), 28.

76 'every intellectual who wrote': Pauley, *From Prejudice to Persecution,* 104.

76 He was now enrolled: Elihu Lauterpacht, *Life of Hersch Lauterpacht,* 26.

77 'extraordinary intellectual capacity': Hans Kelsen, 'Tribute to Sir Hersch Lauterpacht', *ICLQ* 10 (1961), reprinted in *European Journal of International Law* 8, no. 2 (1997): 309.

77 The mark surprised Kelsen: Ibid.

77 In an environment: Norman Lebrecht, *Why Mahler?* (Faber & Faber, 2010), 95.

77 He became president: Elihu Lauterpacht, *Life of Hersch Lauterpacht,* 22.

77 'fallen from heaven': Arnold McNair, 'Tribute to Sir Hersch Lauterpacht', *ICLQ* 10 (1961), reprinted in *European Journal of International Law* 8, no. 2 (1997): 311; Paula Hitler, interview on 12 July 1945, at http://www.oradour.info/appendix/paulahit/paula02.htm.

78 'so quiet, so gentle': Elihu Lauterpacht, *Life of Hersch Lauterpacht*, 31.

78 She said she'd think: Ibid., 32.

80 At the LSE, he studied: Ibid., 41.

80 'his real quality': Ibid., 43.

80 'At our first meeting': McNair, 'Tribute to Sir Hersch Lauterpacht', 312.

81 'strong continental accent': Elihu Lauterpacht, *Life of Hersch Lauterpacht*, 330.

82 'Private Law Sources and Analogies': Ibid., 44.

82 'international progress': Ibid., 55.

83 'Happily for us': Ibid., 49.

83 'be and be seen to be thoroughly British': Philippe Sands, 'Global Governance and the International Judiciary: Choosing Our Judges', *Current Legal Problems* 56, no. 1 (2003): 493; Elihu Lauterpacht, *Life of Hersch Lauterpacht*, 376.

83 'passion for justice': McNair, 'Tribute to Sir Hersch Lauterpacht', 312.

83 'not too well at home': Elihu Lauterpacht, *Life of Hersch Lauterpacht*, 40.

83 'painted nails': Ibid., 157.

83 'I can and must have my private harmless life': Ibid., 36.

84 'By fighting against the Jews': Adolf Hitler, *Mein Kampf* (Jaico Impression, 2007), 60.

84 Poland signed a non-aggression: Antony Alcock, *A History of the Protection of Regional-Cultural Minorities in Europe* (St Martin's Press, 2000), 83.

84 Marriage and sexual relations: Nuremberg Laws (*Nürnberger Gesetze*), passed by Reichstag, 15 September 1935; Anthony Platt and Cecilia O'Leary, *Bloodlines: Recovering Hitler's Nuremberg Laws from Patton's Trophy to Public Memorial* (Paradigm, 2005).

84 In 1933, he'd published: Martti Koskenniemi, introduction to *The Function of Law in the International Community* by Hersch Lauterpacht (repr., Oxford, 2011), xxx.

84 'The well-being of an individual': Lassa Oppenheim, *International Law: A Treatise*, vol. 2, *Disputes, War, and Neutrality*, 6th edn, ed. Hersch Lauterpacht (Longmans, 1944).

86 'The Persecution of the Jews': Reprinted in Hersch Lauterpacht, *International Law*, vol. 5, *Disputes, War, and Neutrality, Parts IX – XIV* (Cambridge University Press, 2004), 728–36.

86 To prepare a strong letter: Oscar Janowsky Papers (undated 1900– and 1916–1933), chap. 17, 367 (on file); see James Loeffler, 'Between

Zionism and Liberalism: Oscar Janowsky and Diaspora Nationalism in America', *AJS Review* 34, no. 2 (2010): 289–308.

86 'I love to see my own work': Janowsky Papers (undated 1900– and 1916–1933), chap. 17, 389.

87 Lauterpacht declined to give a legal opinion: Elihu Lauterpacht, *Life of Hersch Lauterpacht,* 80–81 (the request was from Professor Paul Guggenheim).

88 In late 1937, the boy: Ibid., 82.

89 Philip Noel-Baker, the director: Ibid., 88.

89 'My dearest and beloved son!': Ibid., 86.

89 Tea was served at half past four: Ibid., 424.

90 Farther along, at No. 13: 'The Scenic View', *Times Higher Education Supplement,* 5 May 1995.

90 No. 23 was occupied by: G. P. Walsh, 'Debenham, Frank (1883–1965)', *Australian Dictionary of Biography* (1993), 602.

90 'flew out of the window': Elihu Lauterpacht, *Life of Hersch Lauterpacht,* 85.

90 'What private joke causes': Ibid., 95.

91 known affectionately as 'Lumpersplash': Ibid., 104.

91 Lauterpacht accepted a lecture tour: Ibid., 106.

92 Lauterpacht spent time with British: Ibid., 105.

92 'Do your best; be modest': Ibid., 134.

92 'I'm going to be in Washington': Lauterpacht to Jackson, December 1940; Elihu Lauterpacht, *Life of Hersch Lauterpacht,* 131–32.

92 'What is wanted': Elihu Lauterpacht, *Life of Hersch Lauterpacht,* 142.

92 He got a green light: Ibid., 135.

92 Jackson introduced some: 'An Act to Promote the Defense of the United States', Pub.L. 77–11, H.R. 1776, 55 Stat. 31, enacted 11 March 1941.

93 'extraordinarily significant': 'Text of Jackson Address on Legal Basis of United States Defense Course', *New York Times,* 28 March 1941, 12; the editorial is at 22.

93 Willkie never did make good: Elihu Lauterpacht, *Life of Hersch Lauterpacht,* 137.

93 'our dear old ones have aged': David Lauterpacht to Hersch Lauterpacht, undated, personal archive of Eli Lauterpacht.

94 the 'troublesome' but distracting: Elihu Lauterpacht, *Life of Hersch Lauterpacht,* 152.

94 'all the frying oil I wanted': Ibid., 153.

94 One letter went to Leonard: Ibid.

94 Another was sent to Rachel: Ibid., 152.

94 'in a state of more immediate': Ibid., 156.

94 'the will and exertion': Ibid., 166.

94 'We heartily greet and kiss': Aron Lauterpacht to Hersch Lauterpacht, 4 January 1941, personal archive of Eli Lauterpacht.

94 'Write often to my family': Elihu Lauterpacht, *Life of Hersch Lauterpacht*, 152.

95 'Massacre of the Lwów Professors': Christoph Mick, 'Incompatible Experiences: Poles, Ukrainians, and Jews in Lviv Under Soviet and German Occupation', *Journal of Contemporary History* 46, no. 336 (2011): 355; Dieter Schenk, *Der Lemberger Professorenmord und der Holocaust in Ostgalizien* (Dietz, 2007).

98 'heroic fights against': Elihu Lauterpacht, *Life of Hersch Lauterpacht*, 176.

98 'international lawlessness': Ibid., 180 and n43.

99 'guilty' of and 'responsible' for: Punishment for War Crimes: The Inter-Allied Declaration Signed at St James's Palace, London, 13 January 1942; 'Nine Governments to Avenge Crimes', *New York Times,* 14 January 1942, 6 (with text).

99 The nine governments established: The creation of the United Nations Commission for the Investigation of War Crimes was announced on 17 October 1942. Dan Plesch, 'Building on the 1943–48 United Nations War Crimes Commission', in *Wartime Origins and the Future United Nations,* ed. Dan Plesch and Thomas G. Weiss (Routledge, 2015), 79–98.

99 Churchill authorized British: David Maxwell Fyfe, *Political Adventure* (Weidenfeld & Nicolson, 1964), 79.

99 Within months, the *New York Times*: 'Poland Indicts 10 in 400,000 Deaths', *New York Times,* 17 October 1942.

99 'the best instrumentalities': 'State Bar Rallied to Hold Liberties', *New York Times,* 25 January 1942, 12; speech available at http://www.roberth-jackson.org/the-man/bibliography/our-american-legal-philosophy/.

99 Not much taken by Bette Davis: Elihu Lauterpacht, *Life of Hersch Lauterpacht,* 184.

100 'Singapore may fall': '"*Pimpernel" Smith* (1941): "Mr V", a British Melodrama with Leslie Howard, Opens at Rivoli', *New York Times,* 13 February 1942.

100 'I am slightly depressed': Elihu Lauterpacht, *Life of Hersch Lauterpacht,* 183.

100 'legislation and practices': Hersch Lauterpacht, ed., *Annual Digest and Reports of Public International Law Cases (1938–1940)* (Butterworth, 1942), 9:x.

101 'must be punished': Jurisdiction over Nationals Abroad (Germany)

Case, Supreme Court of the Reich (in Criminal Matters), 23 February 1938, in ibid., 9:294, x.

101 'the ear of the Administration': Elihu Lauterpacht, *Life of Hersch Lauterpacht*, 188.

101 'the question of so-called': Ibid., 183.

101 'Committee on War Crimes': Ibid., 201.

101 'much good . . . for the minorities': Ibid., 204.

101 'on the International Bill of Rights': Ibid., 199.

102 'revolutionary immensity': Hersch Lauterpacht, 'Law of Nations, the Law of Nature, and the Rights of Man', cited in ibid., 252.

105 That same day he sent a memorandum: On file.

105 'I felt I would like': Elihu Lauterpacht, *Life of Hersch Lauterpacht*, 220.

105 'the triumph of the forces': Ibid., 234.

106 'a historic occasion': Ibid., 229.

106 This evoked the possibility: Ibid.

106 'Imagine the study': Ibid., 227.

106 'the greatest victim': Ibid., 247.

107 It should not be the primary focus: *Cambridge Law Journal* 9 (1945–6): 140.

108 Lvov, liberated by the Red Army: Serhii Plokhy, *Yalta: The Price of Peace* (Viking, 2010), 168.

108 'fundamental human rights': Charter of the United Nations, San Francisco, 26 June 1945, preamble.

108 In June, Columbia: Hersch Lauterpacht, *An International Bill of the Rights of Man* (Columbia University Press, 1944).

109 'an echo of the past': Hans Morgenthau, *University of Chicago Law Review* 13 (1945–46): 400.

109 The two men met: Jackson to Lauterpacht, 2 July 1945, Hersch Lauterpacht Archive ('I am so grateful to you for the many courtesies of yesterday and to Mrs Lauterpacht for the delightful hour at tea. Your thought of the junior Jackson was deeply appreciated').

109 'stubborn and deep': Robert H. Jackson's official *Report to the International Conference on Military Trials* (1945), vi (hereafter cited as *Jackson Report*).

110 The Americans wanted: Redrafts of Definition of 'Crimes', submitted by Soviet Delegation, 23 and 25 July 1945, and Redraft of Definition of 'Crimes', submitted by American Delegation, 25 July 1945, in ibid., 327, 373, 374.

110 On his return to London: Revised British Definition of 'Crimes', Prepared by British Delegation and Accepted by the French Delegation, 28 July 1945, in ibid., 390.

110 'as smooth as a tennis court': Katherine Fite to her mother, 5 August 1945, War Crimes File, Katherine Fite Lincoln Papers, container 1 (Correspondence File), Harry S. Truman Presidential Museum and Library.

111 Titles would make it easier: William E. Jackson to Jacob Robinson, 31 May 1961 (on file); Elihu Lauterpacht, *Life of Hersch Lauterpacht*, 272n20.

111 The term was also used: Dan Plesch and Shanti Sattler, 'Changing the Paradigm of International Criminal Law: Considering the Work of the United Nations War Crimes Commission of 1943–1948', *International Community Law Review* 15 (2013): 1, esp. at 11 et seq.; Kerstin von Lingen, 'Defining Crimes Against Humanity: The Contribution of the United Nations War Crimes Commission to International Criminal Law, 1944–1947', in *Historical Origins of International Criminal Law: Volume 1*, ed. Morten Bergsmo et al., FICHL Publication Series 20 (Torkel Opsahl Academic EPublisher, 2014).

111 'the most beautiful thing': Katherine Fite to her mother, 5 August 1945.

111 'We should insert words': 'Notes on Proposed Definition of Crimes' and 'Revision of Definition of "Crimes"', submitted by American Delegation, 31 July 1945, in *Jackson Report*, 394–95; 'I may say that the term was suggested to me by an eminent scholar of international law', ibid., 416.

112 'the best looking man': Minutes of Conference Session of 2 August 1945, *Jackson Report*, 416.

112 'murder, extermination, enslavement, deportation': Charter of the International Military Tribunal, *Jackson Report*, 422.

113 'outraged conscience of the world': Elihu Lauterpacht, *Life of Hersch Lauterpacht*, 274.

113 'I shall be in London': Ibid., 272.

113 'Daddy does not say much': Ibid., 266.

113 This was achieved on 6 October: Protocol to Agreement and Charter, 6 October 1945, *Jackson Report*, 429.

114 'We shall just have': Elihu Lauterpacht, *Life of Hersch Lauterpacht*, 275.

III Miss Tilney of Norwich

121 'became a famous bodybuilder': Frederick Tilney, *Young at 73 – and Beyond!* (Information Incorporated, 1968). Frederick, who became a permanent resident of the United States on 20 June 1920, is

commended by reviewers for his 'timeless advice on physical fitness' and for being 'so enthusiastic about fresh vegetable and fruit juices'.

121 Among the papers: The archive, located at the William Cullen Library, University of the Witwatersrand, Johannesburg, South Africa, includes six letters to and from Miss Tilney, dating from 27 August 1947, to 6 October 1948, http://www.historicalpapers.wits.ac.za/inventory.php?iid=7976.

122 'Elsie M. Tilney': On file.

122 'fearless in pursuing a point': Robert Govett, born 14 February 1813, died 20 February 1901; W. J. Dalby, 'Memoir of Robert Govett MA', attached to a publication of Govett's 'Galatians', 1930.

122 I came across a copy: http://www.schoettlepublishing.com/kingdom/govett/surreychapel.pdf.

124 Dr Codling accompanied: Norfolk Records Office; the archive is divided into three collections: FC76; ACC2004/230; and ACC2007/1968. The online catalogue is available at http://nrocat.norfolk.gov.uk/Dserve/dserve.exe?dsqServer=NCC3CL01&dsqIni=Dserve.ini&dsqApp=Archive&dsqCmd=show.tcl&dsqDb=Catalog&dsqPos=0&dsqSearch=(CatalogueRef=='FC%2076').

124 the 'great' welcome she received: *North Africa Mission Newsletter*, March/April 1928, 25.

124 Someone took a group photograph: *North Africa Mission Newsletter*, September/October 1929, 80.

124 'work amongst Jewish people': Surrey Chapel, Missionary Prayer Meeting Notes, May 1934.

125 'a gentleman pulled her': Surrey Chapel, Missionary Notes, October 1935.

125 'exotic loveliness of flowers': Elsie Tilney, 'A Visit to the Mosque in Paris', *Dawn*, December 1936, 561–63.

125 'I was privileged to help': *Trusting and Toiling*, 15 January 1937.

125 She spoke at meetings: *Trusting and Toiling*, 15 September and 15 October 1937.

126 'Jewish students at Lwów': *Trusting and Toiling*, 16 January 1939.

126 'especially moving, as the largest': André Thobois, *Henri Vincent* (Publications Croire et Servir, 2001), 67, quoting a first-hand account reported in *Le Témoin de la Vérité*, April–May 1939.

126 'people in difficulty waiting': Thobois, *Henri Vincent*, 80.

127 'her Jewish protégés': *Trusting and Toiling*, 15 April 1940.

127 'whose lot is now more bitter': *Trusting and Toiling*, 15 July 1940.

127 'thinking constantly of family': Surrey Chapel, note following prayer meeting, 6 August 1940; Foreign Mission Band Account (1940); *Trusting and Toiling*, 15 October 1940.

127 'presented his compliments': Surrey Chapel Foreign Mission Band Account (1941).

127 In May, she was transferred: On the Vittel camp, see Jean-Camille Bloch, *Le Camp de Vittel: 1940–1944* (Les Dossiers d'Aschkel, undated); Sofka Skipwith, *Sofka: The Autobiography of a Princess* (Rupert Hart-Davis, 1968), 233–36; Sofka Zinovieff, *Red Princess: A Revolutionary Life* (Granta Books, 2007), 219–61. The camp at Vittel is also the subject of a documentary film by Joëlle Novic, *Passeports pour Vittel* (Injam Productions, 2007), available on DVD.

128 'longing for the day': Surrey Chapel Foreign Mission Band Account (1942); *Trusting and Toiling,* 15 March 1943.

128 Most of the women: Bloch, *Le Camp de Vittel,* 10 et seq.; Zinovieff, *Red Princess,* 250–58; see also Abraham Shulman, *The Case of Hotel Polski* (Schocken, 1981).

128 It was said that they held: Bloch, *Le Camp de Vittel,* 18, 22, and nn12–13.

128 In March, a first group: Ibid., 20.

128 'The Song of the Slaughtered': Zinovieff, *Red Princess,* 251 ('The *Song* became one of Sofka's treasured poems, which she repeatedly copied out and distributed. "They are no more. Do not ask anything, anywhere the world over. All is empty. They are no more."')

128 'We felt that Miss Tilney': Skipwith, *Sofka,* 234.

128 'It was only after the camp': Ibid.

129 'always put herself last': *Trusting and Toiling,* 15 December 1944, 123.

129 'outstandingly brave deeds': Ibid.

129 'secretary and hostess': Colonel A. J. Tarr to Miss Tilney, 18 April 1945; Captain D. B. Fleeman to Miss Tilney, 22 May 1945.

IV Lemkin

137 '[A]ttacks upon national, religious and ethnic groups should be made international crimes': Raphael Lemkin, *Axis Rule in Occupied Europe* (Carnegie Endowment for International Peace, 1944), xiii.

139 'I know the words': Nancy Steinson, 'Remembrances of Dr Raphael Lemkin' (n.d., on file).

139 Unable to find a publisher: Raphael Lemkin, *Totally Unofficial,* ed. Donna-Lee Frieze (Yale University Press, 2013), xxvi.

140 'I was born': Ibid., 3.

140 'When the man to the right': Ibid.

140 Josef Lemkin circumvented: John Cooper, *Raphael Lemkin and the Struggle for the Genocide Convention* (Palgrave Macmillan, 2008), 6.

141 To the end of his life: Lemkin, *Totally Unofficial*, 17.

141 'Look how evil oppresses mankind': J. D. Duff, *Russian Lyrics* (Cambridge University Press, 1917), 75.

141 'cloven belly, feather-filled': Paul R. Mendes-Flohr and Jehuda Reinharz, *The Jew in the Modern World: A Documentary History* (Oxford University Press, 1995), 410.

141 Lemkin knew the works: Hayyim Bialik and Raphael Lemkin, *Noach i Marynka* (1925; Wydawnictwo Snunit, 1926).

142 'believe an idea means to live it': Lemkin, *Totally Unofficial*, xi.

143 'More than 1.2 million Armenians': Ibid., 19.

143 'the greatest crime of all ages': Vahakn N. Dadrian, *The History of the Armenian Genocide: Ethnic Conflict from the Balkans to Anatolia to the Caucasus* (Berghahn Books, 2003), 421.

143 'crimes against Christianity': Ulrich Trumpener, *Germany and the Ottoman Empire, 1914–1918* (Princeton University Press, 1968), 201.

143 'A nation was killed': Lemkin, *Totally Unofficial*, 19.

144 After several hours: Government Archive of Lviv Oblast, fund 26, list 15, case 459, p. 252–3.

144 A 1924 document: Ibid.

145 'very conservative place': Marek Kornat, 'Rafał Lemkin's Formative Years and the Beginning of International Career in Inter-war Poland (1918–1939)', in *Rafał Lemkin: A Hero of Humankind*, ed. Agnieszka Bieńczyk-Missala and Sławomir Dębski (Polish Institute of International Affairs, 2010), 59–74; Professor Kornat to author, e-mail, 3 November 2011.

146 He also took a first course: Ludwik Ehrlich, born 11 April 1889, in Ternopil, died 31 October 1968, in Kraków.

147 'undersized, swarthily pale faced': 'Says Mother's Ghost Ordered Him to Kill', *New York Times*, 3 June 1921; 'Armenian Acquitted for Killing Talaat', *New York Times*, 4 June 1921, 1.

148 'I discussed this matter': Lemkin, *Totally Unofficial*, 20.

149 Lemkin returned to the exchange: Herbert Yahraes, 'He Gave a Name to the World's Most Horrible Crime', *Collier's*, 3 March 1951, 28.

149 'lonely, driven, complicated, emotional': Robert Silvers, interview with author, 11 December 2011, New York City.

149 We met on the same day: *Altuğ Taner Akçam v. Turkey* (application no. 27520/07), European Court of Human Rights, judgement of 25 October 2011.

150 'Murdered in the Janowska camp': The Janowska camp was created in October 1941 in a north-western suburb of Lemberg, next to a factory operating at 134 Janowska Street. Leon Weliczker Wells, *The Janowska Road* (CreateSpace, 2014).

150 arch-nationalist with 'ambivalent' feelings: Roman Dmowski, born 9 August 1864, died 2 January 1939.

150 Together we admired: Adam Redzik, *Stanisław Starzyński, 1853–1935* (Monografie Instytut Allerhanda, 2012), 54.

151 Elegant, authoritative, interested: Zoya Baran, 'Social and Political Views of Julius Makarevich', in *Historical Sights of Galicia,* Materials of Fifth Research Local History Conference, 12 November 2010, Lviv (Ivan Franko Lviv National University, 2011), 188–98.

152 He died in 1955: Juliusz Makarewicz, born 5 May 1872, died 20 April 1955.

155 'My old home': Joseph Roth, *The Bust of the Emperor,* in *Three Novellas* (Overlook Press, 2003), 62.

155 Around then, he completed: Rafael Lemkin and Tadeusz Kochanowicz, *Criminal Code of the Soviet Republics,* in collaboration with Dr Ludwik Dworzak, Magister Zdziław Papierkowski, and Dr Roman Piotrowski, preface by Dr Juliusz Makarewicz (Seminarium of Criminal Law of University of Jan Kasimir in Lwów, 1926).

155 Schwartzbard's trial offered: John Cooper, *Raphael Lemkin,* 16.

156 'white-bearded Jews': 'Slayer of Petlura Stirs Paris Court', *New York Times,* 19 October 1927; 'Paris Jury Acquits Slayer of Petlura, Crowded Court Receives the Verdict with Cheers for France', *New York Times,* 27 October 1927.

156 'They could neither acquit': Lemkin, *Totally Unofficial,* 21.

156 'judicial career': Ibid.

156 He published books on the Soviet: http://www.preventgenocide.org/lemkin/bibliography.htm.

157 In the spring of 1933: Raphael Lemkin, 'Acts Constituting a General (Transnational) Danger Considered as Offences Against the Law of Nations' (1933), http://www.preventgenocide.org/lemkin/madrid1933-english.htm.

157 'the life of the peoples': Vespasian Pella, report to the Third International Congress of Penal Law, Palermo, 1933, cited in Mark Lewis, *The Birth of the New Justice: The Internationalization of Crime and Punishment, 1919–1950* (Oxford University Press, 2014), 188, citing *Troisième Congrès International de Droit Pénal, Palerme, 3–8 avril 1933, Actes du Congrès,* 737, 918.

157 The minister of justice: Lemkin, *Totally Unofficial,* 23. Although Rappaport is not named, he fits Lemkin's description of the caller.

157 'It is not difficult': *Gazeta Warszawska,* 25 October 1933.

158 As the *New York Times:* Lemkin, *Totally Unofficial,* xii.

158 Lemkin tried to publish: Keith Brown, 'The King Is Dead, Long Live the Balkans! Watching the Marseilles Murders of 1934' (delivered

at the Sixth Annual World Convention of the Association for the Study of Nationalities, Columbia University, New York, 5–7 April 2001), http://watson.brown.edu/files/watson/imce/research/projects/terrorist_transformations/The_King_is_Dead.pdf.

158 Professor Malcolm McDermott: Lemkin, *Totally Unofficial*, 155.

159 Simon told them about: Ibid., 28.

160 'I do not understand': Ibid., 54.

161 I read the poem: By way of interpretation, see Charlton Payne, 'Epic World Citizenship in Goethe's *Hermann und Dorothea*', *Goethe Yearbook* 16 (2009): 11–28.

163 'I *will* try again': Lemkin, *Totally Unofficial*, 64.

163 'I will be grateful': Lemkin to Monsieur le Director [identity unknown], 25 October 1939; transcribed copy provided by Elisabeth Åsbrink Jakobsen.

164 Such things happen: Lemkin, *Totally Unofficial*, 65.

164 Stopping in Riga: Simon Dubnow, *History of the Jews in Russia and Poland: From the Earliest Times Until the Present Day* (Jewish Publication Society of America, 1920).

164 'the blood red cloth': Jean Amery, *At the Mind's Limits* (Schocken, 1986), 44.

165 'irrefutable evidence': Lemkin, *Totally Unofficial*, 76.

165 His acquaintance said yes: John Cooper, *Raphael Lemkin*, 37.

165 It was a territory: The decree is in Lemkin, *Axis Rule*, 506; Lemkin, *Totally Unofficial*, 77.

166 'Decisive steps': Lemkin, *Axis Rule*, 524.

166 For those who remained: Lemkin, *Totally Unofficial*, 78.

167 The dining table festooned: Ibid., 82.

167 Two days later: Ibid., 86.

168 Dishevelled and unkempt: Ibid., 88.

169 Together the two men fretted: Ibid., 96.

169 'How was it in Europe': Ibid.

169 The porter was taken: Ibid., 100.

170 A sense of idyll: John Cooper, *Raphael Lemkin*, 40.

170 'If women, children': Lemkin, *Totally Unofficial*, vii.

170 Judge Thaddeus Bryson: Andrzej Tadeusz Bonawentura Kościuszko, born February 1746, died 15 October 1817, military leader.

172 There he met with: Lemkin, *Totally Unofficial*, 106.

172 One important introduction followed: Ibid., 108.

172 'be healthy and happy': Correspondence in Yiddish, 25 May 1941, box 1, folder 4, Raphael Lemkin Collection, American Jewish Historical Society, New York.

173 'Keep your chin up': Lemkin, *Totally Unofficial*, 111.

173 'It certainly is important': Address on the observance of the golden anniversary of Paderewski's American debut, 1941, in Ignacy Jan Paderewski, *Victor Recordings (selections) (1914–1941)*.

173 That same month he travelled: 'The Legal Framework of Totalitarian Control over Foreign Economies' (paper delivered at the Section of International and Comparative Law of the American Bar Association, October 1942).

174 'reign of law': Robert Jackson, 'The Challenge of International Lawlessness' (address to the American Bar Association, Indianapolis, 2 October 1941), *American Bar Association Journal*, 27 (November 1941).

175 'When I was reading': 'Law and Lawyers in the European Subjugated Countries' (address to the North Carolina Bar Association), *Proceedings of the 44th Annual Session of the North Carolina Bar Association,* May 1942, 105–17.

175 Lemkin was not listed: *Actes de la 5ème Conférence Internationale pour l'Unification du Droit Pénal* (Madrid, 1933).

175 As word spread: Ryszard Szawłowski, 'Raphael Lemkin's Life Journey', in Bieńczyk-Missala and Dębski, *Hero of Humankind,* 43; box 5, folder 7, MS-60, American Jewish Historical Society.

176 Why was the situation: Lemkin, *Totally Unofficial,* 113.

176 'a coloured man elected': Norman M. Littell, *My Roosevelt Years* (University of Washington Press, 1987), 125.

176 Lemkin was informed: Lemkin, *Totally Unofficial,* 235, xiv.

177 He sent a proposal: John Cooper, *Raphael Lemkin,* 53.

177 He declared that: Franklin Roosevelt, Statement on Crimes, 7 October 1942.

178 This was based on: Jan Karski, *Story of a Secret State: My Report to the World,* updated edn (Georgetown University Press, 2014).

178 'How lucky you are': Littell, *My Roosevelt Years,* 151.

179 He was toying with: Rare Book and Manuscript Library, Columbia University.

179 'New conceptions require new terms': Lemkin, *Axis Rule,* 79.

179 The evolution that led: Uwe Backes and Steffen Kailitz, eds., *Ideokratien im Vergleich: Legitimation, Kooptation, Repression* (Vandenhoeck & Ruprecht, 2014), 339; Sybille Steinbacher and Fritz Bauer Institut, *Holocaust und Völkermorde: Die Reichweite des Vergleichs* (Campus, 2012), 171; Valentin Jeutner to author, e-mail, 8 January 2014.

181 He estimated that nearly: Lemkin, *Axis Rule,* 89.

181 'With the establishment': Proclamation of 26 October 1939, in ibid., 524.

181 Lemkin spent the first: Georgetown Law School, final grades, 1944–1945, box 1, folder 13, Lemkin Collection, American Jewish Historical Society.

182 'Was it something': Vasily Grossman, 'The Hell of Treblinka', in *The Road* (MacLehose Press, 2011), 178.

182 Inaction would cause: 'Report to Treasury Secretary on the Acquiescence of This Government in the Murder of the Jews' (prepared by Josiah E. Dubois for the Foreign Funds Control Unit of the US Treasury, 13 January 1944). Secretary Morgenthau, John Pehle, and Randolph Paul met with President Roosevelt on 16 January 1944, presenting him with a draft executive order to establish a war refugee board tasked with the 'immediate rescue and relief of the Jews of Europe and other victims of enemy persecution'. Rafael Medoff, *Blowing the Whistle on Genocide: Josiah E. Dubois, Jr., and the Struggle for a US Response to the Holocaust* (Purdue University, 2009), 40.

182 The *New York Times:* 'US Board Bares Atrocity Details Told by Witnesses at Polish Camps', *New York Times,* 26 November 1944, 1; '700,000 Reported Slain in 3 Camps, Americans and Britons Among Gestapo Victims in Lwow, Says Russian Body', *New York Times,* 24 December 1944, 10.

182 The War Refugee Board: *The German Extermination Camps of Auschwitz and Birkenau,* 1 November 1944, American Jewish Joint Distribution Committee Archive.

182 'vast majority of the German people': 'Twentieth-Century Moloch: The Nazi Inspired Totalitarian State, Devourer of Progress, and of Itself', *New York Times Book Review,* 21 January 1945, 1.

183 'extremely valuable': Kohr to Lemkin, 1945, box 1, folder 11, MS-60, American Jewish Archives, Cleveland.

184 Lemkin contacted Jackson: Lemkin to Jackson, 4 May 1945, box 98, folder 9, Jackson Papers, Manuscript Division, Library of Congress, Washington DC.

184 'put his foot abroad': Raphael Lemkin, 'Genocide: A Modern Crime', *Free World* 9 (1945): 39.

184 Heading eastward: John Q. Barrett, 'Raphael Lemkin and "Genocide" at Nuremberg, 1945–1946', in *The Genocide Convention Sixty Years After Its Adoption,* ed. Christoph Safferling and Eckart Conze (Asser, 2010), 36n5.

184 These words alone justified: Lemkin to Jackson, 4 May 1945.

184 On 6 May: *Washington Post,* 6 May 1945, B4.

184 Jackson thanked Lemkin: Jackson to Lemkin, 16 May 1945, Jackson Papers; Barrett, 'Raphael Lemkin and "Genocide" at Nuremberg', 38.

184 Jackson's principal lawyer: H. B. Phillips, ed., 'Reminiscences of Sidney S. Alderman' (Columbia University Oral History Research Office, 1955), 817; Barrett, 'Raphael Lemkin and "Genocide" at Nuremberg', 39.

184 Two days later: Draft Planning Memorandum of 14 May 1945, box 107, folder 5, Jackson Papers; Barrett, 'Raphael Lemkin and "Genocide" at Nuremberg', 39.

184 'destruction of racial minorities': 'Planning Memorandum Distributed to Delegations at Beginning of London Conference', June 1945, in *Jackson Report*, 68.

185 Discussing how 'genocide': Barrett, 'Raphael Lemkin and "Genocide" at Nuremberg', 40.

185 This was a contentious: Ibid., 40–41.

185 Nevertheless, the younger Jackson: Phillips, 'Reminiscences of Sidney S. Alderman', 818; Barrett, 'Raphael Lemkin and "Genocide" at Nuremberg', 41.

185 On 28 May, Lemkin: Barrett, Ibid.

185 'top of the refugees': Phillips, 'Reminiscences of Sidney S. Alderman', 842, 858; Barrett, 'Raphael Lemkin and "Genocide" at Nuremberg', 41.

185 'rear echelon Task Force': Barrett, 'Raphael Lemkin and "Genocide" at Nuremberg', 41, at n. 27.

186 'bring all war criminals': 'Declaration Regarding the Defeat of Germany and the Assumption of Supreme Authority with Respect to Germany', Berlin, 5 June 1945, Article 11(a) ('The principal Nazi leaders as specified by the Allied Representatives, and all persons from time to time named or designated by rank, office or employment by the Allied Representatives as being suspected of having committed, ordered or abetted war or analogous offences, will be apprehended and surrendered to the Allied Representatives').

186 but it appears to: Barrett, 'Raphael Lemkin and "Genocide" at Nuremberg', 42.

187 'personality difficulties': Ibid.

187 Colonel Bernays offered: Ibid.

187 No one else was: Ibid., 43.

187 The complaints reached Commander: Ibid., 43–44.

187 'The sooner Lemkin is out': Donovan to Taylor, memorandum, 24 September 1945, box 4, folder 106, Jackson Papers; Barrett, 'Raphael Lemkin and "Genocide" at Nuremberg', 42.

187 A persistent 'bugger': William E. Jackson to Robert Jackson, 11 August 1947, box 2, folder 8, Jackson Papers; Barrett, 'Raphael Lemkin and "Genocide" at Nuremberg', 53.

187   He somehow turned Sidney: On later objections in the United States, see Samantha Power, *A Problem from Hell: America and the Age of Genocide,* rev. edn (Flamingo, 2010), 64–70.

188   The British too were: Telford Taylor, *The Anatomy of the Nuremberg Trials* (Alfred A. Knopf, 1993), 103; Barrett, 'Raphael Lemkin and "Genocide" at Nuremberg', 45.

188   'couldn't understand what the word': Phillips, 'Reminiscences of Sidney Alderman', 818; Barrett, 'Raphael Lemkin and "Genocide" at Nuremberg', 45.

188   'extermination of racial and religious': Indictment, adopted 8 October 1945, *Trial of the Major War Criminals Before the International Military Tribunal* (Nuremberg, 1947), 1: 43.

188   Years of lugging documents: Note from US Army Dispensary, 5 October 1945, box 1, folder 13, Lemkin Collection, American Jewish Historical Society.

189   'I included genocide': Lemkin, *Totally Unofficial,* 68; Barrett, 'Raphael Lemkin and "Genocide" at Nuremberg', 46.

V The Man in a Bow Tie

195   Milein Cosman: Milein Cosman, painter, born 1921, in Gotha, Germany, arrived in England in 1939.

195   a distinguished musicologist: Hans Keller, musician and critic, born 11 March 1919, in Vienna, died 6 November 1985, in London. A personal account of the *Anschluss,* and his own arrest, is in Hans Keller, *1975 (1984 Minus 9)* (Dennis Dobson, 1977), 38 et seq.

196   Inge Trott was ninety-one: Inge Trott, social activist, born 1920, in Vienna, died 2014, in London.

200   It came up instantly: Alfred Seiler, *From Hitler's Death Camps to Stalin's Gulags* (Lulu, 2010).

200   'Emil was able to stay': Ibid., 126.

VI Frank

207   'Community takes precedence': Hans Frank, *International Penal Policy* (report delivered on 21 August 1935, by the *Reich* minister at the plenary session of the Akademie für Deutsches Recht, at the Eleventh International Penal and Penitentiary Congress).

209   As Frank waited: *Jackson Report,* 18–41.

210   After his parents separated: Martyn Housden, *Hans Frank: Lebensraum and the Holocaust* (Palgrave Macmillan, 2003), 14.

210   Two years later: Ibid., 23.

211   Now an insider: Ibid., 36.

211 Four months after: *Neue Freie Presse,* 13 May 1933, 1; 'Germans Rebuked Arriving in Vienna', *New York Times,* 14 May 1933.

212 These specifically targeted: Housden, *Hans Frank,* 49.

212 Frank didn't help with: 'Germans Rebuked Arriving in Vienna'.

213 'to visit the grave': 'Austrians Rebuff Hitlerite Protest', *New York Times,* 16 May 1933, 1, 8.

213 'as if it had': 'Turmoil in Vienna as Factions Clash', *New York Times,* 15 May 1933, 1, 8.

213 A week after Frank's: 'Vienna Jews Fear Spread of Nazism', *New York Times,* 22 May 1933.

213 A year later, Dollfuss: Howard Sachar, *The Assassination of Europe, 1918–1942: A Political History* (University of Toronto Press, 2014), 208–10.

214 In August, he presided: *Proceedings of the XIth International Penal and Penitentiary Congress Held in Berlin, August, 1935,* ed. Sir Jan Simon van der Aa (Bureau of International Penal and Penitentiary Commission, 1937).

214 Judge Emil Rappaport: Hans Frank, *International Penal Policy.* App. 1 lists the participants.

215 A few weeks earlier: Henri Donnedieu de Vabres, 'La répression international des délits du droit des gens', *Nouvelle Revue de Droit International Privé* 2 (1935) 7 (report presented to the Academy for German Law, Berlin, 27 February 1935).

215 'Complete equality': Reck, *Diary of a Man in Despair,* 42.

216 Geoffrey Bing: Geoffrey Bing, 'The International Penal and Penitentiary Congress, Berlin, 1935', *Howard Journal* 4 (1935), 195–98; 'Nazis Annoyed: Outspoken Englishman', *Argus* (Melbourne), 23 August 1935, 9.

216 Four years later: Housden, *Hans Frank,* 78.

216 'be directed by': Decree of the Führer and Reich Chancellor Concerning the Administration of the Occupied Polish Territories, 12 October 1939, Section 3(2).

216 In an early interview: 3 October 1939; William Shirer, *The Rise and Fall of the Third Reich* (Arrow, 1991), 944.

217 From 1 December, all Jews: Housden, *Hans Frank,* 126, citing Frank, Diary, 10 November 1939.

217 From the start of his reign: Frank, Diary, extracts in *Trial of the Major War Criminals,* 29, and Stanisław Piotrowski, *Hans Frank's Diary* (PWN, 1961).

217 By the time he left: During his trial, Frank referred to forty-three volumes (*Trial of the Major War Criminals,* 12:7), but the Polish delegate to the trial, Stanisław Piotrowski, noted that thirty-eight

volumes were preserved but it was 'difficult to determine whether some of the volumes might not have been lost when the International Tribunal first went to work in Nuremberg'. Piotrowski, *Hans Frank's Diary*, 11.

217   'all Jews be evacuated': *Trial of the Major War Criminals,* 3:580 (14 December 1945).

217   Poles would be treated: Housden, *Hans Frank,* 119.

219   'Reich Minister Dr Frank': Frank, Diary, 2 October 1940; *Trial of the Major War Criminals,* 7:191 (8 February 1946).

220   Frank took control: Karl Lasch, born 29 December 1904, died 1 June 1942.

220   Held at Wannsee: Frank, Diary, 16 December 1941, sitting of the cabinet of the General Governments; *Trial of the Major War Criminals,* 22:542 (1 October 1946).

220   The Wannsee Conference met: Mark Roseman, *The Villa, the Lake, the Meeting: Wannsee and the Final Solution* (Allen Lane, 2002).

220   The conference minutes were: The minutes are available on the website of the House of the Wannsee Conference, http://www.ghwk.de/wannsee/dokumente-zur-wannsee-konferenz/?lang=gb.

221   Each time Frank asked a question: Curzio Malaparte, *Kaputt* (New York Review Books, 2005), 78.

222   The Italian didn't report: Curzio Malaparte, 'Serata a Varsavia, sorge il Nebenland di Polonia', *Corriere della Sera,* 22 March 1942.

222   'My one ambition': Malaparte, *Kaputt,* 68.

226   Accused of corruption: Niklas Frank, *In the Shadow of the Reich* (Alfred A. Knopf, 1991), 217, 246–47.

227   'I was surprised': Malaparte, *Kaputt,* 153.

229   His visit: the visit occured on 25 January 1942, although whether he was accompanied by Frank is unclear. Maurizio Serra, *Malaparte: Vies et Légendes* (Grasset, 2011), 366.

233   In June and July: Housden, *Hans Frank,* 169–72. The speeches were given in Berlin (9 June), Vienna (1 July), Munich (20 July), and Heidelberg (21 July).

233   The law must be: Niklas Frank, *Shadow of the Reich,* 219.

234   'A solemn and transfigured': Ibid., 208–9.

234   Mass extermination offered: Ibid., 212–13.

234   'details later but only': Ibid., 213.

237   The *Gazeta Lwowska* reported: *Gazeta Lwowska,* 1 August 1942, 2.

237   Frank's main task: Dieter Pohl, *Nationalsozialistische Judenverfolgung in Ostgalizien, 1941–1944,* 2nd edn (Oldenbourg, 1997), 77–78.

237   'The Higher SS': Frank, Diary, Conference of the District

Standartenführer of the NSDAP in Kraków, 18 March 1942, in *Trial of the Major War Criminals*, 29:507.

237 Schoolchildren lined Opern: *Gazeta Lwowska*, 2/3 August 1942, back page.

238 That evening, Frank inaugurated: Ibid.

238 'shiver in the ecstasy': Housden, *Hans Frank*, 40–41, citing Niklas Frank, *Der Vater* (Goldmann, 1993), 42–44.

238 'We, the Germans': *Gazeta Lwowska*, 2/3 August 1942, back page.

239 The following morning: Frank, Diary, 1 August 1942. Documents in Evidence, in *Trial of the Major War Criminals*, 29:540–42.

239 'I came here': Ibid.

239 The audience erupted: Ibid.

241 His decree meant: Decree of 15 October 1941, signed by Hans Frank, Article 1, para. 4(b) ('Jews who without permission leave the district to which they have been confined are subject to punishment by death').

241 'Frank came for breakfast': Diary of Charlotte von Wächter, Saturday, 1 August 1942, personal archive of Horst von Wächter.

241 *Die Grosse Aktion*: Dieter Pohl, 'Ivan Kalymon, the Ukrainian Auxiliary Police, and Nazi Anti-Jewish Policy in L'viv, 1941–1944' (a report prepared for the Office of Special Investigations, US Department of Justice, 31 May 2005), 92; Pohl, *Nationalsozialistische Judenverfolgung in Ostgalizien*, 216–23.

241 'A lot had to be done': Otto von Wächter to Charlotte, 16 August 1942, personal archive of Horst von Wächter.

242 Heinrich Himmler arrived: Peter Witte, *Der Dienstkalender Heinrich Himmlers, 1941/42* (Wallstein, 2005), 521 (entry for Monday, 17 August 1942, 1830 hours).

242 'One now sees hardly': Frank, Diary, 18 August 1942.

246 The familiar red cover: Karl Baedeker, *Das Generalgouvernement: Reisehandbuch* (Karl Baedeker, 1943).

247 Lemberg got eight pages: Ibid., 157–64.

247 The editors offered: Ibid., 137, 10.

247 The publication of the Baedeker: 'Poland Indicts 10 in 400,000 Deaths'.

248 One account was written: Simon Wiesenthal, *The Murderers Among Us* (Heinemann, 1967), 236–37. ('I saw him early in 1942 in the ghetto of Lwów. He was personally in charge on 15 August 1942, when 4,000 elderly people were rounded up in the ghetto and sent to the railway station. My mother was among them.')

248 Later I found: Narodne Archivum Cyfrove (NAC), http://audiovis.nac.gov.pl/obraz/12757/50b358369d3948f401ded5bffc36586e/.

248 The judge ruled: *United States v. John Kaymon, a.k.a. Ivan, Iwan, John Kalymon/Kaylmun*, Case No. 04-60003, US District Court, Eastern District of Michigan, Judge Marianne O. Battani, Opinion and Order Revoking Order of Admission to Citizenship and Canceling Certificate of Naturalization, 29 March 2007. A deportation order was affirmed by the Board of Immigration Appeals on 20 September 2011, but Kalymon died on 29 June 2014, before he could be deported. See Krishnadev Calamur, 'Man Tied to Nazis Dies in Michigan at Age 93', NPR, 9 July 2014.

248 The judgement relies on: Dieter Pohl, 'Ivan Kalymon, the Ukrainian Auxiliary Police, and Nazi Anti-Jewish Policy in L'viv, 1941–1944' (a report prepared for the Office of Special Investigations, US Department of Justice, 31 May 2005), 16, 27.

248 'Deportation of Jews': Note dated 10 January 1942, regarding the deportation of the Jews from Lemberg, signed by Oberst [Colonel] [Alfred] Bisanz.

249 The second document: Order of 13 March 1942, on the Labor Deployment of Jews, to enter into force on 1 April 1942.

249 Damaging as these two: Heinrich Himmler to State Secretary SS-Gruppenführer Stuckart, 25 August 1942.

251 'I have the honour': Frank, Diary, 25 January 1943, Warsaw, International Military Tribunal, *Nazi Conspiracy and Aggression* (US Government Printing Office, 1946), 4:916.

251 'They must go': Frank, Diary, 16 December 1941; *Trial of the Major War Criminals*, 29:503.

252 In March, the Kraków: Amon Göth, born 11 December 1908, executed 13 September 1946, following trial and conviction by the Supreme National Tribunal of Poland in Kraków.

252 This was implemented: Stroop Report (*The Warsaw Ghetto Is No More*), May 1943, available at https://www.jewishvirtuallibrary.org/jsource/Holocaust/nowarsaw.html.

252 'the mass death rate': Frank, Diary, 2 August 1943, quoted in *Trial of the Major War Criminals*, 29:606 (29 July 1946).

252 'All the others have': Ibid.

252 'We are all': Frank, Diary, 25 January 1943.

253 The words are available: Michael Kennedy, *Richard Strauss: Man, Musician, Enigma* (Cambridge University Press, 1999), 346–47.

253 Some pieces went to Germany: *Trial of the Major War Criminals*, 4:81 (18 December 1945).

254 The picture: *The Lady with an Ermine*, about 1489–90, a portrait of Cecilia Gallerani (1473–1536), mistress of Ludovico Sforza. The ermine is a symbol of purity, and Leonardo is said to have believed

such a painting, which is now the property of the Czartoryski Foundation, could commemorate and inspire love.

257 'a race which must': Frank, Diary, 18 March 1944, Reichshof; *Trial of the Major War Criminals,* 7:469 (15 February 1946).

258 Frank retaliated: Housden, *Hans Frank,* 209; Frank, Diary, 11 July 1944.

258 On 27 July, Lemberg fell: Timothy Snyder, *The Reconstruction of Nations: Poland, Ukraine, Lithuania, Belarus, 1569–1999* (Yale University Press, 2003), 177.

258 On 1 August, an uprising: Norman Davies, *Rising '44: The Battle for Warsaw* (Macmillan, 2003).

258 His diary recorded: Frank, Diary, 15 September 1944 (conversation with Dr Bühler).

258 He watched films: *Die Stadt ohne Juden* (1924, dir. Hans Karl Breslauer). Hans Moser played the character of Rat Bernart.

259 It was only a short trip: Housden, *Hans Frank,* 218.

259 He set up office: Ibid., 218; Frank, Diary, 2 February 1945.

259 Two days later: Niklas Frank, *Shadow of the Reich,* 317.

260 This was the same Frank: Article 175a was adopted on 28 June 1935, adding the crime of severe lewdness (*Schwere Unzucht*) and redefining the crime as a felony. See generally Burkhard Jellonnek, *Homosexuelle unter dem Hakenkreuz: Die Verfolgung von Homosexuellen im Dritten Reich* (F. Schöningh, 1990). Frank had warned that the 'epidemic of homosexuality' was threatening the new *Reich.* Richard Plant, *The Pink Triangle: The Nazi War Against Homosexuals* (Henry Holt, 1988), 26.

260 A vehicle pulled up: Housden, *Hans Frank,* 218.

261 In June, Frank's name: The first meeting of British and American delegates, on 21 June 1945, received a first list of ten possible defendants put forward by David Maxwell Fyfe, selected on the basis that their names were well-known to the public. Taylor, *Anatomy of the Nuremberg Trials,* 85–86.

261 The inclusion of the 'Butcher of Warsaw': Ibid., 89.

261 There he was interrogated: Ann Tusa and John Tusa, *The Nuremberg Trial* (Macmillan, 1983), 43–48.

261 Robert Ley: John Kenneth Galbraith, 'The "Cure" at Mondorf Spa', *Life,* 22 October 1945, 17–24.

261 'unbelievably difficult': Hans Frank, conversation with a US army officer, 4–5 August 1945, http://www.holocaustresearchproject.org/trials/HansFrankTestimony.html.

262 At the end of the month: On 29 August 1945, the chief prosecutors announced a 'first list of war criminals to be tried before the

International Military Tribunal'. Taylor, *Anatomy of the Nuremberg Trials,* 89 (twenty-four defendants were on the first list).

262 A few days later: Interrogation testimony of Hans Frank, taken at Nuremberg, 1, 6, 7, 10 and 13 September, and 3 and 8 October 1945 (by Colonel Thomas A. Hinkel), http://library2.lawschool.cornell. edu/donovan/show.asp?query=Hans+Frank.

VIII Nuremberg

278 Ley had killed himself: Taylor, *Anatomy of the Nuremberg Trials,* 132, 165.

278 'The Tribunal will now enter': Ibid., 143; Tusa and Tusa, *Nuremberg Trial,* 109–10.

279 The man in charge: *Trial of the Major War Criminals,* 1: 1 ('Members and alternate members of the Tribunal').

279 On the far left: Francis Biddle, *In Brief Authority* (Doubleday, 1962; Praeger, 1976), 381.

279 Then John Parker: Ibid., 372–73.

279 The French were seated: Tusa and Tusa, *Nuremberg Trial,* 111; Guillaume Mouralis, introduction to *Juge à Nuremberg,* by Robert Falco (Arbre Bleu, 2012), 13 (at note 2), 126–27.

279 'unique in the history': *Trial of the Major War Criminals,* 2:30.

280 Between 7 September 1941: Ibid., 64.

280 The former governor-general would have known: Taylor, *Anatomy of the Nuremberg Trials,* 132.

280 'authorized, directed, and participated': *Trial of the Major War Criminals,* 2:75.

281 'It was an unforgettable': Elihu Lauterpacht, *Life of Hersch Lauterpacht,* 277.

281 'great satisfaction': Ibid.

281 All that remained: *Illustrated London News,* 8 December 1945.

283 'Tell me, Rosenberg': Gustave Gilbert, *Nuremberg Diary* (New York: Farrar, Straus, 1947), 42.

284 'small cheap face': Martha Gellhorn, 'The Paths of Glory', in *The Face of War* (Atlantic Monthly Press, 1994), 203.

285 'I declare myself': *Trial of the Major War Criminals,* 2:97.

288 'The privilege of opening': Ibid., 98.

288 'That four great nations': Ibid., 99.

289 'a race which has': Ibid., 120.

289 '"leave to live"': Rudyard Kipling, 'The Old Issue', in *Collected Poems of Rudyard Kipling* (Wordsworth Poetry Library, 1994), 307–9.

289 'great personal triumph': Elihu Lauterpacht, *Life of Hersch Lauterpacht*, 277.

290 Such personal concerns: Ibid., 276.

290 I was able to read: On file.

290 'The community of nations': Hersch Lauterpacht, 'Draft Nuremberg Speeches', *Cambridge Journal of International and Comparative Law* 1, no. 1 (2012): 48–49.

292 He allowed himself: Elihu Lauterpacht, *Life of Hersch Lauterpacht*, 276.

292 Shawcross's legal arguments: Ibid.

293 'You spoke with conviction': Ibid., 278.

293 A force of personality: Gilbert, *Nuremberg Diary*, 66; see also John J. Michalczyk, *Filming the End of the Holocaust: Allied Documentaries, Nuremberg, and the Liberation of the Concentration Camps* (Bloomsbury, 2014), 96.

294 'to texts read aloud': Janet Flanner, 'Letter from Nuremberg', *New Yorker*, 5 January 1946, in Drutman, *Janet Flanner's World*, 46–48.

294 'strained attentiveness': Janet Flanner, 'Letter from Nuremberg', *New Yorker*, 17 December 1945, in Drutman, *Janet Flanner's World*, 99.

294 Visitors were attracted by: Ibid., 98.

295 The widow of a Battle of Britain hero: Sir Hugh Dundas, born 22 July 1920, died 10 July 1995.

295 the American judge who: Biddle, *In Brief Authority*.

295 the French judge who: Falco, *Juge à Nuremberg*.

296 'The British papers published': David Low, 'Low's Nuremberg Sketchbook No. 3', *Evening Standard*, 14 December 1945, available at http://www.cartoons.ac.uk/record/LSE1319.

297 'That we sentence 1,200,000': *Trial of the Major War Criminals*, 3:551.

298 In due course, the matter: Tusa and Tusa, *Nuremberg Trial*, 294.

298 'I am a judge': Donnedieu to Lemkin, 28 December 1945, box 1, folder 18, Lemkin Collection, American Jewish Historical Society.

299 Rappaport survived the war: *Law Reports of Trials of War Criminals, Selected and Prepared by the UN War Crimes Commission*, vols. 7, 14, http://www.loc.gov/rr/frd/Military_Law/law-reports-trials-war-criminals.html.

301 He shared vivid dreams: Gilbert, *Nuremberg Diary*, 22.

301 Gilbert was not averse: Taylor, *Anatomy of the Nuremberg Trials*, 548.

302 'I listened to': Gilbert, *Nuremberg Diary*, 81–82 (22 December 1945).

302 'It is as though I am': Ibid., 116 (10 January 1946).

303 'returned from the other world': *Trial of the Major War Criminals*, 8:322.

305 He saw Commander Kurt: Ibid., 328.

306 It was Professor Redzik: Redzik, *Stanislaw Starzynski*, 55.

307 'We tread the earth': Grossman, *Road*, 174.

308 The diaries had been used: Flanner, 'Letter from Nuremberg', 17 December 1945, 107.

308 He followed Alfred Rosenberg: *Trial of the Major War Criminals*, 11:553.

308 'at least 2,500,000 victims': Ibid., 415.

308 'never even occurred to us': Gilbert, *Nuremberg Diary*, 259.

308 Dr Seidl asked a few questions: *Trial of the Major War Criminals*, 12:2–3.

309 'I am possessed': Ibid., 7–8.

310 One step forward: Ibid., 19, 13.

310 'A thousand years will pass': Ibid.

310 'Did you hear him say': Gilbert, *Nuremberg Diary*, 277.

310 'I am glad': Ibid.

310 Other defendants were contemptuous: Ibid., 277–83.

311 'I did not collect': *Trial of the Major War Criminals*, 12:14, 40.

311 Frank's approach generated: Yves Beigbeder, conversation with author, 29 June 2012.

312 'unexpected acknowledgment': Yves Beigbeder, 'Le procès de Nurembourg: Frank plaide coupable', *Réforme*, 25 May 1946.

312 Later I sent a copy: Hans Frank, *International Penal Policy*.

312 'A Nazi Judge on the Nuremberg Tribunal': Falco, *Juge à Nuremberg*, 42.

313 'He has become a Catholic': Christopher Dodd, *Letters from Nuremberg: My Father's Narrative of a Quest for Justice* (Broadway Books, 2008), 289.

313 'A few days ago': Gilbert, *Nuremberg Diary*, 280.

IX The Girl Who Chose Not to Remember

321 There they remained: Gabrielle Anderl and Walter Manoschek, *Gescheiterte Flucht: Der Jüdische 'Kladovo-Transport' auf dem Weg nach Palästina, 1939–42* (Failed flight: The Kladovo transport on the way to Palestine, 1939–42) (Verlag für Gesellschaftskritik, 1993). See also 'The Darien Story', *The Darien Dilemma*, http://www.dariendilemma.com/eng/story/darienstory/; Dalia Ofer and Hannah Weiner, *Dead-End Journey* (University Press of America, 1996).

X Judgement

329 'I should in any event': Elihu Lauterpacht, *Life of Hersch Lauter-pacht*, 293.

329 'Sound realism': Ibid., 285–86; Hersch Lauterpacht, 'The Grotian Tradition in International Law', *British Year Book of International Law* 23 (1946): 1–53.

329 'cry out awfully': Elihu Lauterpacht, *Life of Hersch Lauterpacht*, 278.

330 'We know about you': Lauterpacht to Inka Gelbard, 27 May 1946, personal archive of Eli Lauterpacht.

330 'the main feature': Elihu Lauterpacht, *Life of Hersch Lauterpacht*, 294.

331 'like a bad Hollywood script': Steven Jacobs, ed., *Raphael Lemkin's Thoughts on Nazi Genocide* (Bloch, 2010), 261.

331 So much so: G. Reynolds, 'Cosmopolites Clock the American Femme; Nice, but Too Honest to Be Alluring', *Washington Post*, 10 March 1946, S4.

331 None were obviously addressed: Copies provided by Nancy Steinson.

332 'the needs of under-privileged': Lemkin to Eleanor Roosevelt, 18 May 1946, box 1, folder 13, 5–6, Raphael Lemkin Papers, American Jewish Archives.

332 A similar letter went: Lemkin to McCormick, 19 May 1946, box 1, folder 13, 7–9, Lemkin Papers, American Jewish Archives.

332 'I missed both of you': Lemkin to Pinchot, 20 May 1946, box 1, folder 13, 15–16, Lemkin Papers, American Jewish Archives.

333 'a sudden call': Lemkin to Durward V. Sandifer, 20 May 1946, box 1, folder 13, 13–14, Lemkin Papers, American Jewish Archives.

333 He left for Europe: Identification card issued by the War Department, 22 May 1946, box 1, folder 12, Lemkin Collection, American Jewish Historical Society; Peter Balakian, 'Raphael Lemkin, Cultural Destruction, and the Armenian Genocide', *Holocaust and Genocide Studies* 27, no. 1 (2013): 74.

334 There he met Egon: Schwelb to Lemkin, 24 June 1946, Rafael Lemkin Papers, Rare Book and Manuscript Library, Columbia University.

334 He'd already sent 800,000: *Trial of the Major War Criminals*, 15:164.

334 More than 25,000: Barrett, 'Raphael Lemkin and "Genocide" at Nuremberg', 48.

334 Not formally a member: Lemkin, *Totally Unofficial*, 235.

335 'convict these guys': Power, *Problem from Hell*, 50.

335 as a poste restante: Rafael Lemkin Papers, Rare Book and Manuscript Library, Columbia University.

335 'if the people doomed': Ibid.

336 'that the prosecution did not': 'The significance of the concept of genocide in the trial of war criminals', Thomas Dodd Papers, Box/Folder 387:8580, Thomas J. Dodd Research Center, University of Connecticut.

336 Lemkin met again: Barrett, 'Raphael Lemkin and "Genocide" at Nuremberg', 47–48.

336 It happened on 25 June: Ibid., 48–49.

337 'What you wanted to do': *Trial of the Major War Criminals*, 17:61.

337 'very warm appreciation': John Cooper, *Raphael Lemkin*, 70.

337 Cooper noted that: R. W. Cooper, *Nuremberg Trial*, 109.

337 'was recalled to Poland': Ibid., 110.

339 'a most valuable precedent': Lauterpacht, 'Draft Nuremberg Speeches', 68.

339 'the rights of man': Ibid., 87.

339 'for no other reason': Ibid., 74.

339 Frank was a 'direct agent': Ibid., 76.

340 'Witness . . . defendant Frank': Ibid., 110.

340 'I am naturally inclined': Elihu Lauterpacht, *Life of Hersch Lauterpacht*, 295.

342 On 10 July, Lauterpacht's secretary: Ibid.

342 Dr Alfred Thoma sought: *Trial of the Major War Criminals*, 18:90, 92–94.

342 The unexpected argument: Ibid., 112–13.

342 Rosenberg was aggrieved: Ibid., 114–28.

342 'Presented with all due respect': Lemkin Papers, Rare Book and Manuscript Library, Columbia University.

343 He spent a few days: Office of the Registrar 385th Station Hospital APO 124, US army, Abstract Record of Hospitalization of Raphael Lemkin, box 5, folder 7, 23, Lemkin Papers, American Jewish Archives.

343 It didn't help: *Trial of the Major War Criminals*, 17:550–55.

343 'With one exception': Ibid., 18:140.

343 '5 year struggle': Ibid., 160.

344 As an occupying power: Ibid.

344 'completely irrelevant': Ibid., 152.

344 The Americans first: Ibid., 19:397–432.

344 Then the British: Ibid., 433–529.

344 Then the French: Ibid., 530–618; ibid., vol. 20, 1–14.

344 Robert Jackson opened: Ibid., 19:397.

345 'a thousand years will': Ibid., 406.

345 He addressed the facts: Ibid., 433–529.

345 'We are very apprehensive': Elihu Lauterpacht, *Life of Hersch Lauterpacht*, 295.

346 'If I fail to': Ibid., 296.

346 Shawcross started with: *Trial of the Major War Criminals*, 19:437–57.

347 'Without screaming or weeping': Ibid., 507.

347 A moment of 'living pity': Rebecca West, 'Greenhouse with Cyclamens I', in *A Train of Powder* (Ivan R. Dee, 1955), 20.

347 Shawcross turned his attention: *Trial of the Major War Criminals*, 19:446.

348 'That damn Englishman': Housden, *Hans Frank*, 231.

348 'Genocide' applied to gypsies: *Trial of the Major War Criminals*, 19:497.

349 'International law has in the past': Ibid., 471–72.

349 'The individual must transcend': Ibid., 529.

349 'ultimate unit of all law': Ibid., 472.

349 Shawcross was followed by: Ibid., 530–35.

350 Genocide was 'almost totally': Ibid., 550.

350 'Not one of the defendants': Ibid., 562.

350 He had no time: Ibid., 570.

350 'How vain': Ibid.

351 It contained the photocopied: Taffet, *Holocaust of the Jews of Żółkiew*.

351 'Once they were stripped': Ibid., 58.

353 'Dr Henryk Lauterpacht': Ibid., 8.

354 Among Lemkin's papers: Lemkin Papers, Rare Book and Manuscript Library, Columbia University.

354 Three hundred international lawyers: International Law Association, *Report of the Forty-First Conference, Cambridge* (1946), xxxvii–xliv.

355 He collapsed after his flight: Note on Raphael Lemkin (undated, prepared with input from Lemkin), box 5, folder 7, MS-60, American Jewish Archives, Cleveland.

355 This was British pragmatism: International Law Association, *Report of the Forty-First Conference*, 8–13.

355 'the criminal philosophy of genocide': Ibid., 25–28.

356 'We cannot keep telling': Barrett, 'Raphael Lemkin and "Genocide" at Nuremberg', 51.

356 'I think I succeeded': John Cooper, *Raphael Lemkin*, 73.

356 'distinct technique': 'Genocide', *New York Times*, 26 August 1946, 17.

356 'hurt surprise that the prosecution': Gilbert, *Nuremberg Diary*, 417.

356 'awful crime of genocide': *Trial of the Major War Criminals*, 22:229.

357 Despite Jackson's press release: Ibid., 271–97.

357   The French, by contrast: Ibid., 300.

357   The Soviet prosecutor Rudenko: Ibid., 321.

357   Göring spoke first: Ibid., 366–68.

357   'would act just as': Ibid., 373.

357   Ribbentrop, Keitel: Ibid., 382.

357   'more and more deeply involved': Ibid., 384.

358   'Every possible guilt incurred': Ibid., 385.

358   'Who shall ever judge': Ibid.

359   When their visas ran out: Conversation with Saul Lemkin.

361   'if one emphasizes': Schwelb to Humphrey, 19 June 1946, PAG-3/1.3, box 26, United Nations War Crimes Commission, 1943–1949, Predecessor Archives Group, United Nations Archives, New York; cited in Ana Filipa Vrdoljak, 'Human Rights and Genocide: The Work of Lauterpacht and Lemkin in Modern International Law', *European Journal of International Law* 20, no. 4 (2010): 1184n156.

362   '"I like this"': Gaston Oulmàn, born Walter Ullmann, 5 January 1898, died 5 May 1949, broadcaster and journalist; see Maximilian Alexander, *Das Chamäleon* (R. Glöss, 1978).

364   Khaki Roberts was with them: Taylor, *Anatomy of the Nuremberg Trials,* 103.

364   Lemkin was in Paris: John Cooper, *Raphael Lemkin,* 73.

365   The first day: *Trial of the Major War Criminals,* 22:411–523.

366   'transcend the national obligations': Ibid., 466.

366   The Soviet judge said: Ibid., 497.

366   We were powerless: Ibid., 498.

367   'two thousand wretched': West, 'Greenhouse with Cyclamens I', 53–54.

368   'recalled the madam': Ibid., 6, 58–59.

368   Judge Nikitchenko convicted Rosenberg: *Trial of the Major War Criminals,* 22:541.

368   embroiled in a messy love affair: Lorna Gibb, *West's World* (Macmillan, 2013), 178.

368   Biddle turned to count three: *Trial of the Major War Criminals,* 22:542–44.

368   'It . . . may well be true': Ibid.

369   three were acquitted: Ibid., 574, 584.

370   Of the first six: Ibid., 588–89.

370   Rebecca West noticed the moment: West, 'Greenhouse with Cyclamens I', 59.

370   'Tod durch den Strang': John Cooper, *Raphael Lemkin,* 272.

370   Judge Biddle was surprised: David Irving, *Nuremberg: The Last Battle* (1996, Focal Point), 380 (citing 'Notes on Judgement – Meetings of

Tribunal', Final Vote on Individuals, 10 September 1946, University of Syracuse, George Arents Research Library, Francis Biddle Collection, box 14).

370 'I deserved it': Gilbert, *Nuremberg Diary,* 432.

372 'I hope you will always': Elihu Lauterpacht, *Life of Hersch Lauterpacht,* 297.

372 'Nuremberg nightmare': Letter from Lemkin to Anne O'Hare McCormick, 19 May 1946, box 1, folder 13, Lemkin Papers, American Jewish Archives.

372 'the blackest day': William Schabas, 'Raphael Lemkin, Genocide, and Crimes Against Humanity', in Agnieszka Bienczyk-Missala and Slawomir Debski, *Hero of Humankind,* 233.

373 The pope made a plea: 'Pope Asks Mercy for Nazi, Intercedes for Hans Frank', *New York Times,* 6 October 1946.

373 'the strengthening of international law': Truman to Lawrence, 12 October 1946, Lawrence family album, on file.

373 'Göring is executed first': Lawrence family album.

373 He said a few final words: Kingsbury Smith, 'The Execution of Nazi War Criminals', International News Service, 16 October 1946.

373 'Ça, c'est beau': John Cooper, *Raphael Lemkin,* 301.

Epilogue: To the Woods

377 Desiring to lay the path: UN General Assembly resolution 95 ('Affirmation of the Principles of International Law Recognized by the Charter of the Nürnberg Tribunal'), adopted at the fifty-fifth plenary meeting, 11 December 1946.

377 The General Assembly then adopted: UN General Assembly resolution 96 ('The Crime of Genocide'), adopted at the fifty-fifth plenary meeting, 11 December 1946.

377 On 9 December 1948: Convention on the Prevention and Punishment of Genocide, adopted by the UN General Assembly, 9 December 1948, in force 12 January 1951.

378 This came with agreement: Convention for the Protection of Human Rights and Fundamental Freedoms, 4 November 1950, 213 *United Nations Treaty Series* 221.

378 That summer, more than 150 states: Rome Statute of the International Criminal Court, 17 July 1998, 2187 *United Nations Treaty Series* 90.

379 Two months after agreement: *Prosecutor v. Jean-Paul Akayesu,* Case No. ICTR-96-4-T, Trial Chamber Judgment (2 September 1998).

379 A few weeks later: *R v. Bow Street Metropolitan Stipendiary Magistrate, Ex Parte Pinochet Ugarte* (No. 3) [1999] 2 All ER 97.

379 In May 1999: *Prosecutor v. Slovodan Milosevic et al.,* Case No. IT-99-37, Indictment (ICTY, 22 May 1999).

379 In November 2001: *Prosecutor v. Slobodan Milosevic,* Case No. IT-01-51-I, Indictment (ICTY, 22 November 2001).

379 In March 2007: *United States v. John Kaymon,* Opinion and Order, 29 March 2007

379 In September 2007: Case Concerning Application of the Convention on the Prevention and Punishment of the Crime of Genocide (*Bosnia Herzegovina v. Serbia and Montenegro*) Judgment, *ICJ Reports* (2007), paras. 413–15, 471(5).

379 In July 2010: *Prosecutor v. Omar Hassan Ahmad Al Bashir,* ICC-02/05-01/09, Second Warrant of Arrest (Pre-trial Chamber I, 12 July 2010).

379 Two years later: *Prosecutor v. Charles Ghankay Taylor,* SCSL-03-01-T, Trial Judgment (Trial Chamber II, 18 May 2012).

380 He was sentenced to fifty: *Prosecutor v. Charles Ghankay Taylor,* SCSL-03-01-T, Sentencing Judgment (Trial Chamber II, 30 May 2012), 40.

380 In 2015, the United Nations: Professor Sean Murphy, 'First Report of the Special Rapporteur on Crimes Against Humanity' (17 February 2015), UN International Law Commission, A/CN.4/680; also Crimes Against Humanity Initiative, Whitney R. Harris World Law Institute, Washington University in St Louis School of Law, http://law.wustl.edu/harris/crimesagainsthumanity.

380 'crime of crimes': David Luban, 'Arendt on the Crime of Crimes', *Ratio Juris* (2015) (forthcoming), ssrn.com/abstract=2588537.

380 there emerged a race: Elissa Helms, '"Bosnian Girl": Nationalism and Innocence Through Images of Women', in *Retracing Images: Visual Culture After Yugoslavia,* ed. Daniel Šuber and Slobodan Karamanic (Brill, 2012), 198.

380 'an essential component': Christian Axboe Nielsen, 'Surmounting the Myopic Focus on Genocide: The Case of the War in Bosnia and Herzegovina', *Journal of Genocide Research* 15, no. 1 (2013): 21–39.

380 without contributing to the resolution: Timothy Snyder, *Bloodlands: Europe Between Hitler and Stalin* (Basic Books, 2010), 405, 412–13.

381 'stirs up national outrage': 'Turks and Armenians in Shadow of Genocide', *Financial Times,* 24 April 2015.

381 'the individual, when he comes': Louis Gumplowicz, *La lutte des races* (Guillaumin, 1893), 360.

381 'Our bloody nature': Edward O. Wilson, *The Social Conquest of Earth* (Liveright, 2012), 62.

382 He died there: Request for Delivery of Dr Gustav Waechter for Trial for a War Crime, Wiesbaden, 28 September 1946: 'Subject is responsible for mass-murder (shooting and executions). Under his command as Governor of District-Galicia, more than 100 thousand Polish citizens lost their life.' Wächter was listed as a war criminal on the UN CROWCASS list, file no. 78416, 449, File Bd. 176, in the collection of the Institute of National Remembrance (Warsaw), available at USHMM, RG-15.155M (Records of investigation and documentation of the main Commission to Investigate Nazi Crimes in Poland, Investigation against Dr OTTO WAECHTER Gustaw, Gauleiter of the Kraków district, then the district of Galizien, accused of giving orders of mass executions and actions directed against the Jewish people).

382 His son Horst lives: See Diana Błońska, 'O Muzeum Narodowym w Krakowiew czasie drugiej wojny światowej, 28 Klio' *Czasopismo poświęcone dziejom Polski i powszechnym* (2014), 85, 119 at note 82, ('The Museum suffered major, irretrievable losses at the hands of the wife of the governor of the Kraków Distrikt, Frau Wächter, a Viennese woman aged about 35, with chestnut brown hair. She looted every department of the Museum to decorate the Pod Baranami palace, which was the Distrikt headquarters, taking the most exquisite paintings and the most beautiful items of antique furniture, militaria etc., despite the fact that the Director of the Museum warned her against taking masterpieces for this purpose. Items that went missing included paintings such as: Bruegel's *The Fight Between Lent and Carnival*, [Julian] Fałat's *The Hunter's Courtship* and others; many came back in an extremely damaged state.' Cited in: Archive of the National Museum in Kraków, Office of [Feliks] Kopera, Letter to the personnel department at the Kraków City Administration dated 25 March 1946. 'I do not know whether the list of war criminals includes Lora Wächter, wife of the Kraków governor, who resided at the Potocki Palace known as 'Pod Baranami'. She caused us great harm by taking away to decorate the Wächter residence works including masterpieces by Julian Fałat, as well as a very precious painting by Bruegel, *The Fight Between Lent and Carnival* – of which the latter and Fałat's pictures were lost. I gave her name to the local courts, which demanded information from me about the looting of the Museum, and not knowing if Frau Wächter's name had been entered on the list, I am hereby reporting her harmful activity on behalf of the Museum.' Cited in: Ibid. Dz. p. 407/46 Letter to

the Polish Military Mission for Research into German War Crimes at Bad Salzuflen, dated 9 December 1946.), trans. Antonia Lloyd-Jones.

383 'looks down so challengingly': Wittlin, *City of Lions*, 11–12.

384 Someone suggested I might: Jan Kot, *Chestnut Roulette* (Mazo, 2008), 85.

ILLUSTRATION AND MAP CREDITS

INDEX

Italic page numbers refer to illustrations.